Making Content Comprehensible for Secondary English Learners

The SIOP® Model

Jana Echevarría
California State University, Long Beach

MaryEllen Vogt
California State University, Long Beach

Deborah J. Short
Center for Applied Linguistics, Washington, DC
Academic Language Research & Training, Arlington, VA

Allyn & Bacon
Boston New York San Francisco
Mexico City Montreal Toronto London Madrid Munich Paris
Hong Kong Singapore Tokyo Cape Town Sydney

Executive Editor: Aurora Martínez Ramos
Series Editorial Assistant: Jacqueline Gillen
Marketing Manager: Danae April
Production Editor: Gregory Erb
Editorial Production Service: Nesbitt Graphics, Inc.
Composition Buyer: Linda Cox
Manufacturing Buyer: Megan Cochran
Electronic Composition: Nesbitt Graphics, Inc.
Interior Design: Nesbitt Graphics, Inc.
Cover Designer: Linda Knowles

For Professional Development resources visit www.pearsonpd.com.

Between the time website information is gathered and then published, it is not unusual for some sites to have closed. Also, the transcription of URLs can result in typographical errors. The publisher would appreciate notification where these errors occur so that they may be corrected in subsequent editions.

Library of Congress Cataloging-in-Publication Data was unavailable at press time.

Photo Credits: p. 3, Will Hart/PhotoEdit; p. 25, Robin Sachs/PhotoEdit; p. 55, Frank Siteman; p. 81, Frank Siteman; p. 97, iStock; p. 117, Bob Daemmrich Photography; p. 141, Jeff Greenberg/PhotoEdit; p. 157, iStock; p. 171, David Mager/Pearson Learning Photo Studio; p. 193, iStock; p. 209, Ellen Senisi; inside front cover, Frank Siteman.

Printed in the United States of America

11 12 13 14 BRR 13 12 11

Allyn & Bacon
is an imprint of

www.pearsonhighered.com

ISBN-10: 0-205-62757-9
ISBN-13: 978-0-205-62757-8

For my husband, Casey Vose, for his generosity, support and love.
JE

To my children and grandchildren: Scott, Kevin, Jeff, Karlin, Kyndal, Kameron, True, Arik, and Emerson for their inspiration.
MEV

To my parents and grandmother, for their tradition of strength and determination and for their support and encouragement over the years.
DJS

about the authors

Jana Echevarría is a Professor Emerita of Education at California State University, Long Beach. She has taught in elementary, middle, and high schools in general education, special education, ESL, and bilingual programs. She has lived in Taiwan, Spain, and Mexico. Her UCLA doctorate earned her an award from the National Association for Bilingual Education's Outstanding Dissertations Competition. Her research and publications focus on effective instruction for English learners, including those with learning disabilities. Currently, she is Co-Principal Investigator with the Center for Research on the Educational Achievement and Teaching of English Language Learners (CREATE) funded by the U.S. Department of Education, Institute of Education Sciences (IES). In 2005, Dr. Echevarría was selected as Outstanding Professor at CSULB.

MaryEllen Vogt is Distinguished Professor Emerita at California State University, Long Beach. Dr. Vogt has been a classroom teacher, reading and special education specialist, district reading resource teacher, and university teacher educator. She received her doctorate from the University of California, Berkeley. A co-author of fourteen books, including the SIOP series and *Reading Specialists and Literacy Coaches in the Real World* (2007), Dr. Vogt has provided professional development in all fifty of the United States, and in eight other countries. She served as President of the International Reading Association in 2004–2005.

Deborah J. Short is a professional development consultant and a senior research associate at the Center for Applied Linguistics in Washington, DC. She co-developed the SIOP® Model for sheltered instruction and has directed national research studies on English language learners funded by the Carnegie Corporation, the Rockefeller Foundation, and the U.S. Dept. of Education. She chaired an expert panel on adolescent ELL literacy and co-wrote a policy report. As the director of Academic Language Research & Training, Dr. Short provides professional development on sheltered instruction and academic literacy around the United States and abroad. She has numerous publications, including the SIOP® book series and five ESL textbook series for Hampton-Brown. She has taught English as a second/foreign language in New York, California, Virginia, and the Democratic Republic of Congo.

contents

preface and acknowledgments

It is hard to believe that over fourteen years have passed since we first began our journey with the SIOP® Model. In the beginning, it would have been hard to believe that a decade later the SIOP® Model would be implemented in districts throughout all 50 states in the United States, and in numerous other countries. Whether you are already familiar with the SIOP® Model or are just now learning about it, we hope that you will find this new secondary edition to be informative, helpful, and most important, beneficial to the English learners (ELs) and other students with whom you work. In the earlier editions of the text, we discussed the need for a comprehensive, well-articulated model of instruction for preparing teachers to work with English learners. From this need, the Sheltered Instruction Observation Protocol (SIOP®) was created. Now, with the widespread use of the SIOP® Model throughout the country, we offer this version, written especially for grades 6–12 educators.

Our work on the SIOP® Model began with reviewing the literature and examining district-produced guidelines for English learners to find agreement on a definition of sheltered instruction, or SDAIE (Specially Designed Academic Instruction in English). A preliminary observation protocol was drafted and field-tested with sheltered teachers. A research project through the Center for Research on Education, Diversity, & Excellence (CREDE) enabled us to engage in an intensive refinement process and to use the SIOP® Model in a sustained professional development effort with teachers on both the East and West Coasts.Through this process of classroom observation, coaching, discussion, and reflection, the instrument was refined and changed, and eventually it evolved into the Sheltered Instruction Observation Protocol, or as it has come to be known, the SIOP® (pronounced sī-ŏp). The SIOP® Model operationalizes sheltered instruction by offering teachers a model for lesson planning and implementation that provides English learners with access to grade-level content standards.

Since the first edition of this book was published, we have continued to refine the SIOP® Model, and in our work with thousands of teachers and administrators throughout the country, our own understanding of effective sheltered instruction/SDAIE and the needs of English learners has grown substantially. We believe, and our research confirms, that when teachers use the SIOP® Model for their planning and teaching of English learners, high-quality and effective sheltered instruction results, and student achievement is improved.

As the authors of this book, we have approached our teaching, writing, and research from different and complementary fields. Jana Echevarría's research and publications have focused on issues in the education of English learners, and on ELs with special education needs, as well as on professional development for regular and special education teachers. MaryEllen Vogt's research interests include improving comprehension, especially in the content areas, content literacy for English learners, and teacher change and development. Deborah Short is a researcher and former sheltered instruction teacher with expertise in second-language development, academic literacy, methods for integrating language and content instruction, materials development, and teacher change.

The strength of our collaboration is that we approach the issue of educating English learners from different perspectives. In writing the book, we each provided a slightly different lens through which to view and discuss instructional situations. But our varied experiences have led us to the same conclusion: Educators need a resource for planning and implementing high-quality sheltered lessons for English learners, and the SIOP® Model is fulfilling this need.

Overview of the Book

Over the years, middle and high school teachers have asked for their own SIOP® book, with examples, lessons, instructional activities, and techniques that are especially effective for the ages and needs of the adolescents they teach. In response to these requests, we have revised the original *Making Content Comprehensible for English Learners: The SIOP® Model* (3rd ed.), and now you have your own book! Obviously, we did not revise or adapt the SIOP® Protocol or SIOP® Model because it is intended as a framework for teaching English learners (as well as all other students) of any age.

What is different in this book is that our focus is on teaching students in departmentalized or self-contained secondary classrooms. In this book, you will find many ideas, techniques, and activities for helping your older English learners access the core curriculum as well as teaching them the academic English they need to reach your academic content standards. As always, what is of critical importance is fidelity to the SIOP® Model. Former, recent, and current research studies have shown conclusively that the greater the degree of implementation of the SIOP® Model by teachers, the greater the academic achievement of English learners in their classrooms. To assist you in accessing the information you need from this book so you can be a "high implementer," we provide the following overview.

- **Content and language objectives.** One of the most important aspects of the SIOP® Model is the inclusion of both content and language objectives for each and every lesson. Many teachers have found writing these objectives to be challenging, even as they acknowledge their importance both for their own planning and for their students' understanding of the lesson's content goals and language focus. Therefore, you will find a comprehensive discussion in Chapter 2 (Lesson Preparation) that provides specific guidance for writing a range of content and language objectives, along with recommendations for how to effectively present them orally and in writing to students.
- **Discussion of the eight components and thirty features of the SIOP®.** Each chapter begins with discussion of a component of the SIOP® and its various features. For example, the discussion of lesson planning and preparation is found in the first half of Chapter 2. As you read about each feature in this section, think about how it would "look" in an actual classroom setting and how teachers might use this information to plan and prepare effective SIOP® lessons.
- **Teaching scenarios.** The second half of each chapter includes teaching scenarios. In these vignettes, three teachers, while teaching the same grade level and content, attempt to include the focal SIOP® features, but with varying degrees of success. At the end of each teaching scenario, you will have the opportunity to use that section of the SIOP® to rate the effectiveness of the lesson in implementing the particular SIOP® features. For example, as you read the teaching scenarios in Chapter 2, think about how well the three teachers included the features of the SIOP® component, Lesson Preparation, in their planning and preparation. Note that

the illustrated lessons throughout the book range from grades 6–12, and they cover a variety of content areas.

- **Discussion of the three teaching scenarios.** Following the description of the three teachers' lessons, you will be able to see how we have rated the lessons for their inclusion of the SIOP® features of effective sheltered instruction. We provide detailed explanations for the ratings and encourage you to discuss these with others in order to develop a high degree of inter-rater reliability.

- **Lesson activities.** In each chapter, you will find several ideas and activities identified with the icon shown at left as exemplars for implementing the eight components of the SIOP® Model. The activities are appropriate for both middle and high school classrooms. Some activities will be familiar because you already use them in your own classroom. We hope you'll be motivated to try the others because they represent best practice—those ideas and activities that are included have been found to be especially effective for English learners.
- **Discussion questions.** Based upon input from educators who have used this book, there are discussion questions found at the end of each chapter that reflect actual classroom practice with the SIOP® Model. We hope these questions will promote thinking about your own practice, conversations during professional development, and opportunities for portfolio reflection for preservice university and inservice courses.
- **The SIOP® protocol.** Two versions of the SIOP® protocol are included in Appendix A. The eight components and thirty features of the SIOP® are all the same as in the third edition of *Making Content Comprehensible for English Learners: The SIOP® Model* book.
- **SIOP® lesson plans.** We have been asked frequently for assistance with lesson planning for the SIOP® Model. In this edition, we have included four different formats for lesson plans (see Appendix B); we hope you will find one that is useful for you. In Chapters 2 and 5, you will also find complete plans for two of the lessons featured in the chapter scenarios (for Mr. Cullen and Mr. Montoya). In Chapter 6, you will find another lesson plan written for a technology class. These lesson plans are written with different formats, grade levels, and subject areas. (For additional sample lesson plans, see www.siopinstitute.net; *99 Ideas and Activities for Teaching English Learners with the SIOP® Model* (Vogt & Echevarría, 2008); *Implementing the SIOP® Model through Effective Professional Development and Coaching*, (Echevarría, Short, & Vogt, 2008); *The SIOP® Model for Teaching Mathematics to English Learners* (Echevarría, Vogt, & Short, in press); *The SIOP® Model for Teaching Science to English Learners* (Short, Vogt, & Echevarría, in press); *The SIOP® Model for Teaching History-Social Studies to English Learners* (Short, Vogt, & Echevarría, in press); and *The SIOP® Model for Teaching English/Language Arts to English Learners* (Vogt, Echevarría, & Short, in press).
- **Discussion of reading development and special education for English learners.** In our work with the SIOP® Institutes and in district trainings, we have heard many educators ask questions about English learners who have reading or learning problems and are struggling academically because of them. Based on the published report of the National Literacy Panel on Language-Minority Children and Youth (August & Shanahan, 2006a), and the Response to Intervention (RtI) initiative, we

have updated Chapter 10 with information and recommendations that we hope you will find helpful in SIOP® Model program design and implementation for students with special needs.

- **SIOP® Model research.** In Appendix C, you will find an overview of the findings from the original SIOP® Model research as well as a brief description of recent and current (at the time of this writing) national research studies on the SIOP® Model. We would greatly appreciate hearing about any additional SIOP® studies you are involved with or know about.
- **CD-ROM.** On the inside back cover, you will find a CD with video vignettes of classroom teachers whose instruction exemplifies each of the eight SIOP® components. Keep in mind that even though the CD clips illustrate particular components, you will see a number of features present in each clip. We hope these vignettes will promote reflection and discussion with your colleagues. In addition, you will find brief video clips of the authors speaking about aspects of the SIOP® Model.

Overview of the Chapters

The first chapter in the book introduces you to the pressing educational needs of English learners and to sheltered instruction. In Chapters 2 through 9, we explain the SIOP® Model in detail, drawing from educational theory, research, and practice to describe each component and feature of the SIOP® protocol. Teaching scenarios drawn from secondary classroom lessons of sheltered instruction teachers follow. The features of the SIOP® Model that pertain to each chapter are included for the lesson descriptions in the teaching scenarios. After you read about each of the teachers' lessons, use the SIOP® protocol to rate on the 0 to 4 rubric the degree to which the features are present. The classroom scenarios reflect a different grade level and content area in each chapter and are linked to core curriculum objectives and standards. All the classrooms include English learners, and many also include native English speakers.

In Chapter 10, we discuss the special needs of English learners who have reading problems and learning disabilities. You may wish to read this chapter before you delve into the SIOP® Model, especially if you have had little experience teaching English learners. It will assist you in situating the SIOP® Model in "real" classrooms with English learners who have a wide variety of academic and literacy abilities and needs. Chapter 11 provides a discussion of scoring and interpreting the SIOP® protocol, explaining how the instrument can be used holistically to measure teacher fidelity to the Model and strategically to guide the teacher in planning lessons for one or more targeted SIOP® components. A full lesson from one research classroom is described and rated, revealing areas of strength and areas for improvement that can guide the teacher in future planning and teaching.

As you read each scenario in the chapters that follow, reflect on how effectively the teacher is meeting the linguistic and academic needs of English learners, especially as related to the SIOP® features being described. If you were observing this teacher's lesson, how would you rate it along the five-point SIOP® rubric? Is a particular feature clearly evident in the lesson, thus receiving a rating of 4? Or is the respective feature somewhat evident, thus receiving a 2? Or is it clear that the teacher has not modified teaching practices at all to accommodate the needs of ELs, with the lesson thus receiving 0? Compare your assessment of the lessons with our discussion at the conclusion of the teaching scenarios.

In the appendixes, you will find the Sheltered Instruction Observation Protocol (SIOP®), both the comprehensive and the abbreviated versions. You will also find four lesson planning formats to guide your lesson design and implementation and an overview of research on the SIOP® Model. The book concludes with a Glossary of terms related to the instruction of English learners.

Acknowledgments

Many educators throughout the United States have contributed to this book through their work as SIOP® teachers, bilingual specialists, curriculum coordinators, school and district administrators, and professional developers. We thank them for their insights and critical analyses of the SIOP® Model and protocol. We also appreciate the contributions of those who have participated in the SIOP® Institutes throughout the country (for more information, see www.siopinstitute.net). At each of these Institutes, we gain new understanding about our work from those who participate in them.

We also thank the many teachers and administrators in whose schools we have conducted research on the SIOP® Model, both past and present. Their willingness to let us observe and discuss their teaching of English learners has enhanced our understandings and validated our work. The contributions of these fine educators to the ongoing development of the SIOP® Model are many, and we are grateful for their continued interest and encouragement.

We want to acknowledge a special group of expert teachers who have worked for many years with the SIOP® Model. They are the original cohort of National Faculty of the SIOP® Institute. They have provided input, a critical eye, many exceptional teaching ideas, and unconditional support. They include Melissa Castillo, John Seidlitz, Nicole Teyechea McNeil, Wanda Holbrook, Alvaro Hernandez, Martha Trejo, Kendra Moreno, and Karlin LaPorta.

We found the comments and suggestions from our reviewers to be of great help and we thank them: Julia S. Austin, University of Alabama at Birmingham; Danny Brassell, California State University, Dominguez Hills; Kay Casper, Independence Middle School (OK); and Socorro Herrera, Kansas State University and Madeleine Kingsbury, Overbrook High School (PA). We also appreciate the ongoing support, assistance, and patience of our Allyn & Bacon team, especially that of our editor, Aurora Martínez Ramos.

The original SIOP® work was supported under the Education Research and Development Program, PR/Award No. R306A60001, the Center for Research on Education, Diversity, & Excellence (CREDE), as administered by the former Office of Educational Research and Improvement, now the Institute for Education Studies (IES), National Institute on the Education of At-Risk Students (NIEARS), and U.S. Department of Education (ED). The contents, findings, and opinions expressed here are those of the authors and do not necessarily represent the positions or policies of IES, NIEARS, or ED.

Finally, we express appreciation to our families, whose support has enabled us to pursue our professional interests.

je mev djs

chapter 1

Introducing Sheltered Instruction

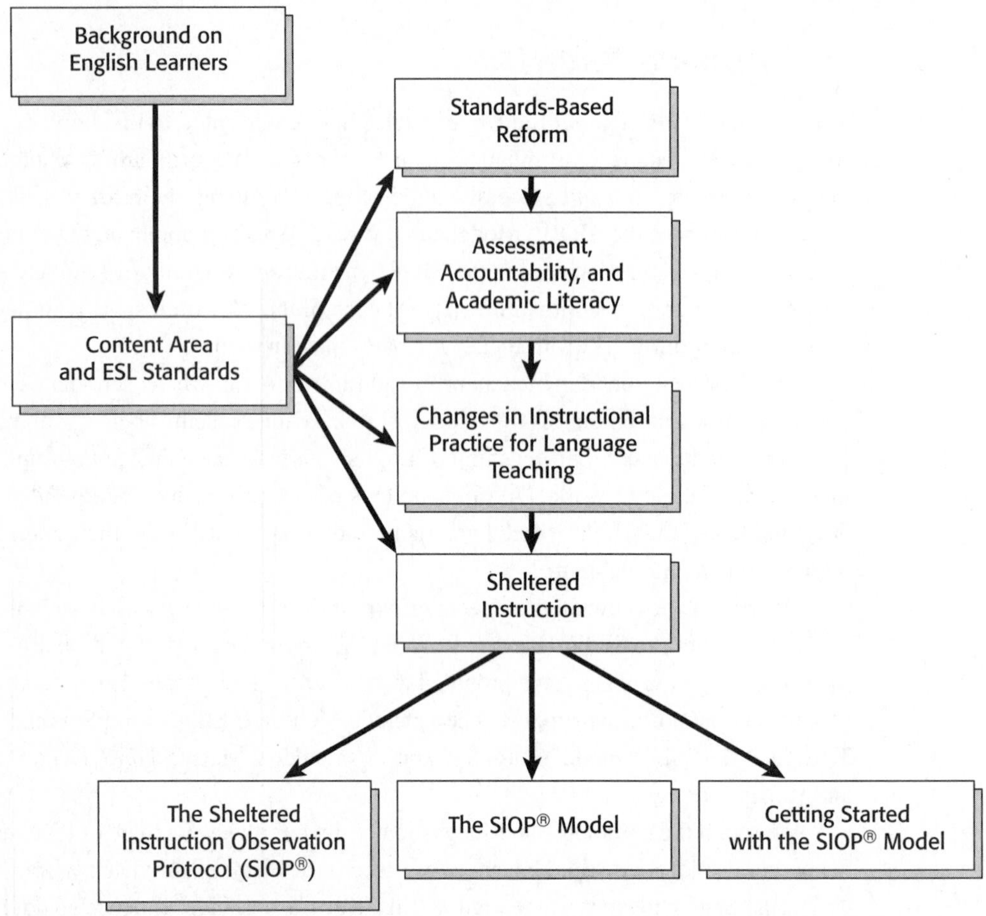

Objectives

After reading, discussing, and engaging in activities related to this chapter, you will be able to meet the following content and language objectives.

Content Objectives

Distinguish between content-based ESL and sheltered instruction.

List characteristics of English learners that may influence their success in school.

Explain the development of the SIOP® Model.

Language Objectives

Discuss the challenges of school reform and its effect on English learners.

Develop a lexicon related to sheltered instruction.

Javier put his head in his hands and sighed. He watched Ms. Barnett standing at the board and tried to understand what she was telling him. He looked at the clock; she'd been talking for 12 minutes now. She wrote some numbers on the board and he noticed his classmates getting out their books. Copying their actions, he too opened his history book to the page matching the first number on the board. He looked at the words on the page and began to sound them out, one by one, softly under his breath. He knew some words but not others. The sentences didn't make much sense. Why was this class so tough? He could understand the teacher much better in science. Mrs. Ontero let them do things. They would all crowd around a table and watch her as she did an experiment and then he got to work with his friends, Maria, Huynh, and Carlos, trying out the same experiment. He even liked the science book; it had lots of pictures and drawings. Mrs. Ontero always made them look at the pictures first and they talked about what they saw. The words on the pages weren't so strange either. Even the big ones matched the words Mrs. Ontero had them write down in their personal science dictionaries. If he forgot what a word meant in the textbook, he would look it up in his science dictionary. Or he could ask someone at his table. Mrs. Ontero didn't mind if he asked for help. This history class just wasn't the same. He had to keep quiet, he had to read, he couldn't use a dictionary, they didn't do things. . . .

Javier is experiencing different teaching styles in his ninth-grade classes. He has been in the United States for 14 months now and gets along with his classmates in English pretty well. They talk about CDs and TV shows, jeans and sneakers, soccer and basketball. But schoolwork is hard. Only science class and PE make sense to him. History, health, math, language arts—they're all confusing. He had a class in English as a second language (ESL) last year, but not now. He wonders why Mrs. Ontero's science class is easier for him to understand than his other classes.

Ironically, Javier is luckier than a number of English learners (ELs). He has one teacher who provides effective instruction as he learns content through English, a new language. If more of Javier's teachers learn the techniques that Mrs. Ontero uses, then Javier will have a chance to develop academic literacy in English and succeed in school. But it will take significant effort on the part of schools, districts, and universities to make this happen for Javier and other students like him.

We know that the foundation for academic success is laid in the elementary schools. If students are not able to read to learn by middle school, we know they will experience significant academic achievement challenges in high school. Consider the following statistics:

- Only 30 percent of all secondary students read proficiently, but for students of color, the situation is worse: 89 percent of Hispanic students and 86 percent of African American middle and high school students read below grade level (Perie, Grigg, & Donahue, 2005).
- Only 4 percent of eighth-grade ELs and 20 percent of students classified as "formerly EL" scored at the proficient or advanced levels on the reading portion of the 2005 National Assessment for Educational Progress (Perie, Grigg, & Donahue, 2005). This means that 96 percent of the eighth-grade limited English proficient (LEP) students scored *below* the Basic level.
- A dramatic, lingering divide in achievement exists between Caucasian students and those from culturally and linguistically diverse groups on state and national measures of achievement (California Dept. of Education, 2004; Kindler, 2002; Siegel, 2002). On the 2007 National Assessment of Education Progress (NAEP) 8th Grade Reading test, the average score for ELs was 42 points lower than the average score for non-ELs (Lee, Grigg & Donahue, 2007). On the 2007 National Assessment of Education Progress (NAEP) 8th Grade mathematics test, the average score for ELs was 37 points lower than the average score for non-ELs (Lee, Grigg & Dion, 2007).
- A recent five-year, statewide evaluation study found that English learners with 10 years of schooling in California had less than a 40 percent chance of meeting the criteria to be redesignated as fluent English proficient (Parish et al., 2006).
- English learners have some of the highest dropout rates and are more frequently placed in lower ability groups and academic tracks than language majority students (Ruiz-de-Velasco & Fix, 2000; Steinberg & Almeida, 2004).
- Only 10 percent of young adults who speak English at home fail to complete high school, but the percentage is three times higher (31 percent) for young adult English learners. If ELs reported speaking English with difficulty on the 2000 U.S. Census, their likelihood of completing high school was 18 percent. However, if they reported speaking English very well, their likelihood of graduating rose to 51 percent (NCES, 2004).

- Since the No Child Left Behind (NCLB) Act was implemented in 2001, there has been an increase in the number of high school ELs not receiving a diploma because they failed high-stakes tests despite fulfilling all other graduation requirements (Biancarosa & Snow, 2004; Edley & Wald, 2002; Kober, et al., 2006; McNeil, et al., 2008).

A number of recent reports have focused attention on the academic literacy crisis in U.S. schools, particularly for adolescent learners, but they offer very little guidance on how best to meet the varied and challenging literacy needs of ELs. Reports such as *Reading Next* (Biancarosa & Snow, 2004), *Reading to Achieve* (National Governors Association, 2005), *Creating a Culture of Literacy* (National Association of Secondary School Principals, 2005), and *Adolescents and Literacy* (Kamil, 2003) have looked at research, student performance, and promising practices. Only *Double the Work* (Short & Fitzsimmons, 2007) has specifically addressed this student population but primarily from a policy perspective.

We need our students like Javier to be successful in school and beyond. In the long run, such success will benefit the communities in which these students live and the national economy as a whole. This book, *Making Content Comprehensible for Secondary English Learners,* offers a solution to one aspect of school reform needed for English learners' acquisition of English and academic achievement, namely classroom instruction. It introduces a research-based model of sheltered instruction (SI) and demonstrates through classroom vignettes how the model can be implemented well.

Sheltered instruction is an approach for teaching content to English learners (ELs) in strategic ways that make the subject matter concepts comprehensible while promoting the students' English language development. It also may be referred to as SDAIE (specially designed academic instruction in English). Sheltering techniques are used increasingly in schools across the United States, particularly as teachers prepare students to meet high academic standards. However, in the past, the use of these techniques had been inconsistent from class to class, discipline to discipline, school to school, and district to district. The model of SI presented here mitigates this variability and provides guidance as to what constitutes the best practices for SI, grounded in more than two decades of classroom-based research, the experiences of competent teachers, and findings from the professional literature.

The goal of this book is to prepare teachers to teach content effectively to English learners while developing the students' language ability. The professional development model evolved from the Sheltered Instruction Observation Protocol (SIOP®), seen in Appendix A, an instrument originally used by researchers to measure teacher implementation of SI. Through subsequent research conducted by the National Center for Research on Education, Diversity, & Excellence (CREDE), the SIOP® Model was field tested and the protocol became a training and observation instrument that codifies and exemplifies the model. The SIOP® Model may be used as part of a program for preservice and inservice professional development, as a lesson planner for sheltered content lessons, and as a training resource for faculty. The protocol can be used as an observation measure for site-based administrators, supervisors of student teachers, and researchers who rate lessons.

The book is intended for teachers of linguistically and culturally diverse students in 6–12 settings, university faculty who prepare such teachers, site-based administrators, and others who provide technical assistance or professional development to 6–12 schools. Our research shows that both language and content teachers can implement the SIOP® Model fully to good effect. The model is best suited for content-based ESL courses and sheltered content courses that are part of a program of studies for English learners, and for mainstream content courses with English learners and struggling readers. Together these courses are proving to be a promising combination when implemented throughout a middle or high school.

Demographic Changes

Each year, the United States becomes more ethnically and linguistically diverse, with more than 90 percent of recent immigrants coming from non-English-speaking countries. From the 1989–1990 school year through 2005–2006, the number of identified students with limited English proficiency in public schools (K–12) grew 149 percent while total enrollment increased by only 21.5 percent (National Clearinghouse for English Language Acquisition, 2008). Thus, the proportion of English learners in the schools is growing even more rapidly than the actual numbers. In 2005–2006, more than five million school-age children were identified as limited English proficient (LEP, a federal designation)—greater than 10 percent of the K–12 public school student population.

The rise in immigrant students conforms to the increase in the immigrant population in the United States. The U.S. Census Bureau determined that in 1999, 20 percent of school-age children had at least one parent who was an immigrant and 5 percent of the students were immigrants themselves (Jamieson, Curry, & Martinez, 2001). When race or origin is considered, 65 percent of Hispanic students and 88 percent of Asian and Pacific Islander students had at least one immigrant parent.

According to Ruiz-de-Velasco & Fix (2000), the geographic distribution of immigrants is concentrated in urban areas, primarily in six states that account for three-fourths of all immigrant children: California (35 percent), Texas (11.3 percent), New York (11 percent), Florida (6.7 percent), Illinois (5 percent), and New Jersey (4 percent). However, the states with the fastest-growing LEP student populations are not the same as the top six traditional immigration states. For example, North Carolina experienced a 500 percent growth between 1993 and 2003, and Colorado, Nevada, Nebraska, Oregon, Georgia, and Indiana all had more than 200 percent increases in that time period (Batalova, Fix, & Murray, 2005). Moreover, many ELs are in linguistically segregated schools. More than half of the LEP students in elementary and secondary schools are in schools where more than 30 percent of the student population is identified as limited English proficient.

Changes in the geographic distribution of ELs present new challenges to the numerous districts in these new destination states that have not served these students in the past. Academic programs are not well-established; sheltered curricula and appropriate resources are not readily available; and most important, many teachers are not trained to meet the needs of these second language learners.

While the number of students with limited proficiency in English has grown exponentially across the United States, their level of academic achievement has lagged significantly behind that of their language-majority peers. As the statistics presented at the beginning of this chapter indicate, there exists growing evidence that most schools are not meeting the challenge of educating these students well. The lack of success in educating linguistically and culturally diverse students is problematic because federal and state governments expect *all* students to meet high standards and have adjusted national and state assessments as well as state graduation requirements to reflect new levels of achievement and to accommodate requirements of the No Child Left Behind Act (2001). In order for students whose first language is not English to succeed in school and become productive members of our society, they need to receive better educational opportunities in U.S. schools.

English Learner Diversity

To develop the best educational programs for ELs, we need to understand their diverse backgrounds. These learners bring a wide variety of educational and cultural experiences to the classroom as well as considerable linguistic differences, and these characteristics have implications for instruction, assessment, and program design. Once we know their backgrounds and abilities in their native language, we can incorporate effective techniques and materials in our instructional practices.

All adolescent English learners in schools today are not alike. They enter U.S. schools with a wide range of language proficiencies (in English and in their native languages) and of subject matter knowledge. In addition to the limited English proficiency and the approximately 180 native languages among the students, we also find diversity in their educational backgrounds, expectations of schooling, socioeconomic status, age of arrival, personal experiences while coming to and living in the United States, and parents' education levels and proficiency in English. All these factors impinge on the type of programs and instructional experiences the students should receive in order to succeed in school.

At one end of the spectrum among immigrant students, we find some secondary school ELs who had strong academic backgrounds before they came to the United States and entered our schools. Some of them are above equivalent grade levels in the school's curricula, in math and science for example. They are literate in their native language and may have already begun study of a second language. For these students, much of what they need is English language development so that as they become more proficient in English, they can transfer the knowledge they learned in their native country's schools to the courses they are taking in the United States. A few subjects, such as U.S. history, may need special attention because these students may not have studied them before. Of all the EL subgroups, these students have the greatest likelihood of achieving educational success if they receive appropriate English language and content instruction in their schools.

At the other end, some immigrant students arrive at our schoolhouse doors with very limited formal schooling—perhaps due to war in their native countries or the remote, rural location of their homes. These students have weak literacy in their native language (i.e., they cannot read or write), and they may not have had schooling experiences such as sitting at desks all day, changing teachers per subject, or taking district or national tests. They have significant gaps in their educational backgrounds, lack knowledge in specific subject areas, and often need time to become accustomed to school routines and expectations. These ELs with limited formal schooling and below-grade-level literacy are most at risk for educational failure. They are entering U.S. secondary schools with weak academic skills at the same time that schools are emphasizing rigorous, standards-based curricula and high-stakes assessments.

We also have students who have grown up in the United States but speak a language other than English at home. Remarkably, 57 percent of adolescent ELs were born in the

United States; that is, they are second- or third-generation immigrants (Batalova, Fix, & Murray, 2005). Some of the students in this group are literate in their home language, such as Mandarin, Arabic, or Spanish, and just need to add English to their knowledge base in school. Others, however, have yet to master either English or the home language. The large numbers of second- and third-generation LEP adolescents who continue to lack proficiency in English in secondary school suggest that many LEP children are not learning the language well even after many years in U.S. schools.

So far, we have been discussing English learners' individual characteristics and the roles they play in educational attainment. Sociocultural factors also have an influence. Poverty level, for example, is a key predictor of school success. Research has shown that poorer students, in general, are less academically successful (Glick & White, 2004). Some ELs come from middle- and upper-class homes, but according to the 2000 U.S. Census, immigrant youth are more likely to be poor than non-immigrants. For instance, 59 percent of adolescent LEP students live in families with incomes 185 percent below the poverty line compared with 28 percent of adolescents in English-only households (Batalova, Fix, & Murray, 2005). Some immigrant ELs are also undocumented, a factor that affects socioeconomic status and often limits postsecondary educational options. Mobility is another factor that can impinge on school success. Glick and White (2004) found that students with a previous move were twice as likely not to complete high school as those who had not moved. Home language experiences, on the other hand, can support academic literacy development (August & Shanahan, 2006). Ethnicity, however, does not appear to be an important factor in second language (L2) educational achievement (Ima & Rumbaut, 1989).

Given the variability in these students' backgrounds, it is clear that there is no simple, one-size-fits-all solution. They need different pathways for academic success. To meet this challenge, fundamental shifts need to occur in teacher development, program design, curricula and materials, and instructional and assessment practices.

School Reform and Accountability in the Twenty-First Century

The educational landscape has shifted in the past two decades. While the focus on standards-based instruction has been growing since the National Governors Association agreed to promote national education goals in 1989 and the National Council of Teachers of Mathematics issued the first curriculum standards for mathematics in that same year, the advent of the No Child Left Behind (NCLB) Act of 2001 has operationalized the goal of high standards and has held schools more accountable for the success of all of their students. States now have standards for mathematics, reading, language arts, English language development, and science, and implement high-stakes tests based on these standards. NCLB calls for annual testing of reading and mathematics achievement for all students in Title I schools in grades 3–8 and once again in high school. Science testing is also required at least once during the grade 3–5 span, the grade 6–9 span, and the grade 10–12 span. English learners are not only included in these assessment measures if enrolled in Title I schools but must also undergo additional testing of their English language development. While they are designated as limited English proficient, they must be tested yearly in grades K–12. Each state, with the approval of the U.S. Department of Education, sets benchmarks for achievement, and students are expected to make adequate yearly progress on all of these assessments.

As Coltrane (2002) points out, this act offers advantages and disadvantages to ELs. On the positive side, standards-based reform has increased academic rigor for all students with a push for academic literacy. This is beneficial for ELs, so teachers integrate content and language development in their lessons. To help teachers do this effectively, more and more districts are offering professional development on this topic. The requirement that districts disaggregate their test scores to measure progress of LEP students can also have a favorable impact in the long term. If schools do not show that all categories of students, including LEP students, are making annual yearly progress as a group over three years, corrective actions can be taken. This situation has led to improved program designs for English learners, new or revised curricula, and enhanced teacher professional development.

Nonetheless, there are negative implications. ELs, especially those at beginning levels, are learning this challenging content in a language they do not speak, read, or write proficiently. The high-stakes tests therefore are more often a test of their English knowledge than their content knowledge or skills (Coltrane, 2002; Menken, 2008). Furthermore, most of the standardized tests that states use have been designed for, and normed on, native English speakers who have spent their educational careers in U.S. schools. Thus, English learners are at a disadvantage.

In addition, the Center on Education Policy reports that twenty-three states require exit exams to graduate from high school, with three more states following suit by 2012 (Zabala, Minnici, McMurrer, & Briggs, 2008). Kober and colleagues (2006) reported that ELs have lower pass rates on these exit exams and lower graduation rates than native speakers, even with test accommodations such as directions provided in their native language and use of bilingual dictionaries or glossaries. Only three of the twenty-three states with these exit exams offer alternative measures specifically designed for English learners (Zabala, et al., 2008).

Furthermore, although NCLB calls for highly qualified teachers in every core academic classroom, it does not require content teachers with LEP students to have any educational background in ESL methodology or second language acquisition theory. Specific qualifications for teachers of "core academic subjects"—English, reading/language arts, mathematics, science, foreign languages, civics and government, economics, arts, history, and geography—are designated by the states, which primarily focus on teachers having a deep understanding of the content area (typically demonstrated by holding a degree in the content area or passing a specialized exam). Despite the rapidly growing numbers of these students, only four states at the time of this writing have policies that require all teachers in preservice programs to have an understanding of how to teach ELs effectively: Arizona, California, Florida, and New York.

The situation at the inservice level has not been any better. In the 1999–2000 Schools and Staffing Survey (National Center for Education Statistics, 2002), 41.2 percent of the 2,984,781 public school teachers reported teaching LEP students, but only 12.5 percent had had eight or more hours of training in the past three years. Eight hours is not even a minimum amount for effective training.

A recent survey that sampled teachers in twenty-two small, medium, and large districts in California (Gandara, Maxwell-Jolly, & Driscoll, 2005) found similar results. In the five years prior to the survey, "43 percent of teachers with 50 percent or more English learners in their classrooms had received no more than one inservice that focused on the instruction of English learners" (p. 13). Fifty percent of the teachers with somewhat fewer students (26–50 percent English learners in their classes), had had no, or only one, such inservice.

Given that LEP students are more than 10 percent of the K–12 student population now, and their proportion of the total student population increases each year, the current status of teacher preparation and development is inadequate for the educational needs of English learners. Indeed, the most desired professional development topics for the secondary teachers in the California survey (Gandara et al., 2005) were training in reading and writing in English, instructional strategies, including those for English language development and for the content areas, and cultural issues related to their students. Unfortunately, at present, many English learners receive much of their instruction from content area teachers or aides who have not had appropriate professional development to address their second language development needs or to make content instruction comprehensible. This situation hinders their academic success.

Because most state certification does not require it and most teacher preparation institutions are not developing all teacher candidates so they can teach linguistically and culturally diverse students appropriately, school districts try to compensate. However, moving toward ongoing, sustained professional development and away from ineffective, one-shot workshops has been a slow process. Research shows that professional development approaches that improve teaching include the following: sustained, intensive development with modeling, coaching, and problem solving; collaborative endeavors for educators to share knowledge; experiential opportunities that engage teachers in actual teaching, assessment, and observation; and development grounded in research but also drawing from teacher experience and inquiry, connected to the teachers' classes, students, and subjects taught (Borko, 2004; Darling-Hammond, 1998; NCTAF, 1997; Weiss & Pasley; 2006).

English learners also have difficulty in school when there is a mismatch among program design, instructional goals, and student needs. Historically, schools offered ESL or bilingual education programs to ELs with specially trained teachers, yet kept those teachers and students separate from regular school programs. Depending on school or state policy and resource availability, ELs were schooled in ESL or bilingual classes and were not a concern of the regular content or classroom teacher until they exited the language support program. In theory, the ELs would make that transition when they were proficient in English and able to perform subject area course work in English-medium classrooms. In practice, however, students would exit before they are proficient in academic English, for several reasons: (1) the number of these students increased without a comparable increase in certified teachers, so it became impossible to relegate the education of these students to separate, specialized classes; (2) policies have been enacted in which the number of years that students are permitted access to language support services is quite limited, such as in Massachusetts, Arizona, and California where the goal is to move students into regular classrooms after one year.

These policies are misguided if ELs are moved into classrooms lacking well-trained teachers and appropriate curricula and materials. Research shows that conversational fluency develops inside and outside the classroom and can be attained in one to three years (Thomas & Collier, 2002). However, the language that is critical for educational success—academic language (Cummins, 2000)—is more complex and develops more slowly and systematically in academic settings. It may take students from four to seven years of study, depending on individual and sociocultural factors, before they are proficient in academic English (Collier, 1987; Hakuta, Butler, & Witt, 2000; Lindholm-Leary & Borsato, 2006; Thomas & Collier, 2002). In their national research study, Thomas and Collier found that there is a large achievement gap between ELs and native English speakers across most program models. For this gap to be closed with bilingual/ESL content programs, students must gain three to four more NCE (normal curve equivalent) points each year than native English speakers gain. The only way to do that is to have well-implemented, cognitively challenging, not segregated, and sustained programs of five to six years' duration. Typical programs of two to three years are ineffective in closing the large achievement gap.

When policies and programs are in place that complement the research on second language acquisition, we see more positive outcomes. For example, recent analyses from New York City and the states of New Jersey, Washington, and California reveal that former English learners outperformed students as a whole on state tests, exit exams, and graduation rates (DeLeeuw, 2008; New York City Department of Education, 2004; State of New Jersey Department of Education, 2006; Sullivan, et al., 2005). These results indicate that when English learners are given time to develop academic English proficiency in their programs and are exited (and redesignated) with criteria that measure their ability to be successful in mainstream classes, they perform on average as well as or better than the state average on achievement measures.

Academic Literacy

The foundation of school success is academic literacy in English. Although not understood by many educators, age-appropriate knowledge of the English language is a prerequisite in the attainment of content standards. We learn primarily through language, and use language to express our understanding. As Lemke (1988, p. 81) explained,

> . . . educators have begun to realize that the mastery of academic subjects is the mastery of their specialized patterns of language use, and that language is the dominant medium through which these subjects are taught and students' mastery of them tested.

Defining academic language or academic literacy has been of interest to educators and researchers in the field of second language acquisition and literacy. Most of the definitions incorporate reading, writing, listening, and speaking skills as part of academic language and refer to a specialized academic register of the formal written and spoken code. Although there is not yet a single agreed-upon definition, each one considers how language is used in school to acquire new knowledge and foster success on academic tasks (Bailey, 2007; Gibbons, 2002; Schleppegrell, 2004; Short, 2002). Without proficient oral and written English language skills, students are hard pressed to learn and demonstrate their knowledge of mathematical reasoning, science skills, social studies concepts, and so forth.

Relationship to second language learning

Academic language is used by all students in school settings, native English speakers (referred to as English-only students or EOs) and English learners alike. However, this type of language use is particularly challenging for English learners who are beginning to acquire English at the same time that school tasks require a high level of English usage. Participation in informal conversation demands less from an individual than joining in an academic discussion (Cummins, 2000). While the distinction is not completely clear, it is widely accepted that the language skills required for informal conversation differ from those required for academic processes such as summarizing information, evaluating perspectives, and drawing conclusions. Certainly, one may converse in a cognitively demanding way—such as debating a current event that requires significant knowledge of both sides of the topic and uses a high-level academic language—but that is not the typical social conversation. The distinction becomes clearer when we consider that students have the ability to converse in English without needing a strong repertoire of academic language skills. In many instances, English learners appear to speak English well in hallways, on playing fields, and in small talk before a lesson begins, but struggle to use English well in classroom assignments or on tests. This situation occurs because they have not yet acquired a high level of academic language which tends to be cognitively demanding and highly decontextualized (Cummins, 1984).

Role in schooling

The relationship between literacy proficiency and academic achievement grows stronger as grade levels rise—regardless of individual student characteristics. In secondary school classes, language use becomes more complex and more content area specific (Biancarosa & Snow, 2004). English learners must develop literacy skills for each content area *in* their second language as they simultaneously learn, comprehend, and apply content area concepts *through* their second language (Garcia & Godina, 2004).

Specifically, English learners must master academic English, which includes semantic and syntactic knowledge along with functional language use. Using English, students, for example, must be able to read and understand the expository prose found in textbooks and reference materials, write persuasively, argue points of view, and take notes from teacher lectures or Internet sites. They must articulate their thinking skills in English—make hypotheses and predictions, express analyses, draw conclusions, and so forth. In content classes, ELs must pull together their emerging knowledge of the English language with the content knowledge they are studying in order to complete the academic tasks. They must also learn *how* to do these tasks—generate the format of an outline, negotiate roles in cooperative learning groups, interpret charts and maps, and such. These three knowledge bases—knowledge of English, knowledge of the content topic, and knowledge of how the tasks are to be accomplished—constitute the major components of academic literacy (Short, 2002).

Although we have yet to determine how best to teach academic language to English learners, there is agreement that it should be done and should include a focus on the lexical, semantic, and discourse levels of the language as they are applied in school settings. Analyses of academic language used in assessments by Bailey and Butler (2007) found that there appears to be content-specific language (such as technical terms like *latitude* and *longitude,* and phrases like "We hypothesize that . . .") and general, or common core, academic language (such as how to structure an argument and use persuasive language) that is useful across curriculum areas. Similarly, there are general academic tasks that one needs to know how to do to be academically proficient (e.g., create a timeline) and more specific tasks (e.g., write a scientific laboratory report). They argue teachers and curricula should pay attention to this full range of academic language. As a result, the enhancement of ELs' academic language skills should enable them to perform better on assessments. This conclusion is bolstered by an older study: Snow et al. (1991) found that performance on highly decontextualized (i.e., school-like) tasks, such as providing a formal definition of words, predicted academic performance, whereas performance on highly contextualized tasks, such as face-to-face communication, did not.

Reviews of research

In recent years, two major syntheses of the research on the education of English learners have been conducted, both with an eye toward academic literacy. The National Literacy Panel on Language-Minority Children and Youth (hereafter NLP) (August & Shanahan, 2006a) analyzed and synthesized the research on these learners with regard to English literacy attainment. Many of the studies that the thirteen-member expert panel examined looked at the reading and writing skills needed for successful schooling. The panel considered second language literacy development, crosslinguistic influences and transfer, sociocultural contexts, instruction and professional development, and student assessment. Figure 1.1 summarizes the findings of the NLP panel that appeared in the executive summary (August & Shanahan, 2006b).

The second major review was conducted by researchers from the National Center for Research on Education, Diversity & Excellence (CREDE), the former federally funded research center. Their focus was on oral language development, literacy development (from instructional and cross-linguistic perspectives), and academic achievement. Both syntheses led to similar findings.

Some of the findings that are closely related to the topics in this book are the following:

- Processes of second language (L2) literacy development are influenced by a number of variables that interact with each other in complex ways (e.g., L1 literacy, L2 oralcy, socioeconomic status, and more).
- Certain L1 skills and abilities transfer to English literacy: phonemic awareness, comprehension and language learning strategies, and L1 and L2 oral knowledge.

FIGURE 1.1 ***Research Findings from the National Literacy Panel on Language-Minority Children and Youth***

1. English language learners (ELLs) benefit from instruction in the key components of reading as defined by the National Reading Panel (NICHD, 2000) as phonemic awareness, phonics, fluency, vocabulary, and text comprehension.
2. Instruction in these five components is necessary but not sufficient to teach ELLs to read and write proficiently in English. Oral language proficiency is needed also, so ELLs need instruction in this area.
3. Oral proficiency and literacy in the student's native language (L1) will facilitate development of literacy in English, but literacy in English can also be developed without proficiency in the L1.
4. Individual student characteristics play a significant role in English literacy development.
5. Home language experiences can contribute to English literacy achievement, but on the whole, the research on the influence of sociocultural factors is limited.

(August & Shanahan, 2006b)

- Teaching the five major components of reading (NICHD, 2000) to English learners is necessary but not sufficient for developing academic literacy. ELs need to develop oral language proficiency as well.
- Oralcy and literacy can develop simultaneously.
- Academic literacy in the native language facilitates the development of academic literacy in English.
- High-quality instruction for English learners is similar to high-quality instruction for other, English-speaking students, but ELs need instructional accommodations and support to fully develop their English skills.
- English learners need enhanced, explicit vocabulary development.

More information on these findings and their implications for developing academic literacy can be found in August & Shanahan (2006a), Genesee et al. (2006), Goldenberg (2008), and Short & Fitzsimmons (2007).

Changes in Instructional Practice for English Learners

The ESL profession has always been sensitive to student needs, and the evolution of ESL methodologies has been a dynamic process over the past five decades (Short, 2006; Stoller, 2004). Teachers have realized that students would benefit from new instructional approaches and have adjusted pedagogical practice and the content of the curriculum over time. But ESL and bilingual teachers alone cannot provide the necessary educational opportunities these learners need.

In the first half of the twentieth century, most language teaching relied on the direct method of instruction or a grammar translation approach. Yet by the 1950s, direct method and grammar translation languished and audiolingual methods surfaced. In the 1970s and after, the audiolingual method was displaced by the communicative method for ESL teaching, preparing students to use functional language in meaningful, relevant ways. As districts implemented communicative curricula, students were given opportunities to discuss material of high interest and topicality, which in turn motivated them to learn and participate in class. Students were encouraged to experiment with language and assume greater responsibility for their learning.

The communicative approach engendered the content-based ESL approach. Viewing the grade-level curricula as relevant, meaningful content for ELs, educators have developed content-based ESL curricula and accompanying instructional strategies to help better prepare the students for their transition to mainstream classes. Content-based ESL classes, in which all the students are ELs, are taught by language educators whose main goal is English language skill development but whose secondary goal is preparing the students for the mainstream, English-medium classroom (Cantoni-Harvey, 1987; Crandall, 1993; Mohan, 1986; Short, 1994). The sophistication of the material presented necessarily varies according to the language proficiency of the students in class, but nonetheless this material addresses key topics in grade-level subjects.

In content-based ESL, content from multiple subject areas is often presented through thematic or interdisciplinary units. For example, in the seventh grade, one theme might be the Impact of the Transcontinental Railroad. In their content-based ESL classes, the middle schoolers might look at letters (in translation) written by Chinese immigrants who worked on the railroad, read diary entries from those who migrated west, sing songs from the period, make maps of the progress of the railroad, and watch video clips depicting changes to the Native Americans' and cattle ranchers' lives. They would thus explore objectives from language arts, social studies, music, and science. For the high school classroom, a theme such as "urbanization" might be selected, and lessons could include objectives drawn from environmental science, geography, world history, economics, and algebra. Students with less proficiency might take field trips around a local city and create maps, transportation routes, and brochures. Advanced students might learn to use reference materials and computers to conduct research on the development of cities and their respective population growth. They might study persuasive language to debate advantages and disadvantages to urbanization. English learners may contribute to this topic because some have lived in cities or rural settings overseas. Some may have experienced moving from small towns to large cities and can express their opinions about the differences.

In general, content-based ESL teachers seek to develop the students' English language proficiency by incorporating information from the subject areas that students are likely to study or from courses they may have missed if they are fairly new to the school system. Whatever subject matter is included, for effective content-based ESL instruction to occur, teachers need to provide practice in academic skills and tasks common to mainstream classes (Chamot & O'Malley, 1994; Mohan, Leung, & Davison, 2001; Short, 2002).

Content-based ESL instruction, however, has not been sufficient to help all ELs succeed academically. So the ESL profession developed the SI approach in conjunction with content teachers, and this process was accelerated by the educational reform movement. Through SI, which is described in more detail in the next section, ELs would participate in a content course with grade-level objectives delivered through modified instruction that made the information comprehensible to the students. The classes may be variously named ESL Pre-Algebra, Sheltered Chemistry, or the like, and a series of courses may constitute a program called Content-ESL, Sheltered Instruction (SI), or SDAIE, yet the goal remains the same: to teach content to students learning English through a developmental language approach. It is generally taught by content area teachers rather than ESL specialists and can be offered to students of all levels of English proficiency.

Sheltered instruction is an approach that can extend the time students have for getting language support services while giving them a jump start on the content subjects they will need for graduation. SI is *not* simply a set of additional or replacement instructional techniques that teachers implement in their classrooms. Instead, it draws from and complements methods advocated for both second language and mainstream classrooms. For example, some techniques include cooperative learning, connections to student experiences, targeted vocabulary development, slower speech and fewer idiomatic expressions for less proficient students, use of visuals and demonstrations, and use of adapted text and supplementary materials (Short & Echevarria, 2004).

Content-based ESL and SI are favored methods for ELs today, as reflected in the national English language proficiency (ELP) standards developed by the Teachers of English to Speakers of Other Languages (TESOL). Four of the five standards in the *PreK-12 English language proficiency standards* (TESOL, 2006) are specifically geared to the academic language of the core subject areas. Standards 2, 3, 4, and 5 state "English language learners communicate information, ideas, and concepts necessary for academic success in the area of _______": language arts (#2), mathematics (#3), science (#4), and social studies (#5), respectively. By late 2008, nineteen states had adopted English language proficiency standards (ELP) similar to TESOL's, known as the WIDA (World-Class Instructional Design and Assessment) standards and the companion ELP test, ACCESS for ELLs® (ACCESS: Assessing Comprehension and Communication in English State to State for English Language Learners), to guide and measure annual gains in English language proficiency (WIDA consortium, 2007). To help their ELs meet the WIDA ELP standards, districts in these states, among others, are training teachers in content-based ESL and SI approaches, especially in the SIOP® Model, which we discuss later in this chapter.

SI plays a major role in a variety of educational program designs (Duff, 2005; Genesee, 1999). It may be part of an ESL program, a late-exit bilingual program, a two-way bilingual immersion program, a newcomer program, or a foreign language immersion program. In some districts, it is the name of the language support program itself. For students studying in content-based ESL or bilingual courses, SI often provides the bridge to the mainstream, and the amount of SI provided should increase as students move toward transition out of these programs. Any program in which students are learning content through a nonnative language should use the SI approach.

In some schools, SI is provided to classes composed entirely of ELs. In others, a heterogeneous mix of native and nonnative English speakers may be present. Bilingual, ESL, and content teachers may be the instructors for these classes (Sheppard, 1995). Depending on school system regulations, a sheltered pre-algebra course, for example, might be delivered by an ESL teacher or a mathematics teacher. Ideally, all content teachers would be trained in areas such as second language acquisition and ESL methodology although, as mentioned earlier, often that is not the case. At the high school level, sheltered content courses are generally delivered by content teachers so that students may receive the core content, not elective, credit required for graduation.

Research has shown, however, that a great deal of variability exists in the design of SI courses and the delivery of SI lessons, even among trained teachers (August & Hakuta, 1997; Berman et al., 1995; Sheppard, 1995) and within the same schools. Some schools, for instance, offer only SI courses in one subject area, such as social studies, but not in other areas ELs must study. By the mid-1990s, it was our experience as well: after two decades of observing SI teachers in class, one SI classroom did not look like the next in terms of the teacher's instructional language; the tasks the students have to accomplish; the degree of interaction that occurs between teacher and student, student and student, and student and text; the amount of class time devoted to language development issues versus assessing content knowledge; the learning strategies taught to and used by the students; the availability of appropriate materials; and more. This situation was the impetus for our research: to develop a valid, reliable, and effective model of SI.

In retrospect, this lack of consistency across SI classes was somewhat predictable. Sheltered curricula for different areas were few in number and varied widely from school district to school district. Commercial publishers offered a relatively small amount of instructional and pedagogical resources for sheltered courses. There was no model to follow. Teachers were encouraged to pick and choose techniques they enjoyed or believed work best with their students, and very few teachers were specially prepared to be SI teachers through undergraduate or graduate work. Few systematic and sustained forms of professional development were available for SI teachers.

The Sheltered Instruction Observation Protocol

The first version of the Sheltered Instruction Observation Protocol (SIOP®) was drafted in the early 1990s in order to exemplify the model of SI we were developing. We used it exclusively as a research and supervisory tool to determine if observed teachers incorporated key sheltered techniques consistently in their lessons. The preliminary instrument was field-tested with sheltered teachers and refined according to teacher feedback and observations in the classrooms. This early draft, like subsequent ones, pulled together findings and recommendations from the research literature with our professional experiences and those of our collaborating teachers on effective classroom-based practices from the areas of ESL, bilingual education, reading, language and literacy acquisition, discourse studies, special education, and classroom management. We sought to determine which combination of best practices in one instructional framework would yield positive achievement results for English learners.

In 1996, the National Center for Research on Education, Diversity & Excellence (CREDE) was funded by the Office of Educational Research and Improvement, U.S. Department of Education, and we designed a study on SI for its research program. The goals of the research project were to (1) develop an explicit model of sheltered instruction; (2) use that model to train teachers in effective sheltered strategies; and (3) conduct field experiments and collect data to evaluate teacher change and the effects of sheltered instruction on LEP students' English language development and content knowledge. (See Appendix C for a discussion of the research study and its findings.) The project built on preliminary versions of the SIOP® protocol as a small cohort of teachers worked with the researchers to refine the features further: distinguishing between effective strategies for beginner, intermediate, and advanced English learners; determining "critical" versus "unique" sheltered teaching strategies; and making the SIOP® more user friendly.

Over the course of the next three years, and with an expanded team of teachers from districts on both the East and West Coasts, the SIOP® continued to be refined, strengthened, and used for professional development with research project teachers (Short & Echevarria, 1999). A substudy confirmed the SIOP® protocol to be a valid and reliable measure of the SIOP® Model (Guarino et al., 2001). During this time, the teacher-researcher cohort suggested that the SIOP® become more than an observation protocol. They recommended that it become a lesson planning and delivery system as well. "If you are going to rate our lessons based on the protocol, shouldn't we use it to plan our lessons?" one of the teachers asked. And so the SIOP® term now refers to both the observation instrument for rating the fidelity of lessons to the model (as shown in Appendix A) and, as will be explained in detail in the following chapters, the instructional model for lesson planning and delivery. Figure 1.2 shows the terminology we will be using in this book to distinguish between these two uses. In addition, we will use SIOP® as a modifier to describe teachers implementing the model (SIOP® teachers)

FIGURE 1.2 ***SIOP® Terminology***

SIOP® Model = the lesson planning and delivery system
SIOP® protocol = the instrument used to observe, rate, and provide feedback on lessons

and lessons incorporating the thirty features (SIOP® lessons). The SIOP® term therefore refers to both the observation instrument for researchers, administrators, and teachers to match the implementation of a lesson to the model of instruction and the instructional model for teachers to plan and deliver lessons.

Specifically, the SIOP® protocol provides concrete examples of the features of SI that can enhance and expand teachers' instructional practice. The protocol is composed of thirty features grouped into eight main components: Lesson Preparation & Building Background, Comprehensible Input, Strategies, Interaction, Practice & Application, Lesson Delivery, and Review & Assessment. These components emphasize the instructional practices that are critical for second language learners as well as high-quality practices that benefit all students.

The six features under Lesson Preparation examine the lesson planning process, including the language and content objectives, the use of supplementary materials, and the meaningfulness of the activities. Building Background focuses on making connections with students' background experiences and prior learning and developing their academic vocabulary. Comprehensible Input considers adjusting teacher speech, modeling academic tasks, and using multimodal techniques to enhance comprehension. The Strategies component emphasizes teaching learning strategies to students, scaffolding instruction, and promoting higher-order thinking skills. The features of Interaction remind teachers to encourage elaborated speech and to group students appropriately for language and content development. Practice & Application provides activities to practice and extend language and content learning while Lesson Delivery ensures teachers present a lesson that meets the planned objectives. In the Review & Assessment component, four features consider whether the teacher reviewed the key language and content concepts, assessed student learning, and provided feedback to students on their output.

From 1999 to 2002, the researchers field-tested and refined the SIOP® Model's professional development program, which incorporates key features of effective teacher development as recommended by Darling-Hammond (1998). The program includes professional development institutes (see *www.siopinstitute.net*), videotapes of exemplary SIOP® teachers (Hudec & Short, 2002a, 2002b), facilitator's guides (Echevarria & Vogt, 2008; Short, Hudec, & Echevarria, 2002), and other training materials.

Since that original CREDE SIOP® study, other research studies have been undertaken or are in progress (see Appendix C). In addition, school districts have conducted evaluations on their implementation of the model. (See *Implementing the SIOP® Model Through Effective Professional Development and Coaching,* Echevarria, Short, & Vogt, 2008, for district information.)

The SIOP® Model

As noted, the SIOP® Model described in this book is the product of several research studies conducted by the authors since the early 1990s. It is grounded in the professional literature and in the experiences and best practice of the researchers and participating teachers who worked collaboratively on developing the observation instrument that codifies it. The theoretical underpinning of the model is that language acquisition is enhanced through meaningful use and interaction. Through the study of content,

To learn about SIOP® implementation in schools and classrooms, please view the corresponding video clip (Chapter 1, Module 1) on the accompanying CD.

students interact in English with meaningful material that is relevant to their schooling. Because language processes, such as listening, speaking, reading, and writing, develop interdependently (Genesee et al., 2006; August & Shanahan, 2006a), SIOP® lessons incorporate activities that integrate those skills.

In effective SIOP® lessons, language and content objectives are systematically woven into the curriculum of one particular subject area, such as sixth-grade language arts, U.S. history, algebra, or life science. Teachers generally present the regular, grade-level subject curriculum to the students through modified instruction in English, although some special curricula may be designed for students with significant gaps in their educational backgrounds or very low literacy skills. Teachers must develop the students' academic language proficiency consistently and regularly as part of the lessons and units they plan and deliver (Echevarria & Graves, 2007; Echevarria & Short, in press; Short, 2002). The SIOP® Model we have developed shares many techniques found in high-quality, nonsheltered teaching for native English speakers, but it is characterized by careful attention to the English learners' distinctive second language development needs.

Accomplished SIOP® teachers modulate the level of English used with and among students and make the content comprehensible through techniques such as the use of visual aids, modeling, demonstrations, graphic organizers, vocabulary previews, adapted texts, cooperative learning, peer tutoring, and native language support. They make specific connections between the content being taught and students' experiences and prior knowledge, and they focus on expanding the students' vocabulary base. Besides increasing students' declarative knowledge (i.e., factual information), SIOP® teachers highlight and model procedural knowledge (e.g., how to accomplish an academic task like writing a science report or conducting research on the Internet) along with study skills and learning strategies (e.g., note-taking and self-monitoring comprehension when reading).

In effective SIOP® lessons, there is a high level of student engagement and interaction with the teacher, with other students, and with text, which leads to elaborated discourse and critical thinking. Student language learning can be promoted through social interaction and contextualized communication as teachers guide students to construct meaning and understand complex concepts from texts and classroom discourse (Vygotsky, 1978). Students are explicitly taught functional language skills as well, such as how to negotiate meaning, confirm information, argue, persuade, and disagree. Teachers introduce them to the classroom discourse community and demonstrate skills like taking turns in a conversation and interrupting politely to ask for clarification. Through instructional conversations and meaningful activities, students practice and apply their new language and content knowledge.

SIOP® teachers also consider their students' affective needs, cultural backgrounds, and learning styles. They strive to create a nonthreatening environment where students feel comfortable taking risks with language. They socialize ELs to the implicit classroom culture, including appropriate behaviors and communication patterns. SIOP® teachers engage in culturally responsive teaching and build on the students' potentially different ways of learning, behaving, and using language (Bartolome, 1994). They also plan activities that tap into the auditory, visual, and kinesthetic preferences of the students. Many effective SIOP® teachers consider the multiple intelligences of their students as well, and provide a variety of assignments that might appeal to the logical/mathematical child, the musical child, the artist, and those with other intelligences (Gardner, 1993).

Depending on the students' proficiency levels, SIOP® teachers offer multiple pathways for students to demonstrate their understanding of the content. For example, teachers may plan pictorial, hands-on, or performance-based assessments for individual students, group tasks or projects, oral reports, written assignments, portfolios, and more common measures such as paper and pencil tests and quizzes to check student comprehension and language growth. In this way, teachers can receive a more accurate picture of most English learners' content knowledge and skills—through an assortment of assessment measures than through one standardized test (TESOL, 2001). Otherwise, student performance may be perceived as lack of mastery of the content when it is actually the normal pace of the second language acquisition process (Abedi & Lord, 2001; Solano-Flores & Trumbull, 2003).

The SIOP® Model is also distinguished by use of supplementary materials that support the academic text. These may include related reading texts (e.g., trade books), graphs and other illustrations, models and other realia, audiovisual and computer-based resources, adapted text, and the like. The purpose of these materials is to enhance student understanding of key topics, issues, and details in the content concepts being taught through means other than teacher lecture or textbook prose. Supplementary materials can also aid teachers in providing information to students with mixed proficiency levels of English. Some students in a mixed class may be able to use the textbook while others may need an adapted text.

The SIOP® Model has been designed for flexibility and tested in a wide range of classroom situations: those with all ELs and those with a mix of native and nonnative English speakers, those with students who have strong academic backgrounds and those with students who have had limited formal schooling, those with students who are recent arrivals and those who have been in U.S. schools for several years, those with students at beginning levels of English proficiency and those with students at advanced levels. The research evidence shows that the SIOP® Model can improve the academic literacy of ELs. In the original CREDE research, using an assessment of student expository writing (using pre- and post-measures), students who participated in classes taught by teachers trained in the SIOP® Model improved their writing skills significantly more than students in classes with non-SI-trained teachers. In the more recent New Jersey SIOP® study, students with SIOP®-trained teachers made statistically significant gains in their average mean scores for oral language, writing, and total proficiency on the IDEA Proficiency Test (IPT), which had been the state assessment of English language proficiency, compared to a comparison group of ELs (Center for Applied Linguistics, 2007).

It is important to recognize that the SIOP® Model does not require teachers to throw away their favored techniques or add copious new elements to a lesson. Rather, this model of SI brings together *what* to teach by providing a framework for *how* to teach it. It reminds teachers to select and organize techniques that facilitate the integration of district- or state-level standards for ESL and for specific content areas.

Implementing the SIOP® Model: Getting Started

The implementation of the SIOP® Model is one key to improving the academic success of English learners: Preservice teachers need it to develop a strong foundation in SI; practicing teachers need it to strengthen their lesson planning and delivery and to provide students with more consistent instruction. Site-based supervisors and administrators use it to

To hear the authors discuss the SIOP® model, please view the corresponding video clips (Chapter 1, Modules 2 and 3) on the accompanying CD.

train and coach teachers, and conduct classroom observations. Teacher education faculty also use the SIOP® Model in their methods courses and in student teacher supervision. As the SIOP® Model has become more broadly established across the United States and abroad, several applications have been put into practice:

- Teacher lesson plan checklist and self-assessment tool
- Research observation tool for fidelity of model implementation
- Supervision and observation tool for student teachers
- Classroom observation tool for administrators
- Program of professional development

If you are a teacher, you may begin using the SIOP® Model as a guide to teaching high-quality sheltered instruction. You may want to assess your areas of strength and your areas for improvement. As you consider your self-assessment, you may decide to focus on one component at a time. If you are unfamiliar with comprehensible input techniques, you may want to practice implementing them as a first step. Or you may need to become accustomed to writing language and content objectives (see Chapter 2) and the way those objectives influence sheltered lessons (see Chapters 8 and 9). As your proficiency in one area of the SIOP® Model is attained, other components of the model should be added to your teaching repertoire. Once you are familiar with the features in the individual components, you should use the SIOP® protocol as a lesson plan checklist to write your lessons and reflect on them after teaching. A new resource (Vogt & Echevarria, 2008) offers a multitude of teaching ideas and activities for enhancing SIOP® components in your lessons. In addition, books detailing SIOP® lessons and units for English-language arts, mathematics, history/social studies, and science are available (Echevarria, Vogt, & Short, in press; Short, Vogt, & Echevarria, in press; Short, Vogt, & Echevarria, in press; Vogt, Echevarria, & Short, in press).

If you are a coach, staff developer, or university field-experience supervisor, you need to understand that learning to implement the SIOP® Model is a process. Not all features will be observed to a high degree in the beginning stages. Working through the SIOP® Model systematically over time will be the most effective way to ensure it will become internalized and present in the teachers' regular classroom practice. We encourage coaches and supervisors to use a collaborative approach with teachers who are implementing SI, including conferencing about observations, setting goals for implementing other features of the model, reflecting on progress in using the SIOP® Model, and so forth. The protocol is an excellent tool for targeted and productive discussions between a teacher and a supervisor. Another new resource, *Implementing the SIOP® Model Through Effective Professional Development and Coaching,* (Echevarria, Short, & Vogt, 2008) offers additional tips for professional development and coaching drawn from the experiences of school districts around the United States that have been implementing the SIOP® Model successfully for several years.

In some districts, school administrators are using the SIOP® protocol in a checklist format when they observe teachers. They mark if the feature is present or absent. It is important to note that we designed the protocol as an observation tool, not an evaluation instrument. The protocol is best used to rate the lesson being delivered and determine how faithful it is to the complete SIOP® Model. Administrators should not use the protocol for teacher evaluation, especially while the teachers are learning the model. In order to change their regular lesson style to the SIOP® Model, teachers must take some risks. Because the process takes time and is challenging, lessons should not be scored during the process. Additional considerations about implementing the SIOP® Model in a school from an administrator's perspective can be found in a third new resource, *The SIOP® Model for Administrators* (Short, Vogt, & Echevarria, 2008).

If you are a researcher, you can measure teachers' level of implementation of the SIOP® Model using the protocol. Because it is the only empirically validated, instructional approach for English learners at the time of this writing, more and more school districts are turning to the SIOP® Model for their staff development plan. However, it is important to determine if the investment in the SIOP® Model is paying off for the students' achievement. One way to check is to see if the teachers who are high implementers of the model are the ones whose students make the most progress.

Summary

Students who are learning English as an additional language are the fastest-growing segment of the school-age population in the United States, and almost all candidates in teacher education programs will have linguistically and culturally diverse students in their classes during their teaching careers. However, most of these future teachers—as well as most practicing teachers—are not well prepared to instruct these learners. Given school reform efforts and increased state accountability measures, this lack of teacher preparation puts ELs at risk of educational failure.

This book describes and illustrates a research-based, professional development model of SI, an effective approach for teaching both academic language and content to ELs that can increase English learners' chances of success in school. The SIOP® Model has been used with positive outcomes in several long-term, collaborative, professional development programs to train and coach teachers in implementing effective SI in their classes in urban, suburban, and rural districts around the United States. (See Appendix C.) The model is operationalized in the SIOP® protocol.

The SIOP® Model does not mandate cookie-cutter instruction, but it provides a framework for well-prepared and well-delivered sheltered lessons for any subject area. As SIOP® teachers design their lessons, they have room for creativity and the art of teaching. Nonetheless, critical instructional features must be attended to in order for teachers to respond appropriately to the unique academic and language development needs of these students. As you read through this book, you will have the opportunity to explore ways to enhance, expand, and improve your own instructional practice through use of the SIOP® Model.

Discussion Questions

1. Consider one class of English learners in high school. Identify the individual and sociocultural factors that may influence the educational success of these students. In what ways might SIOP® Model instruction help them?
2. How would you characterize the type(s) of instruction offered to English learners in your school or schools you know: traditional ESL, content-based ESL, sheltered

content, bilingual content, traditional content? Provide evidence of your characterization in terms of curricula and instruction. Are the ELs successful when they exit English language support programs and are in regular classrooms without support, in either middle or high school? Explain.

3. Many sheltered teachers, whether they had special training in a subject area or in second language acquisition, fail to take advantage of the language learning opportunities for students in sheltered content classes. Why do you think this is so? Offer two concrete suggestions for these teachers to enhance their students' language development.
4. Look at one of your own lesson plans. Which characteristics of the SIOP® Model do you already incorporate? Consider the components and features of the model as found in Appendix A.

chapter 2

Lesson Preparation

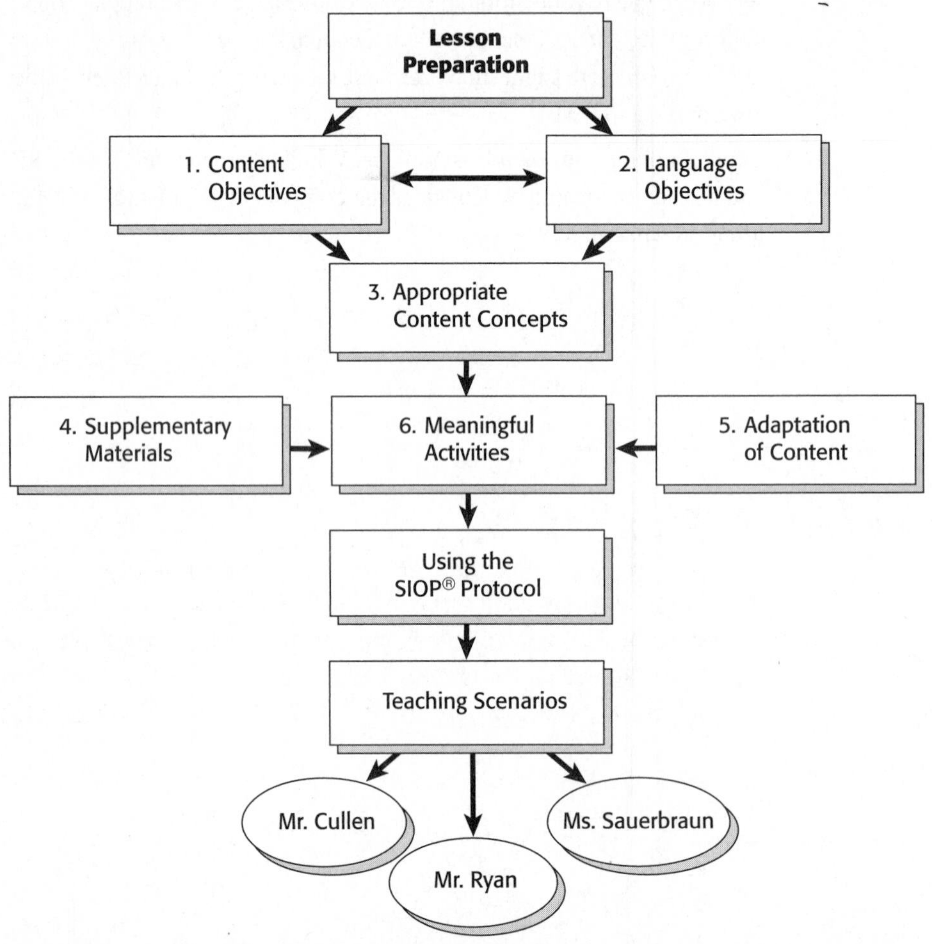

Objectives

After reading, discussing, and engaging in activities related to this chapter, you will be able to meet the following content and language objectives.

Content Objectives

Identify content objectives for English learners (ELs) that are aligned with state, local, or national standards.

Incorporate supplementary materials suitable for ELs in a lesson plan.

Select from a variety of techniques for adapting content to the students' proficiency and cognitive levels.

Language Objectives

Explain the importance of meaningful academic activities for ELs.

Write language and content objectives.

Discuss advantages for writing both language and content objectives for a lesson and sharing the objectives with students.

In this and subsequent chapters, we offer an explanation of each component and feature on the SIOP® (Sheltered Instruction Observation Protocol) protocol. Each chapter begins with the explanation of the SIOP® component, offers classroom activities, and then follows with descriptions of the same lesson taught by three different teachers. The lessons throughout the book are on varied topics and at different secondary grade levels.

This chapter introduces the first component of the SIOP® Model, Lesson Preparation. Following the background information and the rationale for each of the six features in this component, you will find an overview of the lesson topic and then teaching scenarios involving three teachers. As you read these, think about the SIOP® features that have been previously described, and prepare to rate the lessons according to them. Reflect on how effectively the teacher is meeting the needs of English learners (ELs) in relation to each feature. At the conclusion of the teaching scenarios, we offer our assessment of the teachers' efforts to shelter content instruction, and we invite you to compare your appraisal to ours.

Background

As we all know, lesson planning is critical to both a student's and a teacher's success. For maximum learning to occur, planning must produce lessons that enable students to make connections between their own knowledge and experiences and the new information being taught (Rumelhart, 2004). With careful planning, we make learning meaningful

and relevant by including appropriate motivating materials and activities that foster real-life application of concepts studied.

Traditionally, to meet the needs of students who struggled with grade-level reading materials, texts have been rewritten according to readability formulae or lexile levels (Gray & Leary, 1935; Ruddell, 2005; Stenner & Burdick, 1997). The adapted texts included controlled vocabulary and a limited number of concepts, resulting in the omission of critical pieces of information. We have learned that if students' exposure to content concepts is limited by vocabulary-controlled materials, the amount of information they learn over time is considerably less than that of their peers who use grade-level texts. The result is that the "rich get richer and the poor get poorer" (Stanovich, 1986). That is, instead of closing the gap between native English speakers and ELs, the learning gap is increased and eventually it becomes nearly impossible to close. Therefore, it is imperative we plan lessons that are not negatively biased for students acquiring English and that include age-appropriate content and materials.

This component, Lesson Preparation, is therefore very important to the SIOP® Model. If properly prepared, a lesson will include most of the SIOP® features in advance. It is then up to the teachers and class to accomplish them as the lesson unfolds. However, when planning, teachers have asked how they can meet all thirty features in a given period. We explain that a SIOP® lesson may be single day or multiday in length. Over the course of several days, all thirty features should be met. High school teachers with block schedules (e.g., 75–90 minutes long) usually find they can complete full SIOP® lessons in that time frame. See Vogt and Echevarria (2008, pp. 8–9) for a SIOP® lesson-planning flow chart.

As teachers learn the model, we strongly encourage them to write out lessons in detail. They may use the SIOP® protocol as a checklist to ensure they incorporate all of the features. In addition, they may want to try one or more of the lesson plan templates we have included in Appendix B or the templates in Chapter 7 of *Implementing the SIOP® Model Through Effective Professional Development and Coaching* (Echevarria, Short, & Vogt, 2008). All of these templates have been used successfully in classrooms.

"How do I start implementing SIOP® lessons?" is a frequent question from teachers new to the SIOP® Model. We suggest that secondary school teachers begin with one course. Depending on their schedule, they may teach this course over several periods during the day, or they may have it for only one. Nevertheless, it is better to begin on a small scale so they do not have to write multiple SIOP® lessons for different courses each day. In some cases, teachers may learn the SIOP® Model over time, component by component, and they build their lesson planning skills in the same way. Once teachers have internalized the model, they may write less detailed lesson plans.

SIOP® FEATURE 1: Content Objectives Clearly Defined, Displayed, and Reviewed with Students

In effective instruction, concrete content objectives that identify what students should know and be able to do must guide teaching and learning. For the most part, these objectives support school, district, or state content standards and learning outcomes. Frequently, in texts and teachers' guides, content objectives and state standards are complex and not written in a manner that is accessible to ELs. Teachers may or may not present them to students. In other cases, standards are too generic or broad, such as "Explain the geopolitical shifts of countries' alliances in the twentieth century and their economic impact." Given either situation, it is important to write lesson-level objectives (something that can be taught and learned in a lesson or two) and use student-friendly language that suits the age and proficiency levels in the class. Even newcomer students with very limited English skills should be presented with objectives that may have simple phrasings, key words, and/or illustrations, and be read aloud. The bottom line for English learners is that content objectives need to be written in terms of what students will learn or do; be stated simply, orally and in writing; and tied to specific grade-level content standards (Echevarria & Graves, 2007). Also, it may be necessary to limit content objectives to only one or two per lesson to reduce the complexity of the learning task.

Most of us learned about the importance of writing and teaching to content objectives early in our professional preparation. However, it is often easy to overlook sharing the objectives, orally and in writing, with students. One of the sheltered teachers who was learning the SIOP® Model explained her growing awareness of the importance of clearly stated content objectives that are displayed for ELs:

> The objectives are still going on in my class. They're on the board every day and the students are getting used to seeing them, reading them out loud, and evaluating whether or not we achieved them at the end of each class. I still have questions about the wording and what's a good objective . . . but that will come with time and more discussion and study. I just wanted to say that defining the objectives each day definitely brings more focus to my planning and thinking, and it helps bring order to my classroom procedures. So far, it has not been too burdensome and the habit is definitely forming.

We have observed teachers using different approaches when they present the objectives to the class. One science teacher asked the students to focus on the verbs in the statements and generated a discussion about what they would be doing in the lesson. Another teacher asked student partners to discuss one objective at a time and to try to determine what it meant. The student pairs shared their explanations with the class, and, as needed, the teacher paraphrased or gave examples. A high school geometry teacher did a 10-minute, hands-on activity with her students and then asked them to infer what the objectives might be.

Examples of content objectives and language objectives, discussed below, can be found throughout each chapter in this book, in the *99 Ideas and Activities for Teaching English Learners with the SIOP® Model* (Vogt & Echevarria, 2008) resource, in lesson plans presented in *Science for English Language Learners* (Fathman & Crowther, 2006), and in lesson plans on the websites www.cal.org and www.siopinstitute.net.

SIOP® FEATURE 2: Language Objectives Clearly Defined, Displayed, and Reviewed with Students

While carefully planning and delivering content objectives, SIOP® teachers must also incorporate in their lesson plans activities that support students' academic language development (Francis, et al., 2006; Short, 1999; Torgesen, et al., 2007). As with content

FIGURE 2.1 *Process-to-Performance Verbs*

Process-Oriented ---------->-------------->-------------> **Performance-Oriented**				
Explore		Define		
Listen to			Draft	
Recognize				Write
	Discuss in small groups			Give an oral presentation
				Edit

objectives, language objectives should be stated clearly and simply, and students should be informed of them, both orally and in writing.

When considering which language objectives to include in a lesson and how to write them, it is important to keep in mind that acquiring a second language is a long-term process. As such, language objectives may cover a range from process-oriented to performance-oriented statements so that students have a chance to explore, and then practice, before demonstrating mastery of an objective. The following objectives from a SIOP® language arts class show the progression of objectives that might be taught over one week.

Students will be able to

1. Recognize similes in text (day 1)
2. Discuss the functions of similes (day 2)
3. Write three similes (day 3)
4. Write a paragraph that describes a setting using similes (days 4–5)

For the first lesson, students learn to recognize similes in text, perhaps by focusing on the key words *like* and *as*. Then in the next lesson, they develop an understanding, of the purpose of similes. Only after that are they tapped to generate their own similes, first in decontextualized sentences, then in a paragraph.

Figure 2.1 displays possible verbs for objective statements that reflect this process-to-performance continuum.

When determining language objectives, it is also important to distinguish between receptive and productive language skills. English learners tend to develop receptive skills (listening and reading) faster than productive skills (speaking and writing), but all the skills should be worked on in a unified way. Students don't have to learn to speak, for instance, before they learn to read and write (August & Shanahan, 2006a). Moreover, we cannot ignore oral language practice and focus our objectives only on reading and writing. We know from research (Goldenberg, 2008; Guthrie & Ozgungor, 2002) that the absence of planned speaking practice—be it formal or informal—by ELs in content classrooms is detrimental to the development of academic English. Gibbons (2003) argues that skillful teachers should take advantage of oral interaction to move students from informal, everyday explanations of a content topic (e.g., a scientific process) to the more specialized academic register of the formal written and spoken code. Schleppegrell and colleagues (Schleppegrell, 2004; Schleppegrell, Achugar & Orteíza, 2004) have conducted linguistic analysis of the lexical and grammatical forms that construe meaning in written and spoken school discourse and have identified implications for instruction.

SIOP® teachers might make the development of specialized grammar and lexical forms part of their scope and sequence of language objectives.

To see an example of integrating language objectives, please view the corresponding video clip (Chapter 2, Module 1) on the accompanying CD.

A wide variety of language objectives can be planned according to the goals and activities in the lesson. In some cases, language objectives may focus on developing students' vocabulary, which is of critical importance for adolescent ELs who have to close significant gaps in their academic vocabulary knowledge, particularly with polysemous words. Other lessons may lend themselves to practice with reading comprehension skills or the writing process. Students also benefit from objectives that highlight functional language use such as how to request information, justify opinions, negotiate meaning, provide detailed explanations, and so forth. Higher-order thinking skills, such as articulating predictions or hypotheses, stating conclusions, summarizing information, and making comparisons, can be tied to language objectives, too. Sometimes specific grammar points can be taught as well; for example, learning about capitalization when studying famous historical events and persons, or teaching word parts to help ELs develop new vocabulary. These ideas will be expanded upon in the next section.

Teachers are also interested in sources of language objectives. The first place to start is the state English language proficiency (ELP) standards (also known as English language development [ELD] or English as a second language [ESL] standards). National standards for English language proficiency have been developed by the Teachers of English to Speakers of Other Languages (TESOL) association. Four of the five standards in the *Pre-K–12 English language proficiency standards* (TESOL, 2006) address the academic language of the core subject areas and therefore offer an excellent resource for SIOP® language objectives. Nineteen states have adopted a common set of English language development standards similar to TESOL's and formed the WIDA (World-Class Instructional Design and Assessment) Consortium. This consortium has compiled a list of "Can Do" descriptors that can help teachers identify the kind of language tasks students should be able to perform according to five differing levels of English proficiency. (To view these descriptors, go to http://www.wida.us/standards/CAN_DOs/)

Other resources include the state English language arts standards and state content standards that include a strand focused on communication. Ideas for objectives will be found in all of these official documents as well as in local district curricula. Instructional materials are another source. By reviewing course textbooks and other materials, you can see if there are language skills and academic vocabulary that students need to develop in order to comprehend the information.

One final critical source for successful SIOP® lesson implementation is your colleagues. If you are a content teacher, pair up with an ESL or bilingual teacher. Tap his or her expertise for language topics and knowledge of the ELs' academic language needs. (The recent book from the National Science Teachers Association, *Science for English Language Learners* [Fathman & Crowther, 2006] is an excellent resource. Each chapter was a collaboration between a language specialist and a science educator. It includes science lessons with language and content objectives.) If you are an ESL teacher, you have a plethora of language objectives at your disposal. You need to partner with one or more content teachers to identify content objectives they perceive their ELs need assistance with and align them to your language ones. You may want to focus on thematic units to cover a variety of content topics or focus on one subject area per quarter.

Remember, as you teach and assess these language objectives in your lessons, you can plan for multilevel responses from the students according to their proficiency in English.

For example, you might use group response techniques (e.g., thumbs-up/thumbs-down) for students who are in the early stages of English language development. For students who are more proficient English speakers, incorporate activities that involve partner work and small group assignments so that ELs can practice their English in a less-threatening setting. When possible, accept approximations and multiple word responses rather than complete sentences because this supports English development. However, it is also appropriate to require ELs, depending on their level of proficiency, to give answers in one or two complete sentences. This requirement helps develop language skills because it advances students beyond what may be their comfort zone in using English.

Writing Content and Language Objectives

To see an example of writing content and language objectives in lessons, please view the corresponding video clip (Chapter 2, Module 2) on the accompanying CD.

All the content and language objectives should evolve from the lesson topic and be part of the instructional plan. After a teacher writes content and language objectives, posts them, and discusses them with the students at the start of class, at some point in the lesson explicit instruction must be provided on these objectives. Students would then have opportunities to practice with the objectives and be assessed on their progress toward meeting them at the close of the lesson. In other words, each objective is what we want the students to learn, and each needs explicit attention. An objective is not a by-product of an activity but the foundation of one.

Content objectives as mentioned earlier are usually drawn from the state subject area standards. Consider this standard of learning from Virginia: "Students will investigate and understand the basic needs and life processes of plants and animals." It is too broad to be addressed in one lesson, but it is written in a straightforward manner. Surprisingly, however, it is an objective for kindergarten. Posting this objective word for word in the kindergarten classroom would not be successful. Nor would it be comprehensible to a teen at the newcomer or beginning level of English proficiency. How might you rewrite it to present it to these learners? You might write the following on a lesson plan: "Students will identify parts of plants and explain their functions"; but for newcomer students you might write on the board, "Identify parts of a plant. Tell what the parts do." When you explain it, you might elaborate, "Today you will learn about parts of a plant (show a picture or drawing). You will be able to identify the parts (point to the different parts) and tell what the parts do (for example leaves make food for the plant)."

After you have rewritten the state standard as an appropriate content objective for the newcomers, you will need to plan the lesson and determine a language objective. One teacher we worked with combined the science lesson with a walking field trip. In a park near the school, she and the middle school newcomers each found one living plant and sketched it. Then they collected plants and plant parts, such as fallen leaves, twigs, stems, roots, and so forth. Back in the classroom, triads were given one part to become familiar with. They would prepare a poster including a close-up illustration of the plant part and a caption telling what function the part plays for the plant. She had bookmarked some websites for the groups on the class computer and also had some photographic picture books on plants in her classroom library. She taught them the definition of "function." Because her language objective was "Students will represent a plant part visually and write a sentence about its function," she provided a sentence stem for students to use in writing their caption: "This ____ helps the plant because it ____."

Although incorporating language objectives in all content lessons is a hallmark of the SIOP® Model, it is a challenging proposition for many content teachers. It requires a new way of thinking about their subject, specifically both the written and spoken discourse. It also requires them to know their students' proficiency levels so the language objectives can be targeted to what the students need to learn about the academic language of history, science, or mathematics but not be at a level too high for their current understanding. Note that even if you have students with mixed levels of English proficiency in class, we do not suggest you write different language objectives for each proficiency level. Instead, write an objective that all students should attain based on the content concepts in the lesson but adjust the intended outcomes (such as the work product) to match the students' ability levels. Some students may master the objective by the end of the lesson; others will be at some point on a path toward mastery.

Some content teachers have expressed concern that they will have to become grammar experts, but that is not what the SIOP® Model proposes. It is useful for them to be aware of the syntax used in their subject areas (e.g., heavy use of the passive voice in secondary school math textbooks), but not essential that they can explain grammatical rules. Fillmore and Snow (2002) do, however, point out basic linguistic understandings that all teachers should have.

Content-based ESL teachers sometimes face the opposite challenge. They are familiar with language objectives and often have a syllabus that systematically introduces them to students. They need assistance in identifying appropriate content objectives to add to their lessons. In a similar way to content teachers, they may feel unprepared for in-depth instruction on a content topic. For these reasons, we advocate that content and language teachers collaborate closely as they prepare lessons and help their students meet language and content goals.

The six categories in Figure 2.2 on the following pages (adapted from Short, Hudec, & Echevarria, 2002) offer a starting point for generating language objectives. Teachers need to think about how language will be used in their lesson: in their speech, in class discussion, in the reading assignments, in the lesson activities. Then given the content topic and an understanding of the students' degree of academic language acquisition, the teachers write an objective that complements the topic and can be explicitly addressed in the lesson. Sample objectives listed in Figure 2.2 could be incorporated into several lessons throughout a chemistry unit on physical and chemical change.

Sometimes the language and content objectives may be closely linked as in the following pre-algebra math lesson:

- Students will estimate the amount of sales tax and total cost of given items.
- Students will compare and evaluate their estimates with the actual sales tax and total cost.

The first statement is the content objective. It focuses on a mathematical procedure. The second is the language objective. Teachers would teach and then expect students to use comparative and evaluative language phrases.

At other times, the language objective might extend the content knowledge as in this middle school geography lesson:

- Students will identify specific landforms on a map of South America.
- Students will present an oral report about one landform and its influence on economic development.

FIGURE 2.2 *Categories and Examples for Developing Language Objectives*

Consider these six categories as a starting point for generating a language objective. Think about your content topic and how language will be used in your lesson: in your speech, in the reading assignments, and in the lesson activities. Given the content topic and your understanding of the students' degree of academic language acquisition, write an objective that complements the topic and can be explicitly addressed in the lesson. Examples of language objectives are listed below and could occur over several lessons in a chemistry unit on physical and chemical change.

- **Key Vocabulary** refers to the **technical terms, concept words, and other words** needed to discuss, read, or write about the topic of the lesson (e.g., names of important people, places, and events; scientific and mathematical terms; social studies or health concepts) can become language objectives. The "other words" subset includes process words and words like comparatives (e.g., both, are similar, in comparison), conjunctions (e.g., but, however, although), and transition phrases (e.g., first, next, after that, during the second phase).

  An example objective is

  Students will be able to define the terms *chemical reaction, reagent,* and *physical change* orally and in writing.

  Therefore, in this lesson, the teacher will spend time making sure students become familiar with these definitions and can use them, with support as needed.

- **Language Functions** refer to the ways students use language in the lesson. The lesson may call for students to describe, compare, or summarize, for example. Some state standards (e.g., New York's ESL standards) are organized in this way and are a good source for ideas.

  An example objective is

  Students will be able to formulate questions and generate hypotheses before conducting an experiment.

  If a lesson focuses on language functions, the teacher will spend time teaching or reviewing the purpose and procedures for the targeted language use. In this case, the teacher might provide question and hypothesis starters (e.g., What will happen when . . .? How does a . . .? I predict that . . .).

- **Language Skills** are the reading, writing, listening, and speaking skills students need to learn. Skills can be taught directly, practiced, and reviewed; they need to link to the topic of the lesson. In a language arts class, for example, will students need to read and determine a main idea? In social studies, will they need to listen to an audio or video recording and identify the speaker's point of view regarding an historical conflict? In math class, will they have to write an explanation of their solution to a word problem?

  Two example objectives are

  Students will be able to scan directions for a laboratory experiment to identify the necessary equipment.

  Students will be able to draft a lab report.

  In this lesson that revolves around a lab experiment, the teacher may teach scanning skills, using another piece of text, and also teach how to draft a report, perhaps by providing a template and modeling its completion.

- **Grammar or Language Structures** can be taught when they are prevalent in the written or spoken discourse of the class. They might include questioning patterns, past or future tense verbs, paragraph writing, pronoun usage, or sentence formation. Structural clues for words like roots (photo-), prefixes (un-), and suffixes (-tion) can be addressed in this category as well.

  Two example objectives are

  Students will be able to recognize the difference between imperative sentences (like those in lab directions) and declarative sentences (like those in their textbook).

  Students will be able to use adverbs of time in their lab report to describe observations.

  The teacher might introduce or review the types of sentences or the adverbs of time in this lesson on chemical and physical change in passages in the textbook. Beginning-level students may need to understand that a statement like "Turn on the Bunsen burner" is a sentence that calls for an action even though it does not have a recognizable noun subject.

- **Lesson Tasks** are a source for language objectives as well. Teachers consider what language is embedded in a lesson assignment that could be pulled forth and turned into explicit instruction in language. Will the student need language to play a particular role in a cooperative learning group? Will the students have to take notes or explain a procedure to one another?

  An example objective is

  Students will be able to read and summarize a text passage with peers and then teach the main information to another student.

FIGURE 2.2 *Continued*

This example shows how a language objective built around a lesson task might involve multiple areas of language. In this case, the teachers would make sure students knew how to read for the main idea, write a summary, and share key information orally. If not, the teacher might teach one of these three language goals, but we would not suggest the teacher never teach all three at once.

- **Language Learning Strategies** may include corrective strategies (e.g., reread confusing text), self-monitoring strategies (e.g., make and confirm predictions), prereading strategies (e.g., relate to personal experience), or language practice strategies (e.g., repeat or rehearse phrases, visualize). Helping students with Latin-based native languages apply cognates to new academic terms is a very powerful strategy.

  Two example objectives are

  Students will be able to confirm their responses to text questions with a peer.

  Students will be able to represent data graphically.

To help students meet these objectives, the teacher would provide time in class for partners to check their answers but encourage discussion about any disputed responses. Also to help complete the lab report, the teacher may model how to create a chart or graph using the data from the experiment and then have students practice on their own.

For language arts and reading teachers, teasing apart language and content objectives can be tricky. Certain curriculum concepts like *plot* and *setting* are clearly ingredients for language arts content objectives, but some potential objectives like "produce writing that conveys a clear point of view and maintains a consistent tone" could be either a language or a content objective. We encourage language arts and reading teachers to nonetheless consistently identify a content and a language objective for each lesson, even if some might be placed in either category. Because we are aiming for whole-school implementation of the SIOP® Model, having students recognize and expect both types of objectives across all their classes is a valuable goal.

The following objectives are from an eighth-grade language arts class. Which one is the content objective and which is the language objective? Justify your answer.

- Students will be able to (SWBAT) use descriptive adjectives to write sentences about the characters.
- SWBAT compare traits of two characters in a story.

You teach a tenth-grade sheltered World History class with students of intermediate English proficiency. One of your state history standards is "Explain the causes of the economic recovery of Europe and Japan after World War II." You intend to teach about the Marshall Plan. Write a content and a language objective for your class.

As you write your objectives, keep the verbs in Figure 2.3 in mind. Although the verbs are not exclusive to one type or another, they are more common to the category presented. Over time, add to this list to further distinguish between the content and language goals of your lesson.

Once you have written your content and language objectives, you might use this checklist to evaluate them:

The objectives are observable.

The objectives are written and presented in language the students can understand.

The content objective is related to the key concept of the lesson.

The language objective promotes student academic language growth. It is not something most students already do well.

The language objective connects clearly with the lesson topic or lesson activities.

I have a plan for assessing student progress on meeting these objectives during the lesson.

FIGURE 2.3 *Verbs for Writing Content and Language Objectives*

Verbs for Content Objectives	Verbs for Language Objectives
Identify	Listen for
Solve	Retell
Investigate	Define
Distinguish	Find the main idea
Hypothesize	Compare
Create	Summarize
Select	Rehearse
Draw conclusions about	Persuade
.	Write
.	.
.	.
.	.

SIOP® FEATURE 3: Content Concepts Appropriate for Age and Educational Background

SIOP® teachers must carefully consider the content concepts they wish to teach and use district curriculum guidelines and grade-level content standards as guides. In SIOP® classrooms, this entails ensuring that although materials may be adapted to meet the needs of English learners, the content is not diminished. When planning lessons around content concepts, consider the following: (1) the students' first language (L1) literacy, (2) their second language (L2) proficiency, (3) their reading ability, (4) the cultural and age appropriateness of the L2 materials, and (5) the difficulty level of the material to be read (Gunderson, 1991, p. 21).

In some cases, students with major gaps in their educational backgrounds may be placed in newcomer programs or specialized classes that pull objectives and content concepts from earlier grades to provide the foundational knowledge the students need to perform grade-level work successfully and catch up to their classmates (Short & Boyson, 2004). In general, it is inappropriate to use the curriculum materials and books from much earlier grades. Students in high school who are developing literacy for the first time should not be reading about "doggies and birdies," for example. Other materials should be found, and if necessary, the teacher should provide the scaffolding needed to understand the content concepts. Ideally, specialized courses would be developed to accelerate their learning, such as FAST Math developed by Fairfax County (VA) Public Schools (Helman & Buchanan, 1993), which can help students gain several years' worth of mathematics instruction in one subject area in six months to one year.

Additionally, reflect on the amount of background experience needed to learn and apply the content concepts and include ways to activate students' prior knowledge related to them. For example, eighth-grade students typically learn about magnetism, yet some ELs may not have the requisite background knowledge to understand this concept. Rather than diminish the content, use what prior knowledge students do have, perhaps about attraction, and then explicitly build background information as a foundation for their understanding of magnetism.

Providing adequate background requires teachers to perform a *task analysis*—a process in which you carefully analyze the requisite knowledge a student must possess to understand what is being taught. The purpose is to lessen the gap between what a student knows and what he or she must learn. This can be accomplished by modifying the lesson to include substantial background building, or through a small group minilesson that precedes the regular whole-class lesson (Vogt, 2000). This minilesson provides a "jump start" by reviewing key background concepts, introducing vocabulary, leading a picture or text "walk" through the reading material, engaging in simulations or role-plays, or using hands-on experiential activities. The jump-start minilesson develops context and gives access to teens who may lack appropriate background knowledge or experience with the grade-level content concepts. If resources are available, it may be helpful to provide this minilesson in the students' native language. In heterogeneous classes in which ELs study with native English speakers, peer tutors can be used to teach some of the requisite background information as well.

You are the one to decide when to modify content concepts by providing extensive background building for the whole class, or by teaching a brief jump-start lesson to a small group. If you have a large number of English learners who are in the early stages of language development, you may need to include extensive background building. If you have a small group of ELs who have intermediate language proficiency, the jump-start minilesson may provide sufficient scaffolding and access to the content concepts. Alternately, in situations in which an ESL teacher and a content teacher work collaboratively with the same group of students, the ESL teacher can offer lessons that build background and vocabulary before the ELs study the topic in their regular or sheltered content class.

We should also be mindful of concepts our adolescent ELs may have already learned through their life experiences or prior schooling. Sometimes, an illustration or demonstration can help students recall a concept and then the teacher can help them learn new English words to describe the concept and add to their understanding of it. As Torgesen and colleagues (2007) pointed out, "ELLs who already know and understand a concept in their first language have a far simpler task to develop language for the concept in English than do students who lack knowledge of the concept in either language" (p. 92).

SIOP® FEATURE 4: Supplementary Materials Used to a High Degree

Information that is embedded in context allows English learners to understand and complete more cognitively demanding tasks. Effective SIOP® instruction involves the use of many supplementary materials that support the core curriculum and contextualize learning. This is especially important for students who do not have grade-level academic backgrounds and/or who have language and learning difficulties. Because lectures and pencil-and-paper activities centered on a text are often difficult for these students, remember to plan for supplementary materials that will enhance meaning and clarify confusing concepts, making lessons more relevant.

To see an example of the effective use of supplementary materials, please view the corresponding video clip (Chapter 2, Module 3) on the accompanying CD.

A variety of supplementary materials also supports different learning styles and multiple intelligences because information and concepts are presented in a multifaceted manner. Students can see, hear, feel, perform, create, and participate in order to make connections and construct personal, relevant meanings. Supplementary materials provide a real-life context and enable students to bridge prior experiences with new learning.

Examples of supplementary materials that can be used to create context and support content concepts include the following:

- **Hands-on manipulatives:** These can include anything from tangrams for math to microscopes for science to interactive maps for social studies. Manipulating objects physically can reduce the language load of an activity; beginning students in particular can still participate and demonstrate their understanding.
- **Realia:** These are real-life objects that enable students to make connections to their own lives. Examples include bank deposit slips and check registers for a unit on banking, or historial realia such as photos, recordings, and clothing from the 1920's Jazz Age.
- **Pictures:** Photographs and illustrations depict nearly any object, process, or setting, and magazines, commercial photos, and hand drawings can provide visual support for a wide variety of content and vocabulary concepts and can build background knowledge.
- **Visuals:** These can include overhead transparencies, models, graphs, charts, timelines, maps, props, and bulletin board displays. Students with diverse abilities often have difficulty processing an inordinate amount of auditory information and are aided with visual clues.
- **Multimedia:** A wide variety of multimedia materials are available to enhance teaching and learning. These range from simple tape recordings to videos, DVDs, interactive CD-ROMs, and an increasing number of resources available on the World Wide Web. Brief video clips at www.unitedstreaming.com are effective tools. For some students and tasks, media in the students' native language may be a valuable source of information. It is important to preview websites for appropriateness and readability, especially when using them with beginning and intermediate-level students.
- **Demonstrations:** Demonstrations provide visual support and modeling for ELs. If you have a lesson task that includes supplementary materials, then you can scaffold information by carefully planning demonstrations that model how to use the materials and follow directions. Students can then practice these steps in groups or alone, with you or other experienced individuals nearby to assist as needed.

- **Related literature:** A wide variety of fiction and nonfiction can be included to support content teaching. The literature enables readers to create what Rosenblatt (1991) refers to as an "aesthetic response." This type of literature response is characterized by personal feelings about what is read. Aesthetic responses to literature promote more reading of literature, and hopefully, a deeper understanding of the concepts that are depicted—what Rosenblatt refers to as a *transactional experience.* Many content teachers create class libraries with trade books on key topics. Students can read these as supplements to the textbook. They offer a more relaxing way to look at a topic in more depth.
- **Hi-lo readers:** Some publishers are now offering classic literature as well as fiction and nonfiction selections in a hi-lo format. The stories are of high interest but lower readability levels and tend to include many visuals. Some books are grouped thematically and can accompany different content areas and language arts courses. Some have different reading levels within a thematic set. They are useful for students at lower proficiency levels in English.
- **Adapted text:** A type of supplementary reading material that can be very effective for English learners, as well as struggling readers, is adapted text. Without significantly diminishing the content concepts, a piece of text (usually from a grade-level textbook) is adapted to reduce the readability demands. Complicated, lengthy sentences with specialized terminology are rewritten in smaller chunks. Definitions are given for difficult vocabulary, if possible, in context. Please note that we are not advocating "dumbing down" the textbook, an approach that in the past yielded easy-to-read materials with virtually no content concepts left intact. Rather, we suggest that the major concepts be retained and just the readability level of the text be reduced.

SIOP® FEATURE 5:
Adaptation of Content to All Levels of Student Proficiency

In many schools, teachers are required to teach from textbooks that are too difficult for English learners to read. We have previously mentioned the problem of "watering down" text to the point where all students can read it; content concepts are frequently lost when the text is adapted in this way. We also know ELs cannot be expected to learn all content information by listening to lectures.

Therefore, we must find ways to make the text and other resource materials accessible for all students, adapting them so that the content concepts are left intact. Several ways of doing this have been recommended for students who have reading difficulties (Readance, Bean, & Baldwin, 2001; Ruddell, 2005; Vacca & Vacca, 2004; Vogt, 1992), and they work equally well for ELs. These approaches can be used throughout a lesson, as a prereading instructional strategy, as an aid during reading, and as a postreading method for organizing newly learned information.

Suggestions for adapting content to make it more accessible include the following:

- **Graphic organizers:** These are schematic diagrams that provide conceptual clarity for information that is difficult to grasp. They help students identify key content concepts and make relationships among them (McLaughlin & Allen, 2002).

FIGURE 2.4 *Scaffolded Outline*

The Circulatory System

I. Major Organs
   A. Heart
      1. Pumps blood throughout the body
      2. ________________
   B. ________________
      1. ________________
      2. ________________

II. Major Vessels
   A. Artery
      1. Moves blood away from heart
      2. ________________
   B. Vein
      1. ________________
      2. ________________
   C. ________________
      1. Connects arteries and veins
      2. ________________

III. Types of Blood Cells
   A. Red blood cells
      1. ________________
   B. ________________
      1. Fights disease
   C. Platelets
      1. ________________

Graphic organizers also provide students with visual clues they can use to supplement written or spoken words that may be hard to understand. Prior to reading, students can use the organizers as a guide and as a supplement to build background for difficult or dense text. When used concurrently with reading, they focus students' attention and help them make connections between concepts (e.g., Venn diagram), take notes (e.g., T-chart), and understand the text structure (e.g., a timeline informs students the text will be organized chronologically). When used after reading, graphic organizers can be employed to record personal understandings and responses (Buehl, 2009). Graphic organizers include story or text structure charts, Venn diagrams, story or text maps, timelines, discussion webs, word webs, clusters, thinking maps, and so forth. Vogt & Echevarria (2008) include a number of templates for these graphic organizers.

- **Outlines:** Teacher-prepared outlines equip students with a form for note-taking while reading dense portions of text, thus providing scaffolded support. These are especially helpful if major concepts, such as the Roman numeral level of the outline, are already filled in. The students can then add other information to the outline as they read. For some students, an outline that is entirely completed may be helpful to use as a guide to reading and understanding the text. Figure 2.4 shows an example of a scaffolded outline for a reading on the circulatory system in a biology textbook.
- **Leveled study guides:** These study guides are designed specifically for diverse students' needs. All students are expected to master the key concepts in the text; however, depending on students' language and literacy development, the leveled study guides are written differently. For some adolescents who can easily read the text

material, the study guides extend and enrich the subject material and they include challenging questions or tasks. For other students, leveled study guides lead them through the material with definitions and "hints" for unlocking the meaning, and they include fewer challenging questions and tasks. For some ELs and struggling readers, the study guides may include brief summaries of the text along with more manageable questions and tasks. Questions, tasks, and statements on the leveled study guides can be marked with asterisks as follows (from most manageable to most challenging):

*All students are to respond to these questions/statements/tasks

**Group 1 students are required to complete these questions/statements/tasks

***Group 2 students are required to complete these questions/statements/tasks

Of course, the option to try the more challenging questions or statements should be open to all students.

- **Highlighted text:** A few literature anthologies or content textbooks may be marked and reserved for students acquiring English and/or for those with delayed literacy development. Overriding ideas, key concepts, topic sentences, important vocabulary, and summary statements are highlighted (by the teacher or other knowledgeable person) prior to the students using the books. Students are encouraged first to read only the highlighted sections. As confidence and reading ability improve, more of the unmarked text is attempted. The purpose of highlighted text is to reduce the reading demands of the text while still maintaining key concepts and information.
- **Taped text:** Key portions (such as the highlighted text just mentioned) or the entire text is recorded, and students are encouraged to listen to the tape while they follow along in the book. For some students, multiple exposures to the taped text may result in a more thorough understanding. Ideally, tapes should be available for both home and school learning center use. Down loadable books and podcasts are similar options.
- **Adapted text:** As mentioned earlier in this chapter, text adaptation involves rewriting selected sections of text that contain key concepts and information. Although time consuming, rewriting text is an effective modification of curricular materials because information is organized in small sequential steps. Short, simpler sentences are rewritten from long, complex ones. An example of a complex sentence from a science text follows: "Electrons have negative electric charges and orbit around the core, nucleus, of an atom." A simple adaptation of this sentence is, "Electrons have negative charges. They orbit around the core. The core of the atom is called the nucleus."

  Ideally, rewritten paragraphs should include a topic sentence with several supporting details. Maintaining a consistent format promotes easier reading for information-seeking purposes. All sentences included in the rewritten text should be direct and relevant to the subject. In the following example, a paragraph of original text is taken from an anthology theme in a reading series (Cooper et al., 2003). This passage was excerpted from a piece of nonfiction literature, *Into the Mummy's Tomb,* written by Nicholas Reeves.

  Original text: "Tutankhamen's mummy bore a magnificent mask of burnished gold, which covered its face and shoulders. Its headcloth was inlaid with blue glass. The vulture and cobra on its forehead, ready to spit fire at the pharaoh's enemies, were of solid gold" (p. 237).

We have rewritten the original text as follows:

Adapted text: "King Tutankhamen's mummy wore a grand mask, made of very shiny gold. It covered the face and shoulders of the body. The part of the mask over the forehead looked like a gold headcloth. Blue glass was set into the headcloth. Shapes of a vulture (a type of bird) and a cobra (a type of snake) were above the eyes on the mask. They were solid gold. The artist made them look like they could attack the pharaoh's (King Tut's) enemies."

Obviously, adapting text like this takes time and is not easy to do. Note here that the adapted version is slightly longer than the original, which often happens when definitions are included. If you have a large number of ELs in your classroom, adapted text can be very beneficial, and it is worth the time and effort to provide students with more accessible material. Be sure to have a colleague read the adapted text to make sure it clarifies rather than confuses the content.

- **Jigsaw text reading:** Originally designed as a cooperative learning activity for all students, Jigsaw works well with teenaged English learners when there is a difficult-to-read text. One or two members from each cooperative learning group come together to form a new group of "experts." Each new "expert" group is assigned a different section of the text to be read. This group reads the text orally taking turns; partners read to each other; or group members read the text silently. Following the reading, each "expert" group reviews and discusses what was read, determining the essential information and key vocabulary. You need to check carefully with each "expert" group to make sure all members understand the material they have read.

  After you feel sure that the "experts" know their assigned information, they return to their original groups and teach fellow group members what they learned. This process scaffolds the learning of ELs because in both groups they are working with others to understand the text. Some classmates may have more background information on the topic. Text can be read with other students, reducing the demands of lengthy sections. Depending on English proficiency, ELs may join an "expert" group individually or with a partner. It is important that you form the "expert" groups rather than letting the students choose their own group members.
- **Marginal notes:** As with highlighted text, you may wish to reserve a few textbooks for English learners and struggling readers. Print marginal notes directly in the margin of the textbook pages or duplicate notes on a handout that students can put alongside a page they are reading. The marginal notes or handout should include hints for understanding the content, key concepts, and/or key vocabulary and definitions. The notes, whether in the textbook's margin or on a handout, are similar to the ones often found in teachers' guides.

  Most marginal notes deal specifically either with content (e.g., "Cell division includes two types: mitosis and meiosis"), or with hints for reading a passage (e.g., "This paragraph explains why General George Armstrong Custer believed he could win the Battle of Little Big Horn. As you read it, think about whether his reasons make sense."). Marginal notes reduce ambiguity as well as the reading difficulty of the text, making it more accessible and less intimidating.

You may be thinking that marginal notes create an unnecessary burden for the teacher. Please note that once you have completed a set for one textbook, whether in the margins or on handouts, teaching assistants (parent volunteers, other adults, or capable students) can copy them in other student texts. Obviously, this type of scaffolding works only when you have extra textbooks you can write in or when you can assign specific books to particular students.

- **Native language texts:** If some students are literate in their first language, texts written in that language may be used to supplement a textbook or clarify key concepts. Students may conduct research using native language materials and share the information with classmates in English. Increasingly, the Internet offers native language websites, especially for the more commonly taught languages, and authentic materials such as newspapers can be found online. For students who are not literate in their L1, but have oral skills, native language broadcasts, podcasts, and audio books may be additional sources of information.

SIOP® FEATURE 6: Meaningful Activities That Integrate Lesson Concepts with Language Practice Opportunities

To the extent possible, lesson activities should be planned to promote language development in all skills while ELs are mastering content objectives. We want to provide oral and written language practice that is relevant to the lesson concepts, but remember that all activities that generate language practice do not need to be identified as language objectives.

Students are more successful when they are able to make connections between what they know and what they are learning by relating classroom experiences to their own lives. These meaningful experiences are often described as "authentic," because they represent a reality for students. That is, classroom experiences mirror that which actually occurs in the learner's world. Authentic, meaningful experiences are especially important for ELs because they are learning to attach labels and terms to things already familiar to them. Their learning becomes situated rather than abstract when they are provided with the opportunity to actually experience what they are learning about.

Too often, however, English learners are relegated to activities that are not meaningful and are unrelated to the content and activities pursued by the other English-proficient students in their classes. It is essential that content standards that apply to students with English proficiency also apply to ELs, and that the planned activities reflect and support these standards.

Consider a class of middle school students studying insects, butterflies in particular. While the rest of the class learns the scientific names and habitats of varied kinds of butterflies, the teacher has the ELs color and cut out pictures of butterflies to make a butterfly mobile. This activity is neither authentic nor meaningful for these adolescent students. And, in this example, the teacher obviously has not provided meaningful activities that support the grade-level science content standards.

Using the SIOP® Protocol

As you learn to use the SIOP® protocol, both for your own teaching and for coaching other teachers, it is important that you rate each feature as reliably as possible. That is, you need to develop consistency in your rating by having a clear understanding of each feature and how it "looks" during a sheltered lesson. Therefore, it is very important that you discuss with other teachers and/or supervisors how you determined your ratings on the various SIOP® features for the lessons depicted in this book. Some schools have group meetings to discuss the ratings, while other teachers work with a partner to establish reliability. You will probably notice that some ratings for the features will seem quite obvious to you (usually those that fall on 0, 1, or 4 on the scale), while others will be more challenging. As we learned to use the SIOP® protocol in many classroom settings and with many lessons, we developed consistency in our ratings. With practice and discussion about the ratings you give, you will do the same.

Although we organized this book so that you can score the lessons as you read, in real life, you may not want to give scores on each feature, especially as teachers are learning to implement the model. You can record comments and note if a feature is present or absent, and then use the protocol to offer targeted feedback. You will also notice that five of the thirty features have an NA option (see Appendix A). After years of research we determined that those five (such as Adaptation of Content, in Lesson Preparation) might not need to be included in every SIOP® lesson. Adaptation of Content, for example, may not be needed in a class with advanced ELs. Chapter 11 provides more explanation on scoring and interpreting the SIOP® protocol.

The Lesson

The lesson described below is part of a unit on the Italian Renaissance for high school English language learners in a World History course. (For more examples of lesson and unit plans in history, see Short, Vogt, & Echevarria, in press.)

UNIT: Italian Renaissance (Tenth grade)

The classrooms described in these teaching scenarios are found in a metropolitan high school in a suburb located next to the major city. At the district level, approximately 30 percent of the students are English learners or former English learners. At this particular high school, however, the number of students with English as a second language is closer to 60 percent. In the tenth grade classrooms of Mr. Cullen, Mr. Ryan, and Ms. Sauerbraun, the mix of English learners, former English learners who have been redesignated, and native English speakers is about one-third, one-third, one-third. Each class has 25–30 students. The English learners in these rooms are at the intermediate to advanced levels of proficiency. Beginning level ELs study in a separate sheltered World History course.

The Italian Renaissance unit has several main topics, including the political power of the city-states and papacy, the rise of Renaissance art and architecture, the philosophy of Humanism, and the development and use of technology. An essential question students will address throughout the unit is: "What makes someone a Renaissance man or woman?"

Teaching Scenarios

As you read about the tenth grade World History classes of Mr. Cullen, Mr. Ryan, and Ms. Sauerbraun on the cultural and scientific contributions of the Italian Renaissance, consider how they prepared for their lessons. Reflect on the SIOP® Model features for Lesson Preparation: content objectives, language objectives, appropriate content concepts, supplementary materials, adaptation of content, and meaningful activities that integrate language practice with content concepts. The students have already studied the city-state government structure and the influence of trade on Italy's economy.

Mr. Cullen

After the students had entered the room and placed their homework assignments in the basket by the door, Mr. Cullen greeted the class. "Welcome to the city of Florence in the 1500s," he said. He proceeded to introduce a video clip on the cultural and scientific achievements of the Italian Renaissance. When it ended four minutes later, he told the students to do a Think-Pair-Share on this question: "Which achievements in this video interested or surprised you?" The students had a chance to think for one minute; then they discussed ideas with a partner for another two minutes. When the students shared out ideas, he recorded them on the board, including

Building cathedrals
Designing a microscope
Painting scenes of biblical events
Writing books like The Prince
Trying to fly

He used this time to clarify some vocabulary words as well.

Mr. Cullen explained that the class would carry out a project to delve more deeply into one of these accomplishments and to teach others what they found. He reviewed the content and language objectives with the students:

Content: Students will explore major achievements in literature, music, painting, sculpture, architecture, science, and technology in Italy during the Renaissance.

Students will design a representation of one of the achievements.

Language: Students will read and take notes from primary and secondary sources on one of these achievements.

Students will justify orally why the achievement is important.

As they copied these objectives, Mr. Cullen asked the students to paraphrase what the objectives meant, being sure to ask some ELs to focus on the verbs (e.g., explore) and nouns (e.g., achievements). He told the class they would work on this lesson for the rest of the week.

Mr. Cullen called the students' attention to chart paper posted around the room. Each piece of paper had one of the following labels: Aerodynamics, Anatomy, Architecture, Art, Literature, Music, and Technology. "You have seen each of these topics discussed in the video. I'm asking you to choose one that interests you and move to the chart paper."

The students selected an area of interest and were told to generate a KWL (Know-Want-Learn) chart for the topic.

After the students completed the K and W columns, he asked the groups to choose one question from their Want column as a research topic. He explained that he had bookmarked key websites on the classroom computers and had collaborated with the school librarian to build a class collection of books on the Renaissance that reflected a variety of reading levels. He went on to explain that some of the materials were representations of primary sources, such as da Vinci's and Galileo's notebooks, others were photos of major works of art, and some were secondary sources. "None of us read Latin or Italian," he said, "so we can look at primary sources, but mostly we need to see translations of written text. For those of you who can read in another language, you are welcome to look at websites in that language too."

Mr. Cullen then passed out the project assignment sheet and rubric for their written product and oral presentations. Examples of products were listed, such as: (1) Design a tourist brochure for key paintings and buildings in Florence; (2) Write a critique of a Renaissance painting or sculpture; (3) Prepare a museum exhibit showcasing one or more achievements; and (4) Play some Renaissance music and teach the class a dance from the period. The rubric listed assessment categories for their oral presentation, including use of appropriate vocabulary, clear explanation of the importance of the achievement, and relevance of the achievement today.

Mr. Cullen then reviewed with the class ways to take notes on index cards or in a chart. He told the tenth graders that they could begin their research today and then he would meet with each group individually tomorrow to provide further guidance. When the period ended, he reviewed the objectives and told the students they would meet all of the objectives over the next few days.

On the SIOP® form in Figure 2.5, rate Mr. Cullen's lesson on each of the Lesson Preparation features.

Mr. Ryan

When the students entered Mr. Ryan's class, they found a large picture of the *Mona Lisa* projected on the screen at the front of the room. As the students settled, he told them to get out their warm-up journals to copy the learning objective for the day and to answer the warm-up question, both posted on the side blackboard. The learning objective was "Students will learn about the contributions that Italian Renaissance artists made to the world of art." The warm-up question was "What makes this portrait of the *Mona Lisa* special?"

After three minutes, Mr. Ryan asked for volunteers to respond to the question. No one raised his or her hand, so he immediately called on the student in the first desk of the farthest left row. That student had no answer, so Mr. Ryan called upon another. That student, the best in the class, said it was the smile. Mr. Ryan, pleased, agreed and told the class that today they would learn about art during the Italian Renaissance. He told them to take out their notebooks and draw a T-chart, labeling one column Medieval Art and the other Renaissance Art.

For the next 20 minutes, Mr. Ryan showed the students paintings from the Medieval and Renaissance periods through his PowerPoint presentation. He lectured on the aspects of style including realism and symbolism, use of light and shadow, visual perspective, and so forth. He illustrated his points with images of real paintings. He frequently reminded the students to take good notes because they would be writing an essay comparing two of the paintings later.

FIGURE 2.5 *Lesson Preparation Component of the SIOP® Model: Mr. Cullen's Lesson*

4	3	2	1	0	
1. **Content objectives** clearly defined, displayed, and reviewed with students		**Content objectives** for students implied		No clearly defined **content objectives** for students	
2. **Language objectives** clearly defined, displayed, and reviewed with students		**Language objectives** for students implied		No clearly defined **language objectives** for students	
3. **Content concepts** appropriate for age and educational background level of students		**Content concepts** somewhat appropriate for age and educational background level of students		**Content concepts** inappropriate for age and educational background level of students	
4. **Supplementary materials** used to a high degree, making the lesson clear and meaningful (e.g., computer programs, graphs, models, visuals)		Some use of **supplementary materials**		No use of **supplementary materials**	
5. **Adaptation of content** (e.g., text, assignment) to all levels of student proficiency		Some **adaptation of content** to all levels of student proficiency		No significant **adaptation of content** to all levels of student proficiency	NA
6. **Meaningful activities** that integrate lesson concepts (e.g., interviews, letter writing, simulations, models) with language practice opportunities for reading, writing, listening, and/or speaking		**Meaningful activities** that integrate lesson concepts, but provide few language practice opportunities for reading, writing, listening, and/or speaking		**No meaningful activities** that integrate lesson concepts with language practice	

Mr. Ryan was passionate about Renaissance paintings and peppered his talk with descriptions of visits to various museums in Florence two years earlier. He was disappointed when some students started to act out about eight minutes into the presentation, tossing paper wads at one another while the lights were dimmed for the PowerPoint slides.

Mr. Ryan had to stop and reprimand the students twice. Other students doodled or put their heads down on their desks.

When the presentation ended, he posted reproductions of five Medieval and five Renaissance paintings on the front board. He asked the students to come and look at them, row by row. "Choose one of each type," he said "and write a comparative essay. Use your notes. I'll assess these based on your descriptions and comparisons of the artistic styles." When the bell rang, several students were still at the board trying to decide which paintings to select.

On the SIOP® form in Figure 2.6, rate Mr. Ryan's lesson on each of the Lesson Preparation features.

Ms. Sauerbraun

Ms. Sauerbraun entered class wearing a long gown with a headdress and veil down her back. The students giggled as she twirled in front of the room. "I'd like you to see the type of clothing worn by Renaissance women," she said. "Have you any idea what the men wore?" One student raised his hand and said, "I think they wore short pants and tights." "Exactly," said Ms. Sauerbraun. She raised the skirt of her gown to mid-calf and showed them tights she had on underneath. She then told them to open their textbooks to page 84 and look at the illustration.

"We are going to read about some famous people during the time of the Italian Renaissance," she said. "Before we start reading, I want you to complete this anticipation guide. Answer true or false." Using the overhead projector, she showed them the questions.

This chapter will tell us

1. how the Catholic Church supported artists during the Renaissance **T F**
2. how one family held political and cultural power for more than one century **T F**
3. how painters changed from painting realistic portraits to abstract images **T F**
4. how monks copied books by hand to create libraries **T F**

Ms. Sauerbraun told the class they would return to the guide at the end of the lesson to check their predictions. She then explained that today's lesson addressed the state standard that was on the overhead as well, "Analyze the historical developments of the Renaissance, including major achievements in literature, art, architecture, music, and science." She read it aloud and told the class they would study paintings, buildings, and inventions. She continued, "We'll read the chapter and then you will choose one historical person to be. You will write at least six diary entries for that person that can take place over one, ten, or more years." She posted a list of possible people on the overhead transparency: Michelangelo, Leonardo da Vinci, Machiavelli, Lorenzo de'Medici, Catherine de'Medici, Lucrezia Borgia, Galileo, Pope Sixtus IV, Dante Alighieri, Brunelleschi. She showed them a few sample diaries that her class from the prior year had prepared.

She then gave each student an index card. "As you read the chapter, look for answers to the questions on our anticipation guide. Pay attention to the historical figures, and when you find one you want to learn more about, start to take notes on this card. You'll have tomorrow's period to do additional research on your person. If some of you want to work with a partner, you may, but your joint diary will need to have 10 entries."

The students then began reading the chapter in the textbook. Eight students paired up to work together. When the bell rang, most but not all of the students told Ms. Sauerbraun they

FIGURE 2.6 *Lesson Preparation Component of the SIOP® Model: Mr. Ryan's Lesson*

4	3	2	1	0	
1. **Content objectives** clearly defined, displayed, and reviewed with students		**Content objectives** for students implied		No clearly defined **content objectives** for students	
4	**3**	**2**	**1**	**0**	
2. **Language objectives** clearly defined, displayed, and reviewed with students		**Language objectives** for students implied		No clearly defined **language objectives** for students	
4	**3**	**2**	**1**	**0**	
3. **Content concepts** appropriate for age and educational background level of students		**Content concepts** somewhat appropriate for age and educational background level of students		**Content concepts** inappropriate for age and educational background level of students	
4	**3**	**2**	**1**	**0**	
4. **Supplementary materials** used to a high degree, making the lesson clear and meaningful (e.g., computer programs, graphs, models, visuals)		Some use of **supplementary materials**		No use of **supplementary materials**	
4	**3**	**2**	**1**	**0**	**NA**
5. **Adaptation of content** (e.g., text, assignment) to all levels of student proficiency		Some **adaptation of content** to all levels of student proficiency		No significant **adaptation of content** to all levels of student proficiency	
4	**3**	**2**	**1**	**0**	
6. **Meaningful activities** that integrate lesson concepts (e.g., interviews, letter writing, simulations, models) with language practice opportunities for reading, writing, listening, and/or speaking		**Meaningful activities** that integrate lesson concepts, but provide few language practice opportunities for reading, writing, listening, and/or speaking		No **meaningful activities** that integrate lesson concepts with language practice	

had decided on an historical figure to research further. Ms. Sauerbraun asked them to stay put for 30 seconds and had the students confirm or correct their anticipation guide responses.

On the SIOP® form in Figure 2.7, rate Ms. Sauerbraun's lesson on each of the Lesson Preparation features.

FIGURE 2.7 *Lesson Preparation Component of the SIOP® Model: Ms. Sauerbraun's Lesson*

4	3	2	1	0
1. **Content objectives** clearly defined, displayed, and reviewed with students		**Content objectives** for students implied		No clearly defined **content objectives** for students
4	3	2	1	0
2. **Language objectives** clearly defined, displayed, and reviewed with students		**Language objectives** for students implied		No clearly defined **language objectives** for students
4	3	2	1	0
3. **Content concepts** appropriate for age and educational background level of students		**Content concepts** somewhat appropriate for age and educational background level of students		**Content concepts** inappropriate for age and educational background level of students
4	3	2	1	0
4. **Supplementary materials** used to a high degree, making the lesson clear and meaningful (e.g., computer programs, graphs, models, visuals)		Some use of **supplementary materials**		No use of **supplementary materials**
4	3	2	1	0 NA
5. **Adaptation of content** (e.g., text, assignment) to all levels of student proficiency		Some **adaptation of content** to all levels of student proficiency		No significant **adaptation of content** to all levels of student proficiency
4	3	2	1	0
6. **Meaningful activities** that integrate lesson concepts (e.g., interviews, letter writing, simulations, models) with language practice opportunities for reading, writing, listening, and/or speaking		**Meaningful activities** that integrate lesson concepts, but provide few language practice opportunities for reading, writing, listening, and/or speaking		No **meaningful activities** that integrate lesson concepts with language practice

Discussion of Lessons

1. *Content Objectives Clearly Defined, Displayed, and Reviewed with Students*

   Mr. Cullen: 4

   Mr. Ryan: 2

   Ms. Sauerbraun: 3

All of the teachers planned for content objectives based on their state standards and posted them in their classrooms.

After an introductory video clip, Mr. Cullen explicitly reviewed the content objectives with the students and spent time making sure the students understood them. In this way he ensured that the English learners, as well as the other students, would understand what they should learn and be able to do as a result of the lesson. Students would explore major achievements in Italy during the Renaissance and design a representation of one of these achievements. In Figure 2.8 on the following page we see how Mr. Cullen incorporated the objectives in his lesson plan, which received a "4" for content objectives.

Like Mr. Cullen, Mr. Ryan posted his content objective. He did not read it aloud, nor did he explain it, however. He only had the students copy it in their notebooks. The English learners in his class did not necessarily understand what they would be studying. As we mentioned earlier, using verbs like *learn* and *understand* is not recommended in objectives. They are not observable. In this case, a better verb might be *analyze* or *evaluate*. Mr. Ryan's lesson received a "2" on this feature.

In her lesson, Ms. Sauerbraun posted the content objective on an overhead transparency, read it aloud to the students, and gave a brief elaboration ("study paintings, buildings, and inventions"). The students did not have an opportunity to talk about the objective and the English learners may not have been sure how the diary task related to the objectives. Her lesson received a "3" for content objectives.

2. *Language Objectives Clearly Defined, Displayed, and Reviewed with Students*

   Mr. Cullen: 4

   Mr. Ryan: 0

   Ms. Sauerbraun: 2

Mr. Cullen had clearly defined language objectives for the students. Students would read and take notes from primary and secondary sources and would justify orally why a Renaissance achievement was important. He gave the students an opportunity to explain the objectives, and he also taught the note-taking skills. The rubric for their upcoming presentations reinforced the language objectives. His lesson received a "4" for language objectives.

Mr. Ryan did not have any language objectives. He could have prepared one regarding listening comprehension skills, but did not do so. Furthermore, although he required listening and note-taking during the course of his lesson, he did not teach such skills. This lesson received a "0" for language objectives.

Ms. Sauerbraun did not post her language objectives, but she did explain to the students what language skills they would practice in the lesson: reading the chapter and other texts and writing diary entries. Her anticipation guide previewed the reading activity. However, she never stated directly what the students would learn and be able to do, language-wise, as a result of the lesson. Her lesson received a "2" on this feature.

FIGURE 2.8 *Mr. Cullen's SIOP® Lesson Plan*

Date: Dec. 8–12 Grade/Class/Subject: 10 / World History

Unit/Theme: Italian Renaissance Standards: History 10.5 (1–4)

Content Objective(s): Students will explore major achievements in literature, music, painting, sculpture, architecture, science, and technology in Italy during the Renaissance. Students will design a representation of one of the achievements.

Language Objective(s): Students will read and take notes from primary and secondary sources on one of these achievements. Students will justify orally why the achievement is important.

Key Vocabulary		Supplementary Materials
Renaissance	anatomy	PBS video clips
architecture	aerodynamics	chart paper
patronage		presentation rubric & chart, library books, websites

SIOP Features

Preparation	Scaffolding	Grouping Options
✓ Adaptation of Content	___ Modeling	✓ Whole class
✓ Links to Background	✓ Guided practice	✓ Small groups
✓ Links to Past Learning	✓ Independent practice	___ Partners
✓ Strategies incorporated	✓ Comprehensible input	___ Independent
Integration of Processes	**Application**	**Assessment**
✓ Reading	✓ Hands-on	___ Individual
✓ Writing	✓ Meaningful	✓ Group
✓ Speaking	✓ Linked to objectives	✓ Written
✓ Listening	✓ Promotes engagement	✓ Oral

Lesson Sequence

Day 1

Introduce Italian Renaissance through video clips, explain vocabulary. Have students select topic for research, KWL chart, identify research questions. Explain project and presentation rubric. Review note-taking procedures.

Days 2–4

Meet with each group. Check comprehension of references and sources. Present mini-lectures on Renaissance art, architecture, music, literature, technology. Have groups present updates on their research projects. Check status of project. Help students prepare for oral presentations.

Day 5

Have groups present their projects. Assess with language and content rubric. Have observing students record notes on chart.

Reflections:

Student groups worked well throughout the week. Having materials at different reading abilities was a real plus. Great help from librarian when planning this.

3. *Content Concepts Appropriate for Age and Educational Background Level of Students*

   Mr. Cullen: 4

   Mr. Ryan: 3

   Ms. Sauerbraun: 4

Each teacher prepared a lesson that related to the state standards and curriculum topics for this unit on the Renaissance. Because the classes were composed of English learners of intermediate or high proficiency levels—and beginners had a separate sheltered course—the concepts were appropriate for their age and educational levels. The lessons of Mr. Cullen and Ms. Sauerbraun received a "4" for content concepts. Mr. Ryan's lesson primarily focused on one major achievement of the Italian Renaissance—art—so students had less opportunity to explore other accomplishments of the time period. His lesson received a rating of "3" on this feature.

4. *Supplementary Materials Used to a High Degree*

   Mr. Cullen: 4

   Mr. Ryan: 2

   Ms. Sauerbraun: 2

Mr. Cullen used a great deal of supplementary materials in his lessons. He had the video, the KWL charts, the websites already bookmarked, and the classroom library as resources for students to learn about the Italian Renaissance. He supported their project products as well. His lesson was rated a "4" for supplementary materials.

Mr. Ryan incorporated a PowerPoint with photographs of Medieval and Renaissance paintings in his lesson. He also had reproductions of ten paintings displayed for the students to examine. This lesson received a "2" for supplementary materials.

Ms. Sauerbraun wore a Renaissance costume, used an anticipation guide, and showed sample diaries to her students. Other than the guide, students did not interact with the materials very much. The main source of information appeared to be the textbook. Her lesson also received a "2" on this feature.

5. *Adaptation of Content to All Levels of Student Proficiency*

   Mr. Cullen: 3

   Mr. Ryan: 0

   Ms. Sauerbraun: 1

Mr. Cullen made some effort to adapt the content to the students' proficiency levels. He pre-selected books at different proficiency levels and bookmarked websites, including ones that would be useful to his English learners. He encouraged the students to use sites presented in their native languages, if desired. In addition, he allowed students choice in their topic and product, knowing that teens are more motivated to work above their levels when they are interested in the topic. He did not make specific accommodations for all the different proficiency levels in the class, however. This lesson received a rating of "3" on this feature.

Mr. Ryan did not adapt the content for his English learners. He gave a lecture on the differences between Medieval and Renaissance art. Although he did use visuals to illustrate his points, he did not review how to take notes, he did not write key ideas on the board for students to copy, and he did not provide a scaffolding note-taking guide to help those who were learning English as a new language follow along. His lesson was rated a "0" for adaptation of content.

Ms. Sauerbraun, like Mr. Cullen, allowed students choice in their assignment. Nonetheless, in the lesson so far, the textbook has been the main source for information. The English learners may have difficulty learning the key concepts by reading independently. Ms. Sauerbraun offered partnering as an option for the task, but she did not choose partners for the ELs who might have supported their learning. Her lesson received a "1."

6. *Meaningful Activities That Integrate Lesson Concepts with Language Practice*

Mr. Cullen: 4

Mr. Ryan: 1

Ms. Sauerbraun: 3

The lesson that Mr. Cullen prepared was very meaningful for the students. The video helped build background knowledge for the students so that they could choose a relevant topic for their project. The tasks they were asked to accomplish—the KWL charts, the note-taking review, the project planning, and the use of primary and secondary sources—were very applicable to the academic skills they need for success in school. His lesson was rated "4."

Mr. Ryan's lesson was not so meaningful to the students. Although learning about Renaissance painting was one goal of the district curriculum, it was not the only achievement to focus on. The lecture was too long and students were not taught how to take notes. Several students acted out, doodled, or slept. Writing a comparative essay offered a good practice activity, meaningful to school, but the traits of such an essay type were not explicitly taught or reviewed. The lesson received a "1."

Ms. Sauerbraun's lesson was meaningful to the students. The tasks of reading about the Renaissance period and writing diary entries would allow the students to deepen their understanding of the lives and accomplishments of the historical figures while they practiced language skills. What Ms. Sauerbraun did not do, however, was teach or review with the students how a diary entry should be written. This lesson was rated a "3" for meaningful activities.

Summary

We view Lesson Preparation as a critical foundation for delivering a high-quality SIOP® lesson. Thoughtful planning leads to effective teaching—but a great plan does not always guarantee a great lesson for English learners. They require sensitive teachers who realize that curriculum must be grade-level appropriate, based on content standards and learning outcomes. Moreover, all SIOP® lessons need attention to language with at least one objective devoted to furthering the ELs' academic English development. If ELs lack background knowledge and experience with content concepts, effective sheltered teachers provide it through explicit instruction and they enhance student learning with appropriate supplementary materials. They provide scaffolded support by adapting dense and difficult text. They situate lessons in meaningful real-life activities and experiences that involve students in reading, writing, and discussion of important concepts and ideas.

These principles of effective sheltered instruction should be reflected in teachers' lesson plans. As we explore the other features of the SIOP® Model and see how teachers apply many other important principles in their classrooms, remember that the first step in the instructional process is comprehensive and thoughtful lesson design.

Discussion Questions

1. What are some advantages to writing both content objectives and language objectives for students to hear and see? How might written objectives affect teacher and student performance in the classroom?
2. Think of a lesson you have recently taught or one you might teach. What would be an appropriate content objective and language objective for that lesson?
3. What are some ways that curriculum intended for learners at a lower grade level can be used effectively as a supplement for teaching grade-level content concepts? Give examples.
4. Many teachers in sheltered settings rely on paper-and-pencil tasks or lectures for teaching concepts. Think of a curricular area (e.g., science, language arts, math, social studies) and discuss some meaningful activities that could be used to teach a concept in that area. What makes each of these activities "meaningful" and how would they provide language practice?
5. Begin writing a SIOP® lesson. Identify the topic and content and language objectives. Find or create supplementary materials and adapted content as needed. Determine at least one meaningful activity your adolescent students can engage in during the lesson. Decide how many class periods will be needed to complete the lesson. When you finish, share your initial lesson plan with a colleague and garner feedback. Revise your lesson.

chapter 3

Building Background

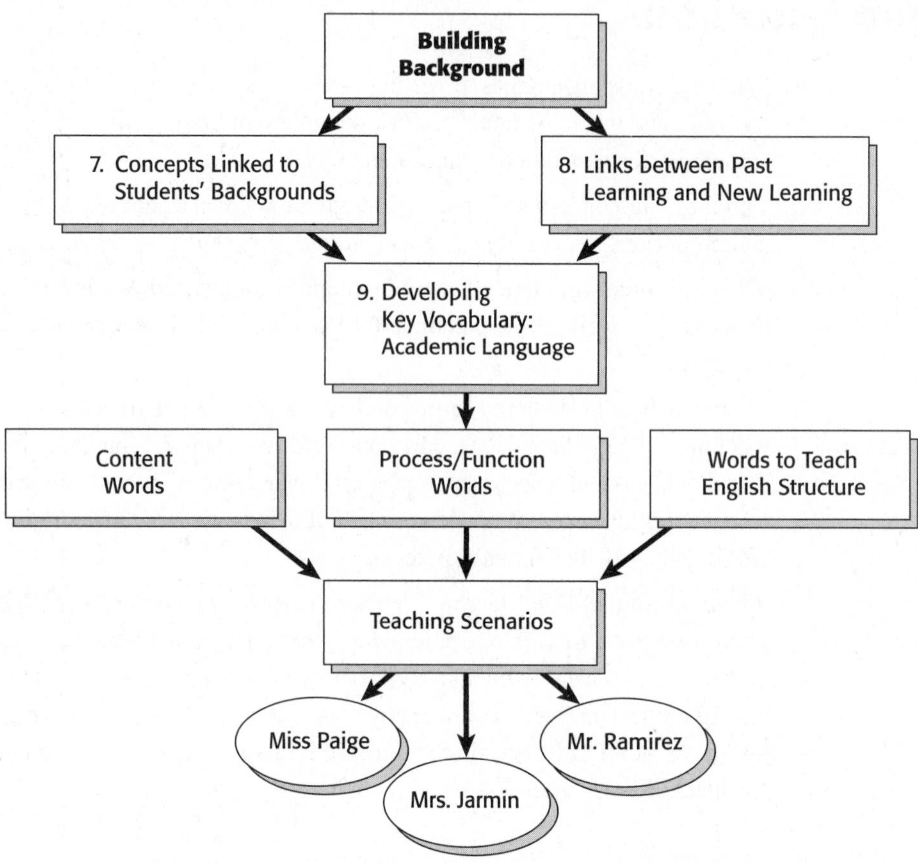

Objectives

After reading, discussing, and engaging in activities related to this chapter, you will be able to meet the following content and language objectives.

Content Objectives

Identify techniques for connecting students' personal experiences and past learning to lesson concepts.

Define the key elements of academic vocabulary (content words, process/function words, and words to teach English structure) and describe their importance for English learners.

Language Objectives

Write a lesson plan incorporating activities that build background and provide explicit links to students' backgrounds, experiences, and past learning.

Identify the academic language in a SIOP® lesson and select key vocabulary words to emphasize.

Background

Have you ever been teaching a lesson that you carefully prepared but with which your students cannot connect? As you are explaining new concepts, you observe confused faces, off-task behaviors, and maybe some students mumbling to each other. While there may be several reasons why your students don't understand what you are explaining, one common cause is a mismatch between what your students have learned and experienced and the concepts that you're teaching. English learners, in particular, are frequently at a disadvantage because their schooling experiences (whether they have had little schooling or exceptional schooling) may be considerably different from U.S. educational contexts. For example, the 6–12 curriculum may be quite different from country to country, and depending on circumstances, some students may have experienced interrupted schooling, especially if they have been refugees. English learners may not have learned the academic language and key vocabulary necessary for understanding content information. It is important that we not assume that all students lack knowledge of academic language; some students may know academic language well in their native language, but not in English.

Effective teaching takes students from where they are and leads them to a higher level of understanding (Krashen, 1985; Vygotsky, 1978). Students learning English must have ample opportunity to use the target language (English); to hear and see comprehensible English; and to read, write, and speak the new language within the context of subject matter learning. But there is a caveat to this: *the language must be meaningful.* It is not only the amount of exposure to English that affects learning, but the quality as well. As we will discuss in the next few chapters of this book, effective SIOP® teachers present information in a way that

students can understand, bearing in mind their language development needs and any gaps in their educational experiences. New information is tied to students' background and experiences, and learning strategies are used to scaffold students' acquisition of knowledge and skills (see Chapter 5 for a detailed discussion). All students benefit from scaffolded instruction, but it is a necessity for English learners. This chapter focuses on *Building Background,* which is closely tied to Lesson Preparation and the teacher's assessment of the students' knowledge of and experience with the topic at hand.

SIOP® FEATURE 7: Concepts Explicitly Linked to Students' Background Experiences

During the past three decades, researchers have investigated how highly proficient readers and writers process new information (Baumann, 2005; Carrell, 1987; Dole, Duffy, Roehler & Pearson, 1991). It is a widely accepted notion among experts that a reader's "schemata"—knowledge of the world—provide a basis for understanding, learning, and remembering facts and ideas found in stories and texts. Individuals with knowledge of a topic have better recall and are better able to elaborate on aspects of the topic than those who have limited knowledge of the topic (Brown, 2008; Chiesi, Spilich, & Voss, 1979; Vogt, 2005).

The importance of background experiences are expressed in the following ways:

> Schemata are the reader's concepts, beliefs, expectations, processes—virtually everything from past experiences—that are used in making sense of things and actions. In reading, schemata are used in making sense of text; the printed work evoking the reader's associated experiences, and past and potential relationships. (John McNeil)
>
> When reading, the learner forms meaning by reviewing past experiences that given images and sounds evoke. (Edmund Huey)

Christen & Murphy (1991) suggested that when readers lack the prior knowledge necessary to read, three major instructional interventions need to be considered: (1) teach vocabulary as a prereading step; (2) provide meaningful experiences; and (3) introduce a conceptual framework that will enable students to develop appropriate background information.

Teach Vocabulary During the Pre-Reading Stage

In this chapter we present ideas for teaching vocabulary before and during a lesson. Some studies suggest that a limited number of words should be taught per lesson or per week, and those words should be key words in the text (Beck, Perfetti, & McKeown, 1982). Others recommend teaching ELs the meanings of basic words, such as those that native English speakers know already (Diamond & Gutlohn, 2006; Stahl & Nagy, 2006). In SIOP® lessons, teachers select words that are critical for understanding the text or material and provide a variety of ways for students to learn, remember, and use those words. In that way, students develop a core vocabulary over time (Blachowicz & Fisher, 2000; Graves & Fitzgerald, 2006).

Provide Meaningful Experiences

In this chapter you will see how a teacher used a videotape to develop background knowledge before students read a challenging, grade-level novel. Connecting students' experiences to a text they will read, developing background knowledge, and teaching key vocabulary are all effective ways to increase comprehension and achievement (Biemiller, 2005; Echevarria, Short, & Powers, 2006; Stahl & Nagy, 2006). Further, throughout a special issue of *Educational Leadership* on high school reform (ASCD, 2008), researchers call for helping adolescents make connections to the real world by providing them with more personalized instruction. The features of the Building Background component foster this type of teaching.

Introduce a Conceptual Framework

This can be accomplished by using techniques such as graphic organizers and chapter previews. As students begin to develop a conceptual framework for their own learning and understanding, they build a repertoire of background experiences from which to draw.

One of the challenges of teaching English learners is that students in the same class vary in the amount of prior knowledge they possess related to a topic. Christen and Murphy (1991) suggest that students generally fall into three categories: much, some, or little prior knowledge. Based on students' levels, the teacher makes specific instructional decisions and differentiates instruction for each level. Some ideas for differentiation include using and teaching superordinate concepts, definitions, analogies, and linking words for students who have much prior knowledge; using and teaching examples, attributes, and defining characteristics for students who have some prior knowledge; and using and teaching associations, morphemes (e.g., base words and word roots), sound-alikes, and firsthand experiences for students who have little prior knowledge.

Students from culturally diverse backgrounds may struggle with comprehending a text or concept presented in class because their schemata do not match those of the culture for which the text was written (Jiménez, Garcia, & Pearson, 1996; Anderson, 1984). In the United States, most school reading materials, such as content area texts, rely on assumptions about students' prior knowledge, especially related to curriculum. Many ELs emigrate from other countries and bring an array of experiences that are quite different from those of the majority culture in the United States, and some have gaps in their education. Even for those English learners born in the United States, culture may have an impact on reading comprehension. As a teacher reads, "The man walked briskly down the dark alley, glancing from side to side," do all children get a sense of fear or danger? Anderson (1994) questions whether we can assume that "when reading the same story, children from every subculture will have the same experience with the setting, ascribe the same goals and motives to characters, imagine the same sequence of actions, make predictions with the same emotional reactions, or expect the same outcomes" (pp. 480–481).

redundant

To see an example of the importance of building background, please view the corresponding video clip (Chapter 3, Module 1) on the accompanying CD.

An actual example of cultural mismatch of schemata occurred in a middle school's self-contained special education class with a small group of English learners. The teacher was participating in a project using instructional conversation, an approach that explicitly links students' background to text (Echevarria, 1995a). The teacher read a passage from a grade-level novel about a young man, Mike, who was reading a magazine (his favorite subscription) while riding a public bus home. He left the magazine on the bus and as he exited, he spoke a quick Russian greeting to some passengers whom he had overheard speaking Russian. The story continues that Mike had learned a few phrases from his brother-in-law who is Russian. After Mike got off the bus, he noticed the bus make its next stop with quite a commotion. He turned to see the Russians running toward him with guns! After taking a circuitous route home, he got to his second-floor apartment, breathing a sigh of relief.

He had no idea why the Russians were so angry with him, but he was relieved that he had lost them. A half-hour later he heard a noise outside, looked out the window, and saw the Russians coming into his building.

At this point, the teacher paused and asked the students how the Russians could possibly have found where Mike lived when the story made it clear that he had lost them. The teacher expected that the students would remember that Mike had left the magazine, with his address label on it, on the bus. However, one student volunteered that the Russians found Mike by asking his brother-in-law. The teacher admitted that she found the answer to be "out in left field" and would ordinarily have tactfully asked someone else for the answer. But the nature of instructional conversation is to discuss ideas, drawing out students' thoughts and linking them to the text. So the teacher asked the student to elaborate. He explained that in his community, which was 99 percent Latino with a small population of Samoans, if he needed to know where a certain Samoan person lived, he'd simply ask someone from the Samoan neighborhood.

The teacher admitted that she had learned an important lesson: the students' schemata were different from hers, yet just as valid. Moreover, she nearly dismissed the student's excellent contribution because she was looking for a specific answer that matched her schemata. In reality, none of the students in her group had any idea about magazine subscriptions and address labels. In the students' experience, if one wanted a magazine, one merely walked to the store and bought it.

This example clearly demonstrates that the students and teacher had very different ideas and assumptions about the characters and events in the story and a different "magazine" schema. Some of the differences might be attributed to cultural variation and a difference in home environments.

Teachers of English learners need to be aware that what may appear to be poor comprehension and a lack of skills may in fact be a lack of experience or a failure to activate background knowledge assumed by a message or a text (Bransford, 1994). Through the SIOP® Model, we urge teachers to activate students' background knowledge explicitly, provide linkages from their experiences to the key concepts, and build additional background when there are gaps. The interactive emphasis of the SIOP® Model (see Chapter 6 for specific features) enables teachers to elicit students' prior knowledge and discuss ideas, issues, concepts, or vocabulary that are unfamiliar to them, in order to develop necessary background information.

Instructional Implications

As you begin to write SIOP® lessons with techniques to develop students' background knowledge, reflect on the following questions:

- What is meant by activating prior knowledge?
- What is meant by building background?
- How do these terms differ instructionally?

In the past, we have used the terms *activating prior knowledge* and *building background* somewhat synonymously. However, we now believe there are some instructional differences that need to be considered when teaching English learners. All students have prior knowledge, gained from schooling and life experiences, and teachers can informally assess what students know and can do, as well as any mismatches in schemata through brainstorming, structured discussion, quick-writes, and techniques such as the familiar KWL (Ogle, 1986).

However, if some ELs have little or no prior knowledge about a content topic (e.g., the American Revolutionary War), brainstorming about it may not be helpful because the brainstormed terms, names, and places will probably be unfamiliar. If students are from countries where there have been revolutions, they may know something about them, but not about the American Revolutionary War. Therefore, it is of critical importance that teachers build background using techniques that fill in the gaps, and help students connect what they do know with what is being taught. And when teachers' explanations are made more concrete with supplementary materials (e.g., photos, models, illustrations, etc.), students are more likely to make the appropriate connections.

To see an example of activating prior knowledge, please view the corresponding video clip (Chapter 3, Module 2) on the accompanying CD.

Additional activities that activate prior knowledge and/or build background include

Read a story, article, play, or book about the topic;

View a video related to the topic;

Use the Insert Method (adapted from the RWCT Project of the International Reading Association; Vogt & Echevarria, 2008). This activity is appropriate for grades 6–12 and all subject areas. First, duplicate a nonfiction article on the topic you're teaching, one per student. In pairs, students read the article. While reading, they insert the following codes directly into the text:

- A check mark (✓) indicates a concept or fact that is already known by the students.
- A question mark (?) indicates a concept or fact that is confusing or not understood.
- An exclamation mark (!) indicates something that is unusual or surprising.
- A plus sign (+) indicates an idea or concept that is new to the reader.

When the partners finish reading and marking the text, they share their markings with another pair of students. If any misconceptions or misunderstandings are cleared up, then the question mark is replaced with an asterisk (*). When groups finish working, the whole class discusses what they have read and learned with the teacher.

Pretest with a Partner (Vogt & Echevarria, 2008). This activity is helpful for students in grades 6–12 and is appropriate for any subject area. The purpose of Pretest with a Partner is to allow English learners the opportunity to preview at the beginning of a lesson or unit the concepts and vocabulary that will be assessed at the conclusion of the lesson or unit. Distribute one pretest and pencil to each pair of students. The pretest should be similar or identical to the posttest that will be administered later. The partners pass the pretest and pencil back and forth between one another. They read a question aloud, discuss possible answers, come to consensus, and write an answer on the pretest. This activity provides an opportunity for students to activate prior knowledge and share background information, while the teacher circulates to assess what students know, recording gaps and misinformation.

SIOP® FEATURE 8:
Links Explicitly Made Between Past Learning and New Concepts

It is also important for teachers to make explicit connections between new learning and the material, vocabulary, and concepts previously covered in class. Research clearly emphasizes that in order for learning to occur, new information must be integrated with what students have previously learned (Rumelhart, 1980). The teacher must build a bridge from previous lessons and concepts to today's lesson. Many students do not automatically make such connections, and all students benefit from having the teacher explicitly point out how past learning is related to the information at hand (Tierney & Pearson, 1994).

Explicit links between past learning and new learning can be made through a discussion—such as, "Who remembers what we learned about _____? How does that relate to our chapter?"—or by reviewing graphic organizers, previously used class notes, transparencies, or PowerPoint slides related to the topic. By preserving and referring to photos, illustrations, word banks, outlines, charts, maps, and graphic organizers, teachers have tools for helping students make critical connections. This is particularly important for ELs who receive so much input through the new language. An explicit, if brief, review of prior lessons focuses on the key information they should remember.

SIOP® FEATURE 9:
Key Vocabulary Emphasized (e.g., introduced, written, repeated, and highlighted for students to see)

Vocabulary development, critical for English learners, is strongly related to academic achievement (Saville-Troike, 1984; Hart & Risley, 2003; Biemiller, 2005; Manzo, Manzo, & Thomas, 2005). In addition, for over 80 years, we have known of the powerful relationship between vocabulary knowledge and comprehension (Baumann, 2005; Stahl & Nagy, 2006). According to Graves & Fitzgerald (2006, p. 122), systematic and comprehensive vocabulary instruction is necessary for English learners because

- content area texts that students must read include very sophisticated vocabulary;
- reading performance tests given to English learners rely on wide-ranging vocabulary knowledge;
- English learners' vocabulary instruction must be accelerated because ELs are learning English later than their native-speaking peers;
- English learners' acquisition of deep understandings of word meaning is very challenging.

Academic Language (or English) and Academic Vocabulary

Many English learners who have been educated in their native countries, come to school in the United States with well-developed vocabularies and an understanding of academic language. Currently, the terms *academic language* or *academic English* are being widely used to describe academic vocabulary and language use in U.S. classrooms, though Stahl & Nagy (2006) refer to it as "literate English." Within the SIOP® Model, we refer to academic vocabulary as having three key elements:

1. **Content Words:** These are the key vocabulary words, terms, and concepts associated with a particular topic being taught (e.g., for the American Revolutionary War: *Redcoats, democracy, Patriots, freedom of religion, Shot Heard 'Round the World, Paul Revere*, etc.).
2. **Process/Function Words:** These are the words that have to do with functional language (e.g., how to request information, justify opinions, state a conclusion, etc.), language used in the classroom for processes and tasks (e.g., *share with a partner, discuss, line up, graph, list, classify*, etc.), and language processes (e.g., *scan, skim, question, debate, argue, summarize*, etc.). Other kinds of words that are included in this category include transition words (*therefore, in conclusion, moreover, furthermore*, etc.), and sequence words (*first, then, next, finally, at last*, etc.).
3. **Words and Word Parts That Teach English Structure:** These are words that enable students to learn new vocabulary, primarily based upon English morphology. Biemiller (2004) suggests students in grade 12 know about 175,000 words with roots; of these, about 15,000 are known by a majority of students. Additionally, students through grade 6 acquire approximately 800–1,200 root words per year. These estimates are based upon *The Living Word Vocabulary* by Dale & O'Rourke (1981). There is no way that English learners can realistically learn all the words they need to know through instruction and memorization. Therefore, all teachers must help students learn that many English words are formed with roots and base words joined to prefixes and suffixes. For example, if a science teacher is teaching photosynthesis, he can help students learn the meaning of *photosynthesis* by introducing the meaning of the root, *photo-* (light). By comparing the words *photosynthesis, photocopy, photograph, photography, photoelectron, photofinish*, and *photogenic*, students can see how these English words are related by both spelling and meaning (Bear, Invernizzi, Templeton, & Johnston, 2007).

To assist with teaching English word structure, especially for those who are not English or language arts teachers, we include in Figure 3.1 some of the most common Latin roots that are found in thousands of English words. The fourteen roots with asterisks provide the meaning of over 100,000 words! By adding suffixes to many of the words that are included with each root (e.g., *disrespectful, extraction, informed*), you can increase further the number of words on this list.

We urge caution about sharing this list with students. It is not included here as a list for having students memorize roots, words, and their meanings. Instead, use what students already know about words: If they know how the words *import, export, portable, transport*, and *porter* are all related (they all have to do with carrying something), they can transfer that knowledge to learning the meanings of *important* (carrying value) and *unimportant* (not carrying value). These roots and words should be used for your reference and for helping students understand how roots work in the English language. (For more information about word parts—morphemes—and English structure, see Bear et al., 2007, and Bear, Helman, Invernizzi, Templeton, & Johnston, 2007).

FIGURE 3.1 *Common Word Roots*

There are hundreds of Latin word roots that are used frequently with prefixes and suffixes. This is only a partial list of the most frequently used roots. The roots with asterisks (*) are the fourteen roots that provide clues to the meaning of over 100,000 words.

Port: to carry
Import, export, portable, transport, porter, deport, report, support, portal, important, importantly, unimportant

Form: to shape
Reform, deform, inform, information, transform, conform, formula, formal, informal, formality, informative

Rupt: to break
Rupture, disrupt, disruptive, disruption, abruptly, bankrupt, corruption, erupted, eruption, interrupt

Tract: to draw or pull
Tractor, attract, abstract, contract, retract, contractual, detract, distract, extract, subtract, tractable, intractable, traction, protract, protractor

*Scrib or script: to write
Scribble, ascribe, describe, description, conscript, inscribe, inscription, superscription, prescribe, prescriptive, script, scripture, transcribe, transcript, transcription

*Spec or spect: to see, watch, observe
Spectator, spectacular, spectacle, respect, spectrum, specter, disrespect, inspect, inspector, retrospective, species, special, specimen

Stru or struct: to build
Structure, structural, construct, construction, destructive, reconstruct, instruct, instructor, obstruct, instrument, construe

Jac or jec or ject: to throw, lie
Dejected, rejection, adjective, conjecture, eject, injection, interjection, object, objective, project, rejection, adjacent

Dic or dict: to say, tell
Dictate, dictator, predict, diction, dictation, contradict, contradictory, edict, indicate, indict, indictment

Flect or flex: to bend
Flex, flexible, flexibility, deflect, inflection, reflect, reflexive, reflective, reflector, circumflexion

Ped or pod: foot (*ped* is Latin; *pod* is Greek)
Pedestrian, pedestal, podium, pedometer, centipede, pedal, expedition, impede, podiatry, podiatrist

*Mit or miss: to send
Mission, missile, missive, admit, admission, commit, dismissed, emissary, intermission, intermittent, remiss, remit, remittance, submit, submission, transmit, transmission, emit, permit, permission, permissive

*Tend or tens or tent: to stretch, strain
Intend, intention, intently, extended, tense, intense, pretense, tension, intensity, attention, inattention, unintentionally, distend, detention, détente

*Ten, tent, or tain: to have, hold
Tenant, tenable, tenacity, tenacious, contents, contended, discontented, contentment, intent, maintain, retain, retentive

*Plic or ply: to fold
Implicit, implicitness, explicit, explicate, implication, replicate, complicated, application, ply, apply, imply, reply

*Fer: to bring, bear, yield
Refer, reference, confer, conference, inference, suffer, transfer, defer, differ, difference, fertile, fertilize, fertilization, circumference, odoriferous

Aud: to hear
Audible, auditory, audience, audio, audiotape, audiovisual, auditorium

Vis: to see
Visual, visa, visor, vision, visible, visitor, visitation, visualize, invisible, evident, provide, providence

Cred: to believe
Credit, credential, credible, incredible, creditable, accredit, credence, incredulity

*Duc, duce, or duct: to lead
Conduct, deduct, educate, induce, introduction, produce, reduce, reduction, reducible, production

Pel or puls: to drive, push, throw
Impulse, compel, compulsion, expel, propel, dispel, impulsive, pulsate, compulsive, repel, repellent

*Fac, fact, fic, or fect: fact, manufacture, faculty, facility, facile, facilitate, satisfaction, factor, beneficiary, amplification, certificate, confection, affect, defective, disinfect, efficacy, magnificent, personification, proficient, sufficient

Vert or vers: to turn
Convert, convertible, revert, reversible, extrovert, introvert, divert, avert, aversion, aversive, vertigo

FIGURE 3.1 *Continued*

Capit or capt: head, chief, leader
Capital, decapitate, capitol, capitalize, captain, caption, recapitulate

*Cept, cap, ciev, or ceit: to take, to seize, to receive
Capable, capsule, captive, captor, capture, accept, deception, exception, intercept, conception, receptable, susceptible, perceptive, precept, receive, receipt, deceive, deceit

Pend or pens: to hang
Pendant, suspend, suspense, pendulum, pending, dependent, perpendicular, appendix

*Pos, pon, or pose: to put, place, set
Compose, composite, dispose, disposable, oppose, component, postpone, proponent, deposit, compound, depose, proposal, preposition, disposal, exposition, exponent, expose, impose, suppose, opponent, proposition, position

*Sist, sta, or stat: to stand, endure
Persist, consistent, consist, desist, assist, resist, assistant, insist, stamina, constant, circumstance, distant, obstacle, standard, substance

Greek Combining Forms

Beginning: auto, phono, photo, biblio, hydro, hyper, hypo, tele, chrom, arch, phys, psych, micro, peri, bi, semi, hemi, mono, metro, demo

Ending: *graph, gram, meter, *ology, sphere, scope, crat, cracy, polis

Examples: photograph, microscope, hemisphere, telegram, chronometer, physiology, metropolis, perimeter, archeology, bibliography, democracy, autocrat

Compiled by M.K. Henry, 1990.

Academic Word List

Another helpful source of words for teachers of English learners, especially those in middle and high school, is the Academic Word List, developed by Averil Coxhead (2000) at Victoria University, Wellington, New Zealand. The list, originally developed for ESL university students, contains 570 word families (or "headwords") contained in four disciplines (arts, commerce, law, and science). Words are listed by the headwords, rather than common roots as in Figure 3.1. They also reinforce for English learners the spelling/meaning connection in thousands of English words, and they provide useful information about which words provide the best academic return for students. In Figure 3.2, you will see examples from Coxhead's Academic Word List. The complete list of 570 headwords and approximately 3,000 words can be found (at the time of this writing) at www.uefap.com/vocab/select/awl.htm. (Note that many of the words on the list have British rather than American spellings; these have been changed in Figure 3.2.) There are also many other websites related to the Academic Word List that you can find using your search engine.

A third source of words for teaching vocabulary is found in a scheme designed by Beck, McKeown, and Kucan (2002). They describe three Tiers of words often taught in U.S. schools:

1. Tier One words are common words, such as simple nouns, verbs, high-frequency words, and sight words. Most students know these words conversationally, and it is usually isn't necessary to focus on them, except for young children who are learning to read. While Beck, McKeown, and Kucan (2002) recommend teachers focus primarily on Tier Two words in their vocabulary lessons, we urge a caution. Teachers of English learners need to be careful that they not assume their students know the Tier One words; newcomers and emergent speakers especially may need explicit instruction and practice with these words. Depending on their ages, they are likely to know the Tier One words in their native language, but they'll most likely need help in learning them in English.

FIGURE 3.2 *Academic Word List Examples*

Accurate: accuracy, accurately, inaccuracy, inaccuracies, inaccurate

Adjust: adjusted, adjusting, adjustment, adjustments, adjusts, readjust, readjusted, readjusting, readjustment, readjustments, readjusts

Analyze: analyzed, analyses, analyzing, analysis, analyst, analysts, analytic, analytical, analytically

Category: categories, categorization, categorize, categorized, categorizes, categorizing

Coincide: coincided, coincides, coinciding, coincidence, coincidences, coincident, coincidental

Constitute: constituencies, constituency, constituent, constituents, constituted, constitutes, constituting, constitution, constitutional, constitutionally, constitutive, unconstitutional

Demonstrate: demonstrable, demonstrably, demonstrated, demonstrates, demonstrating, demonstration, demonstrations, demonstrative, demonstratively, demonstrator, demonstrators

Estimate: estimated, estimates, estimating, estimation, estimations, over-estimate, overestimate, overestimated, overestimates, overestimating, underestimate, underestimating, underestimated, underestimates

React: reacted, reacts, reacting, reaction, reactionaries, reactionary, reactions, reactive, reactivate, reactivation, reactor, reactors

Structure: restructure, restructured, restructures, restructuring, structural, structurally, structured, structures, structuring, unstructured

Vary: invariable, invariably, variability, variable, variables, variably, variance, variant, variants, variation, variations, varied, varies, varying

Coxhead, 2000.

2. Tier Two words can be equated with many of the words in the Academic Word List. They are commonly found in school texts but not in general conversation. Stahl & Nagy (2006) refer to them as "Goldilocks words—words that are not too difficult, not too easy, but just right" (p. 133). These are also considered to be the words students need to know for comprehending school texts and achieving academically, and they should be taught explicitly to English learners, and most native-speaking students.
3. Tier Three words are uncommon words, found rarely in school texts except in particular contexts, such as a discussion of a specific content-related topic. While these words may be interesting, fun to know, and unique to a particular topic, it is recommended that teachers not spend a great deal of time on them. When a Tier Three word is included only once or twice in a story, for example, it's fine to mention the word in its particular context, but then move on.

With all this serious discussion about words and vocabulary development, it's very important to remember that learning about words and playing with words can be great fun, for English learners and native speakers alike. Stahl and Nagy (2006) discuss the importance of developing students' "word consciousness." Word consciousness "is a phrase used to refer to the interest in and awareness of words that should be part of vocabulary instruction. In other words, motivation plays an important role in vocabulary learning, as it does in any other kind of learning" (p. 137). Activities in which students manipulate words, sort words, laugh and giggle about funny words, and choose words they want to know about are as important for vocabulary growth as the more scholarly aspects of vocabulary teaching and word learning. For example, see if you don't chuckle or eye-roll with the following (Stahl & Nagy, 2006, pp. 147–148):

- A bicycle can't stand alone because it is two-tired.
- Time flies like an arrow. Fruit flies like a banana.
- A chicken crossing the road is poultry in motion.
- Those who get too big for their britches will be exposed in the end.

And how about some of these homographs:

- We polish the Polish furniture.
- He could lead if he would get the lead out.
- The present is a good time to present the present.
- I did not object to the object.

Vocabulary Instruction

In a synthesis of twenty years of research on vocabulary instruction, Blachowicz and Fisher (2000) determined four main principles that should guide instruction:

1. *Students should be active in developing their understanding of words and ways to learn them.* Such ways include use of semantic mapping, word sorts (see Figure 3.3a and 3.3b, pp. 66–67), Concept Definition Maps (see Figure 3.4, p. 69), and developing strategies for independent word learning.
2. *Students should personalize word learning* through practices such as Vocabulary Self-Collection Strategy (VSS) (Ruddell, 2007), mnemonic strategies, and personal dictionaries.
3. *Students should be immersed in words* by rich language environments that focus on words and draw students' attention to the learning of words. Word walls, personal word study notebooks and dictionaries, and comparing/contrasting words with the same morphemic element (e.g., photograph, photosynthesis, photogenic) aid students in recognizing and using the words around them.
4. *Students should build on multiple sources of information to learn words through repeated exposures.* Letting students see and hear new words more than once and drawing on multiple sources of meaning are important for vocabulary development.

There is little benefit to selecting 10 or 15 or 20 isolated vocabulary terms and asking ELs to copy them from the board and look up their definitions in the dictionary (Allen, 2007; Fisher & Frey, 2008b). Many of the words in the definitions are also unfamiliar to these students, rendering the activity meaningless. Although using the dictionary is an important school skill to learn, the task must fit the students' learning needs. The number of terms should be tailored to the students' English and literacy levels, and they should be presented in context, not in isolation. The *Oxford Picture Dictionary for the Content Areas* and related books (Kauffman & Apple, 2000) are excellent resources for contextualizing terms. For students with minimal literacy skills, using the dictionary to find words can serve to reinforce the concept of alphabetizing and it familiarizes them with the parts of a dictionary; however, defining words should not be the only activity used. Effective SIOP® teachers support the understanding of dictionary definitions so that the task is meaningful for students. In fact, many effective teachers introduce dictionary skills to students by using words that are already familiar to them.

There are a myriad of meaningful and useful ways that vocabulary can be taught to English learners. The following section describes approaches to vocabulary development and word study that are especially helpful to ELs. When used regularly, they provide students with multiple exposures to key language and vocabulary through meaningful practice and review.

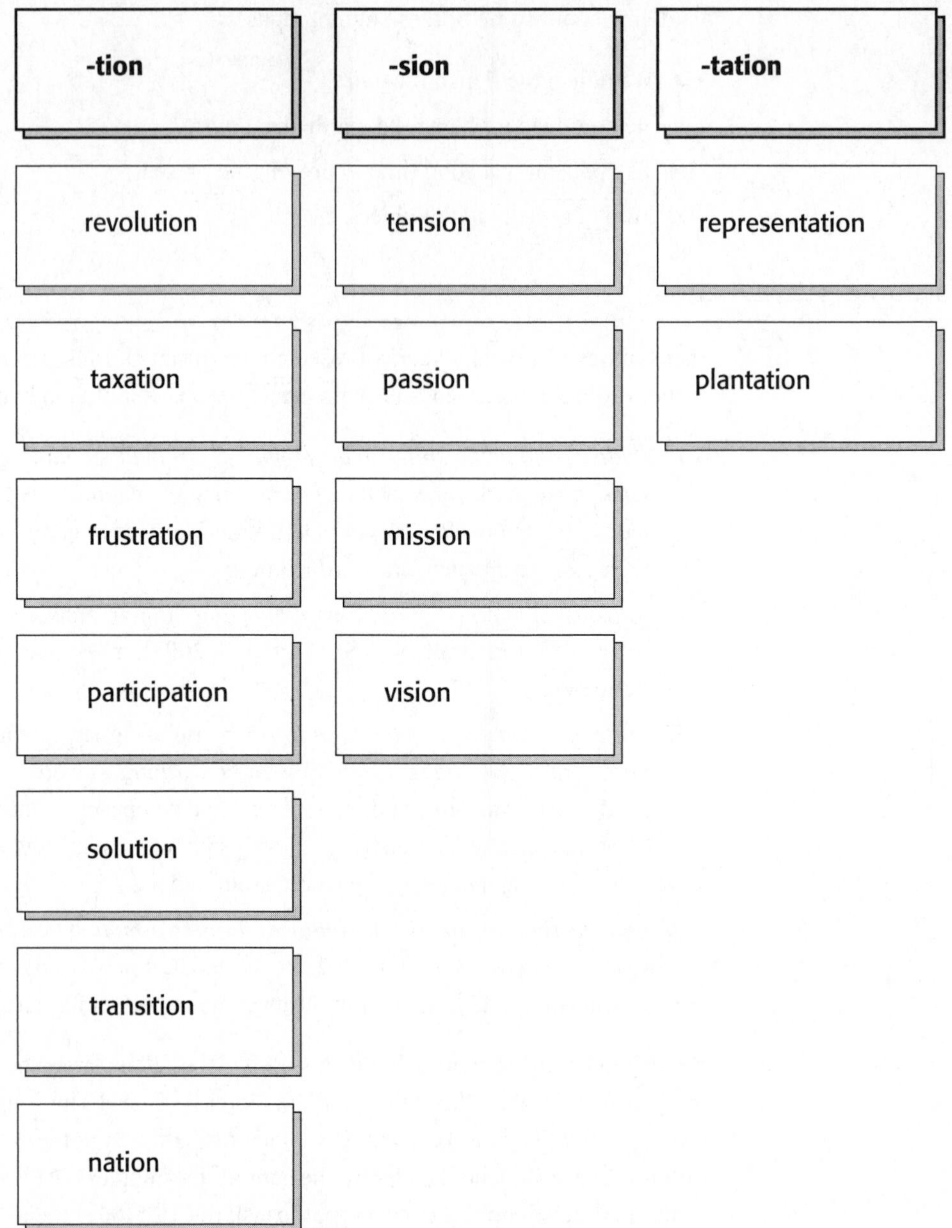

FIGURE 3.3a *Word Sorts: American Revolution–Example 1*

Word Sorts During a Word Sort, students categorize words or phrases that have been previously introduced into groups predetermined by the teacher (Bear, Invernizzi, Templeton, & Johnston, 2007). Words or phrases are typed on a sheet of paper (46-point type on the computer works well). Students cut the paper into word strips and then sort the words according to meaning, similarities in structure (e.g., words ending in -tion, -sion, or -tation), derivations, or sounds.

For example, words related to the American Revolution are listed in mixed order on a sheet of paper: revolution, tension, frustration, taxation, representation, vision, plantation, mission, participation, solution, passion, transition, nation, and so on. After you discuss the meanings of the words, have students cut out each of the words and sort them according to

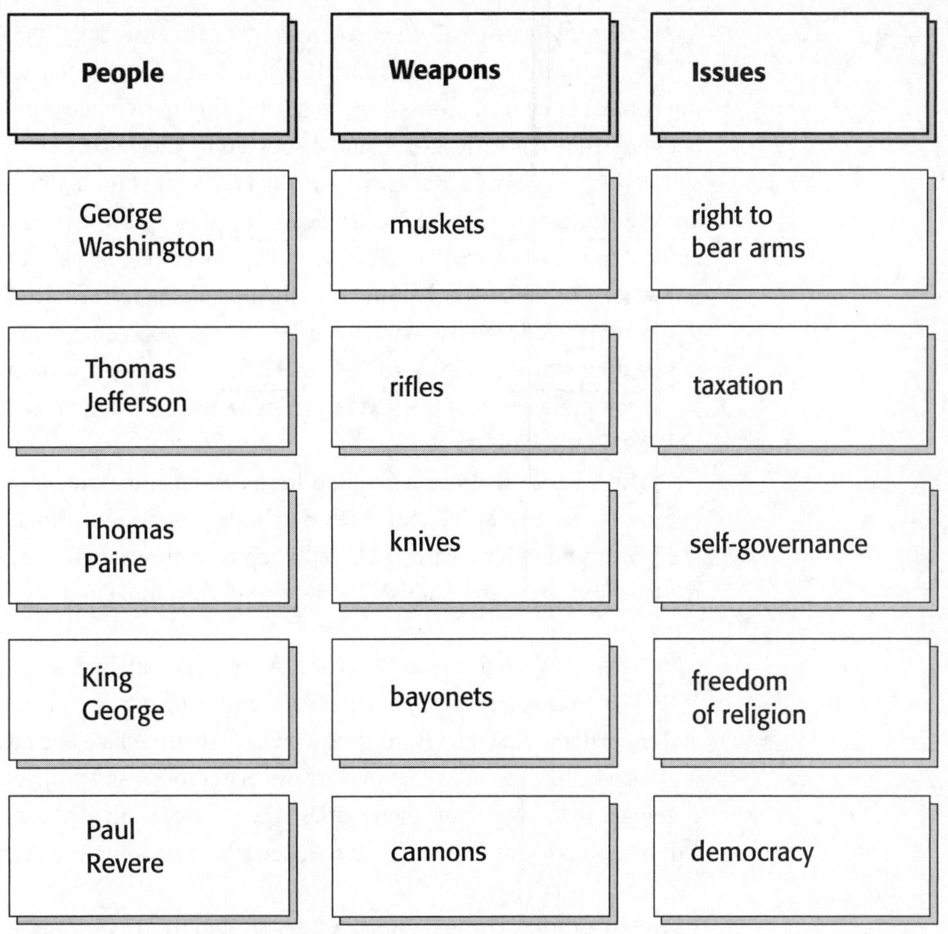

FIGURE 3.3b *Word Sorts: American Revolution–Example 2*

spelling pattern (see Figure 3.3a). The objectives here would be twofold: to introduce words related to content concepts and to reinforce spellings and word structure.

Another example of a Word Sort for the American Revolution might involve words and phrases related to content concepts such as right to bear arms, muskets, George Washington, rifles, Thomas Jefferson, democracy, Thomas Paine, knives, taxation, King George, bayonets, freedom of religion, Paul Revere, self-governance, cannons. After students cut apart the words and phrases, they sort them into groups and identify an appropriate label for each (e.g., People, Weapons, Issues) (see Figure 3.3b).

ACTIVITY *Contextualizing Key Vocabulary* SIOP® teachers peruse the material to be learned and select several key terms that are critical to understanding the lesson's most important concepts. The teacher introduces the terms at the outset of the lesson, systematically defining or demonstrating each and showing how that term is used within the context of the lesson. Experienced SIOP® teachers know that having students understand the meaning of several key terms completely is more effective than having a cursory understanding of a dozen terms.

One way of contextualizing words is to read with students in small groups and, as they come across a term they do not understand, pause and explain it to them, using as many examples, synonyms, or cognates as necessary to convey the meaning.

ACTIVITY *Vocabulary Self-Collection Strategy (VSS)* (Ruddell, 2007). Following the reading of a content text, students self-select several words that are essential to understanding content concepts. Words may be selected by individuals, partners, or small groups, and they are eventually shared and discussed by the entire class. A class list of vocabulary self-collection words for a particular lesson or unit is mutually agreed on by the teacher and the students, and these are reviewed and studied throughout. They also may be entered into a word study notebook, and students may be asked to demonstrate their knowledge of these words through written or oral activities. Ruddell (2007) has found that when students are shown how to identify key content vocabulary, they become adept at selecting and learning words they need to know, and, given opportunities to practice VSS, comprehension of the text improves (Shearer, Ruddell, & Vogt, 2001; Ruddell & Shearer, 2002; Stahl & Nagy, 2006).

The VSS is an effective method for teaching and reviewing content vocabulary because students learn to trust their own judgments about which content words are the most important to learn. This approach is appropriate for students who are high-intermediate and advanced English learners, and for middle and high school students.

ACTIVITY *Personal Dictionaries* Similar to VSS, personal dictionaries are created as an individual vocabulary and spelling resource for students at all levels of English proficiency, and are generally used with students who have intermediate and advanced English proficiency. ELs read together in pairs or small groups and write unknown words they encounter in their personal dictionaries. The teacher works with each group and discusses the words students have written in their dictionaries, providing correction or clarity as needed.

ACTIVITY *Word Wall* During a lesson, key vocabulary is reviewed with a word wall where relevant content vocabulary words are listed alphabetically, usually on a large poster, sheet of butcher paper, or pocket chart (Cunningham, 2004). Originally designed as a method for teaching and reinforcing sight words for emergent readers, word walls are also effective for displaying content words related to a particular unit or theme. The words are revisited frequently throughout the lesson or unit, and students are encouraged to use them in their writing and discussions.

Cunningham (2004) recommends that teachers judiciously select words for a word wall and that the number be limited to those of greatest importance. We would add that teachers should resist the temptation to have multiple word walls in one classroom because the walls quickly become cluttered with words that are difficult to sort through, especially for ELs. One word wall, carefully maintained and changed as needed, is what we recommend. Some teachers, with students' input, regularly remove words from a word wall to keep the number of words reasonable. Every Friday, or every other Friday, for example, the students jointly decide which words they no longer need on the wall. Word wall posters can also be kept and stored for later reference or review.

ACTIVITY *Concept Definition Map* The Concept Definition Map is a great way to learn and remember content vocabulary and concepts (Buehl, 2009). Even though it is a simple graphic, it can be used to discuss complex concepts. For example, a class is studying the American Revolution in social studies. To clarify the meaning of *revolution*, the class could complete a Concept Definition Map, as shown in Figure 3.4. The Concept Definition Map is also an excellent prewriting activity for summarizing. Students can begin the

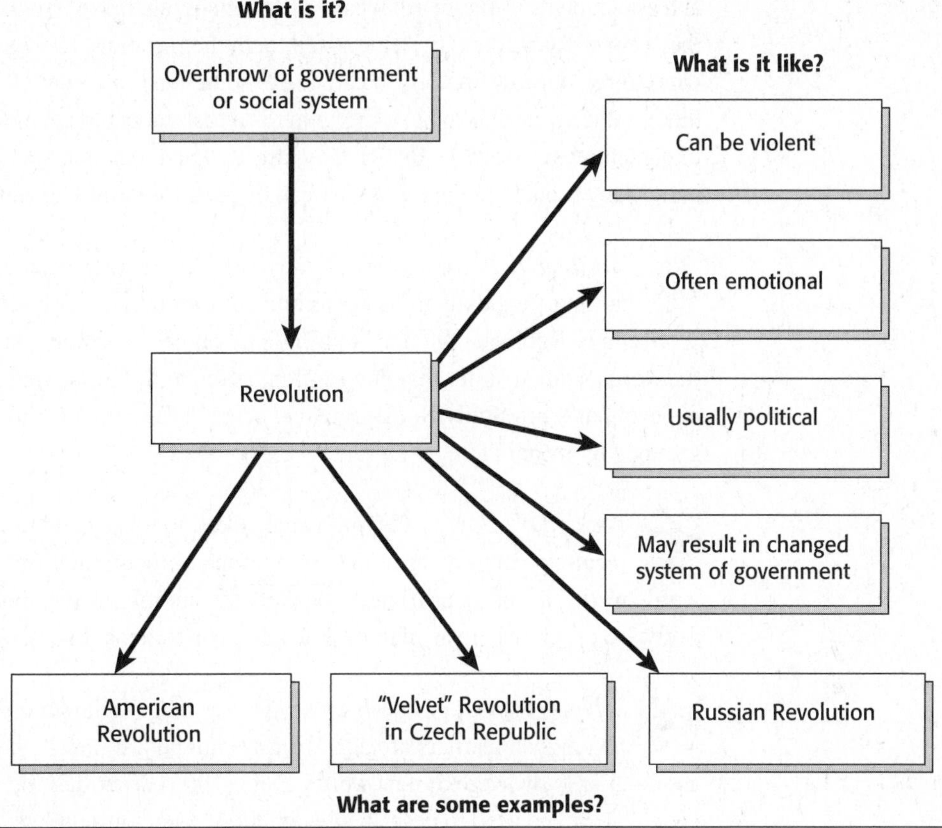

FIGURE 3.4 *Concept Definition Map*

summarizing process by organizing content concepts in the graphic organizer. Then sentences can be created from the information in the Concept Definition Map and subsequently written into paragraph form.

Cloze Sentences Cloze sentences can be used to teach and review content vocabulary. Students read a sentence that has strong contextual support for the vocabulary word that has been omitted from the sentence. Once the meaning of the word is determined and possible replacement words are brainstormed, the teacher (or a student) provides the correct word. For example, "During a _______, which can be violent or peaceful, a group of people tries to overthrow an existing government or social system." *(revolution)*

List–Group–Label This categorizing activity can also be completed as a List–Group–Label activity (Vacca & Vacca, 2004) in which students brainstorm words related to the topic and then determine possible categories or labels for the words. The brainstormed words are then reviewed when they are rewritten under the various categories and labels.

Word Generation This activity helps EL students and others learn and/or review new content vocabulary through analogy. For example, write "-port" on the board. Invite students to brainstorm all the words they can think of that contain "port." Examples might include *report, import, export, important, portfolio, Port-a-Potty, Portland, deport, transport, transportation, support, airport,* and so on. Analyze the meaning of each brainstormed word and ask students to figure out what words containing "-port" might mean ("to carry"). If they cannot figure it out, it's fine to tell them the meaning. Then go back and revisit each word to see if the definition "to carry" has something to do with the word's meaning. Note that we did not define "port" first; rather, we recommend that students generalize meanings of content words from words that they already know that contain the same syllable or word part. Many roots found in Figure 3.1 can be used for Word Generation.

ACTIVITY *Word Study Books* A Word Study Book is a student-made personal notebook containing frequently used words and concepts. Bear et al. (2007) recommend that the Word Study Book be organized by English language structure, such as listing together all the words studied so far that end in -tion, -sion, and -tation. We support this notion and believe that Word Study Books can also be used for content study where words are grouped by meaning.

ACTIVITY *Vocabulary Games* Playing games like Pictionary and Scrabble can help students recall vocabulary terms. Word searches for beginning English speakers and crossword puzzles for more proficient speakers are additional vocabulary development tools. Software programs are available for teachers or students to create crossword puzzles.

ACTIVITY *Self-Assessment of Levels of Word Knowledge* (Diamond & Gutlohn, 2006, p. 5) As English learners are acquiring vocabulary, it may be helpful for them to self-assess their knowledge of new words. Dale (1965) described four levels of word knowledge that can be used to describe the extent of a person's understanding of words:

1. I've never heard or seen the word before.
2. I've seen or heard the word before, but I don't know what it means.
3. I vaguely know the meaning of the word, and I can associate it with a concept or context.
4. I know the word well.

With effective vocabulary instruction and repeated exposures to unfamiliar vocabulary, knowledge of the words increases and they move up the levels from 1 to 4. When teachers introduce the four Levels of Word Knowledge to students, they can self-assess their word knowledge as words are introduced and studied.

The Lesson

UNIT: *Mrs. Frisby and the Rats of NIMH* (Sixth Grade)

The lessons described in this chapter take place in an urban middle school with a large population of ELs. The number of ELs in this school enables classes to be grouped homogeneously by students' English proficiency levels. Students in all three classes described here are a heterogeneous mix of native English speakers and ELs with varied levels of English proficiency. Many of the ELs emigrated from rural areas in Latin America and have low literacy levels due to interrupted schooling experiences.

As part of a literature course, Miss Paige, Mrs. Jarmin, and Mr. Ramirez are required to teach a variety of American literature. The first book in the series is *Mrs. Frisby and the Rats of NIMH*, and the teachers will spend one week to ten days on the unit. The story is about Mrs. Frisby, a field mouse, who is worried about her younger son, Timothy. He has had pneumonia and is too weak and frail to be moved. But if the Frisbys don't move immediately, they'll all be killed. Mrs. Frisby hears about the wonderful Rats of NIMH who are strong, smart, and able to do almost anything. The story chronicles the adventures of the family and the Rats of NIMH.

The goals for this unit include (1) students will read an extended text, and (2) students will use their prior knowledge as a tool for understanding the text. Although these may seem somewhat vague, the teachers felt strongly that these students need to have the experience of reading an extended text, even a challenging one, because materials written at their literacy levels tend to be short, simple stories. They believe that with appropriate instruction, the ELs will be able to participate in reading the novel. The teachers are planning to introduce the novel by showing the video version of the story. Seeing the video prior to reading the text will provide students with an overall understanding of the story and will provide exposure to new vocabulary associated with the text. Following the viewing of the video, the teachers will introduce the text, which the class will read together. The teachers may provide activities of their choosing to reinforce the concepts and vocabulary covered in the story. (For more examples of lesson and unit plans in language arts, see Vogt, Echevarria, & Short, in press.)

Teaching Scenarios

The teachers have prepared their own plans for teaching the unit on *Mrs. Frisby and the Rats of NIMH.* Their individual approaches to teaching the unit and SIOP® ratings are described below.

Miss Paige

Miss Paige began the first lesson of the unit by asking, "Have you ever seen a rat?" and showing the class a picture of one. The students were quite interested in this topic and readily shared their experiences. She then talked with the students about how in some stories and novels, animals take on human characteristics, such as in *Charlotte's Web* (E.B. White, 1974), a book many students had read or listened to in grade 4. She asked students for other examples of stories or books that had animals who behaved like humans. Two students, both English learners, mentioned books they had read in their native languages before moving to the United States. Miss Paige then introduced a semantic map that had the word *survival* written in the center. She asked, "What are some words and ideas you can think of that have to do with survival?" As students orally provided their ideas, she clustered them on the chart: *Survivor TV show, escaping a tsunami, September 11, earthquakes, animals' need for food and water,* and so forth. She then asked students to discuss with a partner the following question: "What would you do if a member of your family was very ill, but you had to move in order to survive?" The students and Miss Paige had a brief and lively discussion about what students thought they would do. Miss Paige then introduced *Mrs. Frisby and the Rats of NIMH*, written by R.C. O'Brien & Z. Bernstein (1986). She told her students that in this book a family of rats who behaved like humans would face the problem of survival. She then began showing the video of *Mrs. Frisby and the Rats of NIMH.*

After watching the video, Miss Paige showed a transparency listing ten key terms from the story that she was certain some students would not know. As she pointed to each word, she asked the class if they knew what the word meant. At least one student knew the meaning of two of the ten vocabulary terms, indicating that Miss Paige had done an

FIGURE 3.5 *Building Background Component of the SIOP®: Miss Paige's lesson*

4	3	2	1	0	NA
7. **Concepts explicitly linked** to students' background experiences		**Concepts loosely linked** to students' background experiences		**Concepts not explicitly linked** to students' background experiences	
4	3	2	1	0	
8. **Links explicitly made** between past learning and new concepts		**Few links made** between past learning and new concepts		**No links made** between past learning and new concepts	
4	3	2	1	0	
9. **Key vocabulary emphasized** (e.g., introduced, written, repeated, and highlighted for students to see)		**Key vocabulary** introduced, but not emphasized		**Key vocabulary** not introduced or emphasized	

adequate job of selecting key vocabulary words for which the students needed direct instruction. She discussed each term and wrote a brief definition next to the word on the transparency. Next, Miss Paige began reading the first chapter of the book with her students. While reading chapters in the book throughout the course of the unit, she made it a practice to pause every few paragraphs to check for understanding, elaborate, define words, and paraphrase parts of the story. Occasionally she reminded students of something they had discussed in another lesson. For example, when Mrs. Frisby is described as a widow, Miss Paige said, "Who remembers what a widow is? We talked about that word when we read *The Witches* by Roald Dahl. Remember the grandma who was a widow? What does that mean?" Then Miss Paige wrote the word on a piece of chart paper that she continued to use as a word wall throughout the unit, adding words the students identified as unfamiliar throughout the course of the unit.

On the SIOP® form in Figure 3.5, rate Miss Paige's lesson for each of the Building Background features.

Mrs. Jarmin

At the beginning of the first lesson of the unit, Mrs. Jarmin began by telling the class that they would be reading an interesting book in which the main characters were rats. Then Mrs. Jarmin asked, "Who has ever seen a rat?" Several students told of their experiences seeing rats or having them as pets. Then Mrs. Jarmin told the class that they would see a video based on the novel *Mrs. Frisby and the Rats of NIMH,* and that they would read the book after seeing the video.

Before showing the video, Mrs. Jarmin wanted to teach the students some terms they would encounter during the unit. Working with small, rotating groups, she introduced reciprocal teaching (Palinscar & Brown, 1984) by posting the following words on a chart: *predicting, clarifying,* and *questioning.* Mrs. Jarmin distributed three index cards that described each of the three terms to each student in the group. First she asked students to

Predicting

Let's look at the title. Look at all the visual clues on the page. What do you think we'll be reading about?

Clarifying

One of the words I wasn't sure about was ________.

Questioning

What is the story about?

FIGURE 3.6 *Activity Based on Reciprocal Teaching*
(Palinscar and Brown, 1984)

look at the card that gave guidelines for predicting. She read, "Let's look at the title." Mrs. Jarmin paused and asked the students what the title was. The students showed her the title of the book. She continued reading, "Look at all the visual clues on the page." Again she stopped to make sure the students understood and she asked the meaning of "visual clues." Because the students weren't sure, she told them the phrase means pictures, graphs, and the like. Then she read, "What do you think we'll be reading about?" Mrs. Jarmin told the students to follow the guidelines and tell her what they predicted the book would be about. (See Figure 3.6.)

She reiterated the information on the card, telling the students to look at the title, look at the pictures, and think about what they'd be reading about. She left the group to think while she checked on another group. When she returned she said, "What do you think we'll be reading about? I . . ." A student began his sentence with, "I think we'll be reading about some rats." Mrs. Jarmin asked him to explain how he came to that answer and then replied, "Good. Who has more information they want to share?" One student made a comment about the mice. The teacher wrote the words *mice* and *rats* on the board and asked what the story would be about. Some students seemed confused about those words so the teacher asked them to look at the title. They had a brief discussion about how mice and rats differ. Once the distinction was made, they moved on to the card about clarifying.

Mrs. Jarmin read, "One of the words I wasn't sure about was ________." She then distributed a photocopy of the summary of the story to the students and told them to use a highlighter to identify the words they didn't understand. The teacher circulated among other groups as the students read the summary and highlighted unfamiliar words. When she returned, she asked the students to tell her their highlighted words as she wrote them on the board. She said, "Let's see if there are other words that can be used in place of the highlighted words. We'll see which words we already know and the ones we don't know we'll look up in the thesaurus. A thesaurus is a book that is like a dictionary that helps us clarify words." The words the students didn't know were:

Vocabulary Word List

NIMH–	a place
Scarce–	______________
Asparagus–	a vegetable
Frail–	______________
Abandoned–	left behind

The group went through the list, with Mrs. Jarmin asking if anyone knew the meaning of the words. One student recognized that NIMH is the name of a place and that asparagus is a vegetable, so the teacher wrote those definitions beside the words. Because nobody knew the meanings of *frail* and *scarce,* Mrs. Jarmin drew a line, indicating that the students would find those words in the thesaurus. Then the students looked up each word together. The first student to find the word called out to the others the page number on which the word was found. As a group, the students decided on a word or two to denote meaning. When they finished defining all the words, the teacher drew their attention to the final card about questioning. She read, "What is the story about?" and said, "Now that we have made some predictions about the story and we've clarified some terms, what do you think this story will be about?"

The students were now familiar with making predictions about a story and knew one way to clarify words they didn't understand. So before starting the video, Mrs. Jarmin showed a transparency on the overhead projector that listed ten words she identified as key vocabulary. Each group of students was asked to look up two of the words in their thesaurus. The class discussed the synonyms that the students read, and Mrs. Jarmin wrote a short definition next to each word on the overhead. She then told the students to copy the words on a piece of paper and to put a check next to each word as they heard it while watching the video. At the conclusion of the video, she asked students which vocabulary words they had heard and marked. Mrs. Jarmin wrote those words on a word wall and then reviewed with the class the meaning of each word, providing synonyms and drawing a picture, if necessary, to convey meaning as they had done in the clarifying exercise. (The word wall remained posted throughout the reading of the novel, and Mrs. Jarmin often drew students' attention to one of the posted words as they came across it in the text.)

After viewing the video, Mrs. Jarmin and the class began reading the story. Mrs. Jarmin paused after the first chapter and brought out a Venn diagram from an earlier lesson that illustrated the way fiction and fantasy are similar, although not all fiction involves fantasy. She asked the students how they would describe this story so far, as fiction or as fantasy. Looking at the descriptors listed on the Venn diagram, they decided

FIGURE 3.7 *Building Background Component of the SIOP®: Mrs. Jarmin's Lesson*

4	3	2	1	0	NA
7. **Concepts explicitly linked** to students' background experiences		**Concepts loosely linked** to students' background experiences		**Concepts not explicitly linked** to students' background experiences	
4	3	2	1	0	
8. **Links explicitly made** between past learning and new concepts		**Few links made** between past learning and new concepts		**No links made** between past learning and new concepts	
4	3	2	1	0	
9. **Key vocabulary emphasized** (e.g., introduced, written, repeated, and highlighted for students to see)		**Key vocabulary** introduced, but not emphasized		**Key vocabulary** not introduced or emphasized	

the story was fantasy. Mrs. Jarmin then told the students that, especially because fantasy can sometimes be confusing, they would construct a graphic organizer as they proceeded through the story to keep track of the characters, as well as to provide visual clues for plot events and vocabulary in the story. She asked students to think of words to describe the characters Timothy, Martin, Cynthia, Teresa, and Mrs. Frisby, from the first chapter. As students mentioned adjectives describing the characters, Mrs. Jarmin began writing them on chart paper as a graphic organizer.

Mrs. Jarmin and the class continued this same type of process until they had completed the novel.

On the SIOP® form in Figure 3.7 rate Mrs. Jarmin's lesson on each of the Building Background features.

Mr. Ramirez

Mr. Ramirez began the first lesson of the unit by distributing the text to the students. He asked what the students thought the book would be about, and they suggested that it would be something about rats. He told them that they would first watch a video based on the book before actually reading the text. He gave an oral summary of the video to provide some background before showing it. He showed the video, then told the students they would begin reading the book the next day.

Mr. Ramirez began the second day's lesson by writing twenty vocabulary terms on the board. He told the students that they were to copy each term in their notebooks and look up the definition of each term in the dictionary. The students spent the second day completing this activity. Most students worked independently, although sometimes they would ask a friend for help.

The third day of the unit Mr. Ramirez read the first chapter with the students. While reading, he asked a number of comprehension questions, cleared up one student's

FIGURE 3.8 *Building Background Component of the SIOP®: Mr. Ramirez's lesson*

4	3	2	1	0	NA
7. **Concepts explicitly linked** to students' background experiences		**Concepts loosely linked** to students' background experiences		**Concepts not explicitly linked** to students' background experiences	
4	3	2	1	0	
8. **Links explicitly made** between past learning and new concepts		**Few links made** between past learning and new concepts		**No links made** between past learning and new concepts	
4	3	2	1	0	
9. **Key vocabulary emphasized** (e.g., introduced, written, repeated, and highlighted for students to see)		**Key vocabulary** introduced, but not emphasized		**Key vocabulary** not introduced or emphasized	

confusion about which character was ill, and reviewed the chapter completely after reading it with the students. He continued this process throughout the book. At the conclusion of the unit, he gave the class an exam to check their understanding.

On the SIOP® form in Figure 3.8, rate Mr. Ramirez's lesson on each of the Building Background features.

Discussion of Lessons

7. *Concepts Explicitly Linked to Students' Background Experiences*

Miss Paige: 4

Mrs. Jarmin: 2

Mr. Ramirez: 1

Miss Paige's lesson received a "4" on the SIOP® for this feature. She elicited information about students' knowledge of rats, but more important, she discussed how animals in stories and novels sometimes take on human characteristics. She also asked students for examples of books they knew that had animals behaving as people. Miss Paige introduced a central theme in the novel, survival, by having students brainstorm words and concepts they knew related to the theme. A novel such as *Mrs. Frisby and the Rats of NIMH* may be difficult for English learners to understand, yet by linking the topic to their own experiences, the teacher helped to enhance student comprehension.

Mrs. Jarmin's lesson received a "2" on the SIOP® for this feature. She made an effort to activate the students' prior knowledge, but it was not done in an explicit or systematic way. While Miss Paige organized the information using a semantic map for students to see and make reference to later, Mrs. Jarmin merely conducted a verbal discussion of a few students' experiences. ELs benefit from visual clues given during a discussion, and Mrs. Jarmin did not provide any visual assistance for those learners with limited English proficiency. Further, she did not organize the information in a useful way that would make the information accessible and meaningful to all the students in class.

Mr. Ramirez's lesson received a "1" on the SIOP® for this feature. Although the video did provide background information for the students, Mr. Ramirez did not provide students with an adequate introduction to the video or the book. While he attempted to provide some background before showing the video, there is little benefit for English learners to hear only an oral explanation of new, unknown information. Further, he did not provide any opportunity to link the students' background or experiences to the unit by tapping into what they already knew.

8. *Links Explicitly Made between Past Learning and New Concepts*

Miss Paige: 3

Mrs. Jarmin: 4

Mr. Ramirez: 0

Miss Paige made several links to past learning by discussing books students had read or listened to (e.g., *Charlotte's Web* and *The Witches*). She also developed a word wall that assisted students' learning by reminding them of the meaning of words used in the story.

Mrs. Jarmin provided a direct link between past learning and new learning by showing the Venn diagram, and she also began constructing a graphic organizer that will be an important tool for activating students' knowledge as they proceed through the book. Each day the students will be oriented to the characters in the story and will be reminded of events covered in the book.

Mr. Ramirez did not make any attempt to link previous learning to what the students were currently reading about, nor did he establish any system for reviewing the material during subsequent lessons.

9. *Key Vocabulary Emphasized*

Miss Paige: 1

Mrs. Jarmin: 4

Mr. Ramirez: 0

Although Miss Paige wrote on a transparency a number of key vocabulary terms and discussed them, there was no further reference to the list nor did she have students copy the list for their own reference. It became a vocabulary-building activity done in isolation of any context, rendering it less effective than if she had used the transparency throughout the unit, reviewing and repeating the words and having them available for students to see.

Mrs. Jarmin took time to introduce students not only to the story and associated vocabulary, but also to ways of "doing school." The introduction took only fifteen minutes or so, and it presented some valuable skills that are required in school but not always explicitly taught. Also, she made new vocabulary words meaningful by defining terms before watching the video, then asking students to identify the terms within the context of the video. The words were written, posted, and referred to frequently. In this way, the key vocabulary terms became an integral part of the unit.

Mr. Ramirez's lesson did a poor job of developing students' vocabulary in any authentic way. First, rather than having a manageable number of key terms, twenty words were selected. The teacher didn't discuss the terms with the students or support their understanding of new vocabulary. Given these students' low literacy and English proficiency levels, an optimal number of new terms would range from five to twelve. The large number of terms, coupled with the vocabulary contained within the definitions, becomes overwhelming. Second, considering the students' academic and English proficiency levels, copying terms from the board and looking up their definitions in the dictionary is not meaningful. Frequently this type of exercise results in papers filled with misspelled words and incomplete sentences because the majority of words—both the vocabulary terms and their definitions—are unfamiliar to these students. Finally, the more decontextualized the activity, the more problematic learning becomes. That is, the more directly related the activity is to the learning objective, the more likely it is that student learning will take place. In this lesson, the activity was not closely aligned to the context of the story. Both the vocabulary terms and their multiple definitions were unfamiliar to the students, as was the formal lexicon of the dictionary that was supposed to clarify the terms. The activity, although probably well-intentioned, had little or no meaning for these students.

Summary

The importance of building background has been well established in the research literature, and is one of the easier components of the SIOP® to incorporate into teaching. Taking a few minutes to jump-start students' schemata and past learning, to explicitly find out what they know or have experienced about a topic, and then explicitly linking their knowledge directly to the lesson's objectives will result in greater understanding for English learners. English learners may have an especially difficult time with academic language, the vocabulary necessary for academic achievement. Therefore, it is of critical importance that the key vocabulary necessary for mastering content and language objectives be explicitly taught and reviewed regularly. Three types of academic vocabulary focused on in the SIOP® Model include content words, process/function words, and words that teach English structure. The traditional method of copying words and writing definitions is ineffective. Activities such as preteaching vocabulary words by highlighting them in context, posting and frequently reviewing words, using visuals to provide concrete meanings, and engaging students in interactive practice with words are effective ways to promote academic language development for English learners.

Discussion Questions

1. Some educators argue the importance of connecting new information to English language learners' own cultural backgrounds in order to make content concepts meaningful. Others disagree, stating that students relate more to popular American influences (e.g., "adolescent culture") than they do to their parents' traditional cultural practices. What are some merits and problems with both positions? What about ELs born in the United States who have never lived in their native cultural setting?

2. Think about a joke or cartoon that you didn't understand, such as from a late-show monologue or a political cartoon. Why was it confusing or unamusing? What information would you have needed for it to make sense? What are the implications for teaching content to all students, including English learners?
3. If you are creating a SIOP® lesson, how will you activate students' prior knowledge and build background? What connections to past learning can you make? What are your key vocabulary words and how will you teach them?

chapter 4

Comprehensible Input

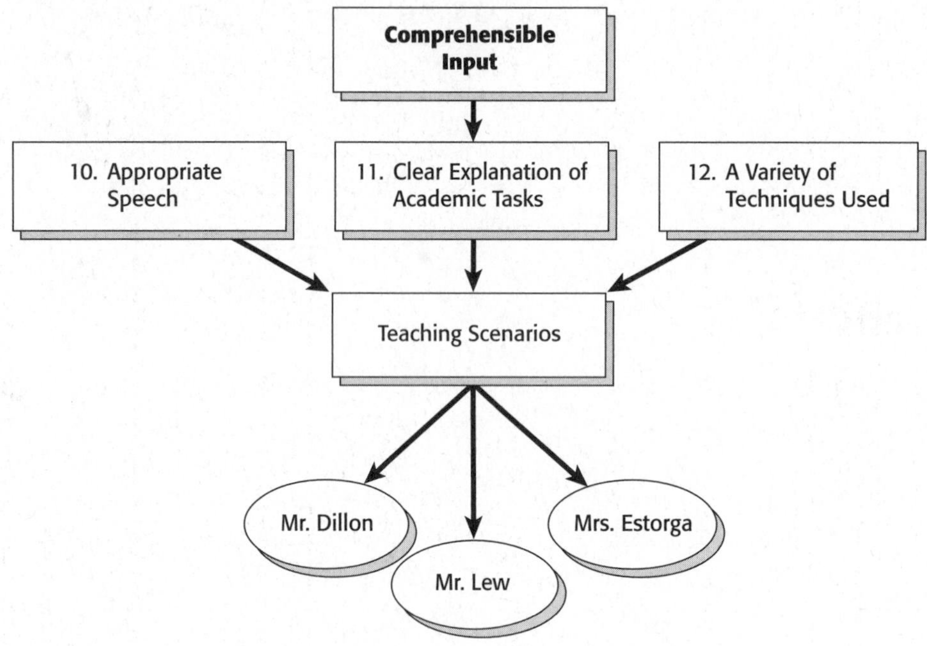

Objectives

After reading, discussing, and engaging in activities related to this chapter, you will be able to meet the following content and language objectives.

Content Objectives

Explore techniques for presenting content information in ways that students comprehend.

Review various ways to model and provide directions for academic tasks.

Language Objectives

Discuss modifications to teacher speech that can increase student comprehension.

Write the steps needed for students to perform an academic task and have a partner perform each step.

While many of the features of the SIOP® Model are indicators of effective instruction for all students, this component comprises some of the features that make SIOP® instruction different from "just good instruction." An effective SIOP® teacher takes into account the unique characteristics of English learners. For these students, the teacher makes verbal communication more understandable by consciously attending to students' linguistic needs. Making the message understandable for students is referred to as comprehensible input (Krashen, 1985). Especially with secondary students, it is important to remember that just because they have difficulty expressing themselves in English—both orally and in writing—this doesn't mean that they can't think about or learn the material. Comprehensible input techniques are essential to help English learners understand what the teacher is saying, and these techniques should be evident throughout the lesson.

Background

Students who are learning rigorous content material in a language they do not speak or understand completely require specialized teaching techniques to make the message understood. Effective SIOP® teachers understand that acquiring a new language takes time and is facilitated by many "clues" and appropriate speech. Comprehensible input is achieved when teachers pay attention to the unique linguistic needs of ELs and consistently incorporate these techniques into their daily teaching routines.

Comprehensible input is much more than simply showing pictures as visual clues during a lesson. It involves a conscious effort to make the lesson understandable through a variety

of means. Communication is made more understandable through speech that is appropriate to students' proficiency levels. The teacher enunciates and speaks more slowly, but in a natural way, for students who are beginning English speakers. More repetition may be needed for beginners and, as students gain more proficiency in English, the teacher adjusts her speech for the students' levels. Teachers will increase students' understanding by using appropriate speech coupled with a variety of techniques that will make the content clear. We will discuss a number of ways to achieve comprehensible input in the next sections. In the scenarios that follow later in the chapter, you will see examples of teachers who use comprehensible input techniques to varying degrees of effectiveness. Further examples of comprehensible input techniques are seen in the classroom footage on the CD.

SIOP® FEATURE 10: Speech Appropriate for Students' Proficiency Levels

For this feature, speech refers to (1) rate and enunciation and (2) complexity of speech. The first aspect addresses *how* the teacher speaks and the second aspect refers to *what* is said, such as level of vocabulary used, complexity of sentence structure, and use of idioms.

To see an example of appropriate speech, please view the corresponding video clip (Chapter 6, Module 1) on the accompanying CD.

Students who are at the beginning levels of English proficiency benefit from teachers who slow down their rate of speech, use pauses, and enunciate clearly while speaking. As students become more comfortable with the language and acquire higher levels of proficiency, a slower rate isn't as necessary. In fact, for advanced and transitional students, teachers should use a rate of speech that is normal for a regular classroom. Effective SIOP® teachers adjust their rate of speech and enunciation to their students' levels of English proficiency.

Likewise, students will respond according to their proficiency level. The following example illustrates the variation in responses that may be expected when students at different levels of English proficiency are asked to describe the setting in a story:

- Beginning: "Cold day."
- Early Intermediate: "The day is cold and there is snow."
- Intermediate: "The day is very cold and heavy snow is falling."
- Advanced: "It is a cold, winter day, and it is snowing more heavily than usual."
- Transitional: "The unusually heavy snow on the day the story takes place causes a number of problems for the characters."

SIOP® teachers carefully monitor the vocabulary and sentence structure they use with ELs in order to match the students' proficiency levels, especially with students at beginning levels of English proficiency. With students at intermediate and advanced levels, teachers should frequently ask students to explain their answers; say it another way; ask why, how, or what if; and require students to connect words, phrases, and short sentences into compound sentences that represent their ideas and thoughts. In this way, students not only use the language but think about how to use it as well. At all proficiency levels, it is important to model what you want students to say before having them produce language. For example, the teacher might say, "Spain, France, and England colonized North America for different reasons. Why did Spain colonize North America? Ask your partner, 'Why did

Spain colonize North America?'" In this way, students know what to say when they turn to their partners because they have heard correct sentence formation. Providing students a model of what to say increases the likelihood that on-point discussion will occur.

Idioms—common sayings that cannot be translated exactly—create difficulty for students who are trying to make sense of a new language. Some common idioms include "below the belt" for unfair; "put one's foot down" meaning to be firm; "see eye to eye" for being in agreement; "get the hang of" meaning to become familiar with; and "get a person's back up" indicating to make someone annoyed. English learners are better served when teachers use language that is straightforward, clear, and accompanied by a visual representation.

Paraphrasing and repetition are useful practices that enhance understanding. English learners require repeated exposures to a word in order to hear it accurately because they often lack the auditory acuity to decipher sounds of English words. Then they need to see and hear the words used repeatedly, preferably in a variety of ways such as on an overhead projector, on a wall, and in context within a text. Brain research tells us that repetition strengthens connections in the brain (Jensen, 2005).

Cognates are often useful in promoting comprehension for students whose native language has a Latin base. For example, using "calculate the mass/volume ratio" (*calcular* in Spanish) may be easier for some students to understand than "figure out the mass/volume ratio." (See Vogt and Echevarria, 2008 for more examples of cognates.)

SIOP® teachers also use simple sentence structures like subject–verb–object with beginning students and reduce or eliminate embedded clauses. For example, in a high school history class, the teacher may use the following sentence structure that is difficult to understand: "By breaking the rules of diplomatic convention and by embarking on his own, he was, he knew, risking ridicule and, in the event that things went sour, disgrace." It might be better stated as, "He decided to break the rules of diplomatic convention and embark on his own. He knew that he might be ridiculed for it and be disgraced if things went badly." Reducing the complexity of language is effective, but should be used judiciously; over-simplification of spoken or written language eliminates exposure to a variety of sentence constructions and language forms (Crossley, McCarthy, Louwerse, & McNamara, 2007).

Using appropriate speech patterns and terms that are easier for ELs to understand contribute to comprehensible input.

SIOP® FEATURE 11: Clear Explanation of Academic Tasks

To hear a student describe the importance of comprehensible input, please view the corresponding video clip (Chapter 6, Module 1) on the accompanying CD.

English learners at all levels (and native English speakers) perform better in academic situations when the teacher gives clear instructions for assignments and activities. The more practice students have with the types of tasks found in content classes, the better they will perform in class and the better prepared they will be when they exit the language support program. It is critical for ELs to have instructions presented in a step-by-step manner, preferably modeled or demonstrated for them. Ideally, a finished product such as a business letter, a research report, or a graphic organizer is shown to students so that they know what the task entails. Oral directions should always be accompanied by written ones so ELs can refer back to them at a later point in time as they complete the assignment or task. Students with auditory processing difficulties also require clear, straightforward instructions posted for them to see.

According to case study data collected from ELs in sheltered classes (Echevarria, 1998), middle school students were asked what their teachers do that makes learning easier or more difficult. The following are some student comments:

- "She doesn't explain it too good. I don't understand the words she's saying because I don't even know what they mean."
- "She talks too fast. I don't understand the directions."
- "He talks too fast. Not patient."
- "It helps when he comes close to my desk and explains stuff in the order that I have to do it."

These students' comments illustrate the importance of providing a clear explanation of teachers' expectations for lessons, including delineating the steps of academic tasks. This point cannot be overstated. In our observations of classes, many "behavior problems" are often the result of students not being sure what they are supposed to do. A cursory oral explanation of an assignment can leave many students without a clue as to what to do to get started. Often, this results in students distracting one another or simply putting their heads down on their desks (usually hiding their heads with a sweatshirt hood!). The teacher, frustrated with all the off-task behavior and chatter, scolds students, exhorting them to get to work. However, students do not know *how* to get to work and often don't know how to articulate that fact to the teacher.

SIOP® teachers go over each aspect of the lesson, showing visuals with each step if needed, e.g., the text and graphic organizer students will complete. For example, in a literature class, the teacher wants students to complete a graphic organizer (GO) with information about the characters, setting, problem, resolution of the problem, and theme of a piece of literature the class has been reading. She writes on the board:

1. Review your notes from yesterday.
2. Use your notes to answer the five questions on the board.
3. Write your answers on your white board.
4. Complete the graphic organizer.

After giving students a few minutes to review their notes, the teacher gives them a set amount of time to answer the first question. She gives them a 30-second warning and then asks the class to "show me" their whiteboards. (See Chapter 9, Review and Assessment, for a description of this technique.) She can see from their white boards who got the right answer and who needs assistance or clarification. This process continues until all questions are answered and then students take the information and use it to complete the GO.

A written agenda for going through a lesson is useful because if students don't understand, weren't paying attention, or simply forgot, they have the written steps to guide them and keep them on task. Depending on the group, the teacher may need to model one or more of the steps for comprehension.

In the area of writing, students need to be shown very specifically—and have opportunities to practice what has been clearly explained—the essential elements of good writing. Showing students what constitutes good writing, explaining it clearly, and providing opportunities to practice will result in improved writing (Schmoker, 2001).

For intermediate and advanced speakers, focused lessons on "voice" or "word choice" may be appropriate while beginning speakers benefit from models of complete sentences using adjectives or forming a question.

SIOP® FEATURE 12: A Variety of Techniques Used to Make Content Concepts Clear

Effective SIOP® teachers make content concepts clear and understandable for English learners through the use of a variety of techniques that make content comprehensible. We have observed some teachers who teach the same way for English learners as they do for native English speakers, except that they use pictures for ELs. We believe that the actual teaching techniques a teacher uses have a greater impact on student achievement than having a lot of pictures illustrating content concepts. High-quality SIOP® lessons offer students a variety of ways for making the content accessible to them. Although it might be impossible for teachers to present a variety of interesting hands-on lessons that include visuals to illustrate every concept and idea in the curriculum each period of every day, there does need to be sufficient planning to incorporate such techniques and activities throughout the week's lessons.

Some techniques include:

ACTIVITY Use gestures, body language, pictures, and objects to accompany speech. For example, when saying, "We're going to review the three forms of water," the teacher holds up three fingers. Showing one finger she says, "One form is liquid," and shows a glass of water. Holding up two fingers she says, "the second form is ice," and shows an ice cube. Holding up three fingers she says, "and the third form is steam," and shows a picture of a steaming cup of coffee. These simple gestures and visual aids assist students in organizing and making sense of information that is presented verbally.

To see an example of effective techniques, please view the corresponding video clip (Chapter 2, Module 2) on the accompanying CD.

ACTIVITY Provide a model of a process, task, or assignment. For example, as the teacher discusses the process of water turning to ice, she shows or draws a model of the process as it is being described. When students are later instructed to record conditions under which the change in ice from a solid to a liquid is accelerated or slowed, the teacher shows an observation sheet that is divided into three columns on the overhead projector. The teacher has a number of pictures (e.g., lamp, sun, and refrigerator), which depict various conditions such as heat and cold. She demonstrates the first condition, heat, with a picture of the sun. She models how students will describe the condition in the first column (e.g., heats). Then she asks students what effect the sun, or heat, has on ice. They answer and in the second column she records how the ice changed (e.g., melted), and in the third column she indicates if the process was accelerated or slowed by the condition (e.g., accelerated). Providing a model as the students are taken through the task verbally eliminates ambiguity and gives the message in more than one way. Students are then able to complete the rest of the worksheet.

ACTIVITY Preview material for optimal learning. When students' attention is focused on the specific information they will be responsible for learning in the lesson, students are able to prepare themselves for the information that is coming, making it more comprehensible for them. Further, they have an opportunity to access prior knowledge and make the connections that they will need to understand the lesson.

ACTIVITY Allow alternative forms for expressing their understanding of information and concepts. Often ELs have learned the lesson's information but have difficulty expressing their understanding in English, either orally or in writing. Hands-on activities and symbolic represenations, such as pictures, pictographs, maps, and diagrams can be used to reinforce the concepts and information presented, with a reduced linguistic demand on these students. In a high school science class, students demonstrated their understanding of concepts such as hydroplaning by drawing a sketch of a car on a wet road, labeling the drawing to show their knowledge.

ACTIVITY Use multimedia and other technologies in lessons. Teachers may use overhead transparencies, PowerPoint slides, or relevant websites as supplements to a presentation. In so doing, they not only provide more visual support but also model the use of the technology.

ACTIVITY Provide repeated exposures to words, concepts, and skills. English learners are learning through a new language, and in order for the input to be comprehensible, they need repetition. However, excessive practice of a single word or skill can become monotonous and defeat the purpose. Jensen (2005) discusses a process for introducing material repeatedly in a variety of ways. He suggests introducing terms and skills well in advance of learning the material (pre-exposure); explicitly previewing the topic at the start of the lesson; exposing students to the target information (priming); reviewing the material minutes after students have learned it; and allowing students to revise or reconstruct information hours, days, or weeks after the lesson to revisit the learning. Research indicates that teachers ought to provide students with the specifics of what they need to learn—the key details of the unit—and then find ways to expose students to the details multiple times (Marzano, Pickening, & Pollack, 2001).

ACTIVITY Use sentence strips. This common technique can be used in a variety of ways at all grade levels. In reading/language arts, students can review events in a story by writing each event on a sentence strip, then sequencing the strips to retell the story. This technique can be applied in science to sequence steps in an experiment or in math to sequence the steps for problem solving.

Provide nontraditional text options for students to learn about a subject such as DVDs, websites, youTube, and easy-to-read books such as _(subject)_ *for Dummies*. Reading widely builds background, and nontraditional information sources can provide access to information that a dense text does not.

ACTIVITY For teenagers, be succinct. Their frontal lobes may not effectively store many ideas at once, so the amount of input should be limited. Instructions should be straightforward and given one at a time. Also, teenagers need concrete, realistic models. They benefit from using hands-on working models and having an opportunity to think through explanations in discussions (Jensen, 2005).

ACTIVITY Use graphic organizers effectively. New ideas and concepts presented in a new language can be overwhelming for English learners. Graphic organizers (GOs) take the information, vocabulary, or concept and make it more understandable by showing the key points graphically. To paraphrase the saying "a picture is worth a thousand words," a graphic organizer can capture and simplify a teacher's many potentially confusing words. While GOs are used commonly in school, they are most effective when they match the task and lead to attaining the lesson's objectives. So if the task is learning definitions, then the GO would be:

	is a		that	

Some GOs may be simple, such as a problem/solution chart or a web with vocabulary definitions. For older students, especially those with learning challenges, some more elaborate GOs such as a Course-Planning Organizer or a Concept Diagram have improved student performance (Deshler & Schumaker, 2006). See Vogt and Echevarria (2008) for many SIOP® -appropriate graphic organizers.

ACTIVITY Audiotape texts for comprehension. A taped version of the text not only allows for multiple opportunities to hear the text, but the reader who records the tape can modify it to proficiency levels. The same passage may be read more slowly with clear enunciation for beginning speakers, or synonyms may be substituted for difficult words.

The techniques we suggest in the SIOP® are critical for providing meaningful, understandable lessons to students learning English, including adapting the content to students' proficiency levels (Chapter 2); highlighting key vocabulary (Chapter 3); using scaffolding techniques and providing opportunities for students to use strategies (Chapter 5); and providing activities that allow students to apply newly acquired content and language knowledge (Chapter 7).

UNIT: Buoyancy (Ninth Grade)

The following lessons take place in an urban high school where English learners make up 35 percent of the school population. In the classrooms described, all the students are beginning to advanced-beginning speakers of English, and they have varying levels of literacy in their native languages.

Ninth-grade teachers Mr. Dillon, Mr. Lew, and Mrs. Estorga are all teaching a unit on *buoyancy,* the ability to float. The science standard that each of the three teachers is teaching requires that students understand why some objects float while others sink. In addition, they review the concepts of *mass,* which is a quantity of matter of nonspecific shape, and *volume,* which is the capacity of a three-dimensional object. The goal is for students to understand that an object will float as long as the mass doesn't exceed the object's capacity, or volume. Students have calculated mass/volume ratios prior to this unit, although the application of these concepts to buoyancy is new. You will see in the scenarios that the teachers have their own ways of helping students understand that an object's ability to float is based on its mass/volume ratio. (For more examples of lesson and unit plans in science, see Short, Vogt, & Echevarria, in press.)

Teaching Scenarios

Mr. Dillon

Mr. Dillon began the lesson by having students open their science texts to the chapter on buoyancy. He told them that in this unit they would learn what makes objects buoyant. He gave a five-minute oral introduction to the concepts behind buoyancy, discussing the fact that if the object's mass exceeds its volume, then it will sink. Mr. Dillon used his normal, somewhat rapid manner, the same speaking style he used with all his classes. He then directed the students' attention to 13 vocabulary terms written on the board and told the class to copy each word, look up the definition in the glossary, and copy the definition onto their papers. After students looked up vocabulary words in the glossary, Mr. Dillon asked them to put the papers in their homework folders. He told them that they needed to take the words home, and their homework assignment was to use each word in a sentence. He emphasized that students needed to complete their homework since he had been frustrated by low homework response rates in this class.

Then Mr. Dillon turned to the science text, telling students to open their books to the beginning of the chapter. He proceeded to lecture from the text, asking students questions to stimulate a class discussion. Most students were reluctant to speak up. After lecturing on the material in the first five pages of the text, Mr. Dillon gave students a worksheet about buoyancy. He told them they could work in pairs or alone, calculating the mass/volume ratio of the objects shown on the worksheet. He said, "You remember how to calculate mass/volume ratios? First you determine the volume of the object, and then you take the mass and divide it by the volume. Okay, just calculate the ratios for each object shown on the worksheet, and when you finish, you may begin doing your homework."

After the class completed the worksheet for calculating mass/volume ratios, Mr. Dillon went over the answers with the whole group. He began by demonstrating how to calculate the first problem. He wrote the numbers on the overhead and went through the process. When he finished he said, "If you got the same answer as I did, raise your hand." About half of the students raised their hands. Mr. Dillon determined that he needed to demonstrate a few more problems so that more students would understand the process. He continued with the next three problems, asking students what they did differently.

Finally, he told the class to work in pairs to review their work, checking the final problems against the process he demonstrated.

On the SIOP® form in Figure 4.1, rate Mr. Dillon's lesson on each of the Comprehensible Input features.

Mr. Lew

As Mr. Lew began the lesson, he drew students' attention to the objective written on the board and told students that the purpose of the unit was to understand why some objects float and others sink. As he said the word "float," he pointed at an orange floating in the aquarium at the front of the room, and as he said the word "sink," he dropped a peeled orange into the water, which sank to the bottom. Then he repeated while pointing at the corresponding object, "Some things float and others sink." He went on to tell the students that at the end of the unit they would be able to calculate and predict whether something has buoyancy. The words "float," "sink," "calculate," "predict," and "buoyant" were

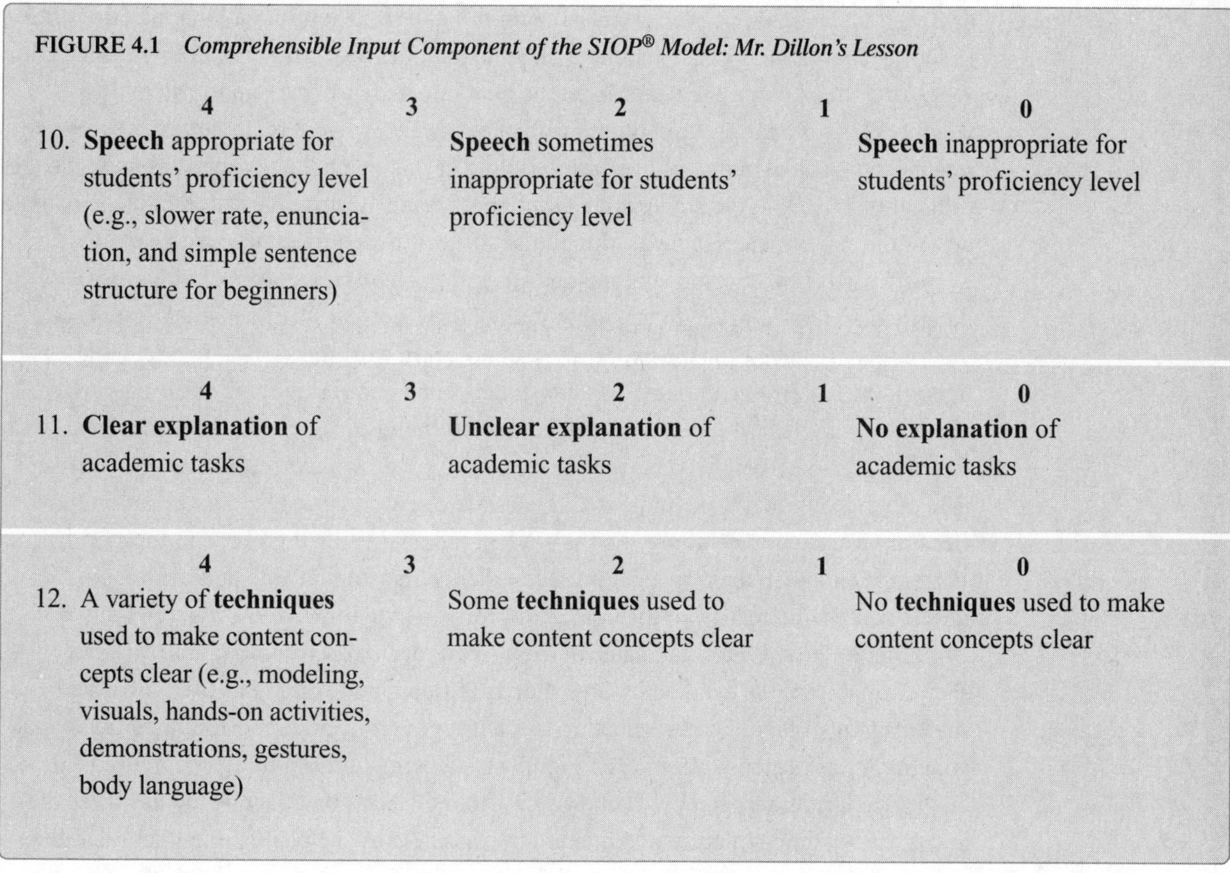

FIGURE 4.1 *Comprehensible Input Component of the SIOP® Model: Mr. Dillon's Lesson*

4	3	2	1	0
10. **Speech** appropriate for students' proficiency level (e.g., slower rate, enunciation, and simple sentence structure for beginners)		**Speech** sometimes inappropriate for students' proficiency level		**Speech** inappropriate for students' proficiency level
4	3	2	1	0
11. **Clear explanation** of academic tasks		**Unclear explanation** of academic tasks		**No explanation** of academic tasks
4	3	2	1	0
12. A variety of **techniques** used to make content concepts clear (e.g., modeling, visuals, hands-on activities, demonstrations, gestures, body language)		Some **techniques** used to make content concepts clear		No **techniques** used to make content concepts clear

written in the Word Bank for students to see. The word list included content vocabulary (buoyant, float, and sink) as well as functional language (calculate and predict). Since many of Mr. Lew's students were recent immigrants and had gaps in their educational backgrounds, Mr. Lew was careful to make sure students not only knew the meaning of content vocabulary, but also knew the meaning of words associated with academic tasks, such as predict and calculate.

Throughout the lesson, Mr. Lew used language structures and vocabulary that he believed the students could understand at their level of proficiency. He spoke slowly, often contextualizing vocabulary words, and enunciated clearly. Also, he avoided the use of idioms, and when he sensed that students did not understand him, he paraphrased to convey the meaning more clearly. He repeated important words frequently and wrote them for students to see.

As the lesson progressed, the students were told to complete an activity while working in small groups. Mr. Lew was very explicit in his instructions. As he gave students instructions orally, he wrote each step on the overhead projector. He said, "First, you will get into your assigned groups and prepare to perform the role that has been assigned to you. Second, you will make shapes out of aluminum foil and try to get them to float (he put a small aluminum foil boat on the water and it floated). Third, you will calculate the object's volume (the students already know how to do this) and write it on the worksheet, and fourth, you will determine the maximum mass the boat will hold before it sinks. Finally, you will calculate the mass/volume ratio. You will write all of these numbers on the worksheet." Then Mr. Lew told the students to watch as he demonstrated. He took a piece of aluminum foil and shaped it into a long, narrow boat. He pointed to #2 on the transparency. Then he took the boat, filled its interior space with water, and then poured the water from the boat into a measuring cup to calculate the volume. He wrote the amount on the worksheet. Mr. Lew went on to determine the maximum mass and the mass/volume ratio, writing each step on the overhead as he made the calculations. He told the students that they must make at least five different boat shapes during the experiment. He wrote the number 5 next to step #2 on the overhead.

After Mr. Lew showed students the steps for calculating mass/volume ratios described above, he gave students thirty seconds to get into their assigned group, get their items organized for the experiments, and begin working. Mr. Lew circulated through the classroom, supervising the students and answering their questions. After about five minutes, Mr. Lew determined that all the groups except one were clear about their assignment. To clarify for that group, Mr. Lew drew the group members' attention to another group that was doing well. He asked one student to stand and explain the steps of what they were doing. As the student talked, Mr. Lew pointed to the step-by-step instructions on the overhead projector. When the student finished explaining, Mr. Lew asked a volunteer from the confused group to explain what they were going to do.

After all groups had calculated at least five boats' mass/volume ratios, Mr. Lew showed a table on the overhead with columns for mass and volume figures. He asked students to pool their data by selecting two boats per group and reporting their mass and volume. A representative from each group wrote their figures in the appropriate columns on the overhead transparency. Then Mr. Lew told the class that they would use these data to construct a graph, plotting the maximum mass held by the boat on the y-axis and the boat's volume on the x-axis. Each student then plotted the mass-to-volume ratios on their individual graphs. At the end of the lesson, Mr. Lew asked the students to look at the objective written on the board and asked each student to write on his or her paper why some objects float and others sink.

On the SIOP® form in Figure 4.2, rate Mr. Lew's lesson on each of the Comprehensible Input features.

Mrs. Estorga

As is her practice, Mrs. Estorga wrote the objective, "Find the mass/volume ratio for objects that float," on the board. She began the lesson by discussing the fact that some things float and others sink, giving examples of objects that float, such as a large ship, and others that sink, such as a small coin. Then she asked the class if they knew what makes some objects float and others sink. A few students guessed, but nobody was able to give an accurate explanation. During the discussion, Mrs. Estorga's rate of speech was normal for her speech style, with a mix of both simple and slightly complex sentences. When the discussion was completed, she noticed that some of the students still seemed confused.

Mrs. Estorga told the students to read the first three pages of their text to themselves and stated that they would discuss it when they'd finished. After the students indicated that they were done reading, Mrs. Estorga asked students if there were any words in the text they did not know. Several students called out unfamiliar words, and she wrote them on the overhead. Then she assigned students at each table a word to look up in the glossary. After several minutes, she asked the students what they had found. Only about half of the words were included in the glossary, since the other words were not science terms per se, but words such as "therefore" and "principle."

FIGURE 4.2 *Comprehensible Input Component of the SIOP® Model: Mr. Lew's Lesson*

4	3	2	1	0	NA
10. **Speech** appropriate for students' proficiency level (e.g., slower rate, enunciation, and simple sentence structure for beginners)		**Speech** sometimes inappropriate for students' proficiency level		**Speech** inappropriate for students' proficiency level	
4	**3**	**2**	**1**	**0**	**NA**
11. Clear **explanation** of academic tasks		**Unclear** explanation of academic tasks		**No** explanation of academic tasks	
4	**3**	**2**	**1**	**0**	**NA**
12. **A variety of techniques** used to make content concepts clear (e.g., modeling, visuals, hands-on activities, demonstrations, gestures, body language)		Some **techniques** used to make content concepts clear		No **techniques** used to make content concepts clear	

Mrs. Estorga orally gave students the definitions of those words that were not in the glossary and then summarized the information the students had read in the text. As she talked, she occasionally spoke rapidly, using long, detail-laden sentences in her summary. When she noticed that students were not paying attention, she slowed her rate of speech to make it understandable and to regain students' interest.

Mrs. Estorga continued the lesson following the same format as described previously. She asked students to read a portion of the text, paused to clarify unknown vocabulary, and summarized the part of the text students read. When they completed the chapter, Mrs. Estorga selected several end-of-chapter questions for students to answer. She let students work in pairs or groups to complete the questions, and then the class discussed the answers together.

On the SIOP® form in Figure 4.3, rate Mrs. Estorga's lesson on each of the Comprehensible Input features.

Discussion of Lessons

10. *Speech Appropriate for Students' Proficiency Level (Rate and Complexity)*

Mr. Dillon: 0

Mr. Lew: 4

Mrs. Estorga: 2

As you can see in the lesson descriptions, the teachers varied in their attention to the unique language needs of the English learners in their classes.

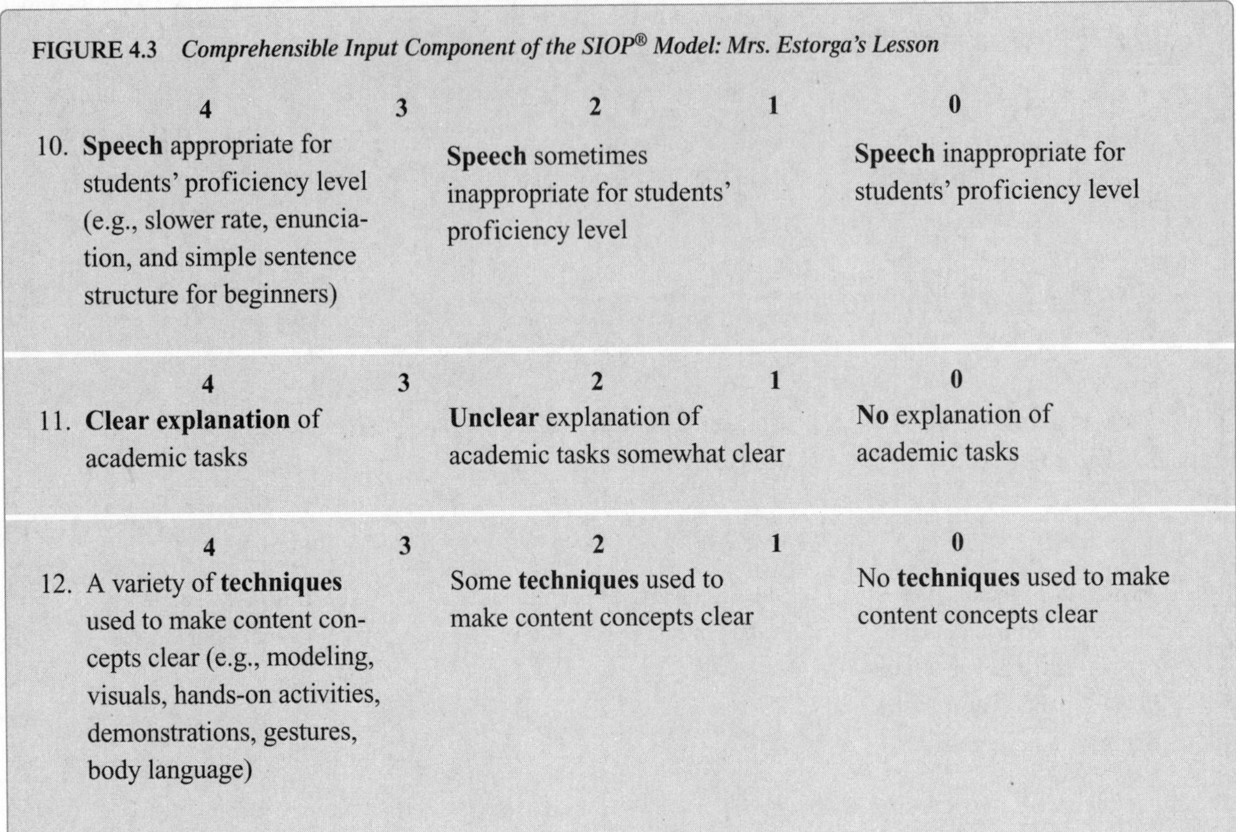
FIGURE 4.3 *Comprehensible Input Component of the SIOP® Model: Mrs. Estorga's Lesson*

4	3	2	1	0
10. **Speech** appropriate for students' proficiency level (e.g., slower rate, enunciation, and simple sentence structure for beginners)		**Speech** sometimes inappropriate for students' proficiency level		**Speech** inappropriate for students' proficiency level
4	3	2	1	0
11. **Clear explanation** of academic tasks		**Unclear** explanation of academic tasks somewhat clear		**No** explanation of academic tasks
4	3	2	1	0
12. A variety of **techniques** used to make content concepts clear (e.g., modeling, visuals, hands-on activities, demonstrations, gestures, body language)		Some **techniques** used to make content concepts clear		No **techniques** used to make content concepts clear

Mr. Dillon seemed unaware that his students would understand more if he adjusted his oral presentation to accommodate the proficiency levels of English learners in his class. He lectured about new, complex concepts without regard to his rate of speech or complexity of speech, variables that impact ELs' ability to comprehend information in class. Also, copying definitions for new terms and creating original sentences are inordinately difficult tasks for ELs. Unwittingly, Mr. Dillon set the students up for failure and then was frustrated by the low number of completed homework assignments. While he believed students chose not to complete assignments, in reality they *could not* complete the type of assignment he gave.

Mr. Dillon did not discuss the lesson content or the class or homework assignments in any meaningful or understandable way for ELs. He thought that discussing the material in the chapter and asking questions during his lecture would make the concepts clear for his students, but the type of language he used did little to facilitate learning for them. His efforts were lost on the English learners who needed richer, comprehensible development of the lesson's concepts to understand the text or lecture. The few students who participated in the discussion gave Mr. Dillon the inaccurate impression that the class was following along.

Mr. Lew was the most attuned to the benefit of modulating his speech to make himself understood by the students. He slowed his rate of speech and enunciated clearly when he addressed beginning speakers; he adjusted his speech for the other, more proficient speakers of English. He used a natural speaking voice but paid attention to his rate of speed and enunciation. Further, Mr. Lew adjusted the level of vocabulary and complexity of the sentences he used so that students could understand. Since most students were beginning English speakers, he selected words that were appropriate to their proficiency level. Although the science book highlighted nearly fifteen terms for the unit on buoyancy, Mr. Lew learned from experience that it is better for his students to learn a smaller number of vocabulary words thoroughly than to give superficial treatment to dozens of content-associated vocabulary words. His students will be able to use and apply the selected words and their concepts since they have a complete understanding of their meaning.

Mrs. Estorga's rate of speech and enunciation vacillated between that used with native speakers and a rate that her students could understand. She didn't consistently adjust her speech (rate or complexity) to the variety of proficiency levels in the class. She was aware that her EL students needed extra attention in understanding the language, but she only addressed their needs by asking for unfamiliar vocabulary. She could have paraphrased, using simpler sentence structure, and she could have used synonyms for words that appeared too difficult for students to understand.

11. *Clear Explanation of Academic Tasks*

Mr. Dillon: 1

Mr. Lew: 4

Mrs. Estorga: 1

Making your expectations crystal clear to students is one of the most important aspects of teaching, and when working with English learners, explicit, step-by-step directions can be critical to a lesson's success. It is difficult for almost any student to remember directions given only orally, and oral directions may be incomprehensible to many English learners. A lesson is sure to get off to a rocky start if students don't understand what they are expected to do. Written procedures provide students with a guide.

As an experienced teacher, Mr. Lew understood the value of being explicit in what he wanted the students to do. He walked them through each step of the buoyancy experiment, demonstrating what they were expected to do. When a group hadn't gotten started, he had other students model the steps of the assignment for the class, drawing their attention again to the instructions on the overhead. The effort that Mr. Lew put into making sure students knew what to do contributed to the success of the lesson and enhanced learning.

Mrs. Estorga, on the other hand, did not explain to the students what was expected during the lesson, although the expectation was implied by the format she used: read material, discuss unknown terms, summarize material. Since Mrs. Estorga followed the same format whenever the class read from the text, the students knew what was expected, however uninteresting the format made the class.

Mr. Dillon had a tendency to be unclear about his expectations but then blamed the students for not completing work. It is obvious that he doesn't understand the importance of making sure students are given explicit instructions at their level of understanding. First, he made unsubstantiated assumptions about the students' knowledge and ability to complete tasks. He said, "You remember how to calculate mass/volume ratios? . . . Okay, just calculate the ratios for each object. . . ." and left them to work independently. Some students did not know how to calculate the ratios but were left on their own.

Second, while he did demonstrate how to calculate ratios, Mr. Dillon should have done that kind of demonstration *before* asking students to do it independently. Teaching is more effective when a good model is demonstrated prior to the exercise, rather than a post hoc review of student work, correcting their mistakes after completion. The process of explaining the assignment *after* students completed the worksheet was particularly confusing for the English learners in his class who struggled to make sense of the assignment only to find out that they had calculated most of the problems incorrectly.

Third, Mr. Dillon did not make his expectations—for in-class assignments and for homework—clear by modeling and discussing what students were to do. He should have provided a step-by-step explanation of the academic tasks he asked the students to complete.

12. *A Variety of Techniques Used*

Mr. Dillon: 2

Mr. Lew: 4

Mrs. Estorga: 0

Concepts become understandable when teachers use a variety of techniques, including modeling, demonstrations, visuals, and body language. Throughout his lesson, Mr. Lew did an excellent job of providing visuals through the use of the tanks and aluminum foil, as well as by using the overhead projector. Not only did he write the vocabulary and assignment for students to see, he consistently referred back to the visual information. In addition to providing a clear explanation of the assignment, this technique teaches students to use visual clues to gain understanding.

Also, Mr. Lew used graphing and writing effectively to review the concepts of the lesson. Notice that these academic tasks came after students were already familiar with the lesson's concepts, which increased the likelihood that students would be able to successfully complete the academic tasks.

Finally, students were able to apply their knowledge through the hands-on activity, making the concepts of mass, volume, and buoyancy tangible, and thus more understandable. Measuring a boat's actual volume and determining maximum mass by adding to the mass by hand makes the concepts come alive for students. Compare the benefit of this hands-on activity to the other scenarios where the students simply went through a paper-and-pencil task. Surely those students learned and remembered less about buoyancy and mass-to-volume ratios than did the students in Mr. Lew's class.

Mrs. Estorga is a compassionate teacher who is concerned about the academic success of the English learners in her class. Her effort to help ELs included clarifying unknown vocabulary (in a somewhat random fashion), paraphrasing or summarizing the chapter (done orally, without visuals or other contextual clues), reducing the number of end-of-chapter questions (done independently by students), and having the students work together in answering questions (with no systematic checks for understanding). Although she had good intentions and wanted her students to understand the concept of buoyancy, Mrs. Estorga did not use the kinds of techniques that facilitate conceptual understanding for these students.

The atmosphere in Mrs. Estorga's classroom was warm and nonthreatening for ELs. She chatted with students throughout the class and showed genuine interest in their well-being. Although it is clear that she enjoys working with students from diverse cultural backgrounds, she needs to develop effective techniques and strategies to further students' learning. The lesson was presented almost entirely orally, which was difficult for the beginning English speakers in her class to follow. Having students read a portion of the text followed by her summary was a good idea, except that there were no techniques used to ensure students understood the text, which was likely too difficult for them to read independently. Also, she did not teach them the necessary skills so that eventually they could read texts on their own. The summary was given orally, which makes it likely that beginning English speakers got little understanding from it. Mrs. Estorga should have had a more structured approach to reading the text and discussing the concepts therein. Finally, she should have adjusted the number of questions students had to answer according to their ability level. The students worked diligently on the assignment because they liked Mrs. Estorga and wanted to please her, but they needed assistance in making the information meaningful—assistance beyond that which Mrs. Estorga provided.

Mr. Dillon attempted to use a number of techniques to make concepts clear, such as using the text as a basis for discussion, providing a worksheet that showed different-size boats and other objects, and some demonstration of the calculations. Also, he let students work in pairs to calculate the mass-to-volume ratios. However, Mr. Dillon should have used more visuals, modeled what he expected from the students *before* he asked them to work independently, and provided a hands-on activity for this lesson. Some lessons, like this one, lend themselves easily to hands-on activities, but Mr. Dillon did not take advantage of the opportunity.

Summary

Although ELs learn in many of the same ways as fluent English-speaking students (August & Shanahan, 2006), they do require special accommodations to make instruction understandable. Effective SIOP® teachers constantly modulate and adjust their speech when teaching English learners to ensure that the content is comprehensible. Concepts are taught using a variety of techniques, including modeling, gestures, hands-on activities, and demonstrations, so that students understand and learn the content material. Finally, effective SIOP® teachers provide explanations of academic tasks in ways that make clear what students are expected to accomplish and that promote student success.

Discussion Questions

1. Have you recently been in a situation where you were not an "insider," and therefore you didn't understand what was being said? Compare that situation and your feelings about it to the way language is used in classrooms where there are English learners. As a teacher, what can you do to make sure all students are able to follow a lecture or discussion?
2. Many times in classrooms, discipline problems can be attributed to students not knowing what they're supposed to be doing. What are some ways that a teacher can avoid having students who are confused about accomplishing academic tasks?
3. If you have traveled in another country, or if you are an English learner, reflect on difficulties you had in understanding others. What are some techniques people used to try to communicate with you? What are some techniques you can use in the classroom?
4. Using the SIOP® lesson you have been developing, add to it so that the Comprehensible Input features in the lesson are enhanced.

chapter 5

Strategies

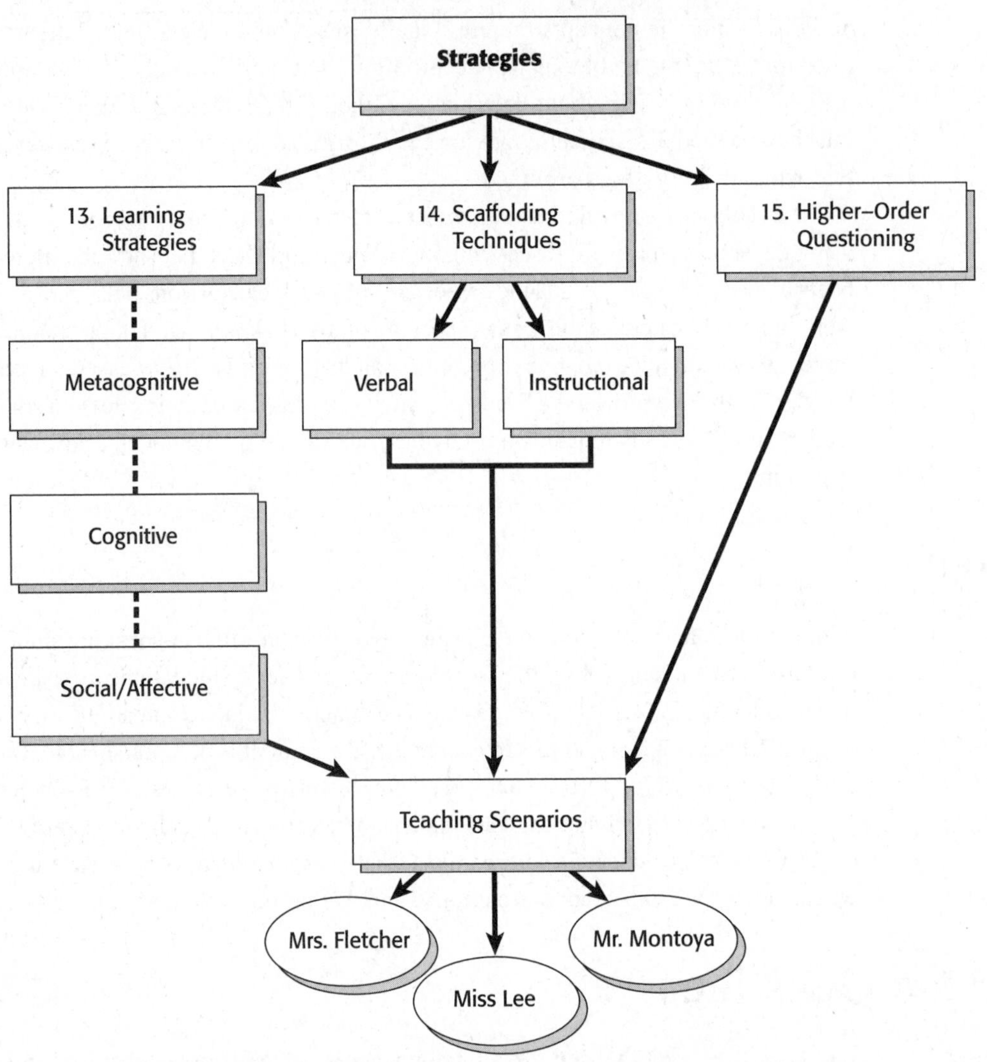

Objectives

After reading, discussing, and engaging in activities related to this chapter, you will be able to meet the following content and language objectives.

Content Objectives

Select learning strategies appropriate to a lesson's objectives.

Incorporate explicit instruction and student practice of metacognitive and cognitive strategies in lesson plans.

Identify techniques for scaffolding verbal, procedural, and instructional understanding.

Language Objectives

Identify language learning strategies to use with students.

Discuss the importance of asking higher-order questions to students of all English proficiency levels.

Write a set of questions with increasing levels of difficulty on a topic.

Up to this point, we have discussed elements of effective planning, background building, and comprehensibility for English learners (ELs). This chapter examines how we teach students to access information in memory, help them connect what they know to what they are learning, assist them in problem solving, and promote retention of newly learned information. This involves the explicit teaching of learning strategies that facilitate the learning process. Techniques and methods for learning and retaining information are systematically taught, reviewed, and assessed in effective SIOP® classrooms.

The lessons on the tropical rain forest found later in this chapter illustrate how three seventh-grade science teachers incorporate the teaching of strategies into their classrooms.

Background

As introduced in Chapter 3, researchers have learned that information is retained and connected in the brain through "mental pathways" that are linked to an individual's existing schemata (Anderson, 1984; Barnhardt, 1997). If the schemata for a particular topic are well developed and personally meaningful, new information is easier to retain and recall, and proficient learners initiate and activate their associations between the new and old learning.

In cognitive theory, this initiation and activation are described as the mental processes that enhance comprehension, learning, and retention of information. Competent language learners actively engage these cognitive skills, and researchers know these learners are effective, in part, because they have special ways of processing the new

information they are learning. These mental processes are called *learning strategies* because they are "the special thoughts or behaviors that individuals use to help them comprehend, learn, or retain new information" (O'Malley & Chamot, 1990, p. 1).

SIOP® FEATURE 13: Ample Opportunities Provided for Students to Use Learning Strategies

There is considerable evidence that explicitly and carefully teaching students a variety of self-regulating strategies improves student learning and reading (Afflerbach, Pearson, Paris, 2008; Fisher, Frey, & Williams, 2002; Neufeld, 2005; Pressley, 2000; 2002; 2005; Shearer, Ruddell, & Vogt, 2001). Self-regulated learning "emphasizes autonomy and control by the individual who monitors, directs, and regulates actions toward goals of information acquisition, expanding expertise, and self-improvement" (Paris, 2001, p. 89).

Three types of learning strategies have been identified in the research literature (O'Malley & Chamot, 1990). These include:

1. **Metacognitive Strategies.** The process of purposefully monitoring our thinking is referred to as metacognition (Baker & Brown, 1984). Metacognition is characterized by (1) matching thinking and problem-solving strategies to particular learning situations, (2) clarifying purposes for learning, (3) monitoring one's own comprehension through self-questioning, and (4) taking corrective action if understanding fails (Dermody & Speaker, 1995). The use of metacognitive strategies implies awareness, reflection, and interaction, and strategies are used in an integrated, interrelated, and recursive manner (Dole, Duffy, Roehler, & Pearson, 1991; Pressley, 2000). Studies have found that when metacognitive strategies are taught explicitly, reading comprehension is improved (Duffy, 2002; McLaughlin, 2003; Snow, Griffin & Burns, 2005; Vogt & Nagano, 2003).
2. **Cognitive Strategies.** Along with metacognitive strategies, cognitive strategies help students organize the information they are expected to learn through the process of self-regulated learning (Paris, 2001). Cognitive strategies are directly related to individual learning tasks and are used by learners when they mentally and/or physically manipulate material, or when they apply a specific technique to a learning task (Pressley, Johnson, Symons, McGoldrick, & Kurita, 1989; Slater & Horstman, 2002). Previewing a story prior to reading, establishing a purpose for reading, consciously making connections between personal experiences and what is happening in a story, taking notes during a lecture, completing a graphic organizer, and creating a semantic map are all examples of cognitive strategies that learners use to enhance their understandings (McLaughlin & Allen, 2002).
3. **Social/Affective Strategies.** These are identified in the research literature on cognitive psychology as the social and affective influences on learning (O'Malley & Chamot, 1990). For example, learning can be enhanced when people interact with each other to clarify a confusing point or when they participate in a group discussion or cooperative learning group to solve a problem.

FIGURE 5.1 *Continuum of Strategies*

Teacher-Centered	*Teacher-Assisted*	*Peer-Assisted*	*Student-Centered*
Lecture Direct instruction Demonstration Recitation	Drill and practice Discovery learning Brainstorming Discussion	Role playing Peer tutoring Reciprocal teaching Cooperative learning	Rehearsal strategies Repeated readings Selective underlining Two-column notes Elaboration strategies Mental imagery Guided imagery Creating analogies Organizational strategies Clustering Graphic organizers Outlining

Muth & Alvermann, 1999

In a somewhat different scheme, Muth and Alvermann (1999, p. 233) suggest there is a continuum of strategies that occurs during the teaching–learning process (see Figure 5.1)—from teacher-centered, teacher-assisted, peer-assisted, and student-centered.

The ultimate goal is for students to develop independence in self-monitoring and self-regulation through practice with peer-assisted and student-centered strategies. Many English learners, however, have difficulty initiating an active role in using these strategies because they are focusing mental energy on their developing language skills. Therefore, effective SIOP® teachers scaffold ELs by providing many opportunities for them to use a variety of learning strategies that have been found to be especially effective.

Whatever strategies are emphasized, learned, and used, it is generally agreed that they should be taught through explicit instruction, careful modeling, and scaffolding (Duffy, 2002). Additionally, Lipson and Wixson (2008) suggest that teaching a variety of strategies is not enough. Rather, learners need not only *declarative* knowledge (What is a strategy?) but also *procedural* knowledge (How do I use it?), and *conditional* knowledge (When and why do I use it?). When teachers model strategy use and then provide appropriate scaffolding while students are practicing strategies, they are likely to become more effective strategy users (Fisher, Frey, & Williams, 2002; Pressley & Woloshyn, 1995).

When teaching learning strategies, effective SIOP® teachers employ a variety of approaches, such as the following:

ACTIVITY

Mnemonics: A memory system often involving visualization and/or acronyms. For example, to help students remember how to spell some challenging words, here are some helpful and fun mnemonics. Hopefully, they'll also remember the phrases!

Because: Big Elephants Can Always Understand Small Elephants

Arithmetic: A Rat In The House May Eat The Ice Cream

Geography: General Eisenhower's Oldest Girl Rode A Pony Home Yesterday

Rhythm: Rhythm Helps Your Two Hips Move

Necessary: Not Every Cat Eats Sardines (Some Are Really Yummy)

Argument: A Rude Girl Undresses; My Eyes Need Taping!

Ocean: Only Cats' Eyes Are Narrow

Potassium: One tea; two sugars

Desserts: Two Sugars Sweet

These mnemonics were found on the website www.fun-with-words.com. Additional mnemonics, word games, tongue twisters, and other spelling and vocabulary ideas are also available on the website.

To see an example of some steps in SQP2RS, please view the corresponding video clip (Chapter 5, Module 2) on the accompanying CD.

SQP2RS ("Squeepers"): An instructional framework for teaching content with expository texts that includes the following steps (Vogt, 2000; Vogt, 2002):

1. **Survey**: Students preview and scan the text to be read for about one minute to determine key concepts that will learned.
2. **Question**: In groups, students generate questions likely to be answered by reading the text; teacher posts student questions on chart paper and marks with multiple asterisks those that are frequently suggested by the groups.
3. **Predict**: As a whole class, students come up with three or four key concepts they think they will learn while reading; the predictions are based on the previously generated questions, especially those marked with asterisks.
4. **Read**: While reading (with partners or small groups, or with the teacher in a small group), students search for answers to their generated questions and confirm or disconfirm their predictions; sticky notes or strips are used to mark answers to questions and spots where predictions have been confirmed.
5. **Respond**: Students answer questions (not necessarily in writing) with partners or group members and formulate new ones for the next section of text to be read (if the text is lengthy); teacher leads discussion of key concepts, clarifying any misunderstandings.
6. **Summarize**: Orally or in writing, alone or with a partner or group, students summarize the text's key concepts, using key vocabulary where appropriate.

Read Mr. Montoya's lesson later in this chapter to see Squeepers in action. Also, for more information on Squeepers, see Vogt & Echevarria, 2008.

GIST: This summarization procedure assists students in "getting the gist" from extended text (Cunningham, 1982; as cited in Muth & Alvermann, 1999). GIST stands for Generating Interactions between Schemata and Texts. Together, students and teacher read a section of text (150 to 300 words) printed on a transparency or handout. After reading, assist students in underlining ten or more words or concepts that are deemed "most important" to understanding the text. List these words or phrases on the board. Without the text, together write a summary sentence or two using as many of the listed words as possible. Repeat the process through subsequent sections of the text. When finished, write a topic sentence to precede the summary sentences; the end result can be edited into a summary paragraph.

ACTIVITY **Rehearsal strategies:** Rehearsal is used when verbatim recall of information is needed (McCormick & Pressley, 1997; Muth & Alvermann, 1999). Visual aids, such as flash cards, engage students during rehearsal; and cognitive strategies, such as underlining and note-taking, help students commit information to memory.

ACTIVITY **Graphic organizers:** These are graphic representations of key concepts and vocabulary. Teachers present them as schematic diagrams of information being taught, and students use them to organize the information they are learning. Barton, Heidama, & Jordan (2002) recommend the use of graphic organizers to help students comprehend math and science textbooks. Examples include Venn diagrams, timelines, flow charts, semantic maps, and so forth. See Buehl (2009), Reiss (2008), and Vogt and Echevarria (2008) for more examples.

ACTIVITY **Comprehension strategies:** Dole, Duffy, Roehler, and Pearson (1991) and Baker (2004) recommend that students' comprehension of text is enhanced when teachers incorporate instruction that includes strategies such as prediction, self-questioning, monitoring, determining importance, and summarizing. These strategies were identified in what has come to be known as the "proficient reader research" because (1) proficient readers use them in all kinds of text; (2) they can be taught; and (3) the more they are taught explicitly and practiced, the more likely students are to use them independently in their own reading. In their studies involving diverse readers, Duffy (2002) and Fisher, Frey, & Williams (2002) report that reading test scores can be elevated through explicit scaffolded instruction of these and other similar metacognitive strategies.

ACTIVITY **Directed Reading-Thinking Activity (DRTA)** (Stauffer, 1969; Ruddell, 2007; Vogt & Echevarria, 2008): DR-TA is a very effective activity for encouraging strategic thinking while students are reading or listening to narrative (fiction) text. It can be used in grades 6–12 with the steps given below; only the difficulty level of the text changes. Reading materials are rich, interesting, and if possible, cliff-hanging stories in which there is some question as to how the story may end. Throughout the reading of a story or book, the teacher and students stop periodically and contemplate predictions about what might follow logically in the next section of the text. Begin the lesson with a question about what the class members think the story or book will be about, based on the title. As students respond, include a variety of probes, such as:

- "With a title like . . . , what do you think this story will be about?"
- "Let's read to find out."
- Revisit predictions: "Did . . . happen? If not, why not?"
- "What do you think is going to happen next? What makes you think so?"
- "Where did you get that idea?"
- "What made you think that?"
- "Tell me more about that . . . "

It is important that teachers revisit previously made predictions after chunks of text are read so that students come to understand how predictions (and their confirmation or disconfirmation) impact their comprehension. Students can "vote" on which predictions are most likely and explain why, as they focus their thinking on character (and author) motivations, problems characters face, reasons for characters' behaviors, and how the plot unfolds.

Note that DR-TA is also effective for longer novels, with chapter-to-chapter discussions focusing on what students think will happen, what really happened, and why.

CALLA: One of the most widely accepted methods for teaching learning strategies to English learners is the Cognitive Academic Language Learning Approach (CALLA) created by Chamot and O'Malley (1987, 1994). It is an instructional model for content and language learning that incorporates student development of learning strategies. Developed initially for intermediate and advanced ESL students in content-based ESL classes, it has had wider application over the years in sheltered classes as well. The CALLA method incorporates the three previously identified categories of learning strategies: metacognitive, cognitive, and socioaffective. Through carefully designed lesson plans tied to the content curriculum, teachers explicitly teach the learning strategies and have students apply them in instructional tasks. These plans are based on the following propositions (Chamot & O'Malley, 1994, p. 196):

1. Mentally active learners are better learners.
2. Learning strategies can be taught.
3. Learning strategies transfer to new tasks.
4. Academic language learning is more effective with learning strategies.

SIOP® FEATURE 14: Scaffolding Techniques Consistently Used, Assisting and Supporting Student Understanding

To see an explanation of scaffolding, please view the corresponding video clip (Chapter 5, Module 1) on the accompanying CD.

Scaffolding is a term associated with Vygotsky's (1978) notion of the Zone of Proximal Development (ZPD). In essence, the ZPD is the difference between what a child can accomplish alone and what he or she can accomplish with the assistance of a more experienced individual. In the classroom, teachers scaffold instruction when they provide substantial amounts of support and assistance in the earliest stages of teaching a new concept or strategy, and then gradually decrease the amount of support as the learners acquire experience through multiple practice opportunities (Vacca, 2002).

For example, when teaching learning strategies, the gradual release of responsibility is manifested when teachers consciously include the following practices (adapted from Brown, 2008, p. 541):

- Emphasize the role of personal choice, effort, and persistence in enacting strategies.
- Motivate students' strategy use by showing how applying strategies improves comprehension.
- Highlight the vital role of prior knowledge activation and connection in comprehension.
- Explain the benefits of strategy use in general and the value of using specific strategies.
- Mentally model (e.g., think-aloud) to make their thinking apparent to students.
- Provide guided and independent practice so that students learn to use strategies when cued by a diverse array of goals, needs, task demands, and texts.
- Promote independent strategy use by shifting responsibility for using strategies to students as quickly as they can do so.

Two types of scaffolding can be used effectively with English learners. One is *verbal scaffolding,* in which teachers, aware of ELs' existing levels of language development, use prompting, questioning, and elaboration to facilitate students' movement to higher levels of language proficiency, comprehension, and thinking. Effective teacher–student interaction promotes confidence when it is geared to a student's language competence. The following are examples of verbal scaffolding:

- **Paraphrasing**—restating a student's response in order to model correct English usage
- **Using "think-alouds"**—carefully structured models of how effective strategy users think and monitor their understandings (Baumann, Jones, & Seifert-Kessell, 1993); for example, when teaching students how to preview a chapter, the teacher might think aloud as follows: "When I'm preparing to read a chapter or article, I ask myself, 'What is the main concept I'm supposed to learn? If I look at the big bold heading at the top of the page, I'll get an idea. The heading might be black, or it could be another color. I see here that it's ________.' Now I need to look at the other headings on the pages to see if they will help me figure out what I'm supposed to learn. Usually I think about what I already know about the topic. If I know something about it, it helps me understand better."
- **Reinforcing contextual definitions**—an example is "Aborigines, the people native to Australia, were being forced from their homes." The phrase "the people native to Australia" provides a definition of the word "Aborigines" within the context of the sentence.
- **Providing correct pronunciation by repeating students' responses**—When teachers repeat English learners' correct responses, enunciating carefully and naturally, students have another opportunity to hear the content information, and correct English pronunciation and inflection are reinforced.
- **Slowing speech, increasing pauses, and speaking in phrases**—Teachers provide scaffolding for ELs' language acquisition when they slow down the rate of speech, pause between phrases, and allow students the wait time they may need to process information in English (see Chapter 4 for more information about Comprehensible Input).

In addition to this important verbal scaffolding, effective teachers incorporate instructional approaches that provide *procedural scaffolding*. These include, but are not limited to, the following:

1. Using an instructional framework that includes explicit teaching, modeling, and practice opportunities with others, and expectations for independent application (see Figure 5.2)

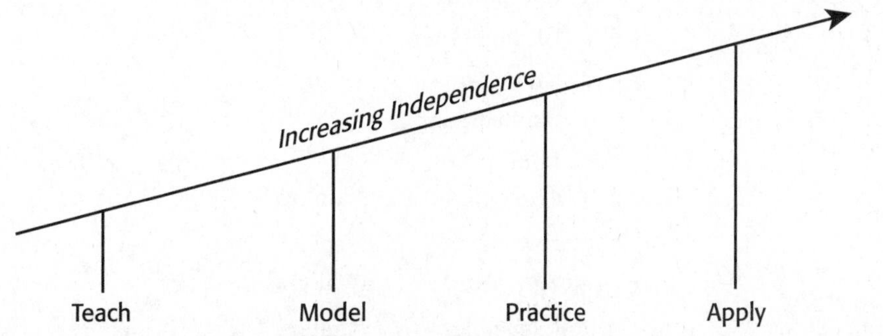

FIGURE 5.2 *Scaffolding Model: Teach, Model, Practice, Apply*

2. One-on-one teaching, coaching, and modeling
3. Small group instruction with students practicing a newly learned strategy with another, more experienced student
4. Partnering or grouping students for reading activities, with more experienced readers assisting those with less experience (Nagel, 2001)

In addition, teachers can use *instructional scaffolding* to enhance student learning. For example, graphic organizers can be used as a prereading tool to prepare students for the content of a textbook chapter. The organizer can also be used to illustrate a chapter's text structure, such as comparative or chronological (Vogt & Echevarria, 2008). Think of how the graphic organizers are used in this book and how they assist you in comprehending and organizing the text content.

SIOP® FEATURE 15: A Variety of Questions or Tasks That Promote Higher-Order Thinking Skills

Another way that effective SIOP® teachers can promote strategy use is by asking questions that promote critical thinking (Fordham, 2006). More than 40 years ago, Bloom and colleagues (1956) introduced a taxonomy of educational objectives that includes six levels: Knowledge, Comprehension, Application, Analysis, Synthesis, Evaluation. This taxonomy was formulated on the principle that learning proceeds from concrete knowledge to abstract values, or from the denotative to the connotative. Educators adopted this taxonomy as a hierarchy of questioning that, when used in the classroom, elicits varied levels of student thinking.

In 2001, D. R. Krathwohl (who originally worked with Benjamin Bloom) and colleagues published a revised taxonomy: *Taxonomy for Learning, Teaching, and Assessing: A Revision of Bloom's Taxonomy of Educational Objectives* (see Anderson & Krathwohl, 2001). In the revised taxonomy the six levels (simplified here) include:

1. Remember
   a. Recognizing
   b. Recalling
2. Understand
   a. Interpreting
   b. Exemplifying
   c. Classifying
   d. Summarizing
   e. Inferring
   f. Comparing
   g. Explaining
3. Apply
   a. Executing
   b. Implementing

4. Analyze
    a. Differentiating
    b. Organizing
    c. Attributing
5. Evaluate
    a. Checking
    b. Critiquing
6. Create
    a. Generating
    b. Planning
    c. Producing

Whichever taxonomy teachers choose to use for their lessons, it is important that they carefully plan higher-order questions prior to lesson delivery. It is just too difficult to think of higher-order questions "on your feet."

In fact, researchers have found that of the approximately 80,000 questions the average teacher asks annually, 80 percent of them are at the Literal or Knowledge level (Gall, 1984; Watson & Young, 1986). This is especially problematic with English learners. As students are acquiring proficiency in English, it is tempting to rely on simple questions that result in yes/no or other one-word responses.

It is possible, however, to reduce the linguistic demands of responses while still promoting higher levels of thinking. For example, in a study of plant reproduction, the following question requires little thought: "Are seeds sometimes carried by the wind?" A nod or one-word response is almost automatic if the question is understood. A higher-level question such as the following requires analysis: "Which of these seeds would be more likely to be carried by the wind: the round one or smooth one? Or this one that has fuzzy hairs? Why do you think so?" Encouraging students to respond with higher levels of thinking requires teachers to consciously plan and incorporate questions at a variety of levels.

Teachers can also assist students in becoming strategic when they teach them how to determine levels of questions they are asked. For example, if a student recognizes that a question is at the literal level, he'll know the answer can be found right in the text. Similarly, if he identifies a question as inferential, he'll know he'll have to "think and search" or read between the lines to find the answer. This process has been named QAR (Question-Answer Relationships; Raphael, 1984; Raphael, Highfield, & Au, 2006). (See a detailed explanation in Vogt and Echevarria, 2008.)

When students are able to determine levels of questions, they can be taught to ask their own questions of varying levels. This complements the goal of developing hypotheses using the scientific method, and it also benefits the research skills students must learn and practice. For example, Burke (2002) explains the importance of students writing their own research questions *before* they use the Internet to find information so that they "steer" rather than "surf" for answers. Also, QAR is a powerful addition to SQP2RS, when students are writing their questions.

Successful learners know how to use question-asking to help them construct meaning while they read (Taboada & Guthrie, 2006). They ask questions and challenge what the author says if something does not make sense to them. Beck and McKeown (2002, 2006), recommend using the instructional approach Questioning the Author (QtA) to develop students' comprehension of textbook material, which sometimes can be disjointed and lacking in connections between ideas and key concepts. QtA values the depth and quality of students' interactions with texts, and their responses to authors' intended meanings. It assists students in developing the ability to read text closely, as if the author were there to be questioned and challenged. We encourage you to learn more about both QAR and QtA in order to enhance your students' comprehension of text material and to assist them in developing self-regulating strategies related to questioning. (See Vogt and Echevarria, 2008, pp. 79–81 for QAR bookmarks.)

The Lesson

The lesson described in this chapter is taken from a seventh-grade unit on the tropical rain forest.

UNIT: The Rain Forest (Seventh Grade)

The three classrooms described in the teaching scenarios in this chapter are heterogeneously mixed with native English speakers and English learners who have mixed levels of fluency. The middle school is in a suburban community, and Hispanic English learners make up approximately 75 percent of the student population.

Mrs. Fletcher, Miss Lee, and Mr. Montoya are each teaching a unit on the tropical rain forest. They are all using the same article taken from a science news magazine designed for middle school students.

State content standards for seventh-grade Earth science include the following:

1. Students know Earth processes today are similar to those that occured in the past and slow geologic processes have large cumulative effects over long periods of time.
2. Students know the history of life on Earth has been disrupted by major catastrophic events (e.g., major volcanic eruptions or the impact of asteroids).
3. Students know how to explain significant developments and extinctions of plants and animals on the geological time scale.
4. Students know how light can be reflected, refracted, transmitted, and absorbed by matter.

(For more examples of lesson and unit plans in science, see Short, Echevarria, & Vogt, in press.)

The following teaching scenarios take place during the first day of the unit on the rain forest.

Teaching Scenarios

To demonstrate how Mrs. Fletcher, Miss Lee, and Mr. Montoya planned instruction for their students, including their English learners, we look at how each designed a lesson on the rain forest.

Mrs. Fletcher

Mrs. Fletcher began her lesson by distributing the rain forest article to the students and asking them to read together the title, "Our Burning Forests." She then directed them to predict from the title and opening photograph what they thought the article would be about. One boy said, "It looks like the jungle." Another said, "I think it's about parrots." One of the girls responded, "I think it's about burning forests." Mrs. Fletcher then began reading the article, stopping once to ask the class, "What do you think will happen to the animals in this rain forest?" When she had finished orally reading the article, she asked the students if they had any questions.

FIGURE 5.3 *Strategies Component of the SIOP® Model: Mrs. Fletcher's Lesson*

4	3	2	1	0
13. Ample opportunities provided for students to use **learning strategies**		Inadequate opportunities provided for students to use **learning strategies**		No opportunity provided for students to use **learning strategies**
4	**3**	**2**	**1**	**0**
14. **Scaffolding techniques** consistently used, assisting and supporting student understanding (e.g., think-alouds)		**Scaffolding techniques** occasionally used		**Scaffolding techniques** not used
4	**3**	**2**	**1**	**0**
15. A variety of **questions or tasks that promote higher-order thinking skills** (e.g., literal, analytical, and interpretive questions)		Infrequent **questions or tasks that promote higher-order thinking skills**		No **questions or tasks that promote higher-order thinking skills**

One of the students asked, "Why do people burn the rain forests if it's so bad?" Mrs. Fletcher replied that the wood is very valuable and people want to make money from the sale of it. Because there were no further questions, she asked each student to write a letter to the editor of the local newspaper explaining why we should save the rain forests. Several of the students began writing, while others reread the article. A few appeared confused about how to start and Mrs. Fletcher helped them individually. When they had finished writing their letters, Mrs. Fletcher asked for volunteers to read their papers aloud. After a brief discussion of the letters, Mrs. Fletcher collected them and dismissed the students for lunch.

On the SIOP® form in Figure 5.3, rate Mrs. Fletcher's lesson on each of the Strategies features.

Miss Lee

Miss Lee introduced the magazine article by presenting a brief lecture on the rain forest and by showing a variety of photographs. She then divided the students into groups of four and asked one person in each group to read the article to the other group members. When the students were finished reading, Miss Lee distributed worksheets. The children were instructed to independently write the answers to the following questions:

1. How much of the Earth's surface is covered by rain forests?
2. What percent of the Earth's species are found in the rain forest?
3. What are three products that come from the rain forests?
4. Why are the rain forests being burned or cut?
5. Who are the people that are doing the burning and cutting?

FIGURE 5.4 *Strategies Component of the SIOP® Model: Miss Lee's Lesson*

4	3	2	1	0
13. Ample opportunities provided for students to use **learning strategies**		Inadequate opportunities provided for students to a use **learning strategies**		No opportunity provided for students to use **learning strategies**
4	**3**	**2**	**1**	**0**
14. **Scaffolding techniques** consistently used, assisting and supporting student understanding (e.g., think-alouds)		**Scaffolding techniques** occasionally used		**Scaffolding techniques** not used
4	**3**	**2**	**1**	**0**
15. A variety of **questions or tasks that promote higher-order thinking skills** (e.g., literal, analytical, and interpretive questions)		Infrequent **questions or tasks that promote higher-order thinking skills**		No **questions or tasks that promote higher-order thinking skills**

6. One of the birds found in the rain forest is a _________________.
7. Global warming is believed to be caused by ______________.
8. I hope the rain forests are not all cut down because ________________.

In addition to their rain forest article, Miss Lee encouraged students to use the class computers to search the Internet for the answers to these questions. She told them to type in "rain forest" on a search engine to begin their search.

When the students were finished writing their responses, they were to compare them to those of their group members. Miss Lee directed them to use the article to fix any answers the group thought were incorrect. She explained that they needed to come to agreement and record their group answer on a clean worksheet. For question #8, students were to decide which of the students' responses in their group was the best.

On the SIOP® form in Figure 5.4, rate Miss Lee's lesson on each of the Strategies features.

Mr. Montoya (see Figure 5.6 for complete lesson plan)

After distributing the magazine article on the tropical rain forest to his class, Mr. Montoya introduced the lesson's content and language objectives that were written on the white board. He then engaged his students in a SQP2RS activity (known as "Squeepers") (see p. 100). First, students were directed to preview and think about the article. He asked them to take one to two minutes individually or with a partner to preview the text material by examining illustrations, photographs, bold or italicized print, charts, and chapter questions

(**Survey**). This was a familiar process for his students because he had previously taught and modeled how to conduct a text survey. After one minute, Mr. Montoya stopped the survey and directed the students to work with a partner to write two or three questions they thought they would find answers to by reading the article (**Question**). When finished, the partners shared their questions with another pair and then with the class. As the groups shared their questions, Mr. Montoya marked with asterisks those questions that were generated by more than one group. From the questions, the class predicted five important things they thought they would learn from the article (**Predict**), and Mr. Montoya recorded them on chart paper.

Mr. Montoya then read aloud the first section of the article while the students followed along in their copies of the text. After he had read four paragraphs, Mr. Montoya referred students to the list of predictions on the board. Next to each prediction that had been confirmed so far in the reading, a "+" was written, while one prediction that was disconfirmed was marked with a "−." One prediction that was unlikely to be discussed in the remainder of the article was marked with a question mark. A few additional questions and predictions were then generated by the class prior to Mr. Montoya's directions to quietly read the next section of the text (about six paragraphs) with a partner or a triad (**Read**).

When students finished the group reading activity, they were directed to find two or three vocabulary words they thought were important to the topic of the rain forest (VSS see p. 68). Mr. Montoya led the class in a brief discussion of the vocabulary words, and the class voted on ten that they felt were most important. These were posted on the board for future discussion during the unit on the rain forest.

In groups, the students then reviewed the questions that had been posed earlier to see if they had found answers in their reading, and they used sticky notes and strips to indicate in the article where the answers could be found. They checked their predictions according to the process Mr. Montoya had previously modeled (**Respond**). Next, each student wrote summary sentences about what they had read, using VSS words (**Summarize**).

Toward the end of the class, Mr. Montoya displayed a transparency with the following questions:

1. Why are we dependent on the rain forests for our survival on Earth?
2. Compare and contrast the arguments of foresters and environmentalists. With which argument do you most agree? Why?
3. Imagine the Earth in one hundred years. How would you describe it if the present rate of deforestation continues?
4. Pretend you are the president of the United States. Write a letter to the president of the lumber company that is responsible for the overseas burning of many acres of rain forest. Try to convince her to stop destroying the rain forest and practice sustainable lumber development.

After reading the questions aloud, Mr. Montoya briefly asked each student to select one. For homework, he asked students to copy the question they chose and to discuss it with parents or caregivers that evening. Students were asked to jot notes as to how they would answer the question, using the information from the article insights they had gained through their discussions at home, and VSS words. He announced that these questions would be debated during the next day's class.

On the SIOP® form in Figure 5.5, rate Mr. Montoya's lesson on each of the Strategies features.

FIGURE 5.5 *Strategies Component of the SIOP® Model: Mr. Montoya's Lesson*

4	3	2	1	0
13. Ample opportunities provided for students to use **learning strategies**		Inadequate opportunities provided for students to use **learning strategies**		No opportunity provided for students to use **learning strategies**
14. **Scaffolding techniques** consistently used throughout lesson, assisting and supporting student understanding (e.g., think-alouds)		**Scaffolding techniques** occasionally used		**Scaffolding techniques** not used
15. A variety of **questions or tasks that promote higher-order thinking skills** (e.g., literal, analytical, and interpretive questions)		Infrequent **questions or tasks that promote higher-order thinking skills**		No **questions or tasks that promote higher-order thinking skills**

FIGURE 5.6 *SIOP® Lesson: Tropical Rain Forests (Science)* *Grade: 7*

Key: SW = Students will; TW = Teacher will; SWBAT = Students will be able to . . .; HOTS = Higher Order Thinking Skills

Content Standards:
Earth and Life History—Earth Sciences

- Students know Earth processes today are similar to those that occurred in the past, and slow processes have large cumulative effects over long periods of time.
- Students know the history of life on Earth has been disrupted by major catastrophic events (e.g., major volcanic eruptions or the impact of asteroids).
- Students know how to explain significant developments and extinctions of plants and animals on the Earth's timeline.

Physical Science

- Students know how light can be reflected, refracted, transmitted, and absorbed by matter.

Key Vocabulary: Vocabulary Self-Collection Strategy (VSS); students will select key vocab after reading; Teacher choices for VSS: *rain forest; deforestation; ozone layer*

HOTS:

1. Why are we dependent on the rain forests for our survival on earth?
2. Compare and contrast the arguments of foresters and environmentalists. With which argument do you most agree? Why?

Visuals/Resources: Article on deforestation of tropical rain forests; photographs from space depicting hole in the ozone layer; chart paper and markers

FIGURE 5.6 *continued*

3. Imagine the Earth in one hundred years. How would you describe it if the present rate of deforestation continues? **4.** Pretend you are the president of the United States. Write a letter to the president of the lumber company that is responsible for the overseas burning of many acres of rain forest. Try to convince her to stop destroying the rain forest and practice sustainable lumber development.	

Connections: Prior Knowledge/ Building Background/Previous Learning
TW review previously taught steps to SQP2RS including how to effectively survey expository text. In small groups, SW list responses to the following: "Based on our reading and discussions from last week, what are three reasons why some animals and plants have become extinct over time?" SW review notes and text for answers, if necessary.

Content Objectives	**Meaningful Activities:** Lesson sequence	**Review/Assessment**
1. SWBAT analyze the impact of deforestation of tropical rain forests on the environment.	TW review SQP2RS process for reading expository texts.	Summative assessment of content objective will be: answers to student-posed questions; class discussion; summary sentences; selection of question for oral debate of HOTS questions; tomorrow's debate
Language Objectives		
2. SWBAT ask questions and predict key concepts prior to reading about tropical rain forests. **3.** SWBAT select and define 2–3 key vocabulary words related to deforestation and rain forests. **4.** SWBAT write summary sentences about deforestation, tropical rain forests, and the impact on the environment. **5.** SWBAT orally defend a position on deforestation of the rain forests.	SW in partners survey rainforest article to generate 2–3 questions they think will be answered by reading article; TW post questions, using asterisks to indicate multiple group responses.	TW monitor questions and predictions about the rain forest posted on chart paper
	Class will predict 4–5 key concepts that will be learned by reading article.	
	TW begin reading; SW read to confirm/disconfirm predictions.	SW show in text answers to questions; where predictions are confirmed.
	SW use sticky notes to find answers to posted questions; SW mark in text answers and confirmed predictions.	SW in small groups compare answers marked by sticky notes.
	SW with partners find and define 2–3 VSS words that are important to the topic of deforestation and the rain forests.	TW check VSS words and definitions
	TW lead discussion of VSS words, clarifying meanings, while SW explain why the selected VSS words related to the rain forest are important to know.	
	SW write summary sentences on the impact of deforestation of rain forests, using key vocabulary selected during VSS.	TW read summary sentences and use of key vocabulary
	SW select a HOTS question to take home and discuss with parents or caretaker in preparation for informal debate tomorrow.	TW review selected questions
	TW review rules of informal debate.	

Wrap-up: Check for understanding of key vocabulary and clarify questions about the debate questions; review content and language objectives. Hold up fingers for level of understanding for each objective: 1 = I can do it; 2 = I think I can do it, but I still have questions; 3 = I need more information or review.

Lesson plan format created by Melissa Castillo & Nicole Teyechea

Discussion of Lessons

13. *Ample Opportunities Provided for Students to Use Learning Strategies*

Mrs. Fletcher: 2

Miss Lee: 2

Mr. Montoya: 4

Mrs. Fletcher's lesson received a "2" for her use and teaching of strategies. She began the lesson by asking her students to make predictions from the title of the article, and three students responded. As typically happens with predictions based on titles, one girl repeated the title of the article in her prediction ("I think it will be about burning forests"), but Mrs. Fletcher did not probe the response to elicit deeper thinking about the topic. Further, she didn't build upon or reinforce the other two students' predictions, nor did she seek other predictions during the text reading. Often, teachers ask for predictions, accept them, and move on without expanding on them or coming back to revisit them later in a lesson.

Mrs. Fletcher's lesson would have been strengthened if she had included additional strategies, and perhaps a graphic organizer or other means for students to organize the information they were learning. She also could have periodically stopped her oral reading to reinforce important concepts, clarify confusing points, and discuss predictions that were confirmed or disconfirmed. Even though Mrs. Fletcher had the students write a letter to the editor at the end of the reading—providing students with a chance to demonstrate their understanding—she missed the opportunity to model summarizing as a strategic process throughout the article. This would have made the letter-writing activity more accessible to English learners and struggling readers.

Miss Lee's lesson also received a "2" for use of strategies. She encouraged her students to evaluate and determine importance during the discussions of the answers to the questions on the worksheet. Students were required to support their responses, clarify misunderstandings, and have consensus on the answers before turning in their papers. Her lesson would have been more effective if she had determined students' prior knowledge about the rain forests, and actively engaged them in drawing on their background knowledge. Instead of just lecturing, she could have shown photographs and generated student predictions and questions about the content of the pictures.

Mr. Montoya's lesson received a "4" on the learning strategies feature. He taught and modeled several important processing strategies when he engaged his students in the SQP2RS/Squeepers activity for the expository text selection: prediction, self-questioning, monitoring and clarifying, evaluating, and summarizing. As Mr. Montoya led his students through the activity, he modeled and provided support in how to survey text, generate questions, make predictions, confirm or disconfirm predictions based on text information, and summarize information. Further, he incorporated Vocabulary Self-Collection Strategy (VSS), during which students carefully select and discuss vocabulary that is key to the topic being studied (Ruddell, 2007). Evidence shows that when students are guided in how to select important vocabulary, and in how to apply strategies through SQP2RS, their comprehension is enhanced (Blachowicz & Fisher, 2000; Shearer, Ruddell, & Vogt, 2001; Vogt, 2000; 2002).

14. *Scaffolding Techniques Consistently Used, Assisting and Supporting Student Understanding*

Mrs. Fletcher: 1

Miss Lee: 3

Mr. Montoya: 4

Mrs. Fletcher's lesson received a "1" for scaffolding. She attempted to scaffold student learning by having the class orally read the title together and by reading the article to the students. This significantly reduced the reading demands of the text. However, if she continues to read everything aloud to the students, she won't be gradually reducing her support, and the students will be less likely to become independent readers. Therefore, her scaffolding might have been more effective if she had begun reading the article to the students and then had them complete the reading with a partner or group. Obviously, this presumes that the text difficulty is such that the students could successfully read it with help from one another.

Miss Lee's lesson received a "3" for scaffolding. She effectively scaffolded student learning in three ways. First, the photographs she displayed during her lecture provided additional support for students who had little background knowledge about the topic of rain forests. Second, by having the students complete the reading in their groups, the reading demands were reduced. Depending on the length of the article, she might have encouraged the reading involvement of more than one student in each group if she had suggested, for example, a "Page, Paragraph, or Pass" approach. With this activity, each student decides whether he or she wishes to read a page, a paragraph, or pass on the oral reading. English learners and reluctant readers may feel more comfortable having the option of choosing whether and how much they'll read aloud to their peers.

Miss Lee also scaffolded the students' answering of the questions on the worksheet. They had to answer the questions independently, but then were allowed to compare their responses to those of the other students and decide on the correct answers together. This provided students the opportunity to demonstrate individual learning of the rain forest material, and also gave them the chance to compare their understandings with those of their peers.

Mr. Montoya's lesson received a "4" for scaffolding. He incorporated a variety of techniques that provided support with the expectation that his students eventually would be able to apply the various strategies independently. He used several grouping configurations during the lesson, including whole class, small groups, triads, and partners. Students had the opportunity to confer with each other, receiving support and assistance if necessary. Mr. Montoya also carefully modeled the strategies for the students prior to requiring application. The reading demands of the article were reduced when students were allowed to read it in pairs or triads. Choice also played a critical role in this lesson when students were encouraged to select key vocabulary and the question for homework that most interested them.

15. *A Variety of Questions and Tasks That Promote Higher-Order Thinking Skills*

Mrs. Fletcher: 0

Miss Lee: 1

Mr. Montoya: 4

Mrs. Fletcher's lesson received a "0" for questioning. She missed several opportunities to use questioning to engage her students' thinking. When the three students made their predictions, she could have probed with questions such as, "What made you think that?" "Tell me more about that," or "Why do you think it's about parrots?" Toward the end of the lesson, when one student asked why people still burn the rain forests, Mrs. Fletcher could have used the student's question to develop inquiry skills in her students, and these questions could then have motivated the letters to the editor. Instead, the letter-writing activity, while potentially meaningful, seemed somewhat removed from the article and brief discussion about the rain forests.

Miss Lee's lesson received a "1" for questioning. Although she incorporated questioning into her lesson by using the worksheet, the questions were essentially written at the literal level, with answers that could be found easily in the rain forest article. The activity would have required greater cognitive work on the part of the students if Miss Lee had written questions at various levels. Question 8 was the only one that required actual application and evaluation of the content concepts.

In addition, although Miss Lee tried to incorporate technology into her lesson, she did not provide enough guidance to help students find the information they needed in a timely fashion. She could have worked with students interested in using the Internet to refine their search procedures; generate some of their own questions about the rain forest; and use several key words to yield the information they were seeking while narrowing the resulting prospective websites.

Mr. Montoya's lesson received a "4" for questioning. He incorporated questioning throughout the lesson, first during the SQP2RS (Squeepers) activity, when students generated their own questions based on the text information, and then with the debate/discussion questions. Note the varied levels of the questions: The first is a literal-level question, the second requires analysis and evaluation, the third requires application and synthesis, and the fourth requires synthesis and evaluation. Mr. Montoya effectively reduced the text's difficulty through the SQP2RS activity, not by lowering the cognitive demand of the questions.

Summary

We frequently remind teachers, "Just because your students can't read well doesn't mean they can't think!" A similar adage to this might be said of English learners: "Just because they can't speak English proficiently doesn't mean they can't think!"

In this chapter, we have described how to promote critical and strategic thinking for all students, but most especially for ELs. Learning is made more effective when teachers actively assist students in developing metacognitive, cognitive, and social/affective strategies, those that promote self-monitoring, self-regulation, and problem solving. We believe that students with developing English proficiency should not be denied effective, creative, and generative teaching while they are learning the language. Therefore, it is imperative that all teachers provide English learners with sufficient scaffolding, including verbal supports such as paraphrasing and frequent repetition, and instructional supports such as the appropriate use of graphic organizers and opportunities to work with more experienced individuals in flexible groups. While English learners are developing English proficiency, teachers must remember to include in their lessons higher-order questions that promote critical thinking.

Discussion Questions

1. Describe a learning situation you participated in or observed in which the teacher modeled how to do something. Describe a recent lesson in which you modeled a process, directions students were to follow, or steps for an experiment. What did you have to do to ensure that students could follow your instruction? What worked and what didn't? How could you have made things more clear?
2. The concept of scaffolding may be somewhat new for you. The definition in the glossary may be helpful, as may be the following construction analogy. Picture a high-rise building as it is under construction. As new stories are added, scaffolding is built along the outside of the previously constructed story (or level). This scaffolding allows access for the construction workers—they need to be able to get into the upper stories in order to continue the building process.

   Think of a content topic that you must teach that is challenging to students acquiring English as a second (or multiple) language. What types of scaffolds must you put in place for your students to successfully access your content and language objectives?
3. Here's a factual question a teacher might ask based on a social studies text: "Who was the first president of the United States?" Given the topic of the presidency, what are several additional questions you could ask that promote higher-order thinking? Why is it important to use a variety of questioning strategies with English learners? Use one of the taxonomies (Bloom's or Anderson and Krathwohl's) to guide you.
4. Using the SIOP® lesson you have been developing, add meaningful activities that develop learning strategies. Determine how to scaffold ELs' access to your objectives. Write several higher order thinking questions/tasks.

chapter 6

Interaction

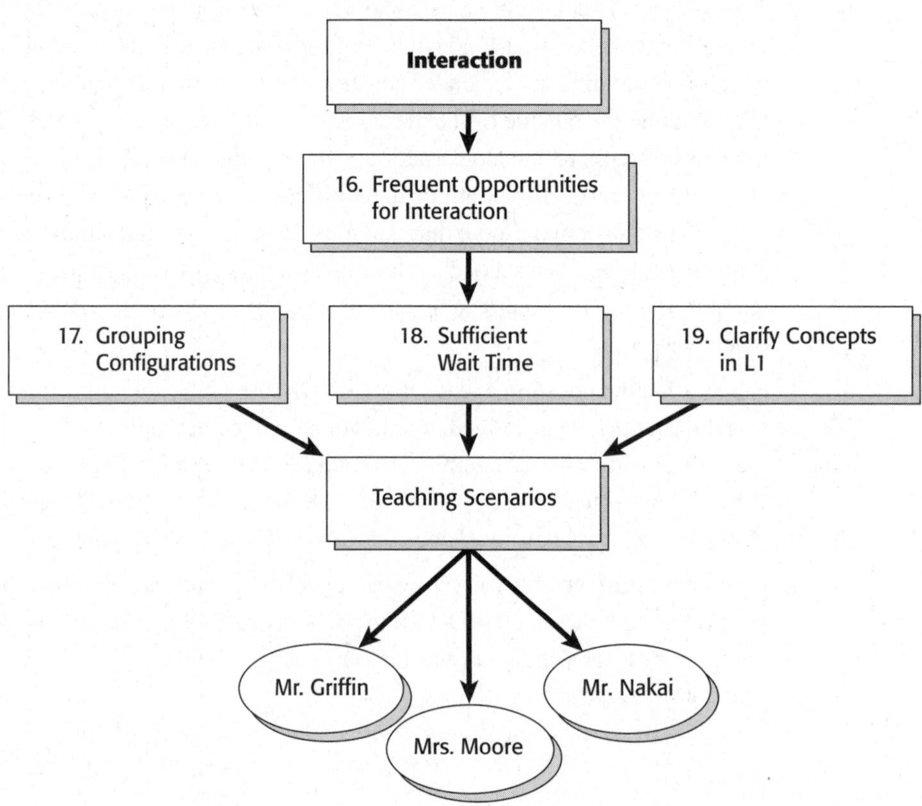

Objectives

After reading, discussing, and engaging in activities related to this chapter, you will be able to meet the following content and language objectives.

Content Objectives

Select from a variety of activities that promote interaction and incorporate them into lesson plans.

Design grouping patterns that support lesson content and language objectives.

Identify techniques to increase wait time.

Identify resources to support student clarification in the native language.

Language Objectives

Explain in writing the purpose of student–student interaction for language development.

Describe techniques to reduce the amount of teacher talk in a lesson.

Practice asking questions that promote student elaboration of responses.

For English learners to become fluent in academic English, we need to provide structured opportunities in all subject areas to practice using the language. Because of the large number of English learners in schools today, *all* teachers are teachers of English, even if their content specialization is science, math, or social studies. The integration of language development across the curriculum is vital. For students learning in and through a new language—English—teachers must create ample opportunities to practice using *academic* language, not just social English. And the language must be meaningful to students; it isn't just the quantity of exposures to English that affects learning, but the quality of these exposures, too (Wong-Fillmore & Valadez, 1986).

For middle school and high school teachers, providing students opportunities to work in small groups may be challenging. Moving away from whole class instruction and sharing responsibility for learning with small groups or partners is an adjustment for many secondary teachers. However, it is clear that if we want students to connect with school and to engage in learning at a level that will result in high achievement, we need to provide students with opportunities to interact with one another, to discuss and "puzzle over" genuine problems (Wiggins & McTighe, 2008). In this chapter we present ways that teachers can use interaction as a way to launch students to higher levels of English proficiency and to improve academic outcomes.

Background

"Use it or lose it" is a saying that conveys what we know from our own experience in learning a second language. If one doesn't practice using the language, it is difficult to maintain it. But what about learning a language in the first place—does speaking it help to develop the language? The answer is a resounding "Yes!" The role that conversation plays in the process of second language teaching and learning is clear (Day, 1998). But discussion also offers important benefits for learning in general. As Gerald Graff puts it, "Talk—about books and subjects—is as important educationally as are the books and subjects themselves" (2003, p. 9).

The issue is, why are there so few opportunities for students to interact in typical classrooms? Studies indicate that, in most classrooms, teachers dominate the linguistic aspect of the lesson, leaving students severely limited in terms of opportunities to use language in a variety of ways (Goodlad, 1984; Marshall, 2000). In a study of programs for ELs (Ramirez, Yuen, Ramey, & Pasta, 1991), it was found that the classes were characterized by excessive teacher talk. When students were given an opportunity to respond, it usually involved only simple information-recall statements, restricting students' chance to produce language and develop complex language and thinking skills. In our own work, we observe teachers doing a significant amount of talking at students rather than providing the impetus for a discussion or sharing, then allowing students to talk to one another.

There are many benefits to having students actively engaged in interaction around subject matter. Some include:

- **Deeper understanding of text.** When teachers use thoughtful questioning to promote discussion, it encourages children to discuss what the passage is about and to think about the text at deeper levels (Echevarria, 1995b; Goldenberg, 1992–1993).
- **Oral language development.** Being exposed to and interacting with language that is just beyond their independent speaking levels moves students to higher levels of language proficiency.
- **Brain stimulation.** Interesting, engaging activities, including discussions, play an important role in learning. When students are engaged, more of the pleasure structures in the brain are activated than when students are simply asked to memorize information (Poldrack, Clark, Pare-Blagoev, Shohamy, Creso Moyano, Myers, & Gluck, 2001).
- **Increased motivation.** Interaction with others is an important component of reading instruction that increases motivation and comprehension (Guthrie & Ozgungor, 2002).
- **Reduced risk.** The typical question-answer sessions where teachers call on students may be threatening to students, particularly those unprepared to respond. Some students cannot focus on the content in this setting because it triggers the brain's "threat response" (Jensen, 2005). Students talking in pairs or small groups minimizes the risk and allows ideas to flow more easily.
- **More processing time.** Students need time to process after learning. Direct instruction should be limited to short increments followed by time for discussion.
- **Increased attention.** Use of pairs or teams can heighten attention levels. Students may be asked to work together to compare/contrast material learned, group and regroup the material, resequence it, or retell it from another point of view (Marzano, Pickering, & Pollock 2001).

To see an example of eliciting interaction, please view the corresponding video clip (Chapter 6, Module 2) on the accompanying CD.

Unfortunately, these practices tend not to be prevalent in secondary classrooms with or without English learners.

We find that it is both interesting and helpful to analyze actual transcripts from lessons to demonstrate the kind of teacher dominance that is so prevalent in classrooms. The following transcripts are from a pilot SIOP® study (Echevarria, Greene, & Goldenberg, 1996) in middle school social studies classes. The teachers were videotaped teaching the same content about consumerism to English learners, the first using a typical approach found in mainstream classes and the other using the SIOP® Model approach. Both classes had approximately twenty-five students, and in this lesson, students were learning how to read labels on clothing and on a bottle of antiseptic.

Mainstream Lesson

TEACHER: Look at the piece of clothing at the bottom. It says *(he reads),* "This shirt is flame-resistant," which means what?

STUDENT: Could not burn.

STUDENT: Won't catch fire.

TEACHER: It will not burn, won't catch fire. Right *(continues reading).* "To retain the flame-resistant properties"—what does "to retain" mean?

STUDENT: *(unintelligible)*

TEACHER: To keep it. All right. *(He reads),* "In order to keep this shirt flame-resistant wash with detergent only." All right *(he reads).* "Do not use soap or bleach. Tumble dry. One hundred percent polyester." Now, why does it say, "Do not use soap or bleach"?

STUDENT: 'Cause it'll take off the . . .

TEACHER: It'll take off the what?

STUDENTS: *(fragmented responses)*

TEACHER: It'll take off the flame-resistant quality. If you wash it with soap or bleach, then the shirt's just gonna be like any old shirt, any regular shirt, so when you put a match to it, will it catch fire?

STUDENT: No.

TEACHER: Yes. 'Cause you've ruined it then. It's no longer flame-resistant. So the government says you gotta tell the consumer what kind of shirt it is, and how to take care of it. If you look at any piece of clothing: shirt, pants, your shirts, um, your skirts, anything. There's always going to be a tag on these that says what it is made of and how you're going to take care of it. Okay. And that's for your protection so that you won't buy something and then treat it wrong. So labeling is important. All right. Let's review. I'll go back to the antiseptic. What did we say indications meant? Indications? Raise your hands, raise your hands. Robert?

STUDENT: What's it for.

TEACHER: What is it for, when do you use this? Okay. What do directions, what is that for, Victor?

STUDENT: How to use . . .

TEACHER: How to use. Okay, so indications is when you use it *(holds one finger up)*, directions is how you use it *(holds another finger up)*, and warnings is what?

STUDENTS: *(various mumbled responses)*

TEACHER: How you don't use it. This is what you don't do.

The teacher in this case tended to finish sentences for the students and accept any form of student comment without encouraging elaborated responses. In examining the exchanges, what did the teacher do when students gave partial or incorrect answers? He answered the question himself. Students learn that they can disengage because the teacher will continue with the "discussion."

SIOP® Model

TEACHER: Most clothing must have labels that tell what kind of cloth was used in it right? Look at the material in the picture down there *(points to picture in text)*.[1] What does it say, the tag right there?

STUDENT: The, the, the . . .

TEACHER: The tag right there.

STUDENT: *(Reading)* "Flame-resis . . ."

TEACHER: Resistant.

STUDENT: "Flame-resistant. To retain the flame-resistant properties, wash with detergent only. Do not use soap or bleach. Use warm water. Tumble dry."

TEACHER: "One hundred percent . . ."

STUDENT: "Polyester."

TEACHER: Now, most clothes carry labels, right? *(pointing to the neck of her sweater)*. They explain how to take care of it, like dry clean, machine wash, right? It tells you how to clean it. Why does this product have to be washed with a detergent and no soap or bleach?

STUDENT: Because clothes . . .

TEACHER: Why can't you use something else?

STUDENTS: *(several students mumble answers)*

STUDENT: *(says in Spanish)* Because it will make it small.

TEACHER: It may shrink, or *(gestures to a student)* it may not be . . . what does it say?

STUDENT: It's not going to be able to be resistant to fire.

TEACHER: Exactly. It's flame-resistant, right? So, if you use something else, it won't be flame-resistant anymore. How about the, uh, look at the *antiseptic (holds hands up to form a container)*—the picture above the shirt, the antiseptic?

STUDENT: Read it?

TEACHER: Antiseptic *(Teacher reads)* and other health products you buy without a prescription often have usage and warning labels. So what can you learn from this label?

[1] The teacher explained then that they would be doing an activity in which they would read labels for information.

Read this label quietly please, and tell me what you can learn from the label. Read the label on that antiseptic. *(Students read silently.)*

TEACHER: What can you learn from this label?

STUDENT: It kills, oh I know.

TEACHER: Steve?

STUDENT: It kills germs.

STUDENT: Yeah, it kills germs.

TEACHER: It kills germs. You use it for wounds, right? What else?

STUDENTS: *(various enthusiastic responses)*

TEACHER: One person at a time. Okay, hold on. Veronica was saying something.

STUDENT: It tells you in the directions that, you could use it, that like that, 'cause if you use it in another thing, it could hurt you.

TEACHER: It could hurt you. Okay, what else? Ricardo?

STUDENT: If you put it in your mouth, don't put it in your mouth or your ears or your eyes.

TEACHER: Very good. Don't put it in your mouth, ears, and eyes. Okay, for how many days should you use it? No more than what?

STUDENT: No more than ten days.

STUDENT: Ten days.

TEACHER: So don't use it—you have to follow what it says so don't use it more than ten days. Now, the next activity you're going to do . . .

The SIOP® teacher allowed for a balance of teacher-to-student talk and encouraged student participation. She asked questions, waited for students' responses, and restated or elaborated on the responses. In this case, what did the teacher do to elicit answers to the question? She scaffolded the answer by encouraging the students to think about it, prompting them to give their responses.

The features of the SIOP® Model within the Interaction component are designed to provide teachers with concrete ways of increasing student participation and developing English language proficiency.

SIOP® FEATURE 16: Frequent Opportunities for Interaction and Discussion

Oral Language Development

To see an example of student-to-student interaction, please view the corresponding video clip (Chapter 6, Module 3) on the accompanying CD.

This SIOP® feature emphasizes the importance of balancing linguistic turn-taking between the teacher and students, and among students. It also highlights the practice of encouraging students to elaborate their responses rather than accepting yes/no and one-word answers.

The findings of the National Literacy Panel on Language Minority Children and Youth (August & Shanahan, 2006) revealed the important relationship between oral proficiency in English and reading and writing proficiency. Specifically, reading comprehension skills and writing skills are positively correlated with oral language proficiency in English (Geva, 2006), two areas that are particularly challenging for English learners. Solid reading comprehension is the foundation for achievement in nearly every subject area in school, and writing proficiency in English is an essential skill as well.

There has long been recognition that language, cognition, and reading are intimately related (Tharp & Gallimore, 1988). As one acquires new language, new concepts are developed. Think about your own language learning with respect to understanding computer functions. Each new vocabulary word and term you learn and understand (e.g., hard drive, memory, and gigabyte) is attached to a concept that in turn expands your ability to think about how a computer works. As your own system of word-meaning grows in complexity, you are more capable of using the self-directed speech of verbal thinking ("Don't forget to save it on the hard drive."). Without an understanding of the words and the concepts they represent, you would not be capable of thinking about (self-directed speech) or discussing (talking with another) computer functions.

Reading comprehension is inseparable from language development. Because an understanding of language makes acquiring knowledge possible, deriving meaning from texts in English will be extremely challenging for English learners who may have difficulty reading unfamiliar words or comprehending their meaning, especially those words that are subject-area specific.

Researchers who have investigated the relationship between language and learning suggest that interactive approaches—where there is more balance in student talk and teacher talk—are effective in promoting meaningful language learning opportunities for English learners (Cazden, 2001; Echevarria, 1995b; McIntyre, Kyle, & Moore, 2006; Saunders & Goldenberg, 1992; Tharp & Gallimore, 1988; Walqui, 2006). Sometimes called instructional conversations (ICs), this mode of instruction emphasizes active student involvement and meaningful language-based teaching. Instructional conversations have been defined as having of a number of elements (Goldenberg, 1992–93) that are consistent with other discussion-based methods (Wilen, 1990). Essentially it is talking about text, which provides opportunities for using language to learn language and concepts. Used mostly, although not exclusively, in reading and language arts classes, an instructional conversation (IC) approach differs from typical teaching because most instructional patterns in classrooms involve the teacher asking a question, the student responding, and the teacher evaluating the response and asking another question (Cazden, 2001).

In contrast, the typical format of an IC begins with the teacher introducing the group to a theme or idea related to the text, then relating the theme to students' background experiences. This aspect of the approach is particularly powerful for middle and high schools students because they have a lot on their minds in terms of social and family relationships. The theme or idea may be introduced by saying something like, "Have you ever had a fight with someone? What was the cause? What happened?" Students share their thoughts and the teacher's questions focus on cause and effect: "But what caused the fight? Then what was the result or effect of the fight on your friendship?" After students contribute, the teacher might say, "Well, today we're going to read about how the Romans began to lose some of the fights for their empire. We'll talk about what caused them to lose battles and what the effect was." Adolescents enjoy learning about subjects that they relate to, and, through a discussion approach, teachers can find any number of ways to "hook" a lesson to student interest.

Next, the teacher shows the text to be read and asks prediction questions. As the text is read, it is "chunked" into sections to provide maximum opportunity for discussion,

FIGURE 6.1 *Contrast Typical Instruction with IC*

Typical Instruction	*Instructional Conversation*
Teacher-centered	Teacher facilitates
Exact, specific answers evaluated by the teacher	Many different ideas encouraged
No extensive discussion	Oral language practice opportunities using natural language
Skill-directed Easier to evaluate Check for understanding	Extensive discussion and student involvement Draw from prior or background knowledge
Mostly literal level thinking and language use	Student level of understanding transparent Fewer black and white responses Mostly higher level thinking and language use

constantly relating the theme and background experiences to a text-based discussion. Figure 6.1 illustrates the contrast in approaches.

A conversational approach is particularly well-suited to middle and high school aged English learners who frequently find themselves significantly behind their peers in most academic areas, usually due to low reading levels and underdeveloped language skills. IC provides a context for learning in which language is expressed naturally through meaningful discussion. In our work, we have seen teenagers who have low reading levels participate fully in grade-level reading groups because of the opportunity to listen to and discuss elements of the text.

The benefits of a rich discussion, or of the conversational approach are many and include:

- It gives students (and teachers) thinking time; pressure to have an instant answer is eliminated.
- Using thoughtful questioning provides opportunities to discuss what the story is about and think about the text at deeper levels.
- Activation of background knowledge occurs naturally as students share their knowledge of the world and about how language works.
- Being exposed to and interacting with language that is just beyond their independent speaking ability moves students to a higher level.
- It fosters a supportive environment, building teacher–student rapport.
- It is easier to determine students' levels of understanding.

Effective SIOP® teachers structure their lessons in ways that promote student discussion, and they strive to provide a more balanced linguistic exchange between themselves and their students. It can be particularly tempting for teachers to do most of the talking when students are not completely proficient in their use of English, but these students are precisely the ones who need opportunities to practice using English the most.

Effective SIOP® teachers also encourage elaborated responses from students when discussing the lesson's concepts. The teacher elicits more extended student contributions by using a variety of techniques that will take students beyond simple yes or no answers and short phrases (Echevarria, 1995b; Goldenberg, 1992–1993). Some of these techniques include asking students to expand on their answers by saying, "Tell me more about that";

and by asking direct questions to prompt more language use such as, "What do you mean by . . ." or "What else. . . ." Another technique is to provide further information through questions such as "How do you know?" "Why is that important?" "What does that remind you of?" Other techniques include offering restatements such as "In other words . . . is that accurate?" and by frequently pausing to let students process the language and formulate their responses. Some teachers call on other students to extend a classmate's response.

It takes time and practice for these techniques to become a natural part of a teacher's repertoire. The teachers with whom we've worked report that they had to consciously practice overcoming the temptation to speak for students or to complete a student's short phrase. The preceding transcript showed how the first teacher spoke for students instead of encouraging students to complete their thoughts. The following segment from the transcript provides another example:

TEACHER: What do "directions" . . . what is that for, Victor?

STUDENT: How to use . . .

TEACHER: How to use. Okay, so "indications" is when you use it, "directions" is how you use it, and "warnings" is what?

STUDENTS: *(various mumbled responses)*

TEACHER: How you don't use it. This is what you don't do.

In this segment, the mainstream teacher could have encouraged a more balanced exchange between himself and the students. First, he did not encourage students to completely express their thoughts; he accepted partial and mumbled answers. Secondly, he answered for the students, dominating the discussion. It is easy to imagine how students could become disinterested, passive learners in a class in which the teacher accepts minimal participation and does the majority of the talking.

The SIOP® teacher approached students–teacher interaction differently:

TEACHER: What can you learn from this label?

STUDENT: It kills, oh I know.

TEACHER: Steve?

STUDENT: It kills germs.

STUDENT: Yeah, it kills germs.

TEACHER: It kills germs. You use it for wounds, right? What else?

STUDENTS: *(various enthusiastic responses)*

TEACHER: One person at a time. Okay, hold on. Veronica was saying something.

STUDENT: It tells you in the directions that, you could use it, that like that, 'cause if you use it in another thing, it could hurt you.

TEACHER: It could hurt you. Okay, what else? Ricardo?

STUDENT: If you put it in your mouth, don't put it in your mouth or your ears or your eyes.

TEACHER: Very good. Don't put it in your mouth, ears, and eyes. Okay, for how many days should you use it? No more than what?

STUDENT: No more than ten days.

STUDENT: Ten days.

TEACHER: So don't use it—you have to follow what it says, so don't use it more than ten days. Now, the next activity you're going to do . . .

The SIOP® teacher let the students have time to express their thoughts (e.g., student says, "It kills . . . It kills germs."). The teacher could have completed the sentence for the student, but she waited for him to complete his answer. Also, the SIOP® teacher encouraged and challenged the students more than the mainstream teacher did by asking twice, "What else?" Finally, the teacher nominated students who volunteered to talk and repeated what they said so that the class could hear a full response (e.g., Veronica).

Effective SIOP® teachers plan instruction so that students have opportunities to work with one another on academic tasks, using English to communicate. Through meaningful interaction, students can practice speaking and making themselves understood. That implies asking and answering questions, negotiating meaning, clarifying ideas, giving and justifying opinions, and more. Students may interact in pairs, triads, and small groups. Literature circles, think-pair-share, Jigsaw readings, debates, and science experiments are only a sample of the types of activities teachers can include in lessons to foster student–student interaction.

Other Opportunities for Interaction

ACTIVITY Interaction need not always be oral. Students can interact with teachers through dialogue journals, sharing ideas and learning from the teacher who models appropriate written text. In secondary classes, students may be partnered with one another. The teacher participates in the dialogue every so often to monitor students' writing and model correct writing.

ACTIVITY Using technology, students can interact with each other through a class electronic list, shared research files on a school network, or a planned pen pal e-mail exchange with another class elsewhere in the world.

ACTIVITY In a discussion of the importance of movement for learning at all ages, Jensen (2005) suggests a number of games such as rewriting lyrics to familiar songs in pairs or teams as a content review, then performing the song; playing Simon Says using content such as "Point to Rome. Point to the first country the Romans conquered," etc.; or role-plays, charades, or pantomime to review main ideas or key points.

ACTIVITY Students may interact by sharing their expertise. For example, in an activity called Expert Stay Stray, students work on an assignment in small groups, such as completing a chart summarizing the key points from a unit of study. Students in the group number off. The teacher calls a number, e.g., #4, and student #4 takes his or her group's chart and goes to another table and shares the information with the new group. Then the student remains with the new group as the teacher calls another number, e.g., #1. Student #1 takes the chart of the student who shared (#4)—which encourages students to listen carefully—and goes to a new group and shares the information from the chart. This activity provides students with an opportunity to discuss the information while completing the chart, then to share the information orally while others listen attentively, and to paraphrase someone else's explanation of the chart. It can be adapted to any content area or grade level.

ACTIVITY

Start the class each day with students in pairs and have them tell each other the day's content objective. Then they move to find another partner and tell them the language objective.

ACTIVITY

Dinner Party is an activity appropriate for all middle and high school levels and most content areas. For instance, in the English Literature course, students would respond to the prompt: "Suppose you could have a dinner party for British authors or poets that we have studied. Whom would you invite? Why would you select them? What would be the seating order of the guests at your table, and why would you place them in that order? What do you think the guests would talk about during dinner? Include specific references to the authors' lives and works in your response." The purpose is for students to act out the questions by assuming personas, such as characters in novels, scientists, historical figures, or artists. During each Dinner Party, specific content must be included and the characters must respond to each other as realistically and accurately as possible (Vogt & Echevarria, 2008).

ACTIVITY

A complete lesson that illustrates interaction is seen in Figure 6.2a. A high school technology teacher on the Arizona-Mexico border, Steve Young, uses an interactive SIOP® approach for making difficult concepts understandable. In this lesson, he uses a visual representation of the four functions of a computer (Figure 6.2b) tying the concepts to something students can relate to: eggs. Eggs are stored in the refrigerator as data are stored on the hard drive. Cooking eggs is like processing data. The output from a computer is information and for the eggs, it is the finished product—cooked eggs.

After students have been taught the four functions of a computer and the related terms, they complete a classification activity (Figure 6.2c) as practice/application.

FIGURE 6.2a *SIOP® Lesson Plan: Four Functions of a Computer*

LESSON TOPIC: *Four Functions of a Computer*

OBJECTIVES

Content

Identify the Four Functions of a computer (Storage, Input, Processing, and Output). Classify computer components according to their functions.

Language

Discuss the difference between long-term and short-term storage.
Distinguish data from information.

CONCEPTS

Data is what the computer understands.
Information is what humans understand.
Data must be processed to become information.
In order for data to be processed it must be in short-term memory.

MATERIALS

Old computer to remove parts from. Four boxes. Four Functions Graphic Organizer (Figure 6.2b). Categorize This worksheets (Figure 6.2c). Cloze summary

STRATEGIES/ACTIVITIES

Think-Pair-Share, Categorize This (classifying), Cloze summary

FIGURE 6.2a *Continued*

VOCABULARY
Prior Vocabulary: *Keyboard, Monitor, Printer, Microphone, Speakers, CPU*
Content Vocabulary: *Storage, Input, Processing, Output, Data, Information, RAM, Hard Drive*
Process Vocabulary: *Identify, Function, Distinguish, Relate, Classify*

MOTIVATION (*Building background*)
The teacher says: *How many of you have a kitchen at home? Think right now about what you use your kitchen for, and when you've thought of at least one function, tell your neighbor. When you and your neighbor have thought of three functions, things you use your kitchen for, one of you stand up to share your ideas with the class.* (When students stand, the teacher calls on students to solicit the responses: keeping food, cooking, and eating. On the board or on the computer projection screen the words *food, keeping food, cooking,* and *eating* are displayed. Next to food, teacher writes "input"; next to "keeping," "storage"; next to "cooking," "processing"; next to "eating," "output.")
How many of you have cooked eggs? I'm going to show you how the four functions of a computer are just like cooking eggs.

PRESENTATION
(Language and content objectives, comprehensible input, strategies, interaction, feedback)

Objectives are presented after background is built, and content words and process words are introduced. Previous vocabulary words, which consist of the basic parts of a computer system, are reviewed.

The teacher says the following:
Let's get back to the eggs. Tell your neighbor where you keep your eggs. The refrigerator? Good. Tell your neighbor what a refrigerator is for. Keeping things in? Good.

Another word for what you keep or put things in is "storage." Everyone say "storage." The refrigerator is for storage. What's the refrigerator for? Tell your neighbor one or two other things you use for storage in your kitchen.

The computer needs storage, too. Discuss with your neighbor why the computer needs storage. Where do you think the computer stores, or keeps, the things you save? Think about it and tell your neighbor what you think . . .

(The teacher selects a pair to remove the hard drive from the parts computer and pass it around to everyone. Then he asks someone to classify the hard drive by placing it in one of the four boxes that are labeled *storage, input, processing,* and *output.*)

Discuss with your neighbor which one of your vocabulary words is what is stored on the hard drive. Stand up when you think you know. Data, very good. You know what data is when we are talking about computers. It's ones and zeroes. That's all the computer understands. What's the only thing the computer understands? What do we call the ones and zeroes the computer understands?

Data is raw like the egg you are going to cook. Would you eat a raw, uncooked egg? No? Well, you won't be able to understand data either unless the computer cooks it for you.

Where do you put everything you get out of the refrigerator before you cook it? Tell your neighbor where you place the ingredients you are going to use as you cook . . . The counter? The table? Good. The refrigerator is long-term storage and the counter or table is short-term storage. We put things on the counter or table to use them but we don't leave them there.

The computer has a counter or table too for short-term storage. It's called RAM, random access memory. When you open a document you want to work with, the computer moves it from the hard drive to RAM. (The RAM picture is now displayed on the graphic organizer.) *This is what RAM looks like. Who wants to find the RAM in our parts computer and take it out for us to see?*

So look at the document you have opened right now on your computer. Is it in long-term or short-term storage? Is it in RAM or on the hard drive?

Let's talk about the eggs again. Tell your neighbor where you got them. Tell your neighbor where you placed them while you got the pan out and the butter or oil to cook them in.

Just like you took your eggs from the refrigerator, which is long-term storage (hold up the hard drive)*, and moved them to the counter or table, which is your short-term storage area* (hold up the RAM)*, raw data has to be moved to RAM so it can be processed.*

Before you can eat the eggs on your counter, you have to cook them. But we don't cook data, we process it. What do we do to data? The data you are looking at on your computer has been processed. That's why all those ones and zeroes appear to you as words. The data has been processed and now it's information. Discuss with your neighbor how processing is like cooking.

(The teacher continues with this approach with all four functions of the computer, relating the computer and its parts to the kitchen and cooking. The teacher uses realia (parts of the computer), a graphic organizer, Tell Your Neighbor, and choral response to keep the students engaged, to practice oral language, and to make the content comprehensible. There is plenty of meaningful interaction and feedback throughout. The teacher also spot checks along the way to make sure ELs comprehend.)

(*continued*)

FIGURE 6.2a *Continued*

PRACTICE/APPLICATION

(Meaningful activities, interaction, strategies, practice/application, feedback)

After the presentation of concepts, students work with their partners to complete the classification activity (Figure 6.2c). The class brainstorms together words and then identifies the categories. Students work to classify words into categories. After they finish, it is checked/reviewed on the big screen.

REVIEW/ASSESSMENT

(Review objectives and vocabulary, assess learning)

If there is time for the following cloze summary, students do it. If not, it is saved for review the following day.

> *The computer has _____ functions. Keeping data is the _____ function. Putting data into the computer is the _____ function. Changing raw data into information is the _____ function. Displaying or printing information is the _____ function.*
>
> *The most common input devices are the k _____ and m _____ . The monitor is an _____ device. D _____ is what the computer understands. I _____ is what humans understand. Data must be p _____ to be changed into Information.*
>
> *The two places where data is stored are the h _____ d _____ and R _____ . The hard drive is for l _____ t _____ storage and RAM is for sh _____ t _____ storage. Data must be moved from the hard drive to R _____ so it can be processed. When the processed data is saved it is moved from RAM to the h _____ d _____.*

At the end of the period, someone in each row must tell the teacher something he or she learned. They can discuss it with their row (Four Heads Together) and when one student gives a response, the row is dismissed. The following day, students write three things they learned the day before in their learning log for focus/review activity.

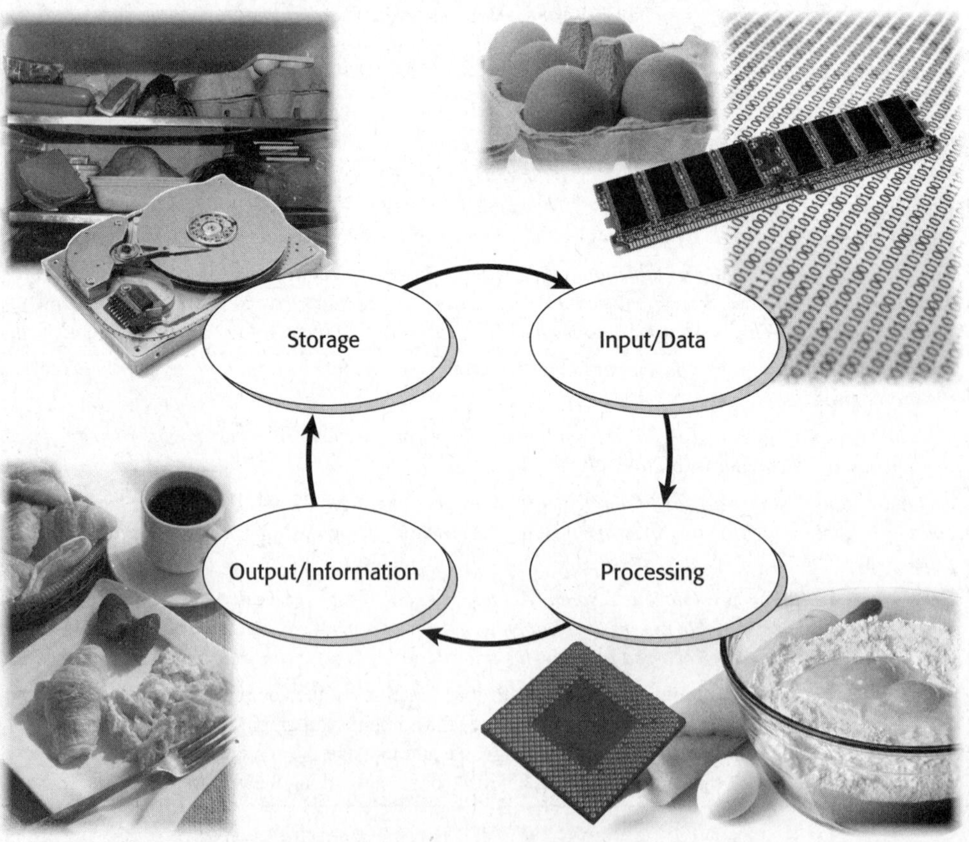

FIGURE 6.2b *Four Functions of a Computer*

FIGURE 6.2c

Categorize This

Directions: Brainstorm words related to your topic. Place these words in the Holding Cell. Then pull your words out of the Holding Cell and put them into categories. Finally, assign your category labels and write a summary sentence (on the back) describing each category.

The Holding Cell

Data, Information, RAM, Hard Drive, Identify, Function, Distinguish, Relate, Classify

STORAGE	INPUT	PROCESSING
OUTPUT	**PROCESS WORDS**	

SIOP®

SIOP® FEATURE 17: Grouping Configurations Support Language and Content Objectives of the Lesson

To maximize achievement, a balance is necessary between whole-group and small-group learning in the classroom. Varying grouping configurations—by moving from whole group to small group, small group to individual assignments—provides students with opportunities to learn new information, discuss it, and process it. Organizing students into smaller groups for instructional purposes provides a learning context that whole-group, teacher-dominated instruction doesn't offer. Fisher and Frey (2008) present a gradual release of responsibility model that slowly and purposefully shifts the workload from teacher to students. As seen in Figure 6.3, the teacher presents information and models "the type of thinking required to solve problems, understand directions, comprehend a text, or the like" (p. 5). The focus lesson is followed by guided instruction; then students are given an opportunity to collaborate. During this phase, students discuss ideas and information they learned during the focus lessons and guided instruction—not new information. Finally, students have acquired background knowledge from the first three phases and are ready to apply the information with independent tasks. When students aren't learning, it is often because there has not been the critical scaffolding that Figure 6.3 represents; teachers go directly from "I do it" to "You do it alone" (Fisher & Frey, 2008, p. 10).

In small guided instruction groups, the teacher naturally differentiates instruction as she works on focused skill instruction, language development, and/or assessment of student progress. Small group instruction provides more opportunity to discuss text (Saunders & Goldenberg, 2007) and increases reading achievement (Vaughn, et al. 2003). While the teacher is working with one group, the other students can work on familiar material in small

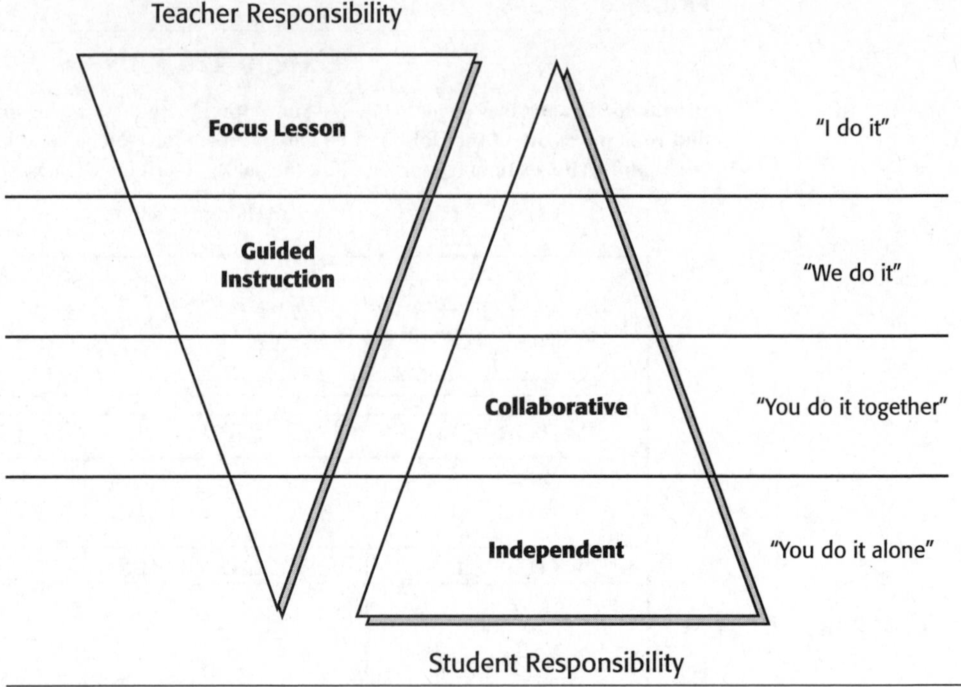

FIGURE 6.3 *A structure for successful instruction (Fisher & Frey, 2008)*

groups, with a partner, or individually either at their desks or at work stations. Activities may include creating graphic representations of vocabulary terms or concepts, summarizing material, practicing word sorts, or reading self-selected leveled readers. These activities are purposeful and meaningful, and lead to increased learning. In our work, we have seen this type of grouping work successfully with all ages, from kindergarten to the upper grades. In their book, *Differentiated Instruction: Grouping for Success*, Gibson and Hasbrouck (2008) provide a wealth of ideas for grouping effectively, including how to organize the classroom and schedule, and how to use a rotation chart for flexible grouping.

But not just any kind of grouping works well. Grouping by ability, which divides students for instruction based on their perceived capabilities for learning (low group, average group, high group) has serious academic and social effects for students who are not in the top group (Hiebert, 1983; Lucas, 1999; Callahan, 2005). Futrell and Gomez (2008) make the point that, "We cannot ignore the fact that for more than five decades, ability grouping has resulted in separation of students by race, ethnicity, and socioeconomic status. Many studies have confirmed that minority and low-income students of all ability levels are overrepresented in the lower tracks and underrepresented in the higher tracks" (p. 76). English learners, who learn from exposure to good language models, are often shut out of the groups with rich academic learning opportunities.

A study of high school English learners revealed that the group—or track—students were in was as strong a predictor of academic achievement as was language proficiency (Callahan, 2005). So attaining English proficiency, while important, is not the only answer if students are shut out of classes with rigorous content-area coverage with its associated discourse and academic learning opportunities. When working with low-achieving groups, teachers have been found to talk more, use more structure, ask lower-level questions, cover less material, spend more time on skills and drills, provide fewer opportunities for leadership and independent research, encourage more oral than silent reading, teach less vocabulary, and allow less wait time during questioning; in addition, they spent twice as much time on behavior and management issues (Oakes, 1985; Vogt, 1989).

In many schools, it has become common practice to group English learners with low-achieving students regardless of their academic ability and performance. However, all students, including ELs, benefit from instruction that frequently includes a variety of grouping configurations. Whole-class groups are beneficial for introducing new information and concepts, modeling processes, and review. Flexible small groups promote the development of multiple perspectives and encourage collaboration. Partnering encourages success because it provides practice opportunities, scaffolding, and assistance for classmates (Flood, Lapp, Flood, & Nagel, 1992; Nagel, 2001; Tompkins, 2006).

Effective SIOP® classes are characterized by a variety of grouping structures, including individual work, partners, triads, small groups of four or five, cooperative learning groups, and whole group. Groups also vary because they may be homogeneous or heterogeneous by gender, language proficiency, language background, and/or ability. There are times that it may be most effective to have students grouped by language-proficiency level. For example, if a teacher's goal is for students at beginning levels of English proficiency to practice using a particular language structure within the context of a social studies lesson, such as present progressive (*-ing* form), then it may be useful to have those students grouped together for that lesson. Likewise, when developing the skills of students with low levels of literacy, it makes sense to have those with similar ability grouped together for a particular lesson. Use of flexible instructional groups in high school is more challenging but essential for accommodating the various academic and linguistic levels of students. Assigning all ELs to the same group regularly is *not* good practice, especially when a bilingual aide teaches them almost exclusively. In SIOP® classes, ELs are given the same access to the curriculum and the teacher's expertise as native English-speaking students.

Using a variety of grouping configurations also facilitates learning in a number of ways. The variety of groups helps to maintain student interest because it is difficult for some students to stay focused when the teacher relies almost exclusively on whole-group instruction or having children work individually. Moving from whole group to cooperative learning groups or partners adds variety to the learning situation and increases student involvement in the learning process.

Another benefit of grouping is that it provides much-needed movement for learners. When students are active, their brains are provided with the oxygen-rich blood needed for highest performance. Movement may be especially important for learners with special needs (Jensen, 2005).

It is recommended that at least two different grouping structures be used during a lesson, depending on the activity and objectives of the lesson.

SIOP® FEATURE 18: Sufficient Wait Time for Student Responses Consistently Provided

Wait time is the length of time between utterances during an interaction. In classroom settings, it refers to the length of time that teachers wait for students to respond before interrupting, answering a question themselves, or calling on someone else to participate. Wait time varies by culture; it is appropriate in some cultures to let seconds, even minutes, lag between utterances, while in other cultures utterances can even overlap one another. In U.S. classrooms, the average length of wait time is clearly *not* sufficient. Imagine the impact of wait time on ELs who are processing ideas in a new language and need additional time to formulate the phrasings of their thoughts. Research supports the idea of wait time and has found it to increase student discourse and more student-to-student interaction (Honea, 1982; Swift & Gooding, 1983; Tobin, 1987).

Effective SIOP® teachers consciously allow students to express their thoughts fully, without interruption. Many teachers in U.S. schools are uncomfortable with the silence that follows their questions or comments, and they immediately fill the void by talking themselves. This situation may be especially pertinent in SIOP® classes where ELs need extra time to process questions in English, think of an answer in their second language, and then formulate their responses in English. Although teachers may be tempted to fill the silence, ELs benefit from a patient approach to classroom participation, in which teachers wait for students to complete their verbal contributions.

While effective SIOP® teachers provide sufficient wait time for ELs, they also work to find a balance between wait time and moving a lesson along. Some adolescents may become impatient if the pace of the class lags. One strategy for accommodating impatient students is to have them write down their responses while waiting, and then they can check their answers against the final answer.

ACTIVITY Another way to help ELs is to allow the techniques made popular by a television show: "50-50" and "phone a friend." Students who are unsure of an answer or are unable to articulate it well might ask to choose between two possible responses provided by the teacher (50-50) or ask a classmate for help (phone a friend). However, to ensure practice with the language, the original student must give "the final answer" to the teacher.

SIOP® FEATURE 19:
Ample Opportunity for Students to Clarify Key Concepts in L1

Best practice indicates that English learners benefit from opportunities to clarify concepts in their first language (L1). In fact, the National Literacy Panel on Language Minority Children and Youth found that academic skills such as reading taught in the first language transfer to the second language (August & Shanahan, 2006). Although SIOP® instruction involves teaching subject-matter material in English, students are given the opportunity to have a concept or assignment explained in their L1 as needed. Significant controversy surrounds the use of L1 for instructional purposes, but we believe that clarification of key concepts in students' L1 by a bilingual instructional aide, peer, or through the use of materials written in the students' L1 provides an important support for the academic learning of those students who are not yet fully proficient in English.

This feature on the SIOP® may have NA circled as a score because not all SIOP® classes need to use students' L1 to clarify concepts for them (especially for advanced ELs).

However, with websites offering word translation capabilities, and the availability of bilingual dictionaries in book and computer program formats, all SIOP® classrooms should have resources in the students' native languages.

The Lesson

UNIT: Economics (Twelfth Grade)

The twelfth grade teachers in this chapter, Mr. Griffin, Mrs. Moore, and Mr. Nakai, work in a suburban high school that has a 24 percent EL population. Their classes have an even distribution of English learners, each with approximately 10 percent ELs. Most of those students are at the intermediate level of English proficiency and still benefit from having teachers use SIOP® techniques to increase their understanding of lessons.

Economics is a course requirement for high school graduation, and it also meets college admissions requirements. Therefore all teachers use a standard course outline that reflects state content standards. The lessons described in the scenarios that follow are part of a unit on Labor Unions. The teachers each have their own methods for making the material accessible for students. (For more examples of lesson and unit plans in history/social studies, see Short, Vogt, & Echevarria, in press.)

Teaching Scenarios

Mr. Griffin

Mr. Griffin likes to begin class with a question on the board that students have to complete to settle them down. He gives students five minutes to complete their writing, and students receive 10 points for the correct answer. Since he is considered a strict teacher, students typically come in and start working immediately. The question for the day was: When was the American Federation of Labor founded and why? The history of the AFL-CIO was covered the previous day and the students' homework assignment was to read the chapter on labor unions. Most students began writing, but some were looking around to see what page in the text contained the information.

After five minutes, Mr. Griffin told students to pass their papers to the front of the class and he picked them up from the person at the front of each row. Calling for volunteers, Mr. Griffin selected a student to answer the question. Few hands went up to volunteer and Mr. Griffin reminded the class to do their homework so that they would be prepared for the daily question. He pointed to a sign on the bulletin board: "Doing homework is YOUR responsibility. You're not in elementary school and I'm not a babysitter—take responsibility for your grade and your graduation."

Mr. Griffin asked students to please open their textbook and he began his lecture on labor union activities, reminding students to take notes. As he spoke about a term, such as strike, open shop, closed shop, or Right-to-Work law, he wrote it on the board. As he explained each term, he paused to ask if there were any questions. Occasionally a student would ask a question and Mr. Griffin patiently answered, asking if everyone understood. When the period was almost over, he reminded students to place their notes in their Economics binder and review them along with the pages in the textbook they were assigned for homework. He mentioned that at the conclusion of the unit, they would watch a movie about labor unions called *Norma Rae*.

On the SIOP® form in Figure 6.4, rate Mr. Griffin's lesson on each of the interaction features.

Mrs. Moore

The previous day the class learned about labor unions, including the AFL-CIO. Then they watched the first half of the movie, *Norma Rae*.

FIGURE 6.4 *Interaction Component of the SIOP® Model: Mr. Griffin's Lesson*

4	3	2	1	0	NA
16. Frequent opportunities for **interaction** and discussion between teacher/student and among students, which encourage elaborated responses about lesson concepts		**Interaction** mostly teacher-dominated with some opportunities for students to talk about or question lesson concepts		**Interaction** teacher-dominated with no opportunities for students to discuss lesson concepts	
4	3	2	1	0	NA
17. **Grouping configurations** support language and content objectives of the lesson		**Grouping configurations** unevenly support the language and content objectives		**Grouping configurations** do not support the language and content objectives	
4	3	2	1	0	NA
18. Sufficient **wait time for student responses** consistently provided		Sufficient **wait time for student responses** occasionally provided		Sufficient **wait time for student responses** not provided	
4	3	2	1	0	NA
19. Ample opportunities for students to **clarify key concepts in L1** as needed with aide, peer, or L1 text		Some opportunities for students to **clarify key concepts in L1**		No opportunities for students to **clarify key concepts in L1**	

Today, as was her usual practice, Mrs. Moore started class by reviewing homework. Students had completed a matching worksheet about the history of the AFL-CIO. Mrs. Moore then told the class they were going to finish watching the movie about labor unions. At the conclusion of the movie, Mrs. Moore divided the class in half and told them that they were going to debate the pros and cons of labor unions. She gave each side some time to discuss its position and to prepare arguments. Many of the students started talking about the assignment, but the groups were large and quite a few students were left out of the discussion. Some passively listened while others put their heads down on their desks. Mrs. Moore circulated among the groups and encouraged all students to participate. To the off-task students she made comments such as, "Come on, Minerva, join in the discussion. Why do you think unions are a good idea?" With some students this approach worked and with others it didn't. In general, Mrs. Moore didn't wait for an answer; instead, she answered her own question in an attempt to help the student and move the lesson along.

After the students on each side had prepared their arguments, the class debated the topic. Only four or five students from each side defended their positions, and the others listened. A couple of times points that students made were slightly inaccurate, so Mrs. Moore used the opportunity to clarify facts about labor unions. The debate continued until the bell rang.

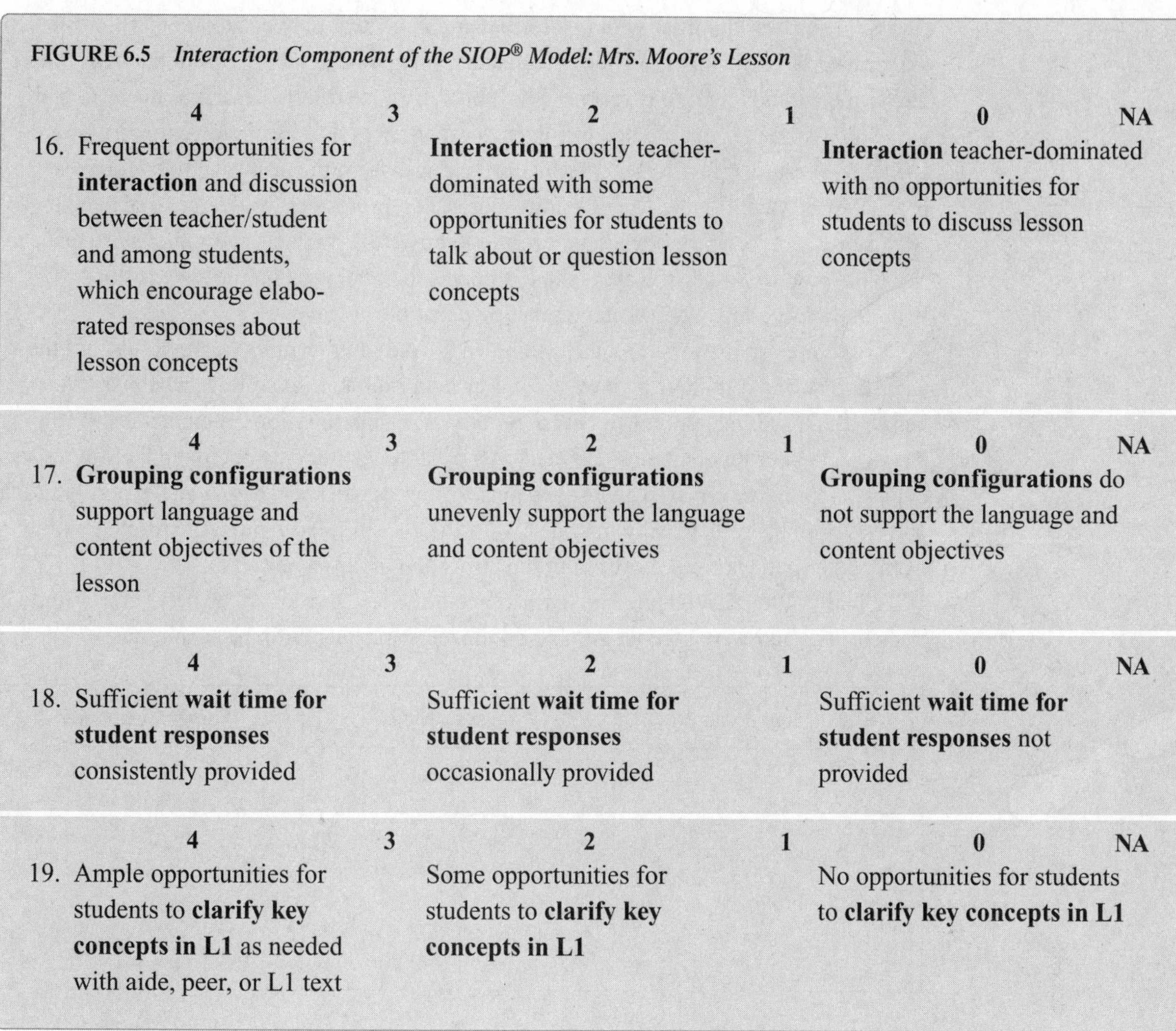

FIGURE 6.5 *Interaction Component of the SIOP® Model: Mrs. Moore's Lesson*

4	3	2	1	0	NA
16. Frequent opportunities for **interaction** and discussion between teacher/student and among students, which encourage elaborated responses about lesson concepts		**Interaction** mostly teacher-dominated with some opportunities for students to talk about or question lesson concepts		**Interaction** teacher-dominated with no opportunities for students to discuss lesson concepts	
4	**3**	**2**	**1**	**0**	**NA**
17. **Grouping configurations** support language and content objectives of the lesson		**Grouping configurations** unevenly support the language and content objectives		**Grouping configurations** do not support the language and content objectives	
4	**3**	**2**	**1**	**0**	**NA**
18. Sufficient **wait time for student responses** consistently provided		Sufficient **wait time for student responses** occasionally provided		Sufficient **wait time for student responses** not provided	
4	**3**	**2**	**1**	**0**	**NA**
19. Ample opportunities for students to **clarify key concepts in L1** as needed with aide, peer, or L1 text		Some opportunities for students to **clarify key concepts in L1**		No opportunities for students to **clarify key concepts in L1**	

On the SIOP® form in Figure 6.5, rate Mrs. Moore on each of the interaction features.

Mr. Nakai

When the bell sounded, Mr. Nakai pointed to the board where his PowerPoint presentation was reflected. As was their routine, the class read together the content and language objectives to set the purpose for the lesson. The content objective was: Students will define labor union terms: open shop, closed shop, primary boycott, secondary boycott, strike, mediation, collective bargaining, and arbitration. The language objective was: With a partner, students will discuss and categorize labor union activities.

Mr. Nakai began by reviewing the previous day's lesson on the AFL-CIO. As he did, he pointed to the timeline summarizing events in the history of the AFL-CIO that students had completed on chart paper. As students looked at the chart, he asked what event was associated with a particular date. After this review, he told the class that they had already learned a little about some of the terms they would focus on in the lesson and that each of the pods (four desks together) would become an "expert" on one term and teach the others. He assigned each pod a term, such as arbitration.

Students were familiar with this format and knew that they needed to take notes on all the terms. Mr. Nakai showed slides that had a term and page number from the book where the term could be found (e.g., primary boycott p. 79). He briefly described the term and gave some examples that related to student's experiences. For example, a primary boycott is when protestors refuse to buy products or services from the primary provider of that product or service. If Nike were having labor issues, protestors would quit shopping at Nike stores. A secondary boycott is refusing to buy Nike products at another store that carries Nike products. As Mr. Nakai talked, students took notes using the slide to copy the term and wrote a few words to remember the example he gave.

Next, the groups were given ten minutes to find their term in the book, discuss the term, and define it in their own words and give an example (to solidify what Mr. Nakai had said). During this time, Mr. Nakai circulated around the room, monitoring student work and answering questions. He made it a point to let students complete their thoughts before jumping in to answer their questions. At the signal, the designated "expert" in each pod stayed in his or her seat while the rest of the class rotated around the room, going from pod to pod learning more about the terms and taking notes.

Finally, after all students had learned about the terms from an "expert," they returned to their pods and were given a graphic organizer worksheet with three columns:

Work Environment	Protest Activities	Problem Resolution

Students worked together in pairs and discussed under which category each of the terms belonged. Each student had a copy of the GO to complete, ensuring participation by all.

With ten minutes left in class, Mr. Nakai told the students that for homework, they were to write a definition of each term on the GO, and he showed a sample of a completed worksheet:

Work Environment	Protest Activities	Problem Resolution
Open Shop: Employees of an "open shop" may choose to join the local union or not join the union. Union membership is NOT required. **Closed Shop:** If an employee accepts a position within a "closed shop," it is required that the employee be a member of the union.	**Primary Boycott:** This is when protestors, or union members, refuse to buy products or services directly from a company that is having issues with its employees (union issues). They stop buying from the PRIMARY provider of that product or service.	**Mediation:** When a neutral (unbiased) third party comes in to help resolve disputes between employers and the union (employees). The recommendations made are merely strong suggestions, but do not need to be followed.

FIGURE 6.6 *Interaction Component of the SIOP® Model: Mr. Nakai's Lesson*

4	3	2	1	0	NA
16. Frequent opportunities for **interaction** and discussion between teacher/student and among students, which encourage elaborated responses about lesson concepts		**Interaction** mostly teacher-dominated with some opportunities for students to talk about or question lesson concepts		**Interaction** teacher-dominated with no opportunities for students to discuss lesson concepts	
4	**3**	**2**	**1**	**0**	**NA**
17. **Grouping configurations** support language and content objectives of the lesson		**Grouping configurations** unevenly support the language and content objectives		**Grouping configurations** do not support the language and content objectives	
4	**3**	**2**	**1**	**0**	**NA**
18. Sufficient **wait time for student responses** consistently provided		Sufficient **wait time for student responses** occasionally provided		Sufficient **wait time for student responses** never provided	
4	**3**	**2**	**1**	**0**	**NA**
19. Ample opportunities for students to **clarify key concepts in L1** as needed with aide, peer, or L1 text		Some opportunity for students to **clarify key concepts in L1**		No opportunity for students to **clarify key concepts in L1**	

He then told the class that they would use the information the following day as they watched the movie, *Norma Rae*. Mr. Nakai planned to give an outline of events in the movie, and students, based on what they had learned about labor unions, would critique the events by relating facts to the fictionalized story.

On the SIOP® form in Figure 6.6, rate Mr. Nakai on each of the Interaction features.

Discussion of Lessons

16. *Frequent Opportunities for Interaction and Discussion between Teacher/Students and among Students*

Mr. Griffin: 0

Mrs. Moore: 2

Mr. Nakai: 4

Mr. Griffin represents a "traditional" style of teaching that is characterized as a transmission of knowledge from teacher to student. His lecture approach didn't allow for student questions, even though that was his intent. He frequently asked if anyone had questions, but the class environment precluded students from speaking up, and he interpreted this as the students not needing clarification or additional instruction. Also problematic was reliance on students to gain information independently by reading dense text for homework. Few students were able to answer the "daily question" because (1) the new, challenging information had not been scaffolded for them and (2) it was nearly impossible to know what fact he wanted students to remember from the seven pages of difficult text he assigned.

Mrs. Moore attempted to involve students in an interactive lesson by planning a debate, but it was less successful than she had hoped. First, the groups were too large for quality discussion. With only some of the students participating, the others were left out, especially less confident students and English learners. Second, there was no guided discussion about the ideas presented in the movie; students had some misconceptions or misinformation about labor unions and there wasn't a phase of the lesson for instruction prior to presenting points in the debate. Further, the activity wasn't structured enough for students. A worksheet to guide the process would have helped—such as a graphic organizer with five bullet points that students would complete with a partner, then share with the group, selecting the strongest points to use in the debate. Another option for structure would have been to assign students roles to ensure their participation. Because the activity lacked intentional planning, the lesson ended up being mostly teacher-dominated with some opportunity for interaction.

Mr. Nakai provided lots of opportunities for students to discuss the information, make decisions about it (e.g., how to define terms in their own words, what example best represented the terms), and think about it using higher levels of cognition such as discussing and categorizing the terms. There was plenty of interaction with peers and with the teacher. The interactive nature of the class encouraged students to ask questions and seek clarification.

17. *Grouping Configurations Support Language and Content Objectives of the Lesson*

Mr. Griffin: 0

Mrs. Moore: 1

Mr. Nakai: 4

The type of whole-class instruction that Mr. Griffin used doesn't provide opportunities for teachers to address specific instructional needs of students, nor does it allow for students to collaborate, negotiate, discuss, or engage in inquiry with peers about what they learned in the lesson. Mrs. Moore moved from the whole class to groups, but the two large groups were ineffective in supporting the lesson's objectives. Mr. Nakai's classroom arrangement facilitated interaction as students in pods easily formed groups of two or four. In addition, the "expert" activity allowed for students to experience multiple groups. In his lesson, Mr. Nakai's students went from whole class to small groups to partners.

Perhaps most importantly, Mr. Nakai's lesson covered the same material as Mr. Griffin's in the same amount of time, but his students undoubtedly learned the material at a deeper level and retained it better than those students in Mr. Griffin's class.

18. *Sufficient Wait Time for Student Responses Consistently Provided*

Mr. Griffin: 2

Mrs. Moore: 0

Mr. Nakai: 4

Mr. Griffin enjoys teaching and wants students to ask and answer questions. When they did so during this lesson, he patiently waited for their responses. However, his style didn't allow time for students to formulate questions before he moved on to his next point. Mrs. Moore wasn't aware of the importance of wait time and thought that if she answered for the students, it helped maintain the pace of the lesson. Mr. Nakai consistently provided wait time for students.

19. *Ample Opportunities for students to Clarify Key Concepts in L1*

Mr. Griffin: 0

Mrs. Moore: 0

Mr. Nakai: 4

Since there was virtually no peer interaction and Mr. Griffin didn't speak another language, there wasn't opportunity for English learners to talk with one another in their first language to discuss, clarify, or apply information. The same was true for Mrs. Moore's lesson. The lack of structure in the debate activity precluded participation of ELs in either language. They sat passively while the more confident students did all the talking. In Mr. Nakai's class, the format of the lesson allowed for use of L1 if needed. This particular lesson was made comprehensible with a high level of SIOP® features, but if some students needed information or clarification from a peer in L1, there was opportunity to do so.

Summary

SIOP® teachers create ample opportunities for English learners to practice using academic English, both among themselves and with teachers. Incorporating a number of grouping configurations into lessons often facilitates using English in ways that support the lessons' objectives.

The evidence is clear that for most secondary teachers, it is challenging to balance the interchange between themselves and their students. Effective SIOP® teachers plan for and incorporate structured opportunities for students to use English in a variety of ways.

Discussion Questions

1. Think of a content concept that you might be teaching. Describe three different grouping configurations that could be used for teaching and learning this concept. How would you organize the members of each group? How would you monitor student learning? What would you want students to do while working in their groups? How would the grouping configurations facilitate learning for ELs?
2. Either videotape your own classroom while you're teaching a lesson or observe another teacher's classroom for a 15-minute segment. Estimate the proportion of teacher talk and student talk. Given the ratio of teacher–student talk, what are some possible ramifications for English learners in the class?
3. Adolescent English learners are often reticent to contribute to class discussions. An important role for an SIOP® teacher is to encourage ELs to participate in nonthreatening ways. What are some specific techniques you can use to encourage students to elaborate on their responses and express their thoughts fully? What can you do to ensure sufficient wait time for students to formulate and express their thoughts?
4. Using the SIOP® lesson you have been developing, add activities and grouping configurations to enhance interaction.

chapter 7

Practice & Application

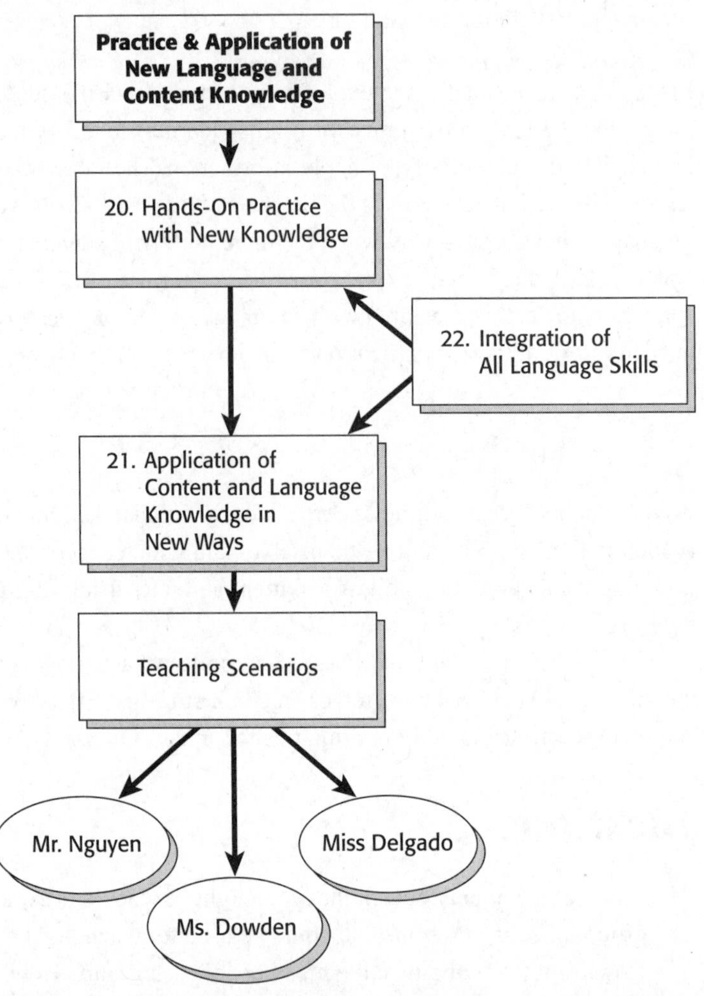

Objectives

After reading, discussing, and engaging in activities related to this chapter, you will be able to meet the following content and language objectives.

Content Objectives

Identify a variety of ways for students to enhance their learning through hands-on practice.

Create application activities that extend the learning in new ways and relate to language or content objectives.

Language Objectives

Design activities that integrate different language skills as students practice new content knowledge.

Discuss the importance of linking practice and application activities to specific lesson objectives.

One common memory that most adults share is of learning to ride an adult bike. Even after riding smaller bicycles with training wheels, most of us were unprepared for the balancing act required for us not to fall down when riding a regular bike. If you had an older brother or sister who talked you through the process, showed you how to balance, and perhaps even held on to the bike while you were steadying yourself, your independent practice time with the big bike was probably enhanced. Talking about the experience, listening to someone else describe it, observing other riders, and then practicing for yourself all worked together to turn you into a bicycle rider. That feeling of accomplishment, of mastering something new through practice and applying it to a bigger bike, or perhaps a motorcycle in later years, is a special feeling that most of us have experienced as learners.

Background

Up to this point in a SIOP® lesson, a teacher has introduced content and language objectives, built background or activated prior knowledge, introduced key vocabulary, selected a learning strategy and higher-order questions for students to focus on, developed a scaffolding approach for teaching the new information, and planned for student interaction. In the Practice & Application component, the teacher gives the students a chance to practice with the new material, and, with careful teacher oversight, demonstrate how well they are learning it. In the same lesson or a subsequent one, the teacher plans a task so students

apply this new knowledge in new ways. It is well established that practice and application helps one master a skill (Fisher & Frey, 2008; Jensen, 2005; Marzano, Pickering, & Pollock, 2001). For SIOP® instruction, however, both the practice and application tasks should also aim for practice of all four language skills: reading, writing, listening, and speaking.

For English learners, this stage of a SIOP® lesson is very important, especially for academic language development. As Saville-Troike (1984) pointed out, both language and academic learning occur through language use in the classroom. Second language acquisition research has shown repeatedly that for an individual to develop a high level of proficiency in a new language, he or she must have opportunities not only for comprehensible input (Krashen, 1985) but also targeted output (Swain, 1985), namely, oral and written practice. In the chapter on oral language development in the recent research synthesis conducted by CREDE researchers (discussed in Chapter 1), Saunders and O'Brien (2006) conclude "ELLs are most likely to use the language used to deliver instruction in their interactions with peers and teachers" (p. 41). They further explain that

> . . . while use and exposure are necessary conditions, they may not be sufficient conditions, especially when it comes to achieving higher levels of proficiency involving more academic uses of language. The content and quality of L2 exposure and use are probably of equal, if not greater, importance than L2 exposure and use per se (p. 41).

What this says to us as SIOP® teachers is that we need to carefully choose the activities we include in our lessons. The activities must support the students' progress in meeting or mastering the content and language objectives. If a language objective calls for ninth-grade students to argue a point of view, for example, then an activity might have the students write a letter to the editor of a school or local newspaper on the content topic of a lesson (or a related one for application), such as keeping or removing vending machines from the school for a health unit. If the class includes students with multiple proficiency levels, the Practice & Application component of the SIOP® Model is the ideal place to differentiate instruction. In the lesson we are developing here, the teacher might facilitate a whole-class brainstorming of pros and cons for the argument. Then some advanced-level students might write individual letters, intermediate-level students might write in pairs or triads, and beginners might work with the teacher to prepare a group letter.

Indeed, it is within this component that teachers can incorporate activities that explore multiple intelligences (Gardner, 1993), project-based learning, or other methods for meeting the different language needs of students (Vogt & Echevarria, 2008). As teachers plan these practice and application activities, they should consider the structure of the task and degree of difficulty for the resulting product, the grouping configurations, the type of feedback that will be provided so it is geared to proficiency level, and the expectations for student achievement (Vogt, 2000). As Tomlinson (2005) explains, instruction may be differentiated in terms of the content material, the learning process (e.g., aural versus kinesthetic), or the task and product. In *Implementing the SIOP® Model Through Effective Professional Development and Coaching* (Echevarria, Short, & Vogt, 2008, pp. 152–161), we provide guidance on implementing differentiated instruction in SIOP® classrooms.

To see an example of practical application of SIOP® features, please view the corresponding video clip (Chapter 7, Module 1) on the accompanying CD.

In this chapter, we discuss how sheltered teachers provide English learners (ELs) with the types of hands-on experiences, guidance, and practice that can lead to mastery of content knowledge and higher levels of language proficiency. The teaching vignettes demonstrate how three high school general biology teachers, all of whom have large numbers of ELs in their classes, designed biology lessons on ecosystems.

SIOP® FEATURE 20: Hands-On Materials and/or Manipulatives Provided for Students to Practice Using New Content Knowledge

As previously mentioned, riding a bike is usually preceded by practicing with training wheels and working with a more experienced bike rider. Obviously, the more practice one has on the bike, the more likely one is to become a good bike rider. Now think about learning to play a musical instrument.

Some years ago, an entrepreneur decided to market a piano-teaching course that included a cardboard sheet printed with piano keys. Students were supposed to practice the piano on the paper keyboard by following the directions printed in the course manual. The black-and-white keys on the keyboard were printed, and dotted lines represented where students were supposed to place their fingers during practice sessions. It was little surprise that the paper keyboards didn't catch on, even though the course manual clearly described in incremental steps how to play the piano, because even with hours of practice on the paper keyboard, students were still unable to play the piano well. In this case, it wasn't just the *practice* that was important. Without hearing the sounds during practice, learning to play the piano was an artificial and nearly impossible task.

When learning to ride a bicycle, play the piano, or write a research report, students have a greater chance of mastering content concepts and skills when they are given multiple opportunities to practice in relevant, meaningful ways. When this practice includes "hands-on" experiences like using manipulatives, practice sessions are enhanced. Madeline Hunter (1982), a renowned expert in teaching methods, coined the term "guided practice" to describe the process of the teacher leading the student through practice sessions prior to independent application. She suggested that we keep the following four questions (and their answers) in mind as we plan lessons involving hands-on practice for students (pp. 65–68):

1. How much material should be practiced at one time? *Answer:* A short meaningful amount. Always use meaning to divide your content into parts.
2. How long in time should a practice period be? *Answer:* A short time so the student exerts intense effort and has intent to learn.
3. How often should students practice? *Answer:* New learning, massed practice. Older learning, distributed practice. [Hunter explains that massed practice means several practice periods scheduled close together. Distributed practice means spacing practice periods farther and farther apart, such as when we review previously learned material.]
4. How will students know how well they have done? *Answer:* Give specific knowledge of results (i.e., specific feedback).

Although all students benefit from guided practice as they advance to independent work, English learners make more rapid progress in mastering content objectives when they are provided with multiple opportunities to practice with hands-on materials and/or manipulatives. These may be organized, created, counted, classified, stacked, experimented with, observed, rearranged, dismantled, and so forth. We would also include kinesthetic activities in a broad definition of this feature. Manipulating learning materials is important for ELs because it helps them connect abstract concepts with concrete experiences. Furthermore, manipulatives and other hands-on materials reduce the language load for students. Students with beginning proficiency in English, for instance, can still participate and demonstrate what they are learning.

Obviously, the type of manipulative employed for practice depends on the subject being taught. For example, in a tenth-grade geometry class in which students are learning how to solve proofs, content objectives might justify paper-and-pencil practice. However, if it is possible to incorporate hands-on practice with manipulatives, such as geoboards, compasses, and rulers, students' learning will be enhanced. Fortunately, publishers are making more manipulatives and other supplementary materials available for students in secondary schools. Some have been designed for specific content areas, such as manipulatives and foldables for math, science, and history (e.g., Zike, 2000a, 2000b, 2003, 2004).

ACTIVITY For a kinesthetic example, instead of having students fill out a worksheet on a timeline about Ancient China, they could form a physical timeline. Some students might have a card displaying a date; others might have one displaying an event. The students would organize themselves, first pairing the dates and events, and then forming the human timeline in the front of the room.

ACTIVITY In *99 Ideas and Activities for Teaching English Learners with the SIOP® Model* (Vogt & Echevarria, 2008), the "Bingo" (p. 130) and the "Piece O' Pizza" (p. 148) activities offer other examples where students create the hands-on materials as part of their practice or application time. Students build a bingo chart with teacher guidance and then play the game. Individual students or small groups create a pizza slice with information that differs from their peers. They put their slices together to address the main points of a key topic.

Being told how to ride a bike or play the piano, reading about how to do so, or watching a DVD of someone else engaged in bike riding or piano playing is much different from riding down the sidewalk or listening to musical sounds you have produced yourself. Whenever possible and appropriate, use hands-on materials for practice.

SIOP® FEATURE 21: Activities Provided for Students to Apply Content and Language Knowledge

Think again about the relationship between actually riding a bicycle and just watching someone else ride it, or about actually playing a piano and just reading step-by-step piano-playing instructions. As Hunter (1982) said:

> The difference between knowing how something should be done and being able to do it is the quantum leap in learning . . . new learning is like wet cement, it can be

easily damaged. A mistake at the beginning of learning can have long-lasting consequences that are hard to eradicate (p. 71).

We all recall our own learning experiences in elementary, middle, and high school, and the university. For many of us, the classes and courses we remember best are the ones in which we applied our new knowledge in meaningful ways. These may have included activities such as writing a diary entry from the perspective of a character in a novel, creating a semantic map illustrating the relationships among complex concepts, or completing comprehensive case studies on children we assessed and taught. These concrete experiences forced us to apply new information and concepts in a personally relevant way. We remember the times when we "got it," and we remember the times when we gave it our all but somehow still missed the point. Consider this as you do the activity below.

ACTIVITY Think about a college or graduate school course. What is one activity you remember well? What made it memorable? Did it involve different learning styles or senses? Now think about a recent lesson you taught or observed. Was there an activity that would be memorable for the students? If not, how could the activity have been more engaging and unforgettable?

For students acquiring a new language, the need to apply new information is critically important because discussing and "doing" make abstract concepts concrete. Application can occur in a number of ways, such as using graphic organizers to synthesize information, solving problems in cooperative learning groups, writing a journal, engaging in literature circles, or a variety of other meaningful activities (Peregoy & Boyle, 2005). Fisher and Frey (2008), in their model for gradual release of responsibility (by the teacher), argue that collaborative learning is an important bridging step between guided practice and independent work. They state that "collaborative learning should be a time for students to apply information in novel situations or to engage in a spiral review of previous knowledge" (p. 7). Mainly we must remember that we learn best by involving ourselves in relevant, meaningful application of what we are learning.

For English learners, application must also include opportunities for them to practice language knowledge in the classroom. Opportunities for oral interaction promote language development, and these include discussion, working with partners and small groups, and "reporting out" information orally and in writing. For example, it is appropriate, depending on students' language proficiency, to ask them to explain a process to a peer using a newly learned sentence structure. Activities such as describing the results of an experiment, specifying why a character reacted in a particular way, and justifying the steps for solving an algebraic equation all help ELs produce and practice new language and vocabulary while they are in a supportive environment.

Consider a middle school science class with mixed-proficiency ELs and native English speakers. To apply new vocabulary from the unit, the teacher might plan a scaffolded listening cloze dictation. The native English speakers might record what the teacher says as a regular dictation. The ELs might have two different dictation forms with more or fewer words already written down. (See Figure 7.1.) All the students listen to the paragraph the teacher reads on Gregor Mendel and the study of genetics, all participate in the listening task, but the task format is slightly adjusted to the students' English abilities.

FIGURE 7.1 *Scaffolded Listening Cloze Dictation Forms*

More Proficient Students	Less Proficient Students
Fill in the blanks with the missing words while the teacher reads a passage aloud. You will hear the passage twice.	Fill in the blanks with the missing words while the teacher reads a passage aloud. You will hear the passage twice.
Gregor Mendel ________________ ________ from parent to ________. This ____________ is called ____________. Mendel used ______________ in his ________ experiments. ________________ always ________________ with the same form of a ____________. In one of his experiments, __________ ________________________. He put the ____________________ of tall pea plants on the ____________ ________ of the short pea plants. He discovered that ________________ ________________________.	Gregor Mendel studied how ________ are passed on from parent to ________. This passing on of traits is called ____________. Mendel used ____________ pea plants in his heredity experiments. ____________ plants always produce ____________ with the same form of a trait as the parent. In one of his experiments, he ________ ________________ pea plants. He put the pollen from the __________ of tall pea plants on the ____________ of the flowers of the short pea plants. He ________ that none of the ________ ____________________ were short.

SIOP® FEATURE 22: Activities Integrate All Language Skills

Reading, writing, listening, and speaking are complex, cognitive language processes that are interrelated and integrated. As we go about our daily lives, we move through the processes in a natural way, reading what we write; talking about what we've read; and listening to others talk about what they've read, written, and seen. Most young children become grammatically competent in their home language by age five, and their continuing language development relates primarily to vocabulary, more sophisticated grammar usage (e.g., embedding subordinate clauses), and functional as well as sociocultural applications of language (e.g., using different language registers according to their audience, and developing rhetorical styles) (Peregoy & Boyle, 2005; TESOL, 2006). Proficiency in reading and writing is achieved much later, and differences exist among individuals in levels of competence. Students in particular need to learn academic language for use in school settings (see Chapter 1 for a detailed discussion).

For English learners, students may achieve competence in written language earlier than oral language, and ELs do not need to be proficient speakers before they start to read and write (August & Shanahan, 2006a). In fact, the language processes—reading, writing, listening, and speaking—are mutually supportive. Although the relationships among the processes are complex, practice in any one promotes development in the others (Hinkel, 2006).

Effective sheltered teachers understand the need to create many opportunities for English learners to practice and use all four language processes in an integrated manner. Throughout the day, ELs benefit from varied experiences that incorporate reading, promote interactions with others, provide the chance to listen to peers' ideas, and encourage writing about what is being learned. Because students have different preferred learning styles, when teachers teach through different modalities and encourage students to practice and apply new knowledge through multiple language processes, they have a better chance of meeting students' needs and furthering both their language and content development.

We do want to clarify that although all identified language objectives in a lesson need to be practiced and applied as the lesson advances, not all language skills that are practiced need to be tied to an objective. In other words, a language objective represents a key skill, language structure, or strategy the teacher plans to teach explicitly and intends for students to learn. In a SIOP® lesson, the teacher teaches to this objective and assesses, formally or informally, how well students are meeting it. The objective may focus on one language domain, such as writing, but in the course of the lesson, students may have additional opportunities to read, speak, and listen. These should be carefully planned but need not be assessed in the same way an objective would be.

Teachers are sometimes unsure whether to correct ELs' language errors during practice time or not (Peregoy & Boyle, 2005). In general, consider students' stages of English language development when deciding. For beginning English speakers, errors may be developmental and reflect students' native language use (e.g., not remembering to add past tense inflected endings to English verbs). Other errors may deal with placement of adjectives, sentence structure, plurals, and so forth. If errors impede communication, you can gently correct them by restating the sentence in correct form. Otherwise, leave the errors alone. If you notice, however, that many students make the same error and it does not seem to be due to the language acquisition process, it is reasonable to plan a minilesson on the issue for a later day. This practice conforms to recommendations from second language acquisition research studies that offer evidence that "corrective feedback is important for learning grammar" (Ellis, 2006, p. 102).

For example, Meeli, who recently emigrated from Estonia, told her teacher, "My parents sends congratulations to you." She meant that her parents sent their greetings. In reply, Meeli's teacher responded, "Thank you. I think you mean 'greetings.' Please tell your parents I send them my greetings, too." Note that the confusion over the nouns, "congratulation" and "greetings" was corrected, but the teacher did not correct the form of the verb *send* because acquisition of these verb endings occurs later in the second language development process. What is most important is that you be sensitive to errors that confuse communication; these usually can be corrected in a natural and nonthreatening way.

The Lesson

The biology lessons below are drawn from a unit on ecosystems. (For more examples of lesson and unit plans for science, see Short, Vogt, & Echevarria, in press.)

UNIT: Ecosystems (Eleventh Grade)

The three eleventh-grade general biology classrooms described in the teaching vignettes in this chapter are located in a large urban high school. Approximately 65 percent of the students in the classes are English learners, and they are nearly all in the beginning and advanced-beginning stages of English language fluency. The other students in the classes are heterogeneously mixed.

The general biology standards for the eleventh grade require that teachers include the study of ecosystems, water and nutrient cycling, symbiosis, life cycles, and decomposition. Scientific processing

UNIT: Ecosystems (Eleventh Grade) *continued*

skills include making observations, recording data, forming hypotheses, making models, designing projects, and experimenting. For the scenarios described in this chapter, the teachers have designed an extended unit on *ecosystems* (ecological communities that, together with their environment, form a unit) and *symbiosis* (a close relationship between two or more species that may or may not benefit each other). The lessons extend over several days.

Teaching Scenarios

Mr. Nguyen

Mr. Nguyen approached the subject of ecosystems by asking students to read the textbook chapter with a partner. He then provided photographs, illustrations, and procedural steps for creating an ecosystem that was essentially a covered terrarium—a container for plants and small animals. The materials he used to build the ecosystem included a glass tank, a variety of small plants, some sand, small rocks, soil, a turtle, a horned toad, and mealworms. He poured a small amount of water into the system and put the terrarium under a soft sunlamp. He presented a brief lecture on how the various species within the ecosystem might support each other within it.

Mr. Nguyen then showed a video on a variety of ecosystems that exist on Earth. Students were given a study guide to use during the video that included two columns for structured note-taking. Over the next two weeks, each student was required to complete a standard lab observation report about the changes that occurred within the newly created ecosystem. Throughout, students were encouraged to work in groups on writing up their observations and findings, and the most vocal students were enthusiastic participants during the shared discussions.

On the SIOP® form in Figure 7.2, rate Mr. Nguyen's lesson on each of the Practice & Application features.

Ms. Dowden

Ms. Dowden decided that the best way for her students to understand and apply newly learned content about ecosystems was to have them read, discuss, write detailed observations, and create their own models of ecosystems. After reading and explaining the content and language objectives, she began the first lesson by introducing content vocabulary. Then students read the section of the biology textbook on ecosystems in small groups. After that, Ms. Dowden reviewed the key concepts by writing them on the board.

Because Ms. Dowden realized that many of the content concepts and key vocabulary in this unit were new and complex, she believed she could best meet everyone's needs, including ELs and English proficient students, by dividing the class into two groups. As older adolescents, her students were able to work independently, and most had experience with computers and the Internet, even though the amount of experience they had varied. Ms. Dowden directed students with higher levels of academic English proficiency to some library references and Internet websites related to science and biology. These students were instructed to read and research the topic of ecosystems and symbiosis and design a method for creating an

FIGURE 7.2 *Practice & Application Component of the SIOP® Model: Mr. Nguyen's Lesson*

	4	3	2	1	0	NA
20.	**Hands-on materials and/or manipulatives** provided for students to practice using new content knowledge		**Few hands-on materials and/or manipulatives** provided for students to practice using new content knowledge		**No hands-on materials and/or manipulatives** provided for students to practice using new content knowledge	
21.	Activities provided for students to **apply content and language knowledge** in the classroom		Activities provided for students to **apply either content or language knowledge** in the classroom		No activities provided for students to **apply content and language knowledge** in the classroom	

	4	3	2	1	0
22.	Activities integrate all **language skills** (i.e, reading, writing, listening, and speaking)		Activities integrate some **language skills**		Activities do not integrate **language skills**

ecosystem using a variety of inexpensive and accessible materials they could find around their homes. Ms. Dowden pledged her assistance in helping them with the research and the project, but she arranged for them to work together as partners and in groups to create sustainable ecosystems. She explained how students were to write and submit their plans including materials, timeline, and so forth. Once they created their ecosystems, they were to monitor the changes that occurred within them, and eventually, they would include their findings on the districtwide general biology website.

While a third of the students were independently researching the library and the Internet, Ms. Dowden worked with the English learners and a few other students. She introduced them to a website on the classroom computer that included information about ecosystems. She had printed a few pages from the website and together students read these, comparing the information to what they learned in their textbooks. Ms. Dowden then introduced a project in which students were to create their own "ecocolumns"—stacked ecosystems made from plastic bottles (*Bottle Biology,* 1993). Simplified directions in the form of an illustrated sequence map provided steps for creating the ecocolumns along with a list of materials that were needed. The ELs volunteered to bring materials from home, including soil, water, plants, compost, spiders, fruit flies, snails, and two large plastic soda bottles for each ecocolumn.

The following day, while Ms. Dowden modeled the process, the ELs began creating their own ecocolumns from the soda bottles that were each cut into three sections. Chambers were created using the sections of the plastic bottles, and an aquarium with water and rocks was prepared for the bottom section of the ecocolumn. Above it was a soil or decomposition unit, and above that was a plant or animal habitat. The top of the system included air holes and a precipitation funnel. Ms. Dowden modeled the creation of the ecocolumns, demonstrating each step of the process.

The students then created their own ecosystems; as they were doing so, Ms. Dowden encouraged them to discuss what was working and what wasn't, and why. Over the next two weeks, all students were expected to observe their ecosystems, including root and soil changes and the effects of light and water. Ms. Dowden provided models of data-recording sheets that showed what students might be observing and what they should record on the overhead. All students, including those who independently created their ecosystems, used the models as guides. The ELs used specially designed data sheets on which they recorded their data in a simplified format.

The students who designed their own ecosystems completed a "bioessay" to explain the effects of different substances on seed germination and plant development (*Bottle Biology,* 1993, p. 79). The ELs were encouraged to list the changes that occurred as a result of competition among the species in their ecosystems; that is, "Did one species do better than another, and if so, how do you know? Which appeared to be symbiotic? How do you know?" The ELs were also encouraged to contribute their findings to the general biology website.

Throughout this unit, Ms. Dowden emphasized to all students that there was no right or wrong way to build the ecosystem or the ecocolumn. Change was considered to be a natural part of the experience, and students were encouraged to work together to determine what happened with their own systems and why.

On the SIOP® form in Figure 7.3, rate Ms. Dowden's lesson on each of the Practice & Application features.

FIGURE 7.3 *Practice & Application Component of the SIOP® Model: Ms. Dowden's Lesson*

4	3	2	1	0	NA
20. **Hands-on materials and/or manipulatives** provided for students to practice using new content knowledge		**Few hands-on materials and/or manipulatives** provided for students to practice using new content knowledge		**No hands-on materials and/or manipulatives** provided for students to practice using new content knowledge	
4	**3**	**2**	**1**	**0**	**NA**
21. Activities provided for students to **apply content and language knowledge** in the classroom		Activities provided for students to **apply either content or language knowledge** in the classroom		No activities provided for students to **apply content and language knowledge** in the classroom	
4	**3**	**2**	**1**	**0**	
22. Activities integrate all **language skills** (i.e, reading, writing, listening, and speaking)		Activities integrate some **language skills**		Activities do not integrate **language skills**	

FIGURE 7.4 *Practice & Application Component of the SIOP® Model: Miss Delgado's Lesson*

	4	3	2	1	0	NA
20.	**Hands-on materials and/or manipulatives** provided for students to practice using new content knowledge		**Few hands-on materials and/or manipulatives** provided for students to practice using new content knowledge		**No hands-on materials and/or manipulatives** provided for students to practice using new content knowledge	
	4	3	2	1	0	NA
21.	Activities provided for students to **apply content and language knowledge** in the classroom		Activities provided for students to **apply either content or language knowledge** in the classroom		No activities provided for students to **apply content and language knowledge** in the classroom	
	4	3	2	1	0	
22.	Activities integrate all **language skills** (i.e, reading, writing, listening, and speaking)		Activities integrate some **language skills**		Activities do not integrate **language skills**	

Miss Delgado

Miss Delgado taught the lessons on ecosystems by having students work as partners to read the textbook chapter. She pointed out key vocabulary and orally reinforced the key concepts. To illustrate an ecosystem, she drew a layered ecosystem on the blackboard that included decaying plant matter, insects, and small animals. Students were directed to copy her illustration from the board and to label the various species within the ecosystem. Miss Delgado then showed a video on ecosystems and symbiosis. Each student was required to write a paragraph explaining how various species on the earth support and contribute to each other's sustenance and viability.

On the SIOP® form in Figure 7.4, rate Miss Delgado's lesson on each of the Practice & Application features.

Discussion of Lessons

Mr. Nguyen, Ms. Dowden, and Miss Delgado differed substantially in how they taught their units on ecosystems. As you read our ratings, compare them to your own and those of colleagues.

20. *Hands-On Materials and/or Manipulatives Provided for Students to Practice Using New Content Knowledge*

Mr. Nguyen: 2

Ms. Dowden: 4

Miss Delgado: 1

Mr. Nguyen's lesson received a "2" for Hands-On Manipulatives and Practice. Although he modeled the creation of an ecosystem (the covered terrarium), the students did not have hands-on practice. He incorporated a "one-size-fits-all" approach by having everyone do the same task. Because native English speakers represented one-third of his class and the rest of the students were in the beginning to advanced-beginning stages of English proficiency, the most vocal and competent English speakers assumed primary responsibility for monitoring the changes in the ecosystem (terrarium). Therefore, ELs may have concluded the unit with few opportunities to participate in a hands-on manner and most likely had limited mastery of the content and key vocabulary concepts.

Ms. Dowden's lesson received a "4" for Hands-On Manipulatives and Practice. All students in her class, regardless of English proficiency, were expected to master the content concepts related to ecosystems and symbiosis. Also, all students were expected to create their own ecosystems; however, the ELs were provided with materials and clear directions, including modeling, to assist them in building their ecocolumns. The hands-on experimentation by all students reinforced the content concepts and key vocabulary, and the meaningful practice made concrete what could have been abstract for the English learners.

Miss Delgado's lesson received a "1" on the SIOP® protocol for Hands-On Manipulatives and Practice. Although she illustrated an ecosystem on the board, students were mostly passive while they copied her illustration and when they watched the video. The class did partner reading but few of the students had the opportunity to practice using their newly learned content information or key vocabulary. It is therefore doubtful that ELs had a clear understanding of ecosystems or that students could apply what they had learned in any meaningful way.

21. *Activities Provided for Students to Apply Content and Language Knowledge*

Mr. Nguyen: 3

Ms. Dowden: 4

Miss Delgado: 1

In his lesson on ecosystems, Mr. Nguyen provided his students with photographs, illustrations, and procedural steps for creating a terrarium. Even though he was the one who actually created the terrarium, his students noted changes within the ecosystem and reported on examples of symbiosis. Further, they completed data reports on their observations and Mr. Nguyen discussed them with students. They were encouraged to ask questions and to share their observations and hypotheses with other students.

Therefore, Mr. Nguyen's lesson received a "3" on the SIOP® protocol for Applying Content and Language Knowledge. Students were involved as observers in the creation of the ecosystem, and they applied what they learned through their data sheets and in their discussions. Language knowledge was applied through oral interactions and in the writing of the data reports; however, there were few opportunities for students to engage in student–student interactions, which provide language practice and develop language proficiency. The video reinforced the textbook content concepts and the demonstration provided another level of scaffolding.

Ms. Dowden's lesson received a "4" for Applying Content and Language Knowledge. Throughout the lessons, students were required to apply what they were learning, not only during the creation of their ecosystems, but also during discussion and through their submitted data sheets. ELs had multiple opportunities to apply their new knowledge and to practice English (e.g., sharing observations of changes with partners and groups). While Ms. Dowden provided independent research opportunities for English-fluent students, she carefully scaffolded the learning for ELs; but she did not lessen her expectations that all her general biology students would master the content and language objectives.

After students read the textbook chapter, Miss Delgado drew an illustration of a layered ecosystem on the board. Students copied the drawing and labeled the species. They watched the video on ecosystems and symbiosis, and each wrote a paragraph about what they had learned.

Miss Delgado's lesson received a "1" for Applying Content and Language Knowledge. Although there was no opportunity for students to apply their content knowledge in a hands-on way, they could demonstrate what they knew through their written paragraph. There were very few opportunities for students to practice or apply their language knowledge orally.

22. *Activities Integrate All Language Skills*

Mr. Nguyen: 3

Ms. Dowden: 4

Miss Delgado: 2

Mr. Nguyen's lesson received a "3" on the SIOP® protocol for Integrating All Language Skills. Throughout their lesson on ecosystems, English learners were given the opportunity to read, write, listen, and discuss the content concepts. However, because he did not differentiate his instruction for ELs, his less vocal students may have felt reluctant to fully participate in class discussions. In addition, Mr. Nguyen's lesson was teacher dominated, so students' opportunities for language practice were somewhat limited.

For all of her students, Ms. Dowden facilitated the reading of the textbook chapter and the information on the website about ecosystems. The ELs followed her demonstration on how to build their ecocolumns, discussing their work throughout. Each student kept a data sheet on observed changes in the ecocolumns, and they were expected to talk about their findings with each other.

Therefore, Ms. Dowden's lesson received a "4" on the SIOP® protocol for this feature. Throughout the lessons in this unit, English learners were reading, discussing, and writing about the process of building their ecosystems. The language processes were well integrated into the delivery of the biology content because students were not only reading and writing about what they were learning, but also speaking with the teacher and with each other.

Miss Delgado's lessons on ecosystems involved partner reading for the textbook chapter and a lecture with a blackboard illustration on the process of decomposition of plant material. Independently, students copied her illustration from the board and labeled the various species within the ecosystem. After she showed the video on ecosystems and symbiosis, students wrote paragraphs explaining how various species on the earth support and contribute to each other's sustenance and viability.

Miss Delgado's lesson received a "2" for Integrating All Language Skills. Her students read the textbook, listened to the mini-lecture, watched the video, and wrote paragraphs about their understandings. However, students had few chances to connect reading and writing activities with discussion, either with the teacher or each other. There were few opportunities for students to practice language and content concepts with each other.

Summary

With any type of new learning, practice and application of newly acquired skills are needed to ensure mastery of content concepts. Hands-on activities and materials, including manipulatives, enable students to forge connections between abstract and concrete concepts. Students make these connections most effectively when they use all language processes, including reading, writing, listening, and speaking, during practice and application.

Discussion Questions

1. Compare and contrast the following two teachers' approaches to teaching a lesson on nutrition.
   a. One teacher's approach involves a lecture about the nutritional content of different foods while showing a food pyramid diagram. The teacher then gives the middle schoolers a list of appropriate foods for each food group in the pyramid and the calories associated with each food. Students are then tested about their knowledge of the food pyramid and the caloric count of common foods.
   b. The other teacher's approach begins with students' maintaining a food diary for a week. Copies of the food pyramid are distributed and explained, and all students must analyze their food consumption according to the recommendations on the pyramid. With a partner, students must design a nutritionally sound weekly menu for each day of the following week, and they must be prepared to defend their food choices to peer group members.

   Which of the approaches to teaching this content concept is most appropriate for English learners? How do you know? Be as specific as you can.
2. One way to ensure practice and application of new knowledge is through project-based learning. Develop a unit project that students in one of your courses can build incrementally as the series of lessons progress over several days or weeks. Identify the steps to completion that students will accomplish in each lesson of the unit. Determine which language objectives can be taught, practiced, and applied in the project. Plan a culminating presentation or performance to enhance oral language practice.
3. English learners benefit from the integration of reading, writing, listening, and speaking. For those with limited English language proficiency, tell what may be

difficult. Is it performance of all four skills, or just some? What adjustments and techniques can a teacher use to provide ELs with successful experiences while they read, write, listen, and speak about new information they are learning? Include specific activities and examples in your answer.

4. With district curriculum pacing guides and a large number of content standards in each subject area for which teachers and students are accountable, how is it possible to provide direct application and hands-on practice for lessons? What can teachers do to alleviate the conflict between "covering the content" and making it "accessible" for English learners?
5. Using the SIOP® lesson you have been developing, write some activities for students to practice and then apply the key language and content concepts.

chapter 8

Lesson Delivery

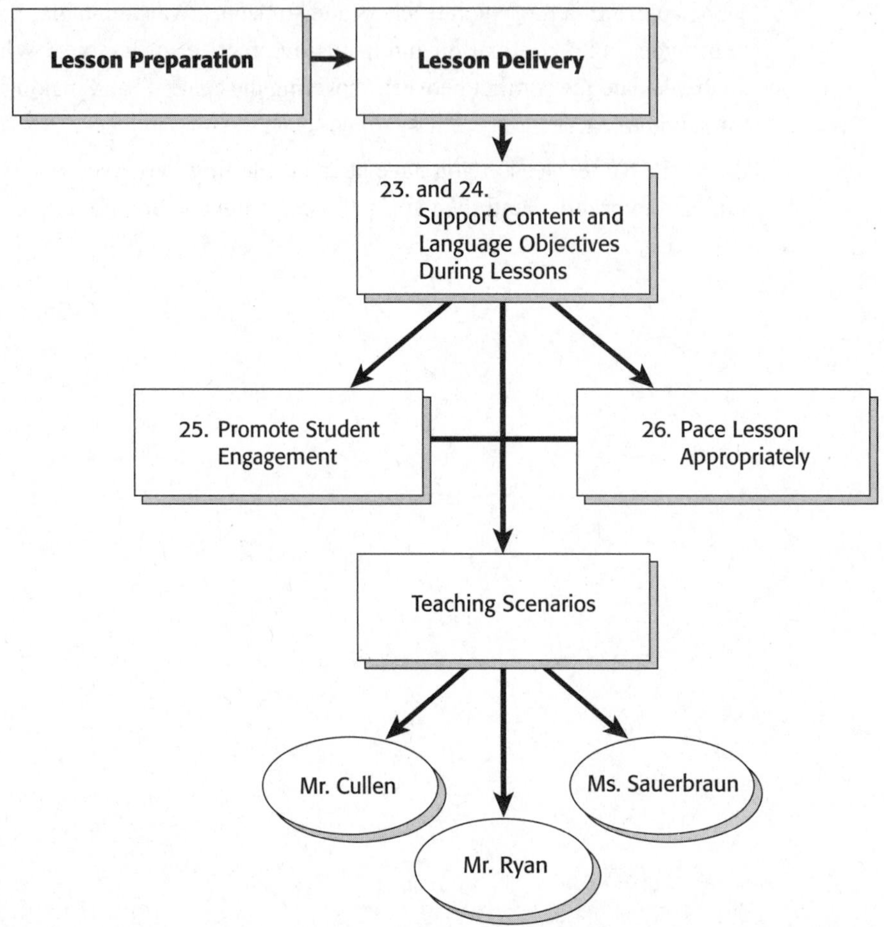

Objectives

After reading, discussing, and engaging in activities related to this chapter, you will be able to meet the following content and language objectives.

Content Objectives

Monitor lessons to determine if the delivery is supporting the objectives.

List strategies for improving student time on task throughout a lesson.

Explain how a focus on a lesson's objectives can aid in pacing.

Generate activities to keep English learners engaged.

Language Objectives

Evaluate a situation where a well-designed lesson plan is not enacted successfully and explain what might have gone wrong and what could be improved.

Compare pacing considerations in classes that have only native English speakers with classes that have English learners.

Discuss characteristics of effective SIOP® lesson delivery.

Background

As we mentioned, good preparation is the first step in delivering a lesson that leads to student learning. However, a lesson can go awry, even if it is well written. Activities might be too easy or too difficult for the students. The lesson might be too long or too short. A student might ask an interesting but tangential question, and the ensuing class discussion consumes ten unexpected minutes. The Lesson Delivery component of the SIOP® Model is included to remind teachers to stay on track, and in this chapter we provide some guidance for doing so.

To see an example of using the SIOP® model for lesson delivery, please view the corresponding video clip (Chapter 8, Module 1) on the accompanying CD.

This chapter addresses the way a lesson is delivered, how well the content and language objectives are supported during the lesson, to what extent students are engaged in the lesson, and how appropriate the pace of the lesson is to students' ability levels. You will see that this chapter parallels Chapter 2, Lesson Preparation, because the two components are closely related. The effectiveness of a lesson's delivery—the level of student participation, how clearly information is communicated, students' level of understanding reflected in the quality of their work—often can be traced back to the preparation that took place before students entered the classroom. We will meet the teachers from Chapter 2 again and discuss how their level of preparation was executed in their lesson delivery.

SIOP® FEATURE 23: Content Objectives Clearly Supported by Lesson Delivery

As we discussed in Chapter 2, content objectives must be stated orally and must be displayed for students and teachers alike to see. From the content perspective, this is no longer an unusual proposition. Since the No Child Left Behind Act has raised the level of school accountability, teachers and principals are more comfortable with posting objectives tied to state standards. We caution against any inclination to list the standard in an abbreviated form, like CA History 5.2.3, as an objective because it would be meaningless to the students and is unlikely to be at the level of a lesson goal. Adolescents may recognize the shorthand as representing a standard, but listing the standard number would not be informative, nor would it guide their learning. Rather, written, student-friendly objectives serve to remind us of the focus of the lesson, providing a structure to classroom procedures. Written objectives also allow students to know the direction of the lesson and help them stay on task. The posted objectives provide a buffer when it comes to the interesting but tangential questions middle and high schoolers are sometimes known to pose. Instead of taking the lesson discussion off in a new direction, a teacher can remind students of the objectives, offer to address the question once the lesson is completed, and maintain the appropriate focus and pace. Throughout the lesson and at its conclusion, the teacher and students can evaluate the extent to which the lesson delivery supported the content objectives.

SIOP® FEATURE 24: Language Objectives Clearly Supported by Lesson Delivery

As you now know, language objectives are an important part of effective sheltered lessons. Teachers and students benefit from having a clear language objective written for them to see and reviewed with them during the lesson. The objective may be related to an English language proficiency standard such as "Students will produce a variety of writing forms using register appropriate to audience" (WIDA Consortium, 2007, p. 42); or it may be related to teachers' scope and sequence of language skills that their own students need to develop, such as "Students will make connections between text and self, and text and world." No matter which language objective is written for a lesson, as we stated in Chapter 2, a teacher needs to address it explicitly during instruction. For example, if ninth graders in a language arts class have to "defend a position" as their language objective in a lesson on *To Kill a Mockingbird* by Harper Lee and the task is to argue in favor of Atticus's decision to act as the lawyer for Tom Robinson, then we would expect the teacher to spend some of the period discussing or modeling persuasive speech.

Meeting Content and Language Objectives

A SIOP® lesson is effective when it meets its objectives. Although we have experienced some teacher reluctance to write both kinds of objectives for each lesson and to post them and review them with the students, our research results give evidence of their value.

When presenting a SIOP® lesson, the objectives should be noticeable throughout—in terms of the activities students are asked to accomplish and the questions and comprehension checks the teachers perform. The objectives should always be reviewed at the end of the lesson too.

Some teachers have explained that they don't want to write out and discuss the objectives with the students because they can't write them in a manner that students understand or because they fear not completing the full lesson. Both of those arguments are easily overcome with practice and support. A SIOP® coach or a fellow SIOP® teacher can advise a teacher on writing student-friendly objectives. The students themselves will confirm if they understood the objective when it is presented in class. And as a teacher gets to know his or her students, writing for their age and proficiency level becomes easier. If the problem is that the objectives are not being met by the end of the lesson, then the teacher and students can discuss why as they review them. It may be that the activities took longer than planned or class discussions veered off track, but the presence of objectives can actually impose discipline on the pacing of each lesson. If a teacher consistently does not meet objectives, however, it may also be that too many objectives are planned for the time frame of the lesson or time is lost during activity transitions or at the start or end of the period.

We acknowledge that it takes time to determine good objectives for every lesson, but the investment in writing them and then teaching to them pays off in student achievement.

SIOP® FEATURE 25: Students Engaged Approximately 90% to 100% of the Period

This feature in the Lesson Delivery component calls on teachers to engage students 90 percent to 100 percent of the class period. By this we mean that the students are paying attention and on task. It does not mean they need to be highly active (writing, reading, moving) the entire time, but they are following the lesson, responding to teacher direction, and performing the activities as expected. When students are in groups, all are participating. Lessons where students are engaged less than 50 percent of the time are unacceptable. This situation tends to occur when teachers have not provided clear explanations of the assignment or have not scaffolded the process well.

Engagement, motivation, and identity are important factors in successful lessons for adolescents, native, and non-native English-speaking teens alike (Short & Fitzsimmons, 2007, Tatum, 2008; Torgesen et al., 2007). When older learners are actively engaged, they are involved in tasks that challenge them and allow them to gain confidence. Adolescents prefer to see connections between school topics and their current or future lives, and they will engage with text above their reading level if it is of interest to them. Offering choices in task, text, or partner, and differentiating instruction are key methods for accommodating classrooms with English learners of varying proficiency levels as well as those with both native English speakers and English learners. It is often through such modifications to a curriculum that student engagement can be enhanced (Buck, Carr, & Robertson, 2008; Tomlinson, 2005).

ACTIVITY Student engagement is enhanced, for example, when a teacher incorporates a **Think-Pair-Share** technique during a class discussion. Instead of asking questions to the whole class and calling on two or three students to respond, the teacher asks everyone to think of an answer, then tell it to a partner before calling on some students to share responses with the whole class. This relatively simple and quick technique gives *all* of the students a chance to think and speak, instead of two or three. Another activity called **Chunk and Chew** (see Vogt & Echevarria, 2008, p. 164) encourages teachers to pause after every ten minutes of input to give students time to discuss or reflect.

English learners are the students who can least afford to have valuable time squandered through boredom, inattention, socializing, and other off-task behaviors. Time also is wasted when teachers are ill prepared; have poor classroom management skills; spend excessive amounts of time making announcements and passing out and handing in papers; and the like. The most effective teachers minimize these behaviors and maximize time spent actively engaged in instruction (Mastropieri & Scruggs, 1994). English learners who are working to achieve grade-level competence benefit from efficient use of class time. Further, many of these adolescent learners have had uneven schooling experiences in their past, missing time in school due to circumstances beyond their control, and are then further disadvantaged by inefficient use of class time.

There are actually three aspects to student engagement that should be considered: (1) allocated time, (2) engaged time, and (3) academic learning time (Berliner, 1984). *Allocated time* reflects the decisions teachers make regarding the amount of time to spend studying a topic (e.g., math versus reading) and doing a given academic task (e.g., how much time to spend on reading comprehension versus decoding skills). As we have discussed throughout this book, effective sheltered instruction teachers plan for and deliver lessons that are balanced between teacher presentation of information and opportunities for students to practice and apply the information in meaningful ways. Effective sheltered instruction teachers use instructional time wisely.

Engaged time refers to the time students are actively participating in instruction during the time allocated. The engaged time-on-task research has consistently concluded that the more actively students participate in the instructional process, the more they achieve (Schmoker, 2006). As Bickel and Bickel (1986) explained: "Students learn more when they are attending to the learning tasks that are the focus of instruction" (p. 493). Instruction that is understandable to ELs, that creates opportunities for students to talk about the lesson's concepts, and that provides hands-on activities to reinforce learning captures students' attention and keeps them more actively engaged.

Academic learning time focuses on students' time-on-task, when the task is related to the materials they will be tested on. Creative, fun activities are not effective if they are unrelated to the content and language objectives of the lesson. According to Leinhardt and colleagues (1982):

> When teachers spend their time and energy teaching students the content the students need to learn, students learn the material. When students spend their time actively engaged in activities that relate strongly to the materials they will be tested on, they learn more of the material (p. 409).

Of course, sheltered teachers need to be explicit in their expectations and make certain that their English learners understand how activities and materials relate to standards and upcoming assessments.

In summary, effective SIOP® teachers need to plan to use the entire class period efficiently, teach in ways that engage students, and make sure students are engaged in activities that specifically relate to the material on which they will be assessed.

SIOP® FEATURE 26: Pacing of the Lesson Appropriate to Students' Ability Levels

Pacing refers to the rate at which information is presented during a lesson. The pace of the lesson depends on the nature of the lesson's content, as well as the level of students' background knowledge. When working with ELs, it can be challenging to set a pace that doesn't present information too quickly yet is brisk enough to maintain students' interest, especially when a variety of English proficiency levels are represented in the same classroom. Finding an appropriate pace requires practice but becomes easier as teachers develop familiarity with their students' skills.

Middle and high school content area teachers are often constrained by the school's bell schedule and the district's curriculum pacing guide. Teachers do not want to move so quickly through the curriculum that they leave their ELs behind. Collaborating with the ESL teacher, if the ELs have that additional support, can augment instructional time. The ESL teacher might introduce key vocabulary and build background on topics before they are covered in the content classroom, or provide additional practice and application activities afterward.

When content teachers have classes mixed with ELs and native English speakers, it can take some effort and experience to pace the lessons well. Investing in instructional routines and teaching task procedures during the first quarter of the year are two strategies that will reap dividends later. Adolescents also enjoy working with peers, so collaborative learning projects with tasks geared to proficiency level and interest are beneficial. On occasion, interdisciplinary projects could be planned, such as a project on the Harlem Renaissance that involves U.S. history (e.g., the migration of African Americans from the South to the North), English literature (e.g., poems by Langston Hughes and Zora Neale Hurston), and music (e.g., the Jazz Age). Such projects not only spiral the content but also introduce and reinforce key language terms, functions, and sentence structures, allowing English learners time over the course of a unit and across several content areas to develop the academic English skills they need for success.

Using differentiated instruction techniques and prorating the task are other options for managing a lesson with multiple proficiency levels. Some other related ideas can be found in *99 Ideas and Activities for Teaching English Learners with the SIOP® Model* (Vogt & Echevarria, 2008) and in *Implementing the SIOP® Model Through Effective Professional Development and Coaching* (Echevarria, Short, & Vogt, 2008).

One important fact to remember is this: If a teacher wastes five minutes of a class period daily, perhaps by starting the lesson late or finishing early, over the course of 180 days, 15 hours of instructional time will be lost! Sometimes little routines can help the pacing: a basket by the door where students deposit homework when they enter or classwork when they leave, a materials manager for each group of desks who distributes books or worksheets to everyone in the group, or a classroom timer set to ring when an activity should end. If you finish a lesson early, don't let students chat or do homework; instead, play a game to review vocabulary or key concepts. We need to maximize the way we use time when we have English learners in the classroom.

The Lesson

The lesson below is a continuation of the three lessons we first read about in Chapter 2. The lesson is part of a unit on the Italian Renaissance for high school English learners in a World History course. (For more examples of lesson and unit plans in history, see Short, Vogt, & Echevarria, in press.)

UNIT: Italian Renaissance (Tenth Grade)

Recall that the classrooms of Mr. Cullen, Mr. Ryan, and Ms. Sauerbraun are found in a metropolitan high school in a suburb located next to the major city. At the district level, approximately 30 percent of the students are English learners or former English learners. At this particular high school however, the number of students with English as a second language is closer to 60 percent. In the tenth grade classrooms of these three teachers, the mix of English learners, former English learners who have been redesignated, and native English speakers is about one-third, one-third, and one-third. Each class has 25–30 students. The English learners in these rooms are at the intermediate to advanced levels of proficiency. Beginning-level ELs study in a separate sheltered World History course.

The Italian Renaissance unit has several main topics, including the political power of the city-states and papacy, the rise of Renaissance art and architecture, the philosophy of Humanism, and the development and use of technology. An essential question students will address throughout the unit is: "What makes someone a Renaissance man or woman?"

Teaching Scenarios

In these vignettes, we return to the tenth grade World History classrooms of Mr. Cullen, Mr. Ryan, and Ms. Sauerbraun as they discuss the cultural and scientific contributions of the Italian Renaissance. We reflected on their lesson preparation in Chapter 2. Here we will summarize what has taken place and then discuss how the lesson concluded. As you read, consider how well the teachers delivered their lessons. The SIOP® Model features for Lesson Delivery are meeting content objectives, meeting language objectives, engaging students 90–100% of the time, and pacing the lesson appropriately for students' ability levels.

Mr. Cullen

In the scenario in Chapter 2, Mr. Cullen's class had watched a brief video about achievements during the Italian Renaissance, chosen an area of achievement to work on, developed a research question with their groups, and conducted research using websites and books in the classroom library gathered specifically for this unit. The student groups were given a choice of a project to work on that would reflect a major contribution and were provided with the rubric on which their oral presentations would be assessed. Mr. Cullen's objectives, which he had posted and explained to the students, were the following:

Content: Students will explore major achievements in literature, music, painting, sculpture, architecture, science, and technology in Italy during the Renaissance.
Students will design a representation of one of the achievements.

Language: Students will read and take notes from primary and secondary sources on one of these achievements.

Students will justify orally why the achievement is important.

The day after the lesson described in Chapter 2 took place, Mr. Cullen met with the students in each group to discuss their plans and offer guidance. The groups worked fairly independently over the next two days, although Mr. Cullen gave additional support to the groups that contained ELs with lower proficiency levels. He particularly helped the groups make sense of some of the primary sources. Each successive day in the week, he began class with one or two groups sharing what they had learned so far. He encouraged the others to ask questions or make comments. He also gave 5–7 minute mini-lectures on Renaissance contributions in art, architecture, music, literature, and technology. His goal was to set the stage for the group presentations to come, so that the class would not view each project in a vacuum.

On the final day of the week, the groups took turns presenting their projects to the class. The whole class was given a chart to complete as they listened to the presentations. On the chart they could record the type of achievement, examples of the achievement, names of historical figures who were involved with the achievement, and a new question that the presentation had generated for them about the achievement. Underneath the chart, the students were asked to respond to the following question: Of the historical people you learned about today, who represents a Renaissance man or woman and why?

On the SIOP form in Figure 8.1, rate Mr. Cullen's lesson on each of the Lesson Delivery features.

FIGURE 8.1 *Lesson Delivery Component of the SIOP® Model: Mr. Cullen's Lesson*

4	3	2	1	0
23. **Content objectives** clearly supported by lesson delivery		**Content objectives** somewhat supported by lesson delivery		**Content objectives** not supported by lesson delivery
4	**3**	**2**	**1**	**0**
24. **Language objectives** clearly supported by lesson delivery		**Language objectives** somewhat supported by lesson delivery		**Language objectives** not supported by lesson delivery
4	**3**	**2**	**1**	**0**
25. **Students engaged** approximately 90% to 100% of the period		**Students engaged** approximately 70% of the period		**Students engaged** less than 50% of the period
4	**3**	**2**	**1**	**0**
26. **Pacing** of the lesson appropriate to the students' ability level		**Pacing** generally appropriate, but at times too fast or too slow		**Pacing** inappropriate to students' ability levels

Mr. Ryan

In Mr. Ryan's classroom described in Chapter 2, the students experienced an art history lesson as Mr. Ryan showed slides of paintings and lectured on the similarities and differences between Medieval and Renaissance art. His learning objective was "Students will learn about the contributions that Italian Renaissance artists made to the world of art." He did not have a defined language objective, although his tasks required listening comprehension and comparative writing. After his 20-minute lecture, in which some students misbehaved or tuned out, he gave them an assignment to select one Medieval and one Renaissance painting from those he had displayed and to write a comparative essay about their artistic styles.

The next day, Mr. Ryan spent five minutes showing the students additional paintings at the start of the lesson to determine if the students had understood the information provided the day before. For each example, he asked the students to identify the painting as a Medieval or a Renaissance piece of art and to explain their answers. The students were to write down their ideas individually first. After he showed five paintings, he encouraged the students to pair up and share their responses with a partner. They then reviewed the exercise as a class.

Next, Mr. Ryan had the students begin their essays on the paintings they had chosen. He told them that the essays would be evaluated on how well they conveyed the students' knowledge of the differences between the two styles of art and how accurate their explanations were. The students worked on these essays for the rest of the period, with varying degrees of engagement, while Mr. Ryan graded papers at his desk. Some students finished in 10 minutes; others looked into space for half the period, and others were still writing when the bell rang. From time to time, Mr. Ryan walked around the room and exhorted the students to "Get to work!" and "Add more to that."

On the SIOP form in Figure 8.2, rate Mr. Ryan's lesson on each of the Lesson Delivery features.

Ms. Sauerbraun

In Chapter 2, Ms. Sauerbraun's class began researching historical figures in order to write diary entries. The class read the chapter in the text after doing an anticipation guide. As they read, they were to decide which historical person they would like to learn about. Ms. Sauerbraun had posted and reviewed her content objective: "Analyze the historical developments of the Renaissance, including major achievements in literature, art, architecture, music, and science." She also told the class the language skills they would practice—reading the chapter and writing at least six diary entries for a historical Renaissance figure.

On following day, Ms. Sauerbraun reviewed the chapter with the students for the first 15 minutes by playing a Jeopardy-style game. The categories were Art, Architecture, Literature, and Science, and each category had four questions of increasing value. Students formed three teams and thus could consult their textbooks within the one minute allotted for providing an answer to each question. Afterward, the students worked on their research and writing. Ms. Sauerbraun met with each student or pair to review their progress. She allowed students to go to the school library to look for reference material and made the computers in her room available for those who wanted to check information online.

On the third day, she reminded the students that their diary entries should be written in the first person. She gave examples, "I set up my easel in the garden. We walked to the cathedral on Sunday." She told the students to use neat handwriting and suggested that

FIGURE 8.2 *Lesson Delivery Component of the SIOP® Model: Mr. Ryan's Lesson*

	4	3	2	1	0
23.	**Content objectives** clearly supported by lesson delivery		**Content objectives** somewhat supported by lesson delivery		**Content objectives** not supported by lesson delivery
24.	**Language objectives** clearly supported by lesson delivery		**Language objectives** somewhat supported by lesson delivery		**Language objectives** not supported by lesson delivery
25.	**Students engaged** approximately 90% to 100% of the period		**Students engaged** approximately 70% of the period		**Students engaged** less than 50% of the period
26.	**Pacing** of the lesson appropriate to the students' ability level		**Pacing** generally appropriate, but at times too fast or too slow		**Pacing** inappropriate to students' ability levels

they could decorate the diary if they wanted to. She reminded them that their entries should reveal why the person they chose was considered a representative Renaissance Man or Woman. She told them to turn in their diaries at the end of the period. Some students (many of whom were English learners) balked at this and requested additional time to finish the diary entries for homework. Ms. Sauerbraun agreed. The students and pairs worked diligently for the rest of the period. Ms. Sauerbraun assisted students as necessary. She read a few of the entries and gave some feedback.

On the SIOP form in Figure 8.3, rate Ms. Sauerbraun's lesson on each of the Lesson Delivery features.

Discussion of Lessons

23. *Content Objectives Clearly Supported by Lesson Delivery*

Mr. Cullen: 4

Mr. Ryan: 2

Ms. Sauerbraun: 3

When implementing the SIOP® Model for teachers, it is very important not only to plan content and language objectives, but also to follow through with them during the lesson. Our research shows this attention to helping students acquire the subject area knowledge and the needed academic language skills is very beneficial and should occur each day.

FIGURE 8.3 *Lesson Delivery Component of the SIOP® Model: Ms. Sauerbraun's Lesson*

4	3	2	1	0
23. **Content objectives** clearly supported by lesson delivery		**Content objectives** somewhat supported by lesson delivery		**Content objectives** not supported by lesson delivery
4	3	2	1	0
24. **Language objectives** clearly supported by lesson delivery		**Language objectives** somewhat supported by lesson delivery		**Language objectives** not supported by lesson delivery
4	3	2	1	0
25. **Students engaged** approximately 90% to 100% of the period		**Students engaged** approximately 70% of the period		**Students engaged** less than 50% of the period
4	3	2	1	0
26. **Pacing** of the lesson appropriate to the students' ability level		**Pacing** generally appropriate, but at times too fast or too slow		**Pacing** inappropriate to students' ability levels

Mr. Cullen's lesson received a "4" for meeting the content objectives. He had posted and explained them to the students, so they knew what they were supposed to learn. He then supported these objectives throughout the extended lesson as they conducted their research, reviewed primary and secondary sources, and developed their projects. He also gave mini-lectures each day on different achievements of the Renaissance period. When the groups presented their work, each student had a chart to complete in order to highlight the diverse contributions that the Renaissance contributed to life in the fourteenth to sixteenth centuries.

Mr. Ryan's use of visuals during the art history lecture helped illustrate his content concepts as he lectured on the paintings. However he did not ensure that the students, particularly the English learners, could take appropriate notes on his discussion of Medieval and Renaissance art. In order to clearly support these objectives, he needed to teach note-taking skills or check on the notes the students were taking. Because his assessment of their learning was based on their essays, which in turn were based on their notes, the note-taking process was of critical importance. This lesson was rated a "2."

Ms. Sauerbraun's lesson plan called for students to gain in-depth knowledge about one Renaissance figure. The tasks assigned to the students enabled this type of learning to take place (and English learners could work with a partner), but they did not conform entirely with the stated content objective, namely to analyze major achievements of the Renaissance period. Across the whole class, major achievements were analyzed, but the students did not have an opportunity to share their individual pieces of the whole. While they researched only one person, they did not interact systematically with classmates who focused on another person or achievement. The bulk of their overall understanding of the Renaissance period came from the textbook reading and Jeopardy game. This lesson received a score of "3."

24. *Language Objectives Clearly Supported by Lesson Delivery*

Mr. Cullen: 4

Mr. Ryan: 0

Ms. Sauerbraun: 2

The language objectives in Mr. Cullen's class were clearly supported by the lesson delivery. He introduced and clarified key vocabulary with the video clip. He preselected text and bookmarked websites to accommodate the language abilities of his students and supported them as they reviewed primary and secondary sources. He taught note-taking skills and provided a rubric for the students' oral presentations in advance. By calling on the groups to share what they were learning as the week continued, he offered them a dress rehearsal for their later presentations. The rating for Mr. Cullen's lesson on this feature was a "4."

Mr. Ryan's lesson received a "0" for clearly supported language objectives. He did not have a defined language objective, but as his lesson was enacted, we saw that he could have developed a listening comprehension objective or a comparative writing one. He offered a T-chart for the students to take notes, but he did not consciously instruct them on how to listen and take notes. He required a comparative essay, but he did not review comparative phrases (e.g., Both X and Y are ____; X is ___, but Y is ___; They are similar because ___; In contrast, ___) or provide a prewriting tool such as another T-chart or Venn diagram for the students to organize their ideas. It is unlikely that the students improved their academic literacy skills during this lesson.

In Ms. Sauerbraun's class, the students were assigned reading and writing tasks, although they were not identified as learning objectives. The students read the chapter without support, but they did have a review Jeopardy game. They conducted research with reference materials, but again Ms. Sauerbraun did not provide support. Unlike in Mr. Cullen's lesson, where print materials and websites were carefully selected in advance so students of differing reading levels could have access, Ms. Sauerbraun's students were on their own to find information they could comprehend and use to complete the diary entries. Although Ms. Sauerbraun showed the students models of the diaries, she did not teach or review the style for writing an entry, except on the third day when she told them to use the first-person narrative. This lesson was rated a "2" for clearly supported language objectives.

25. *Students Engaged Approximately 90% to 100% of the Period*

Mr. Cullen: 4

Mr. Ryan: 2

Ms. Sauerbraun: 3

In Mr. Cullen's lesson, the students were highly engaged. He built background for the topic through the video clips and gave the students a significant amount of choice in selecting both their topics for research and their products. Research has shown that adolescent students' motivation increases when they have choice and assume responsibility for their work. The tasks and procedures were well scaffolded, too, so students conducted the research step by step with materials geared to their individual ability levels. By requiring each student to record information while the groups presented their products, he also kept the class engaged at a time when off-task behavior could have occurred. Overall, he maximized the academic learning time the students experienced. This lesson was rated a "4" for student engagement.

Mr. Ryan was passionate about his topic and had a great deal of information to share. However, his method for doing so did not engage all of his students. Recall that during the 20-minute lecture on the differences between Medieval and Renaissance art, several of his students acted out, lost interest, or seemingly took a nap. For tenth graders, 20 minutes for a slideshow lecture on an unfamiliar topic is too long. The essay-writing task also was not very engaging for some of the students. The reason may partly be the lack of preparation the students had for accomplishing the task successfully. This lesson received a "2" for student engagement.

Ms. Sauerbraun engaged the class with her costume and introduction to the Renaissance topic. The students enjoyed the Jeopardy game the second day as well. She provided students choice in their selection of a Renaissance figure to portray through the diary entries. Although not all of the English learners could do the research on their own, she allowed them to work with a partner. All of the students were on task and completed the assignment. Her lesson was rated a "3."

26. *Pacing of Lesson Appropriate to Students' Ability Levels*

Mr. Cullen: 4

Mr. Ryan: 1

Ms. Sauerbraun: 2

Mr. Cullen's lesson was well paced. The students were required to accomplish different tasks leading up to their projects and oral presentations, and the teacher allocated a week for this project. The project groups included English learners and native English speakers. Mr. Cullen checked with the groups each day and had some give updates about the information they were uncovering. No time was wasted trying to find reference materials in the library or on the Web because Mr. Cullen had gathered reference books and had bookmarked sites before the project began. His lesson was rated a "4" for pacing.

Mr. Ryan's lesson needed a better pacing plan. The first day, the 20-minute lecture on art styles was too long for the tenth graders and too difficult for some of the English learners to follow because he did not review vocabulary or guide the students' note taking. The second day devoted the bulk of the period to essay writing—but without support for the writing process. Some students finished quickly, others did not. This lesson received a "1" on the pacing feature.

Ms. Sauerbraun's lesson moved along each day with students responsible for a good deal of independent work. Some students lost time looking for reference material. This loss of learning time could have been reduced if Ms. Sauerbraun had identified in advance some basic sources for students to use. Because not all of the students had finished by the third day, she allowed some to complete the assignment for homework. The pacing of the lesson was rated a "2."

Summary

The importance of setting and meeting objectives cannot be overemphasized. Many teachers may feel comfortable having a general objective in mind and moving along with a lesson's flow, but that approach is not helpful for English learners. Delivering a lesson geared to objectives that have been made clear to students benefits all. The teacher stays on task, and the students know what is important to focus on and remember. By incorporating a variety of techniques that engage students throughout the lesson, teachers not only give students opportunities to learn, practice, and apply information and language skills, but they also help to ensure that the lesson's objectives are met.

Pacing is another important aspect of lesson delivery, and appropriate pace is critical for English learners. Information that is presented at a pace suitable for native English speakers may render that information meaningless, especially for beginning English speakers. Finding the right pace for a lesson depends in part on the content of the lesson and students' prior knowledge about the topic. It may also depend on the task—whether the product has been prorated or whether students were able to work in cooperative groups. As illustrated in the lessons here, effective sheltered instruction teachers can meet the lesson objectives, at the same time while accommodating the language and learning needs of their students.

Discussion Questions

1. Reflect on a lesson that you taught or observed that did not go well. What happened? Can you identify a feature in Lesson Delivery that might have caused the lesson to be less successful? Or a feature from another SIOP® component? In retrospect, how might the lesson delivery have been improved?
2. Suppose three new middle school students, all with limited English proficiency, joined a social studies or history class midyear. The other students in the class include a few former ELs and native English speakers. What are some language objectives the teacher could write for each of the following content concepts?
   a. Economic trends during the Great Depression
   b. Migration of people from the Dust Bowl of Oklahoma

   How might the teacher prorate the tasks associated with the language objectives to meet the different academic development needs of the students?
3. How does a secondary school teacher or supervisor determine whether a majority of students, including English learners, are engaged during a lesson? What techniques could be used to sustain engagement throughout the period? What should the teacher do if he or she senses that students are off task? Why is sustained engagement so critical to ELs' academic progress?
4. Look over a SIOP® lesson you have been working on. Write down the amount of time you expect each section (or activity) of the lesson to take. Teach the lesson and compare your expectations with reality. Do you have a good handle on pacing? If not, review your lesson for tightening or extending. Where did you lose or gain time? What can you add or take away? List some routines you could implement in your classroom so that you do less talking, or less distributing and collecting. Share with a colleague your ideas for maximizing time-on-task and student engagement.

chapter 9

Review and Assessment

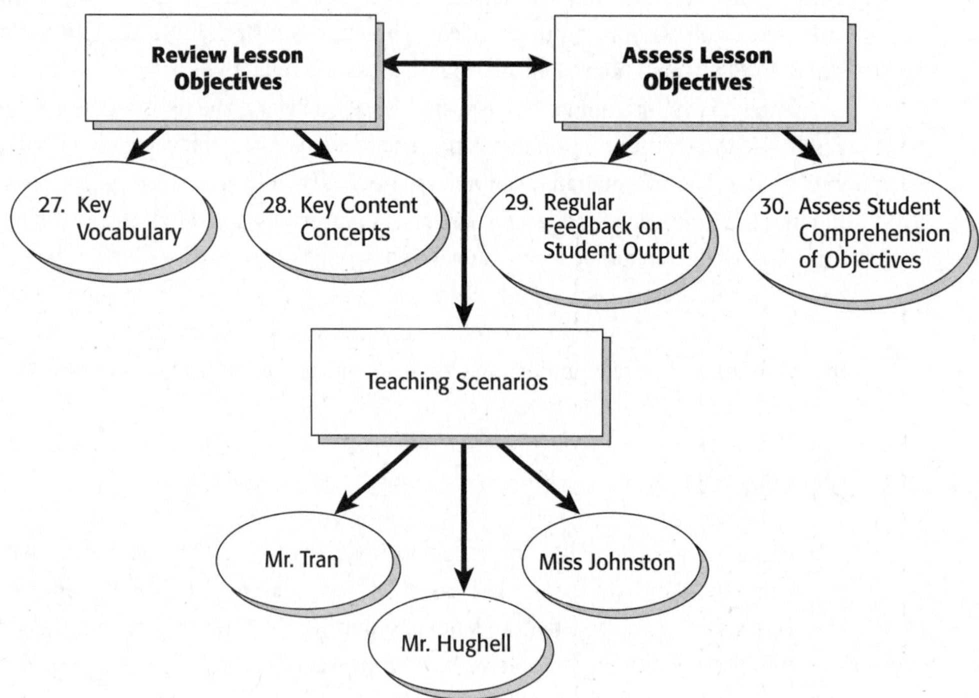

Objectives

After reading, discussing, and engaging in activities related to this chapter, you will be able to meet the following content and language objectives.

Content Objectives

Select techniques for reviewing key content concepts.

Incorporate a variety of assessment techniques into lessons.

Describe the challenges in assessing the content learning of students with limited English proficiency.

Language Objectives

Write a lesson plan that includes review of key vocabulary.

Teach a lesson with group response techniques.

Orally provide feedback to ELs that enhances language development.

Use oral, written, and physical means to provide specific feedback to students on their performance.

Over the years, teachers have asked us why Review and Assessment is the eighth component in the SIOP® Model. Usually the question is preceded by a comment such as "Shouldn't the assessment of students' strengths and needs precede any instruction?" Our response is always "Of course!" Clearly, assessment and instruction are inexorably linked (Vogt & Shearer, 2007). Effective teachers use assessment findings to plan their lessons according to student needs and strengths, and to evaluate how effectively their lessons have been delivered. Effective SIOP® teachers also realize the importance of ongoing and continuous assessment of a lesson's content and language objectives throughout the lesson. We've all experienced that feeling of frustration when we realize, sometimes too late, that students have not understood what it is we were trying to teach. That is precisely what we hope to avoid with the Review and Assessment component.

So why is Review and Assessment the eighth component? The simple answer is that other than the Preparation component, there is no particular hierarchy or order to the eight SIOP® components. For example, as you begin to write SIOP® lesson plans, you'll see that the features of Comprehensible Input are necessary from the beginning to the end of a lesson and that students must engage in Interaction throughout if they're going to learn to speak English proficiently. The components and features of the SIOP® Model are interrelated and integrated into each and every lesson. In fact, as you become more familiar with each of the components and features, you may find that you decide to implement them initially in an order other than the one presented in this book. That is just fine—as is beginning to implement them in the order presented in the SIOP® protocol. What is

important is that you see that all 8 components and 30 features eventually need to be present in your lessons for English learners.

Background

The component of Review and Assessment is not only about what teachers do at the end of a lesson to see if students have learned what was intended. Rather, reviewing and assessing occur throughout each lesson and then again as the lesson concludes. During each step of a lesson, throughout each meaningful activity, we have an opportunity to assess students' progress toward meeting the lesson's content and language objectives.

For English learners review is essential. During class, ELs receive forty minutes, fifty minutes, perhaps seventy-five minutes of input in a new language. Unless the teacher takes the time to highlight and review key information and explicitly indicate what students should focus on and learn, English learners may not know what is important. Students, especially those at the early stages of English proficiency, devote considerable energy to figuring out what the teacher is saying or the text is telling them at a basic level. They are much less able to evaluate which pieces of information among all the input they receive are important to remember. That is why the teacher must take the time to review and summarize throughout a lesson and particularly as a wrap-up at the end.

To teach students effectively, teachers need information about their learning from multiple indicators. One single assessment approach is insufficient for all students, but especially those who may have difficulty articulating their level of understanding through English, their new language. As teachers gather information about what students understand or do not understand, they can adjust their instructional plan accordingly. *Scenarios for ESL Standards-Based Assessment* (TESOL, 2001) is an excellent resource for classroom assessment ideas that are linked to standards and can measure student academic performance. Effective sheltered instruction involves reviewing important concepts, providing constructive feedback through clarification, and making instructional decisions based on student response. In the end, you must have enough information to evaluate the extent to which students have mastered your lesson's objectives. This teach, assess, review, and reteach process is cyclical and recursive (see Figure 9.1).

To see an explanation of the relationship between assessment and instruction, please view the corresponding video clip (Chapter 9, Module 1) on the accompanying CD.

SIOP® FEATURE 27: Comprehensive Review of Key Vocabulary

In Chapter 2, we stated that effective teachers incorporate in their lesson plans techniques that support ELs' language development. In Chapter 3, we discussed the importance of building background through teaching academic language, key content vocabulary, language structure, and functional language. We suggested that language objectives should be identified in lesson plans, introduced to students at the beginning of a lesson, and reviewed throughout the lesson.

We can help develop academic language and key vocabulary by teaching and then reviewing terminology and concepts through *analogy*—the process of relating newly learned words to other words with the same structure or pattern. In Chapters 2 and 3, we gave the example of *photo* (meaning *light*) in a lesson on photosynthesis, and suggested referring students to other words with the same morpheme (e.g., photography).

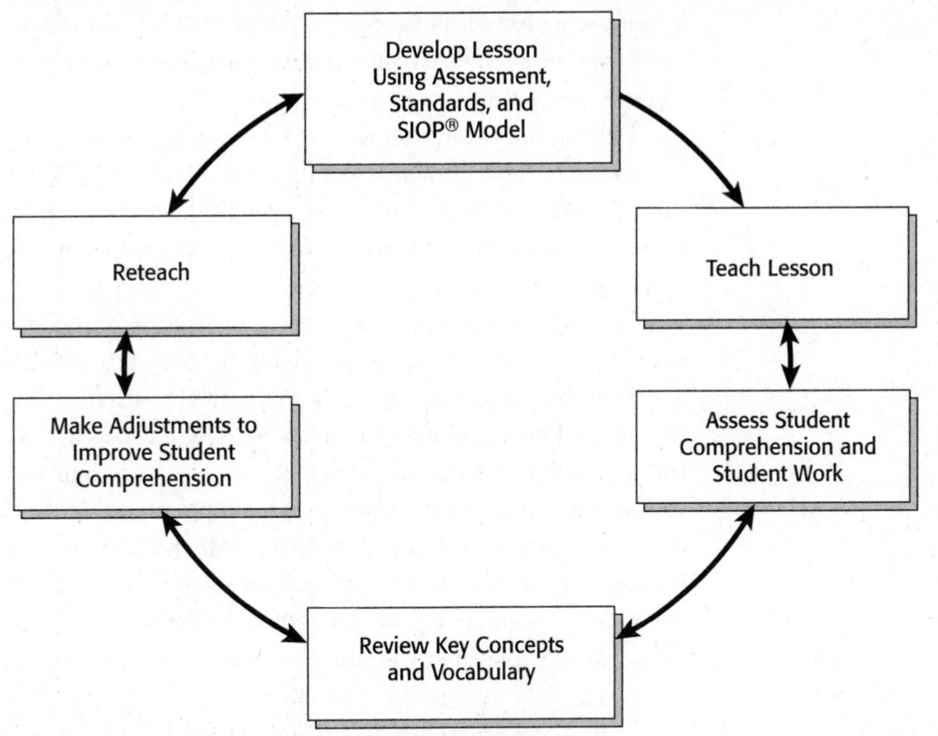

FIGURE 9.1 *Effective Teaching Cycle for English Learners*

Reviewing key vocabulary also involves drawing students' attention to tense, parts of speech, and sentence structure. Repeating and reinforcing language patterns helps students become familiar with English structures.

Multiple exposures to new terminology also build familiarity, confidence, and English proficiency. Words and concepts may be reviewed through paraphrasing, such as "Remember to *share your ideas*; that is, if you have something you want to say, tell it to the others in your group." Another example of a paraphrase (and contextualized sentence) is "The townspeople were *pacifists,* those who would not fight in a war." Paraphrasing as review provides an effective scaffold for ELs, especially after words and phrases have been previously defined and discussed in context.

Key vocabulary also can be reviewed more systematically. It is important to remember that it is ineffective to teach vocabulary through the "dreaded word list" on which students must write (or copy) dictionary definitions (Ruddell, 2007). Research findings are very clear—as stated previously, isolated word lists and dictionary definitions alone do not promote vocabulary and language development. We also know that students do not learn vocabulary words when the teacher just orally introduces and defines them and then expects students to remember the definitions. The more exposures students have to new words, especially if the vocabulary is reinforced through multiple modalities, the more likely they are to remember and use them.

An effective way to incorporate ongoing vocabulary study and review is through the use of individual Word Study Books (Bear, Invernizzi, Templeton, & Johnston, 2007). A Word Study Book is a student-made personal notebook that includes frequently used words and concepts. Vocabulary in Word Study Books might be organized by English language structure, such as listing together words with similar plural endings (e.g., *s, es, ies*). We also believe Word Study Books can be used for content study where words are grouped by topic (e.g., American Revolution words related to protest or government). Some students may benefit by creating semantic maps of the words, for example, linking events to related verbs, adjectives, adverbs, and so forth.

Helping students review and practice words in nonprint ways is beneficial as well. Students may draw a picture to depict a concept or to remember a word. They may demonstrate the meaning through physical gestures or act out several words within the context of a role-play. Pictionary and charade-like games at the end of a lesson can stimulate an engaging review of vocabulary.

Remember that we also need to help students become comfortable with academic language by introducing and modeling academic tasks throughout lessons and units. For example, if you are planning to have ELs engage in discussion it is important to review what "discussion" means, what "turn-taking" is, what it means to "share ideas," how questions are asked and answered, and so forth. Reviewing this terminology provides the necessary scaffolding so that students understand the expectations for their participation in routine activities. This also includes language that is found in test directions or question prompts. Increasingly, our English learners need exposure, practice, and review of those types of terms and phrasings (e.g., "Which of the following is *not* an herbivore?") to help prepare them for the accountability measures they will be called upon to perform.

SIOP® FEATURE 28: Comprehensive Review of Key Content Concepts

Just as it is important to review key vocabulary periodically throughout a lesson, and especially at its conclusion, it is also essential that English learners have key content concepts reviewed during and at the end of a lesson. Understandings are scaffolded when you stop and briefly summarize, along with students' help, the key content covered up to that point. For example, in a lesson on Egyptian mummification, you might say something like the following: "Up to this point, we learned that little was known about Mummy No. 1770 until it was donated to the museum. After the scientists completed the autopsy, they discovered three important things. Who remembers what they were?" This type of review is usually informal, but it must be planned carefully. It can lead into the next section of the text or to a discussion: "Let's read this next section to see what else the scientists learned." Or if predictions about an upcoming section of a text have been made or hypotheses about an experiment developed, teachers should always refer to these afterward and assess their validity with the students.

One favorite wrap-up technique of several SIOP® teachers is Outcome Sentences. A teacher can post sentence starters on the board or transparency, such as:

I wonder . . .

I discovered . . .

I still want to know . . .

I learned . . .

I still don't understand . . .

I still have a question about . . .

I will ask a friend about . . .

To see how one teacher assesses her students' understanding, please view the corresponding video clip (Chapter 9, Module 2) on the accompanying CD.

Students take turns selecting and completing an outcome sentence orally or in writing in a journal. The students can also confer with a partner.

A more structured review might involve students summarizing with partners, writing in a journal, or listing key points on the board. It is important to link the review to the content objectives so that you and the students stay focused on the essential content concepts. Toward the end of the lesson, a final review helps ELs assess their own understandings and clarify misconceptions. Students' responses to review should guide your decisions about what to do next, such as a summative evaluation or, if needed, additional reteaching and assessing.

SIOP® FEATURE 29: Regular Feedback Provided to Students on Their Output

Periodic review of language, vocabulary, and content enables teachers to provide specific academic feedback to students that clarifies and corrects misconceptions and misunderstandings. Feedback also helps develop students' proficiency in English when it is supportive and validating. For example, teachers can model correct English usage when restating a student's response: "Yes, you're correct, the scientists *were confused* by what they thought was a skull lying next to the mummy." Paraphrasing also supports students' understandings and validates answers if we add after the paraphrase, "Is this what you're thinking (or saying)?" If ELs are only able to respond to questions in one or two words, you can validate their answers in complete sentences: "You're right! *Mummification* is the process of preserving dead bodies."

Specific feedback is generally given orally or in writing, but teachers can also provide it through facial expressions and body language. A nod, smile of support, pat on the shoulder, or encouraging look can take away fear of speaking aloud, especially for students who are beginning to develop English proficiency. Additionally, students can provide feedback to each other. Partners or groups can discuss among themselves, giving feedback on both language production and content understanding, but then report to the whole class. The teacher can facilitate feedback by providing appropriate modeling.

SIOP® FEATURE 30: Assessment of Student Comprehension and Learning of All Lesson Objectives Throughout the Lesson

Within the context of lesson delivery for English learners, we see review and assessment as an ongoing process, especially related to a lesson's language and content objectives. Historically, educators have blurred the line between assessment and evaluation, generally using the term *evaluation* for both formative and summative judgments. The teacher's role in evaluation was primarily as a judge, one who conveyed a value on the completion of a given task. This value was frequently determined from the results of periodic quizzes, reports, or tests that served as the basis for report card grades in elementary and secondary schools.

Today, however, many educators distinguish between assessment and evaluation, (Lipson & Wixson, 2008). *Assessment* is defined as "the gathering and synthesizing of information concerning students' learning," while *evaluation* is defined as "making judgments about students' learning. The processes of assessment and evaluation can be viewed as progressive: first, assessment; then, evaluation" (McLaughlin & Vogt, 1996, pp. 104, 106).

Assessment occurs throughout a lesson, as evidenced in lesson plans and in periodic review to determine if students are understanding and applying content concepts. Assessment must be linked to the instruction, and it needs to target the lesson objectives. Just as students need to know what the objectives are, they also need to be informed about how and what types of assessments they will have. Toward the end of the lesson, students' progress is assessed to see whether it is appropriate to move on or whether it is necessary to review and reteach. This type of assessment is *informal, authentic, multidimensional,* and includes *multiple indicators* that reflect student learning, achievement, and attitudes (McLaughlin & Vogt, 1996; O'Malley & Pierce, 1996; Lenski, Ehlers-Zavala, Daniel, & Sun-Irminger, 2006; Lipson & Wixson, 2008).

Informal assessment involves on-the-spot, ongoing opportunities for determining the extent to which students are learning content. These opportunities may include teacher observations, anecdotal reports, teacher-to-student and student-to-student conversations, quick-writes and brainstorming, or any number of tasks that occur within regular instruction and that are not intended to be graded or evaluated according to set criteria.

Authentic assessment is characterized by its application to real life, where students are engaged in meaningful tasks that take place in real-life contexts. Authentic assessment is usually *multidimensional* because teachers use different ways of determining student performance. These may include written pieces, audiotapes, student and parent interviews, videotapes, observations, creative work and art, discussion, performance, oral group responses, and so forth.

These multidimensional student performances usually involve *multiple indicators,* specific evidences related to the language and content objectives or standards. For example, a student may indicate proficiency with an objective through a piece of writing, through active participation in a group activity, and through insightful questions he or she asks during discussion. The teacher thus has more than one piece of evidence indicating the student is progressing toward mastery of the particular content or language objective.

Periodic assessments before and during lessons can eventually lead to evaluation of a student's demonstrated performance for an objective or standard. This evaluation, while summative, also may be informal and take a variety of forms. Often, rubrics (such as the SIOP® protocol) are used to ascertain a developmental level of performance for a particular goal, objective, or standard. For example, on a developmental rubric, student performance may be characterized as "emergent," "beginning," "developing," "competent," or "proficient." Other rubrics may communicate evaluative information, such as "inadequate," "adequate," "thorough," or "exceptional." Whichever rubric is used, results of assessment and evaluation are often shared with other interested stakeholders, such as parents and administrators, and with the students themselves.

As you are preparing to informally assess your English learners' oral language proficiency, reading, and writing to differentiate instruction appropriately, you may find a paucity of assessment instruments that are practical, quick, and easy to use. This represents an acute need, not only for teachers and their students, but also in terms of research findings that can guide us to assessment instruments that are reliable, valid, and appropriate for diverse students who are English learners (IRA & NICHD, 2007). Additional research is needed on how to assist teachers of ELs in becoming experts in using various assessment measures, including how to best organize all the assessment data, and how to monitor progress and design instruction based on the informal and formal assessment data (Edwards, Turner, & Mokhtari, 2008; IRA & NICHD, 2007; Mokhtari, Rosemary, & Edwards, 2008).

Assessments can be individual or group administered. Individual oral or written responses tell you how one student is performing, while group responses may quickly tell you how the entire group is progressing. Group response is especially sensitive to the needs of ELs, and there is a variety of methods for eliciting group responses, including some of our favorites:

ACTIVITY **Thumbs up/thumbs down:** Generally, this is used for questions that elicit "agree/disagree" responses. (If students agree, they raise their thumbs.) It can also be used for yes/no questions or true/false statements. Older students may be more comfortable responding with "pencils up/pencils down" (point of pencil up or down). Students can also indicate "I don't know" by making a fist, holding it in front of the chest, and wiggling it back and forth. The pencil used by older students can also be wiggled to indicate that the answer is unknown.

ACTIVITY **Number wheels:** A number wheel is made from tag board strips (5″ × 1″) held together with a round-head brass paper fastener. Each strip has a number printed on it, with 0 to 5 or 0 to 10, or a-d, depending on your needs and students' ages. Students use their individual number wheels to indicate their answers to questions or statements that offer multiple-choice responses. Possible answers are displayed on the board, overhead, or pocket chart, and the teacher asks the questions or gives the statements orally.

For example, if you are teaching a lesson on possessives, you could write the following on the board:

1. policemans
2. policemen's
3. policeman's

Each student has a number wheel and you say, "Show me the correct use of the word 'policemen's in the following sentences. Remember that you can show me a '0' if you don't know the answer. "The policemen's squad cars were parked in front of the doughnut store." Think. Get set. Show me."

Students then find the number 2 strip, and holding their number wheels in front of their chests, they display their answers. They repeat the process as you give the next sentence. Be sure to give the cues (Think, Get Set) before giving the direction, "Show me!"

You may think that number wheels are appropriate only for younger students, but middle school and high schools students enjoy working with them too, and they provide you with much needed information about students' understandings of language and content concepts.

ACTIVITY **Response boards:** Either small chalkboards or dry-erase boards can be used for group responses. Each student has a board and writing instrument. You ask a question, students respond on their boards, and then turn them to face you when you say, "Show me!" Older students seem to prefer working with the dry-erase boards and will willingly use them in a classroom in which approximations are supported and errors are viewed as steps to effective learning. Dry-erase boards (12″ × 12″) can be inexpensively cut from "bathroom tile board," which is available at home and building supply stores.

Group response activities are very effective for assessing, reviewing, and providing feedback. By looking around the room, teachers can quickly gauge how many students understand what is being assessed. If students are having difficulty with language and content concepts, and this is obvious from individual answers given during a group response activity, review and reteaching are necessary.

Number 1 to 3 for self-assessment: It's one thing for the teacher to assess student progress toward meeting objectives; it's something entirely different for students to assess their own progress and understandings. From our experience teaching students of all ages, when we ask English learners (and native speakers as well) if they have met a particular objective, the usual response is generally a grunt, a nod, or a "Yeah," often in unison. This activity (Vogt & Echevarria, 2008) is a quick and easy way to have students self-assess the degree to which they think they have met a lesson's content and language objectives. At the end of the lesson as you review the objectives with the students, ask them to indicate with one, two, or three fingers how well they think they met them:

1 = I didn't (or can't) meet (or do) the objective.

2 = I didn't (or can't) meet (or do) the objective, but I made progress toward meeting it.

3 = I fully met (or can do) the objective.

Another example is, "I can teach the key concepts to someone else."

Depending on how students indicate their understandings of a lesson's key concepts (the objectives), the teacher can reteach, provide additional modeling, group students for further instruction and practice, and so forth. We have found that self-assessments that are directly related to a lesson's content and language objectives are far more informative than the typical students' "yeah" or "no" or "sorta" comments that arise when teachers ask whether the lesson's objectives have been met.

Stock Market (grades 3–12): (Created by MaryEllen Vogt)

1. Stock Market is great for an end-of-unit review prior to an exam because it provides the teacher with information about student misconceptions, factual errors, etc. It's also lots of fun!
2. Prepare Monopoly or other "play" money in denominations of $5, $10, $20, $50, $100.
3. Generate content questions (some from an actual quiz or test you're going to give) so that you can assess your students' readiness to take the test. Mix challenging and easier questions so that you'll have at least 10 to 15 to choose from, depending on the grade you teach.
4. Also write some trivia questions of interest to the grade level of your students (such as the principal's first and last name; the U.S. president's first name, the street name where your school is located, the correct spelling of the school's name, etc.). Students also enjoy questions about popular culture, such as the names of musicians, actors, etc., but take care to ask questions on varied topics so that your immigrant English learners are not at a disadvantage because they lack background knowledge about

American popular culture. On Stock Market day, group students heterogeneously (4 to 5 per group). This is very important so that all groups have a mix of students, languages, abilities, etc.

5. Provide each table group with one worksheet with two columns:
   a. for dollar "investments"
   b. for students to write answers to the questions you will be asking
6. Each group must write an "investment" dollar amount on the Stock Market handout *prior* to the teacher asking a question. Groups cannot risk more than 50 percent of what they have in their groups' "bank." For example, if they have $120, the most they can invest is $60. You don't want to have any group "go broke" so they can't continue to play.
7. Ask the question (either content-related or trivia). If a group's answer is correct, the "bank" pays; if not the "bank" (you, the teacher) takes the investment.
8. Use both content and trivia questions, but don't let students know what kind of question you'll be asking. Alternate frequently, but don't let students know which type of question will be asked. If students miss several content questions in a row, you know you'll need to do some reteaching later. To keep everyone in the game, switch to a few easier trivia questions that all groups are sure to answer correctly.
9. Reward groups that are behaving well and are cooperating by giving bonuses (e.g., slipping them extra money). It's also fun to give bonuses to groups ($25 or more) for the correct spelling of answers to particular questions, either trivia or academic content. You don't need to "fine" groups for misbehavior or spelling; just reward or bonus them when they're on task, working well together, and conscientiously answering the questions.
10. If a group falls perilously behind, slip them some money so they won't go broke. If you do this discretely, no one notices and the group receiving the bank's assistance won't say a word.
11. For the final question, make it about content (not trivia) and tell groups they can invest all or some of their earnings—it's their choice. After the question is asked and answered, the group with the most money in the end is declared the winner for that day's Stock Market.

As teachers plan for formal and informal assessments, they should keep in mind that because language and content are intertwined in SIOP® classes, separating one from the other in the assessment process is difficult. It is, however, necessary to do so. When students have difficulty, teachers need to determine if it is the content that has not been mastered, or if it is a lack of English proficiency that is interfering with their acquisition and application of information.

A general rule of thumb is to plan multiple assessments. Having students perform a test on one day only provides limited information. Alternative assessment techniques balance the norm- and criterion-referenced tests teachers are required to give. These alternative techniques include performance-based tasks, portfolios, journals, and projects. All of these assessments allow students to demonstrate their knowledge more fully than would be possible on a multiple-choice test. Although all students benefit from a wide range of assessment procedures, variety is particularly important for ELs because they (1) may be unfamiliar with the type of tests usually required in U.S. schools and (2) may need to demonstrate their knowledge in ways other than using academic English.

Teachers who are learning to implement the SIOP® Model often express concern about having varied content assessments, in part because of the perceived amount of work it takes to create them, and because some believe it is unfair if students are not assessed equally. High school teachers' assessment policies, in particular, are further constrained by issuing grades that impact students' future opportunities for graduation and college admission. While acknowledging all this, we also believe that for English learners, adaptations must be made if teachers are to ascertain accurately the extent to which content objectives and standards are met. Often, English learners do know the information on which they are being assessed, but because of language proficiency issues, including vocabulary, reading, and writing, they are unable to demonstrate their knowledge.

The Center for Intercultural and Multilingual Advocacy (CIMA) at Kansas State University, based on recommendations made by Deschenes, Ebeling, & Sprague (1994), summarized nine types of assessment adaptations that permit teachers to more accurately determine students' knowledge and understanding. We have modified them somewhat to enable teachers to assess more accurately, and give grades when necessary, to English learners. The following are possible assessment adaptations for English learners that are congruent with the SIOP® Model and that hold high academic expectations for ELs:

- **Range:** Adapt the number of items the English learner is expected to complete, such as even or odd numbers only (see Leveled Study Guides in Chapter 2 as another example). Determine percentages of correct responses based on the number of items assessed.
- **Time:** Adapt the amount of time the English learner has for completing a task, such as providing more processing time and/or breaking tasks into manageable chunks. Unless there is a requirement to have a timed test, allowing additional time should not affect a student's score or grade.
- **Level of support:** Adapt the amount of scaffolding provided to an English learner during assessments, by asking an aide, peer assistant, or parent volunteer to read and/or explain the task, or even read aloud (and translate, if necessary and possible) the items for the assessment. Remember the difference between assessing an EL's ability to *read* and follow *written* directions and his or her ability to complete a task or answer questions about a content topic. If you are looking for a student's content knowledge (not his or her ability to read directions), it is fine to have someone else help with reading or clarifying what the expectation for the task is.
- **Difficulty:** Adapt the skill level, type of problem or task, and the process for how an English learner can approach the task, such as allowing a calculator, dictionary, or simplified instructions. Once again, you are not reducing the expectation that the English learner should know the material—you're just making it easier for him or her to demonstrate understandings.
- **Product:** Adapt the type of response the English learner is allowed to provide, such as permitting drawings, a hands-on demonstration, a verbal, and, if necessary, a translated response. Whereas native speakers may be required to write a paragraph summary or essay, it may be reasonable for an English learner to submit an illustration, poster-board explanation, or other kind of product that doesn't rely so much on sophisticated English usage.

- **Participation:** Adapt the degree of active involvement of an English learner in assessment, such as encouraging individual self-assessment, assistance in creating rubrics, and cooperative group self-assessment. As you have read often in this book, content learning is enhanced for all students, but especially for English learners, through interaction and group work. English learners can certainly be involved in their own assessment progress, particularly in the upper grades.

Finally, to the extent possible, students should be assessed on their personal progress to determine if learning has taken place. In sheltered classes in particular, where students may have different levels of language proficiency, the value of this approach becomes apparent. If teachers gather baseline data on what their students know and can do with the content information before instruction occurs and then what they know and can do afterward, teachers can identify student growth.

The Lesson

UNIT: Egyptian Mummies (Eighth Grade)

The classrooms described in the teaching vignettes in this chapter are all in a large urban middle school with a heterogeneously mixed student population. English learners represent approximately 45 percent of the students who are in the teachers' eighth-grade classes; the majority are native Spanish speakers, most of whom are at an intermediate level of English proficiency.

The three eighth-grade language arts/social studies core teachers, Mr. Tran, Mr. Hughell, and Miss Johnston, are teaching an extended unit on Egypt. The lessons illustrated here are on the topic of Egyptian mummies. Each of the teachers has planned a three-day lesson using the chapter titled "Mummy No. 1770: A Teenager" (Cooper et al., 2003). This chapter tells of a mummy that was in the possession of the Manchester Museum in England. Because very little was known about this mummy, the museum made it available to a group of scientists who wanted to use modern techniques for determining its age, its mummification process, and how the person had lived. The chapter describes what the scientists learned, including when the thirteen year-old lived (A.D. 260), what she had eaten, what her life was like, how she died, and how her body was preserved.

The following teaching vignettes represent the second day of the lessons taught by Mr.Tran, Mr. Hughell, and Miss Johnston. (For more examples of lesson and unit plans in history/social studies lessons, see Short, Vogt, & Echevarria, in press.)

Teaching Scenarios

The following vignettes illustrate how Mr. Tran, Mr. Hughell, and Miss Johnston reviewed the language and content objectives of their second day's lesson on the chapter "Mummy No. 1770: A Teenager" and assessed student learning. As you read, think about the SIOP® features for Review and Assessment: Review of Key Vocabulary, Review of Key Concepts, Feedback on Student Output, and Assessment of Student Understanding of Lesson Objectives.

Mr. Tran

In Mr. Tran's lesson plan, he listed the following language and content objectives for English learners: "The learner will be able to (1) describe how scientists learned about Mummy No. 1770, (2) identify major discoveries scientists made during the autopsy of the mummy, and (3) define and correctly use the following vocabulary words: mummy, autopsy, evidence, embalming, amputation, and tissue." Mr. Tran's lesson plan for the first day included the following activities:

1. Brainstorming words about mummies that students already knew
2. Creating a word wall with the brainstormed words
3. Group reading of the first five pages of the chapter
4. Adding of new words to the word wall, selected by students from the reading (Vocabulary Self-Collection Strategy—VSS)
5. Completing the first section of a sequence chain (graphic organizer) listing initial steps used by the scientists
6. Including on the sequence chain words from the word wall (mummy, evidence, and autopsy)

On the second day of the lesson (the one observed for the SIOP® rating), Mr. Tran began by referring back to the word wall. First, the whole class read the words aloud in sequence and again in random order. To assess student comprehension, Mr. Tran asked for volunteers to give informal definitions for a few of the words, focusing on the key vocabulary he had selected to emphasize (mummy, evidence, autopsy) while reminding them of the reading from the day before. When needed, he clarified definitions, assisted students with pronunciations, and gently corrected errors.

Mr. Tran then asked students to review the sequence chains they had begun the previous day with their partners. Feedback was provided by peers as they shared their graphic organizers with each other in order to make corrections or additions about the steps scientists took in analyzing Mummy No. 1770. Students were prompted to include words from the word wall, especially the key vocabulary (mummy, evidence, autopsy). Mr. Tran circulated and listened to the discussions of several pairs. After the partner sharing, the entire class discussed the information on their sequence chains and Mr. Tran informally assessed the students' knowledge.

Next, students reviewed the major discoveries of the scientists described to this point in the reading, and two were listed on the board. The teacher referred to illustrations on pages 5–7 of the chapter and asked students to predict what they think happened to the teenage girl and how scientists might have reached conclusions about her death. He wrote on the board, "What *evidence* did the scientists discover during the *autopsy* of the *mummy*?" as a focal question for the rest of the lesson.

Students were directed to look for additional scientific discoveries as they read the next four pages with partners. They were told to complete a T-chart with the following column headings: "Evidence scientists discovered about No. 1770's life" and "Evidence scientists discovered about No. 1770's death." As a matter of practice, Mr. Tran walked around the room while students were working. He frequently smiled, voiced encouragement, answered questions, and provided support for his students' efforts. When this task was completed, Mr. Tran asked students to share their ideas as a class so he could determine what they had learned and make sure all students could complete their charts.

The lesson continued as students reviewed their papers and the text to find additional words for the word wall. Among the words added were "embalming," "amputation," and "tissue." (See Figure 9.2.) Mr. Tran wrote "embalm," "embalmer," and "embalming" on the board and discussed the differences in meaning. He also asked a volunteer to differentiate

Word Wall: Mummies

archaeologists	jewels	sarcophagus
amputation		spirits
artifacts		
autopsy		
	linen	
		tissue
		tombs
coffin		Tutankhamen
	mummification	
	mummy	
drying-out-process		
		X-ray
	oils	
embalming		
evidence		
	perfumes	wrappings
	pharoahs	
	preservation	
	pyramids	
gold		

FIGURE 9.2 *Use of Word Wall*

between the meaning of "tissue" in the text and the more common meaning—something one uses to blow one's nose.

Students then completed the second section of their sequence chains, indicating the subsequent steps the scientists had taken to gather evidence from the mummy. Mr. Tran encouraged students to include the new key vocabulary (embalming, amputation, and tissue) on the graphic organizer. He concluded the lesson by asking students to review with their partners the steps taken by the scientists and to determine two more major discoveries detailed in the text. These were then discussed and added to those on the board from the previous day. Finally, Mr. Tran highlighted in yellow on the word wall the six key vocabulary words, and these were reviewed one last time before the bell rang.

On the SIOP® form in Figure 9.3, rate Mr. Tran's lesson for each of the Review/Assessment features.

Mr. Hughell

Mr. Hughell's lesson plan noted the following objectives: "(1) Write a paragraph on what mummies teach scientists about how Egyptians lived; (2) Explain how mummies were preserved; and (3) Match twenty vocabulary words with their definitions."

The plan for the first day of the lesson included the following activities:

1. Distributing a list of twenty words and definitions related to mummies along with page numbers on which the words could be found in the chapter text

FIGURE 9.3 *Review & Assessment Component of the SIOP® Model: Mr. Tran's Lesson*

4	3	2	1	0
27. Comprehensive **review of key vocabulary**		Uneven **review of key vocabulary**		No **review of key vocabulary**
28. Comprehensive **review of key content concepts**		Uneven **review of key content concepts**		No **review of key content concepts**
29. Regular **feedback** provided to students on their output (e.g., language, content, work)		Inconsistent **feedback** provided to students on their output		No **feedback** provided to students on their output
30. **Assessment** of student comprehension and learning of all lesson objectives (e.g., spot checking, group response) throughout the lesson		**Assessment** of student comprehension and learning of some lesson objectives		No **assessment** of student comprehension and learning of lesson objectives

2. Reading aloud one-half of the chapter while students follow along
3. Having students find the first group of ten vocabulary words in the chapter
4. Having students work with a partner to write an original sentence related to the topic of mummies for each word

Mr. Hughell began the second day of the lesson by asking volunteers to read several of their vocabulary sentences written the previous day. As students read, Mr. Hughell corrected language errors when needed. He clarified content misconceptions, modeled appropriate pronunciation, and reminded students of the correct definitions for the vocabulary. Mr. Hughell then gave students five minutes to review what had been read the previous day. He asked volunteers to summarize what they had learned about Mummy No. 1770 and how mummies were prepared. Several students responded briefly, and Mr. Hughell prompted others to elaborate. He highlighted key points by writing them on the board and made additions to the students' summaries.

He then asked for volunteers to read the next set of ten words and definitions from the vocabulary list. He informed students that they would have a vocabulary matching quiz on these words the following day. Students were then directed to read the rest of the chapter silently and encouraged by Mr. Hughell to ask for help if they found words they did not understand. Following the reading, students worked with partners to write ten more sentences for the remaining words on the vocabulary list.

FIGURE 9.4 *Review & Assessment Component of the SIOP® Model: Mr. Hughell's Lesson*

4	3	2	1	0
27. Comprehensive **review of key vocabulary**		Uneven **review of key vocabulary**		No **review of key vocabulary**
4	3	2	1	0
28. Comprehensive **review of key content concepts**		Uneven **review of key content concepts**		No **review of key content concepts**
4	3	2	1	0
29. Regular **feedback** provided to students on their output (e.g., language, content, work)		Inconsistent **feedback** provided to students on their output		No **feedback** provided to students on their output
4	3	2	1	0
30. **Assessment** of student comprehension and learning of all lesson objectives (e.g., spot checking, group response) throughout the lesson		**Assessment** of student comprehension and learning of some lesson objectives		No **assessment** of student comprehension and learning of lesson objectives

At the end of the period, Mr. Hughell called on a few volunteers to read their sentences aloud quickly and asked if anyone had questions. Because not everyone had finished writing the sentences, he assigned the remaining ones for homework and reminded students of the vocabulary quiz planned for the next day. He suggested that students review the entire chapter at home because in addition to the vocabulary quiz, they were going to be writing a paragraph in class on what scientists have learned from mummies. He would evaluate the students' comprehension of the chapter with the written paragraph and quiz the following day.

On the SIOP® form in Figure 9.4, rate Mr. Hughell's lesson for each of the Review & Assessment features.

Miss Johnston

Miss Johnston's lesson plans revealed one objective for the three-day lesson on mummies: "The learner will understand how mummies were made." The plan included the following for all three days: "(1) Read chapter on Mummy No. 1770 and (2) complete the worksheet questions."

Miss Johnston began the second day of the lesson by calling on a student to summarize the chapter that had been read aloud the previous day. The student responded, "We took turns reading about how some guys in a museum unwrapped an old mummy."

Another student added, "And scientists learned the mummy was a girl with no legs." Although the responses were brief and only related simple facts, Miss Johnston offered no further explanation or review.

Miss Johnston then distributed a worksheet to students that had multiple-choice and fill-in-the-blank questions covering information in the text chapter, along with two short essay questions. Students worked individually but were allowed to use their books while completing the worksheets. If they finished early, they were given a word search puzzle and asked to find ten words related to mummies. The teacher circulated through the room, answering questions and keeping students on task.

Toward the end of the period, to assess their learning, she asked students to exchange papers. She read the correct answers for the multiple-choice and fill-in-the-blank questions aloud, and students marked their peers' papers. When she asked how many students had only one or two wrong answers, no one raised a hand. She did not pursue the discussion to see if some questions were problematic for most of the class. The lesson concluded with students turning in their essays so Miss Johnston could grade them. She told them to bring in shoe boxes and craft materials for dioramas that each student would make on the following day as a culminating activity.

On the SIOP® form in Figure 9.5, rate Miss Johnston's lesson for each of the Review and Assessment features.

FIGURE 9.5 *Review & Assessment Component of the SIOP® Model: Miss Johnston's Lesson*

4	3	2	1	0
27. Comprehensive **review of key vocabulary**		Uneven **review of key vocabulary**		No **review of key vocabulary**
28. Comprehensive **review of key content concepts**		Uneven **review of key content concepts**		No **review of key content concepts**
29. Regular **feedback** provided to students on their output (e.g., language, content, work)		Inconsistent **feedback** provided to students on their output		No **feedback** provided to students on their output
30. **Assessment** of student comprehension and learning of all lesson objectives (e.g., spot checking, group response) throughout the lesson		**Assessment** of student comprehension and learning of some lesson objectives		No **assessment** of student comprehension and learning of lesson objectives

Discussion of Lessons

27. *Comprehensive Review of Key Vocabulary*

 Mr. Tran: 4

 Mr. Hughell: 1

 Miss Johnston: 0

The emphasis on vocabulary and content instruction, practice, review, and assessment varied across the three classrooms.

Mr. Tran had clearly defined language and vocabulary objectives, and throughout the lesson his instruction and activities were congruent with these objectives. He built upon what students already knew about mummies, incorporated student selection of important terms, and ensured the key vocabulary words were included on the word wall. He pointed out similarities in word structure and differences in word meaning (e.g., embalm/embalming and tissue/tissue).

Mr. Tran's English learners were challenged to articulate orally and in writing the key vocabulary. However, even though many terms and phrases related to mummies were introduced, discussed in the text, and included on the Word Wall, sequence chain, and worksheet, Mr. Tran limited to six the number of words students were expected to master. It is important to note that he repeatedly reinforced these words, at the beginning, in the middle, and again at the end of the lesson. By using the vocabulary in context, repeating the words orally, and writing the question on the board ("What *evidence* did the scientists discover during the *autopsy* of the *mummy*?"), Mr. Tran reviewed the pronunciation, meanings, and usage of the words.

Finally, Mr. Tran expected students to use the new key vocabulary orally and in their writing during partner, small-group, and whole-class discussion. As he listened, he could readily determine who had met the vocabulary objectives and who had not.

Mr. Hughell reviewed the vocabulary sentences from the first day, provided definitions and page numbers, and allowed students to write their sentences with partners. However, it is unrealistic to expect English learners, as well as struggling readers, to master such a large number of vocabulary words (i.e., twenty words) using the approaches he selected. He did not assist students in learning the words through analogy, pictorial representations, or exploration of language structure, and he provided very few exposures to the words. The sentences that the partners were writing were not expected to result in connected text; thus, the students only used the words in isolated instances. Moreover, many students did not complete the assignment in class, so Mr. Hughell was unable to review or assess student understanding of the words.

Mr. Hughell ran out of time at the end of the period and expected students to conduct their own review of the chapter at home. Obviously, this did not provide the type of scaffolding that English learners need and did not represent effective review of language, vocabulary, and content.

Miss Johnston had no language objectives for the lesson plan and did not introduce, teach, or review any key vocabulary to assist students in completing the worksheet. There may have been words in the multiple-choice questions that students were unfamiliar with, reflecting "test language," but she gave them no opportunity to ask about them, nor did she explain the words to the students in advance. Some students (those who finished the worksheets early) practiced finding vocabulary on the word search. However, English learners and struggling readers were least likely to complete the word search because it was intended only for those who completed the worksheet quickly. It is important to note that word searches, while engaging, do not constitute effective review of vocabulary because students are expected to simply match spellings without knowing pronunciations or meanings and they do not receive any teacher support.

28. *Comprehensive Review of Key Content Concepts*

Mr. Tran: 4

Mr. Hughell: 1

Miss Johnston: 1

Most teachers, if they review at the end of a lesson, focus on the content concepts. In these three scenarios, the teachers did so to varying degrees.

Throughout the lesson, Mr. Tran consciously and consistently reviewed content directly related to his objectives. Students reviewed the information they learned the previous day and the new information from this lesson both as a class and with partners. Mr. Tran created opportunities for students to correct errors or add information to the sequence chains and T-charts so that he could clarify misunderstandings. At the conclusion of the lesson, Mr. Tran had students review the major discoveries.

Mr. Hughell provided a basic review of the previous day's reading. He gave students time to focus on their previous learnings and had volunteers summarize what had been read. He asked others to elaborate and wrote the information on the board so all students could follow along. Most important, he clarified points and added information to their summaries. But these efforts were primarily directed to the Building Background component of the SIOP®. In terms of reviewing the day's key concepts, Mr. Hughell was less successful. He ran out of time at the end of the period and consequently failed to review content concepts adequately before the lesson concluded. It was inappropriate for him to require English learners to review at home an entire text chapter that had specialized terminology. The *teacher* is the one to provide this review or scaffold student efforts to review by themselves, prior to assessment and evaluation.

Miss Johnston took a different approach in reviewing content concepts with the students, but it yielded little success with English learners. Initially, she asked students to summarize the chapter they had read. Although two students made an attempt, each stated only one sentence, which recalled a fact but did not summarize the information. Miss Johnston's major effort at concept review was through an individualized paper-and-pencil assignment. This was, however, an assessment of student knowledge and reading comprehension, but not a true review of content concepts for her students. Students could peruse the textbook to find information, but neither the class as a whole nor students in groups had an opportunity to discuss and clarify understandings about the content material. Moreover, Miss Johnston's only objective was vague ("Students will understand how mummies were made") and did not provide clearly defined content concepts for the students.

29. *Regular Feedback Provided to Students on Their Output*

Mr. Tran: 4

Mr. Hughell: 2

Miss Johnston: 1

Mr. Tran, Mr. Hughell, and Miss Johnston had some similar and different techniques for providing feedback to the students during their lessons.

Mr. Tran scaffolded students' learning by clarifying, discussing, and correcting responses. He encouraged peer support and feedback when the graphic organizers were shared, and he used explanation and discussion to help students understand how to evaluate the importance of the scientists' discoveries. He moved around the classroom during the lesson, offering support and encouragement. Mr. Tran clearly used review, assessment, and feedback to develop his students' language proficiency and content knowledge.

Mr. Hughell frequently clarified misconceptions and gave clear corrections for students' errors. However, his feedback would have been more effective had it better scaffolded students' developing language proficiency and content knowledge. That is, Mr. Hughell's feedback was primarily corrective rather than supportive. He essentially told students their answers were incorrect and then gave them the correct ones, rather than assisting them in formulating the correct responses themselves. Mr. Hughell also directed students to read the text independently and ask for help if needed. Many students, English learners especially, may be reluctant to ask for help for fear of appearing incapable or because they don't know how to formulate the questions they need to ask.

Because Mr. Hughell's classroom was quite teacher centered (he delivered instruction mostly by standing at the front of the room), students had little opportunity to work together to provide each other with helpful feedback. His teaching would be more effective for English learners if he created a more supportive classroom environment. He could begin by providing more sensitive feedback to his students' responses.

Miss Johnston attempted to help students by answering questions while they were completing their worksheets. She also corrected the papers in class, providing the answers for the questions. However, the amount of feedback she provided students was very limited, and not particularly supportive. When she gave the correct responses to the worksheet questions, she provided little or no explanation, and she did not consider student output on an individualized basis during the lesson. In all, English learners received very little supportive feedback during the observed lesson.

30. *Assessment of Student Comprehension and Learning of All Lesson Objectives*

Mr. Tran: 4

Mr. Hughell: 2

Miss Johnston: 1

Assessing student learning is a critical step in the teaching and learning cycle. The three teachers in these vignettes all conducted some assessment, but in different ways.

As his lesson unfolded, Mr. Tran's assessment opportunities included group response, partner, and whole-class reporting, as well as individual written work. His assessments occurred throughout the lesson and were authentic, multidimensional, and included multiple indicators. Most important, his assessment was directly linked to his content and language objectives.

Mr. Hughell did not assess student understanding well in the observed lesson. He called upon a few students to read their vocabulary sentences aloud, so for those students he was able to assess their sense of the words' meanings, but he had no way of knowing whether the rest of the students, particularly the English learners, understood the vocabulary terms. When students read the chapter silently, he did not assess their reading comprehension of the content. He planned some summative assessments, namely the vocabulary matching test and the written paragraph, and tried to match assessment to his objectives ("Write a paragraph on what mummies teach scientists about how Egyptians lived; Explain how mummies were preserved; Match twenty vocabulary words with their definitions"). However, these assessments were scheduled for the following day, too late to guide review, feedback, and reteaching during instruction. By the time he discovered who had met the language and content objectives and who had not, the three-day lesson would be completed.

Miss Johnston was less successful on this SIOP® feature. The factual recall sentences elicited from the two students at the start of the lesson yielded no information about the understanding of the rest of the students. Although the worksheet constituted summative evaluation, there was no ongoing assessment throughout the lesson. Students responded to the worksheet individually, and only after she collected the papers, looked at the scores, and graded their essays—after the lesson had ended—would she have a sense of what students had learned. As with Mr. Hughell, this information would arrive too late to guide review and reteaching. There was no learning objective related to the creation of the dioramas, and students were not provided with a rubric or criteria upon which their projects would be assessed. It is doubtful the dioramas would tell Miss Johnston much about her students' understanding of key vocabulary and content concepts. Finally, her one objective ("The students will understand how mummies were made") was too general and not directly measurable.

Summary

Review and assessment are integrated processes, essential for all students, but they are critical to the success of English learners. Effective SIOP® teachers carefully plan for periodic review and informal formative assessment throughout lessons. This informal assessment is authentic, multidimensional, and includes multiple indicators of students' performance. Effective SIOP® teachers also design appropriate summative evaluation of key vocabulary and content concept objectives at the conclusion of the lesson. Assessment adaptations that provide for effective differentiated instruction include the time ELs need to complete a task; the level of support they need during practice and application; the difficulty level of the task and the process by which ELs can approach it; the type of response or product an EL is allowed to provide; and the degree of active participation. These adaptations do not reduce the level of cognitive involvement of English learners, but rather provide them with the opportunity to demonstrate their knowledge and understanding. Most important, review and assessment guide teaching and reteaching, inform decision making, lead to supportive feedback, and provide for fair and comprehensive judgments about student performance.

Discussion Questions

1. Many teachers introduce key vocabulary at the beginning of the lesson, but often neglect to revisit the new terms systematically throughout the lesson and review them at its conclusion. How can you ensure that a SIOP® lesson's key academic vocabulary is reviewed at the end of each lesson? Describe a variety of ways you

would review the terms, as well as the techniques you could put in place to build a vocabulary review into each lesson. Which of the activities introduced in this chapter would you select? Why?

2. Research has shown that gratuitous compliments to students (e.g., "Good job" or "Keep up the good work") do little to motivate them or assist with their learning. Instead, teachers should give regular, substantive feedback to students on their verbal contributions and on their academic work. What are some ways to provide constructive, specific academic feedback to students? Consider class size and English proficiency levels as you answer this question.
3. Reflect on the ideas presented in this chapter, as well as all the other activities you have used to assess student learning of specific lesson objectives. How much time do you think you should allocate for review and assessment during each lesson? What if you discover (as is often the case) that some students are ready to move on, while others need more review and/or reteaching? Using the SIOP® lesson you have been creating, provide specific provisions for students at varying levels. Plan multiple indicators throughout the lesson that will enable you to assess on-the-spot progress toward meeting the lesson's content objectives. Then determine what you will do for (1) independent or partner work for students who are ready to move on and (2) a reteaching or review minilesson for those who need additional assistance from you. This is probably the most challenging aspect of providing differentiated instruction, not only for English learners, but for all students. How will you assess who is ready to move on? How will you assess the students in the reteaching/review group to determine if and when they're ready to move on? What will you do if a few students are still struggling? These are the *big* questions to ask (and answer) when planning for a lesson's review and assessment.

chapter 10

Issues of Reading Development and Special Education for English Learners

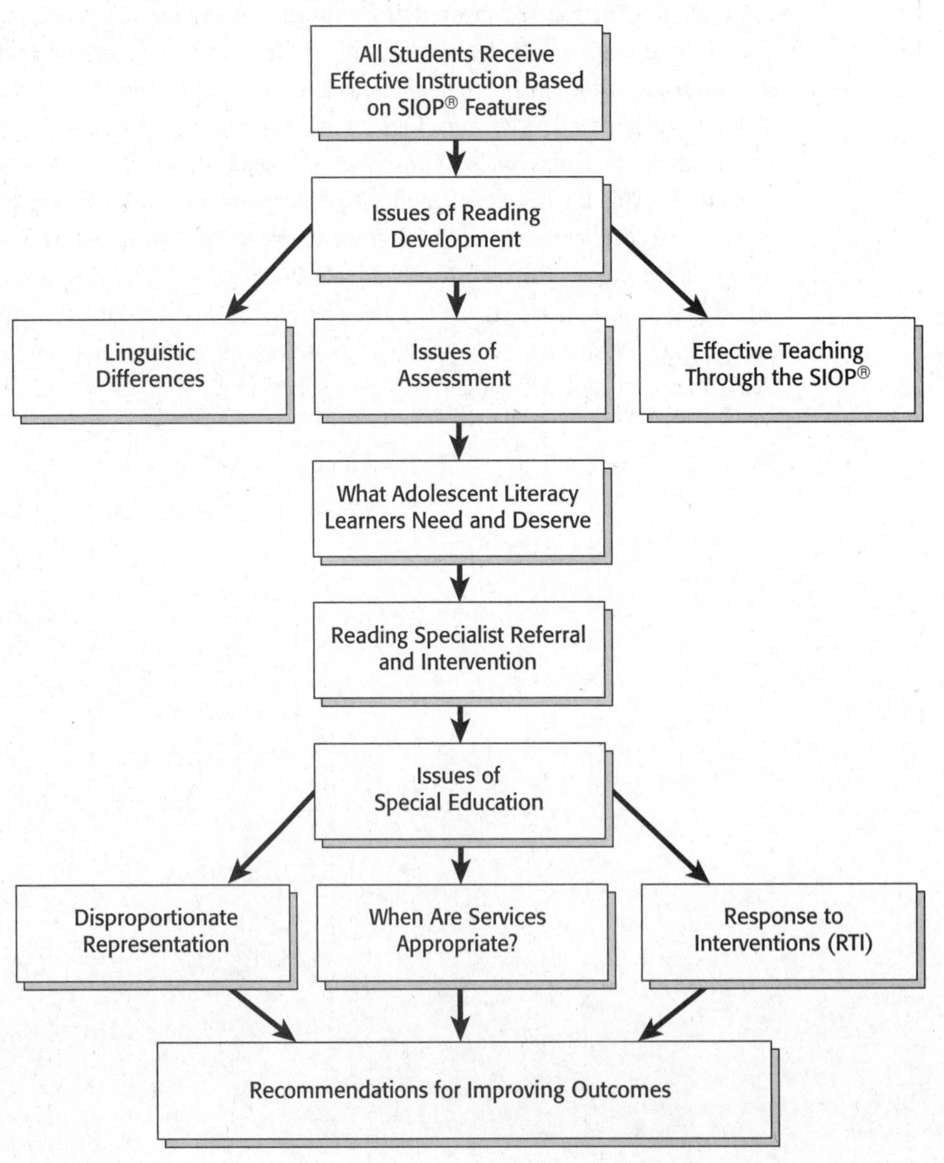

Objectives

After reading, discussing, and engaging in activities related to this chapter, you will be able to meet the following content and language objectives.

Content Objectives

Explain how linguistic differences in home languages and English can affect English learners' reading and writing development.

Describe in-class interventions that content teachers can provide to struggling readers and learners.

Delineate a sequence of steps teachers and other educators can take to assure appropriate placement of English learners in regular and special education classes.

Language Objectives

Discuss with a group how to plan appropriate instruction for English learners who may have reading and learning difficulties.

Write a lesson plan that develops vocabulary and reading proficiency for English learners who struggle to read and learn.

In our work with teachers and administrators throughout the United States, a persistent question concerns appropriate instruction for older English learners who exhibit difficulties with reading and learning. Teachers often feel ill-prepared to provide content instruction for these students because they're not sure whether a student's difficulty is due to a reading problem, a learning disability, lack of schooling, or limited English proficiency. Unfortunately, the result of this confusion has been both under- and overrepresentation of English learners in remedial and special education classes (Gunderson & Siegel, 2005).

In this chapter, we discuss issues of assessment, identification, and instruction for students who may be experiencing reading and/or learning problems. It is beyond the scope of this book to provide a comprehensive treatment of this topic (For a full discussion see Echevarria and Graves, 2007). Instead, we hope to stimulate your thinking and discussion with colleagues about these issues, especially as they affect English learners. We begin with a discussion of reading development and assessment for English learners and then move on to issues related to special education.

Issues of Reading Development and Assessment for Adolescents

Teachers face many challenges related to the literacy development of their adolescent English learners. The task of teaching ELs to read is made difficult in part due to the complexity of learning to read and write in a language one does not understand completely. However, it is not always possible for students to learn to read first in their primary language. Many older English learners, including those who are native-born Americans, have been schooled almost exclusively in the United States, yet their home language differs from the language of instruction. A large number of these students are not fully literate in either their L1 or English, and most have not been successful in school. Sadly, 30 percent of secondary students in the United States are not graduating from high school, but our language minority students are failing to graduate in even higher numbers. Eighty percent of the English learners in the United States are Hispanic, and of these only 52 percent graduate from high school. The unfortunate truth is that every day, approximately 3,000 middle and high school students walk out of their schools and never return (National Center for Educational Statistics, 2002).

In a study of struggling middle school readers, Vogt (1997) confirmed the insights of earlier investigators who looked into the nature of struggling adolescent readers. Their findings indicate (Ruddell, Shearer, & Vogt, 2001; Vogt & Shearer, 2007, p. 93):

- Most adolescent struggling readers have had difficulty with reading since the beginning of their schooling.
- Many have adopted complex strategies to avoid situations in which they are required to read aloud, often acting out or withdrawing during literacy-related activities.
- The majority have had poor grades, low self-esteem, and little interest in school or extracurricular activities.
- Although many have limited decoding skills, most can read one-syllable regular words; most have difficulty with multisyllabic and irregular words (those most often found in secondary content textbooks). Adolescent, native-born English learners with reading problems also are very likely to have difficulty with these words.
- By middle school, many adolescent struggling readers have given up hope of ever improving their reading ability and openly proclaim their distaste for reading extended text.

Think for a moment about the students you teach who have serious reading problems, both those who are native-English speakers and those who are English learners. Are the above outcomes descriptive of your students?

In another study, Vogt (1989) uncovered a number of disturbing incongruities between teachers' attitudes and practices toward middle and high school low- and high-achieving students. When compared to opportunities given to their lower-achieving peers, higher-performing students (Vogt & Shearer, 2007):

- Spend more classroom time engaged in silent rather than oral reading.
- Are provided with more instructional time related to comprehension.
- Are given more opportunities to engage in higher levels of thinking and strategic learning and more independent research and synthesis projects.
- Are asked questions requiring higher levels of thinking, followed by more wait time.
- Are provided with richer, comprehensive, grade-level texts and supplemental materials.
- Are offered greater opportunities for leadership.

Such discrepant opportunities led Keith Stanovich (1986) to describe a phenomenon he called the "Matthew Effect," borrowed from the book of Matthew in the Bible. When it comes to literacy development, "The rich get richer, and the poor get poorer." Given what we know about struggling adolescent readers in general, how can we assist adolescent English learners who are demonstrating reading deficiencies?

Older English learners may need explicit instruction in the aspects of English that differ from their native languages, including the phonology, morphology, and syntax of English (Goldenberg, 2008). Clearly, English learners benefit when they learn to read and write in both their native language and in English (August & Shanahan, 2006; Genesee, Lindholm-Leary, Saunders, & Christian, 2006; Lenters, 2005; Slavin & Cheung, 2004), but this may not be possible for all students.

An additional challenge when teaching ELs to read in English is determining their reading proficiency. Students who arrive in the United States with well-developed reading skills in their native language have mastered many of the essentials of reading (Tabors & Snow, 2005). They have learned that print carries meaning, and if their home language is alphabetic, they have learned that phonemes (sounds) are represented by graphemes (letters and letter combinations), and that when put together, these graphemes create words and meaning (the alphabetic principle). They have also learned the syntax (structure) of their first language, and though they may be challenged by learning English syntax, they can use their knowledge of their first language's structure to make connections with English. Also, once students have learned what it means to strategically comprehend text in their native language, they are able to transfer these thinking strategies from their home language to English (August, 2006; Gutiérrez, 2004). English learners whose first language is nonalphabetic (such as Mandarin) will need to learn an alphabetic sound–symbol system in order to speak, read, and write English, but will carry over their understandings of the reading and writing processes to their new language.

Therefore, students who read satisfactorily in their primary language do not have to relearn how to read or write. However, they do need to learn English. With comprehensible input and explicit instruction in the structure of English they have a better chance of transferring their existing reading skills to the reading of English. For example, for students whose primary language is Spanish, there are many cognates that link English vocabulary and spelling with Spanish (estudiar = study; excepción = exception). Using dictionaries in Spanish, English, French, and German as resources helps students make these connections as they explore similarities in the languages (Bear, Templeton, Helman, & Baren, 2003). It is also clear that English learners need to be immersed in print, with many opportunities to read appropriate books, stories, and informational texts, ideally in their home language as well as in English (Krashen, 2003).

In contrast to those ELs who have well-developed literacy skills in their primary language, other students enter American schools with little or no reading instruction in their primary language, or find reading and writing very difficult. These students are often referred to special education programs inappropriately, when other interventions, such as longer exposure to high-quality, scaffolded instruction; more direct, small group, or individual instruction; or referral to a reading specialist may be more appropriate. It is important for teachers to know whether their English learners can read in their primary language and to be able to ascertain whether difficulty in content subjects may be due to a reading problem or a lack of English proficiency.

Many teachers, rightly, want to know the "reading level" of their students. This information helps the teacher match texts to students. For example, if a seventh-grade student is reading at approximately the fourth-grade reading level, he is likely to have difficulty comprehending his seventh-grade social studies textbook without instructional modifications and scaffolding. Either the too-difficult text will need to be adapted or the student will require considerable assistance in accessing the content information from the text. It is challenging enough to teach struggling readers who are native English speakers. With English learners, the problem of struggling readers is even more complex. According to Tabors and Snow (2005), "Knowing what a child knows—and in what language—is necessary before any informed placement or program decisions can be made. Often, however, assessment—if it occurs at all—only occurs in English, providing no information about possible early literacy strengths that have been developed in the child's first language" (p. 263).

Classroom teachers and reading specialists use a variety of assessments to determine their students' reading proficiency. However, commonly used assessments that yield a particular reading level (such as fourth grade) may be inappropriate for English learners (Jiménez, 2004). For example, a common diagnostic instrument for assessing students' fluency and comprehension is an informal reading inventory (IRI). During this assessment, a student reads silently or orally a series of increasingly difficult, leveled passages. The teacher or reading specialist marks reading errors, asks comprehension questions, and, based on a student's reading proficiency, determines approximate *independent, instructional,* and *frustration* reading levels.

Think of your own reading. If you read for pleasure and enjoy lying in a hammock with a favorite book during the summer, you'll most likely select an independent-level text that doesn't require you to look up the meaning of words, take notes, or work very hard while reading. However, if you're taking a graduate course, your textbook should be at your instructional level. You expect to have assistance from your professor, and after a lecture or class discussion on the topic, the text is more accessible for you. You may experience frustration-level reading when you read detailed and complex directions that accompany a new computer, confusing income tax forms, or a text on a subject for which you have very little knowledge or experience.

What we know is that it is futile to assign any students, native English speakers and English learners alike, text that is written at their frustration level (Snow, Burns, & Griffin, 1998). Instead, we need to select texts that are written at the student's instructional level, if possible, and that account for students' different experiential bases (Goldenberg, 2008) and then provide additional assistance so that the text becomes accessible. If this level of text isn't available, then we must adapt the grade-level text through rewriting, providing a detailed study guide, highlighting the key concepts, or providing detailed marginal notes. Without these, the instructional- and frustration-level texts will be largely inaccessible, especially for English learners.

It's important to remember that successful reading of any text is also dependent on a number of other variables, including familiarity with the topic being read; vocabulary knowledge; the flexible use of a variety of reading skills and strategies; motivation; and purpose-setting. For students who are reading in their native language, these variables are relatively easy to assess, and the selection of appropriate text materials can be made with a reasonable amount of confidence. However, many of our usual battery of reading assessments may not yield reliable results for English learners, and selection of appropriate texts is considerably more difficult. A student who is assessed at grade level in his native language may be assessed as reading at a considerably lower level in English. Using results from an IRI (or, a standardized achievement test printed in English) in English might suggest that the student has a serious reading problem. However, if the student doesn't have difficulty reading in his native language, it's unlikely he'll have a serious reading problem in his new language. Likewise, if the student has a reading problem in his first language, he may very well have difficulty reading in English.

So how do we determine whether a student's academic difficulties are due to a reading problem or English proficiency? First, we need to recognize that the phonology of a student's native language may differ substantially from that of English. Although we may teach phonics explicitly and effectively, some ELs may not hear or be able to reproduce the sounds of English because these sounds do not exist in their primary language. The consonant sounds may be considerably different, the number of vowels may vary, and such things as vowel combinations, commonly found in English *(ea, ie, oa)*, may be nonexistent in the students' home languages (such as Spanish).

Most secondary content area teachers will not be expected to teach phonemic awareness and phonics to their English learners or struggling readers, but recognizing that there are differences in the phonology (sound system), morphology (word structure, such as the prefixes, suffixes, and roots of English), and syntax (sentence structure) of various languages will be helpful as you work with your students. Teachers' accepting approximations ("coming close") in pronunciation, reading, and writing also will help English learners develop confidence and a willingness to try. Teachers of adolescent literacy learners will benefit from the recommendations given in Table 10.1.

How many of you can define blog, IM, fanfic, manga, MUDs, MOOs? The answer to this question may depend on your age or interest in current technology, but they are the world of the typical adolescent in the United States today. By the time this book is published, these terms will most likely have been replaced by others. As with all tools, new literacies are being invented and old ones transformed in response to the needs of communicators (Vogt & McLaughlin, 2005). As teachers, it is imperative that we stay abreast of these of ever-evolving literacies.

Even when we provide adolescent literacy learners with effective content and literacy instruction, there will be students who need more. These students need intensive intervention by a reading specialist, especially if they have never learned how to read effectively in either their home language or English. But before your refer students for diagnostic

TABLE 10.1 *What Adolescent Literacy Learners Need and Deserve*

1. *Adolescents need direct, explicit comprehension instruction that is imbedded in rich content.* This can occur most effectively in classrooms with content area teachers and with authentic content. If you need to brush up on some of the more recent effective techniques to developing reading skills and strategies in your content area, see Doug Buehl's *Classroom Strategies for Interactive Learning* (3rd ed., 2009), and Jeff Zwiers's *Building Reading Comprehension Habits in Grades* 6–12 (2004), and Marty Ruddell's *Teaching Content Reading and Writing* (5th ed., 2007).
2. *Adolescents need instruction that incorporates focused strategy instruction within rich, relevant texts that are aligned with clear academic goals and assessment evidence.* If we want to find out what students can do, then we have to have them "doing." Combining formative, summative, and authentic assessment using their results to guide what to teach and how to teach it gives teachers direction and focus.
3. *Adolescents need opportunities to access and produce a variety of rich text materials across genres and literacies.* For example, there are big differences in how we think, read, and write about photosynthesis as opposed to the Civil War. Therefore, the texts describing each of these content topics will also be different because how we read and write about a scientific process in which plants utilize light differs considerably from how we compare and contrast the North and South's economic, military, and social realities in 1863. Students, especially English learners, need assistance in learning how to deal with these differences in their reading and writing. Graphic organizers can greatly assist students in recognizing these differences.
4. *Adolescents need a curriculum that provides appropriate support while capitalizing on the diverse funds of knowledge and literacy needs of all learners.* As mentioned previously (see Chapter 3), some students from diverse backgrounds have not had access to the vast amount of cultural and academic "capital" that the majority of mainstream students bring to school. Therefore, it is critically important to be able to assess and provide background knowledge for those who have gaps. Further, Shearer & Ruddell (2006), in writing about their research on motivation and its impact on adolescent literacy development, found that personal identification with and investment in an activity increases and sustains learner persistence and productivity.
5. *Adolescents need to engage in rich collaboration that promotes motivation and self-directed learning.* Think about a classroom experience in which you were participating as a student, and you became so engrossed that you lost all sense of time and space. It was, perhaps, a group activity or project where you were collaborating with other students, and everything just came together. Perhaps you can even remember the teacher who helped make this happen. Secondary content teachers are in a unique position to create classroom conditions that lead to sustained engagement and high levels of student motivation, and this seldom occurs with daily lectures.
6. *Adolescents need instruction that fosters critical literacy skills.* Our students, perhaps as no others, have unprecedented access to information, complex media, persuasive advertising, and web-based sources, many of which are intent on manipulating them. One thing we can help adolescents control is how they approach sources on the Internet and in print. Secondary teachers can model for their students how to analyze and question who is the source of the information they are citing, and show them how to ask the right questions about possible perspective or bias. Leu (2005) suggests requiring students to cross-check all information from the Internet with at least three different sources, comparing the messages for accuracy and verification.
7. *Adolescents need instruction in technologies that facilitate students' ability to use literacy for in-school purposes as well as for out-of-school practices.* Leu (2005), in his presidential address for the National Reading Conference, suggested three ideas that might reframe the way educators think about technology:
   a. In every age, our technologies define our culture and our literacy.
   b. The Internet is this generation's defining technology for learning and literacy.
   c. The Internet is a reading and literacy issue, not a technology issue.

(Adapted from Vogt & Shearer, 2007, pp. 146–151)

remediation, think about the following questions that can guide your inquiry about how to best help these students.

1. What evidence do you have that a particular student is having difficulty with reading?
2. Do you have any evidence that this student has difficulty reading in his or her home language? If not, how might you gather some? If you are not fluent in the student's

language, is there another student who is? Is there a community liaison or family member who can provide information about the student's L1 literacy development?

3. If your evidence points to a reading problem, what have you and other teachers done to accommodate the student's needs?
   a. Are the student's teachers adapting content and texts to provide greater accessibility (see Chapter 2)?
   b. Are the teachers using instructional techniques that make the content and expectations understandable for English learners (see Chapter 4)?
   c. Are the student's teachers incorporating cognitive and metacognitive strategy instruction in the language arts and content subjects (see Chapter 5)?
   d. Are the student's teachers scaffolding instruction through flexible grouping (see Chapters 5 and 6)?
   e. Are the student's teachers providing multiple opportunities for practice and application of key content and language concepts (see Chapter 7)?
   f. Are the student's teachers using effective assessment to determine what the student knows and can do related to content and language objectives, and to plan subsequent reteaching lessons (see Chapter 9)?

At this point, we hope you're getting the idea that appropriate instruction for this student involves all of the components of the SIOP® Model: those listed above as well as appropriate pacing, meaningful activities, sufficient wait time, and so forth. Certainly, a student with reading problems will benefit from the effective practices advocated in the SIOP® Model, while he or she receives an appropriate intervention for the reading problems.

Will this type of instruction overcome a serious reading problem? Probably not, although recent research on effective literacy instruction for young English learners is consistent with the features of the SIOP® Model (Graves, Gersten, & Haager, 2004). But, here's the key: If you (and your colleagues) have done all you can to provide effective English language development and content instruction using the SIOP® Model and a student is still struggling with reading, it is appropriate and important that the student be referred to a reading specialist. The reading specialist can do a thorough, diagnostic assessment and implement an intervention designed for the student's literacy needs. If the student is still struggling with school after the intensive intervention, then further intervention and referral to special education might be warranted (Haager, Dimino, & Windmueller, 2007).

Issues Related to Special Education

The previous discussion of reading is closely related to any discussion of special education because approximately 80 percent of referrals to special education are for reading problems. It is critically important that school personnel provide the support and assistance necessary when English learners exhibit learning difficulties and exhaust every option before considering referral to special education. (See discussion of response to intervention that follows.) There has been a long history of disproportionate representation of minority students in special education, especially those from low socioeconomic backgrounds (Artiles, 1998; Dunn, 1968; Lee, 2006; Trent, Kea, & Oh, 2008). A number of factors may contribute to the disproportionate number of minority students referred to and placed in special education.

One factor is that teachers and administrators in general education often fail to provide effective instruction in fundamental subjects of reading and math—content areas basic to learning in other areas—and also fail to manage their classrooms effectively (Orfield, Losen, & Edley, 2001). This is more often the case in urban schools where students have the greatest needs. When teachers feel unprepared to work with students who struggle academically or who exhibit inappropriate classroom behaviors, referral to special education is often the first option to which they turn.

Another factor may be a mismatch between minority-learner characteristics and the materials and teaching methods presented in school, which contributes to underachievement among this group of students (Powers, 2001; Vogt & Shearer, 2007). Much of what students understand and are able to do in school is based on their culture and background, and most academic tasks and curricula reflect middle-class values and experiences (see Chapter 3 for more discussion). Reliance on paper-and-pencil tasks, independent reading of dense text, and information presented orally are only some of the types of academic tasks that create difficulties for English learners. Also, students who are culturally and linguistically diverse may not have the requisite background knowledge and experience to perform well academically, nor do they have behaviors that are consistent with the values of school. In general, students achieve better educational outcomes if they have been reared in a culture that has expectations and patterns of behaviors that are consistent with those of the school (Comer, 1984). If that is not the case, then instruction such as that characterized in the SIOP® Model provides the best opportunity for English learners to participate successfully in the academic program of school.

Underachievement among minority youth, which often leads to special education referral and placement, may also be explained by outside factors such as the effects of poverty (Smith, 2006), low teacher expectations (Callahan, 2005), poor study habits and poor time management (Ford, 1998), cultural differences in students' and teachers' behavioral expectations (Neal, McCray, Webb-Johnson, & Bridgest, 2003; Patton & Townsend, 1999), and language differences (Cummins, 1984; Echevarria & Graves, 2007; Genesee, 1994). Obviously, all the complexities of underachievement cannot be ameliorated with good instruction alone; however, quality of instruction is a variable that makes a difference, and it is something that is under the control of school personnel.

It should be mentioned that English learners are also sometimes underreferred for special education services for many of these same reasons: (1) teachers may be unsure whether to refer ELs to special education (2) low expectations allow ELs to languish without services, or (3) district policies require an arbitrary amount of time to pass before students can be referred for the services they need.

Teachers and administrators must understand the critical relationship between quality of instruction and student performance. For a complete discussion of these issues, see Echevarria and Graves, 2007.

Special Education Services: When Are They Appropriate?

Disproportionate representation of minority students in special education is most pronounced among the mild and moderate disability categories, such as learning disabilities and speech and language disorders. For example, more than 17 percent of Hispanic students are labeled as learning disabled although they account for only about 12 to 13 percent of the population while 61 percent of white students have the LD label but they make up 75 percent of the population (Office of Special Education Programs, 2002).

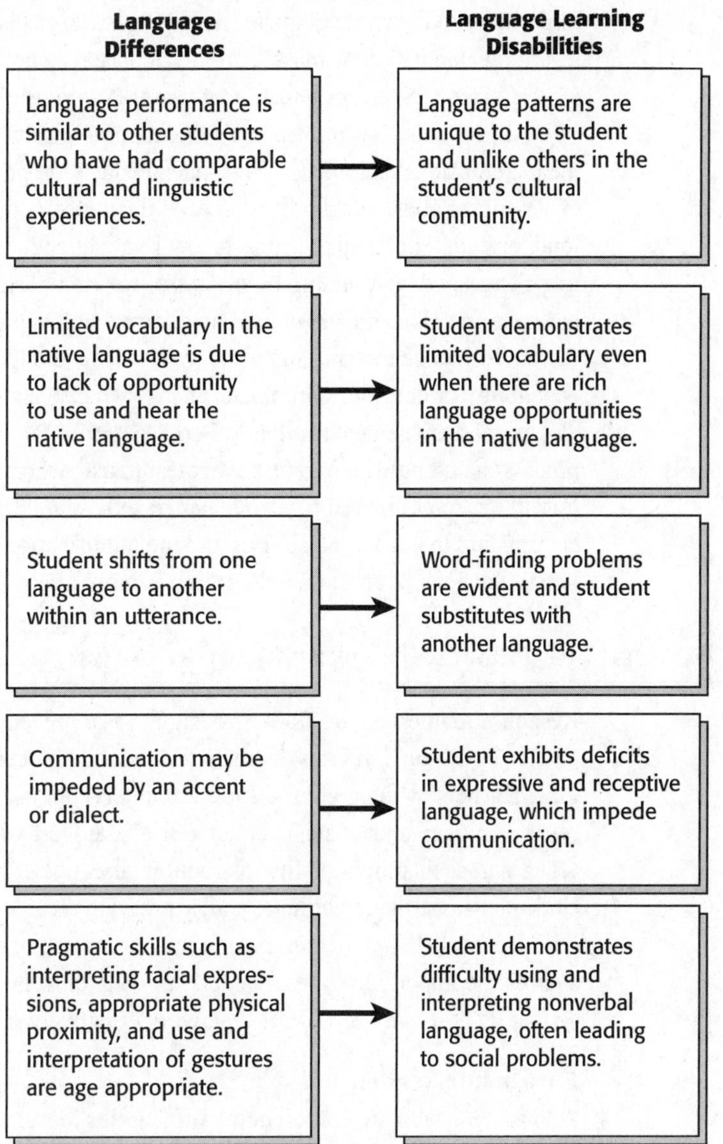

FIGURE 10.1 *Causes of Confusion in Assessing Students with Language Differences and/or Language Learning Disabilities*

The characteristics of students in these categories are not as easily identifiable as they are in students with more significant disabilities and therefore require subjective judgment. Recent research indicates that it is very difficult for school personnel to distinguish between the challenges associated with acquiring a second language and a language-based learning disability (Klinger & Harry, 2006; Lesaux & Geva, 2006). The distinctions can be fairly subtle, as you can see in Figure 10.1. The subjectivity of identification is exacerbated because mild to moderate disabilities do not have a clear biological cause, prompting some to argue that the disabilities themselves are socially constructed (Barnes, Mercer, & Shakespeare, 1999). What is considered "normal" is influenced by a number of factors, including culture, age, community practice, point in history, and school expectations. The labels associated with mild disabilities are assigned arbitrarily and are subject to extreme variability in identification rates. American Indians/Alaskan Native children are about one and a half times more likely to be identified as having learning disabilities than the proportion of the rest of the population, while Asian/Pacific Islanders are much less likely to receive an LD label (Office of Special Education Services Programs, 2002).

All students placed in special education programs have gone through a referral, assessment, and placement process. The special education process is initiated once a student is experiencing considerable difficulties in the general education program—academic, behavioral, or both. For English learners, low English language proficiency, gaps in educational experience, and cultural differences influence the referral process. The reality is that teachers have a tremendous impact on who is referred and who is not. Research indicates that two factors influence referral: (1) teacher tolerance and (2) the interaction of perceived student ability or behavior with the teacher's own expectations and approach to instruction and classroom management (Podell & Soodak, 1993). Subjectivity is part of the evaluation process including whom to test, what test to use, when to use alternative assessments, and how to interpret the results (Losen & Orfield, 2002). So if teachers have an appreciation of cultural and linguistic differences and the modifications those differences require, intervention in the general education classroom is more likely.

Assisting Struggling Learners: Response to Intervention

Response to intervention (RTI) is designed as a prevention system so that fewer students are labeled as disabled. It is a systematic schoolwide process for addressing the needs of struggling learners by integrating instruction, intervention, and assessment, which can ultimately result in higher student achievement (Brown & Doolittle, 2008; Johnson & Smith, 2008). RTI assumes that high-quality instruction takes place in general education and that those students who struggle within a quality program receive an immediate response. Before we describe an RTI approach in detail, there are some related issues we want you to consider, such as the importance of early intervention and the need for improved teacher preparation, so that RTI—or any approach—can work effectively (Echevarria, Powers, & Elliott, 2004).

Earlier Intervention

Adolescents who are experiencing difficulties require systematic interventions to enable them to participate fully in the academic and social opportunities offered in middle and high schools. Currently, before students are eligible for specialized support services, they must exhibit significant academic or behavior problems. Why should students have to establish a pattern of failure before assistance is provided? In the case of ELs, many teachers delay referral so that students have ample opportunity to learn English (Limbos & Geva, 2002). However, at the secondary level, these students have limited time in which to receive the kinds of intervention that will help them graduate.

Better Training

Professional preparation programs for all school personnel should address effective instruction for English learners—general education, special education, reading specialists, school psychologists, and administrators. Preparing general education and special education personnel to work together effectively with English learners begins at the preservice level. Teacher preparation programs (general and special education) that address issues of diversity, social equity, second language acquisition, culturally relevant instruction methods, and empirically supported interventions contribute to a teaching force that implements meaningful and appropriate instruction for students with differing abilities (Echevarria & Graves, 2007).

However, in the past decade, there has not been considerable progress in incorporating into preservice general education or special education programs practices for addressing diverse learners. There have been numerous calls for change but few actual changes (Trent, et al., 2008). Working effectively with diverse populations should be a priority for teacher preparation programs, especially given demographic trends. In many ways, a teacher is the key to a child's success or failure. Students' interactions with their teacher can be either disabling or empowering, and the quality of teacher–student interaction has a significant impact on academic performance and classroom behavior (Kea & Utley, 1998). In a recent study on teacher–student interaction (Yoon, 2008), it was found that when teachers treat English learners with respect and have positive interactions with them, English-speaking peers follow suit. In addition, ELs participate in class to a greater extent and learning opportunities are enhanced in such settings.

Effective SIOP® teachers reflect on their practice and are mindful of the interaction between the learner and the instructional setting, materials, and teaching methods, and make adjustments as needed to facilitate learning. The importance of context to learning cannot be overstated; characteristics of the classroom and school can increase the risk for academic and behavioral problems. Teachers need training in understanding the interaction between learning and context, avoiding the deficit model that views academic and behavior problems as a within-child problem. We have empirical and anecdotal evidence that many academic and behavioral difficulties can be attributed to the impact of the instructional setting (teacher, materials, methods) on the student, rather than some inherent problem of the learner.

In fact, in our observation of classrooms, it seems that the best option for struggling students may be gifted classes. In those classes, teachers tend to capitalize on students' strengths, allow students time to interact and discuss ideas, and teach in creative, stimulating ways. Too many classes for low-performing students are devoid of an excitement for learning, and teachers seem to be simply trying to keep students in their seats.

Search for Interventions Rather Than Disabilities

When English learners struggle in school, they are referred to a site-based team that considers the reason for the referral and makes recommendations for interventions to be implemented in the general education program (Ortiz, 2002; Rinaldi & Samson, 2008). A site-based team approach offers the best way to address problems the student is experiencing because they know the context of the school and have the potential to provide appropriate, effective instructional interventions for English learners, especially when the membership of the team is diverse, and includes parents and members who are knowledgeable about issues related to diverse learners (Klinger & Harry, 2006). Site-based intervention teams have been shown to decrease referral and special education placement (Fuchs, Fuchs, & Bahr, 1990; Ysseldyke & Marston, 1999), and even reduce disproportionate referrals of minority students to special education (Powers, 2001). Too often, when students struggle, the focus is on naming the student's problem rather than searching for solutions.

Response to intervention (RtI) is a multi-tiered service delivery model that is founded on the principle that *all children can learn*. As you can see in Figure 10.2, all students receive high-quality core instruction in general education, while some receive additional services for as long as there is evidence that they need those services. The focus is on finding ways to change instruction (or student behaviors) so the learner can be successful beginning in the general education classroom using evidence-based practices that work for the individual child. RtI involves documenting a change in behavior or performance

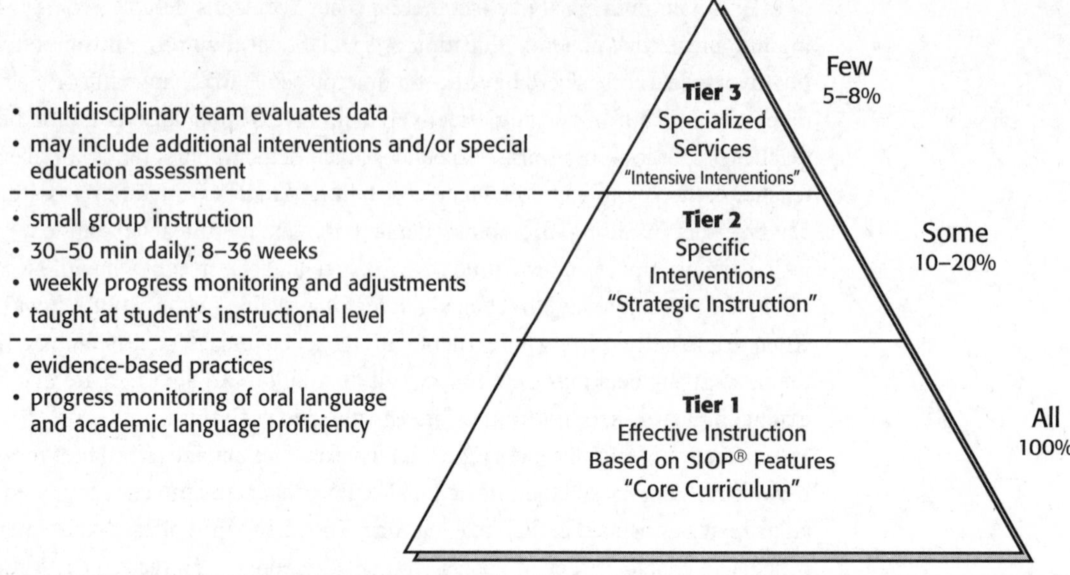

FIGURE 10.2 ***Response to Intervention for ELLs***

Adapted from Echevarria & Graves (2007). *Sheltered Content Instruction: Teaching English Language Learners with Diverse Abilities Third Edition.*

as a result of intervention and assessments. In the IDEA 2004 reauthorization (Individuals with Disabilities Education Act), RtI was approved as an option for schools to use, and resources may be allocated from a number of sources such as Title I and special education funds (Tilly, 2006).

Tier One represents general education. All students should receive high-quality, appropriate instruction and progress monitoring in their general education classroom. For English learners, that would be the type of instructional practices featured in the SIOP®. Students in Tier One who are not keeping up may need extra support, such as some of the supplemental interventions listed below. For many students, the extra attention will be enough to catch them up. However, a subset of students (approximately 10 to 20 percent) who have received effective instruction will require more intensive interventions to meet their learning needs (Tier Two). Interventions should, to the extent possible, be scientifically validated through research. Some examples include:

- specialized materials
- small-group or individualized instruction
- family involvement
- primary language support
- explicit teaching of learning strategies for students who need assistance in "learning how to learn"
- more intensive English language development
- modification of assignments
- counseling services
- reading specialist services
- classroom-based reading interventions
- Saturday school or after school sessions

The difference between Tier One and Tier Two is the individualized nature of the instruction, level of intensity of the intervention, and frequency of assessments. Based on progress monitoring, the team may find some students (approximately 5–8%) who have had systematic, effective interventions yet do not respond (Brown & Doolittle, 2008; Leafstedt, Richards, & Gerber, 2004). These students are eligible for Tier Three, which may include special education services. Few students would be in this category, and this consideration is based on a student's documented insufficient response to general education and Tier Two interventions and the team's informed determination that an additional level of support is needed to increase achievement.

One of the main advantages of an RtI model is its emphasis on ensuring appropriate learning opportunities for all students, beginning in the general education classroom. All students receive instruction in the core curriculum, even those who receive additional services. By focusing on interventions rather than disability, more students' needs will be met in the least restrictive environment, and decisions about student placement will be based on documented evidence over time. The result should be that fewer students from diverse backgrounds will be inappropriately identified as disabled; for those who require special education services, their IEPs will include instructional strategies and modifications that are tailored to their demonstrated needs (Echevarria, Powers, & Elliott, 2004).

Students with Special Needs

Many of the features of the SIOP® are effective for students with learning differences. In a study with middle school students with learning disabilities, students made significant growth in writing when teachers used the SIOP® Model (Echevarria, 1998). However, it is also important to keep in mind the unique individual characteristics of students with learning and behavior problems.

- Focus students' attention by limiting the clutter and excessive visual stimuli in the classroom. While we advocate word walls and other visuals to assist students in information recall and vocabulary development, they must be used with discretion. Students with special needs are often distracted by artwork and projects hanging around the room.
- Repetition is essential. Students will retain more information if it is repeated and reviewed frequently. Poor memory is often a characteristic of students with special needs, especially memory that is associated with symbols, (e.g., letters and numbers).
- Allow extra time for students to process information. Students with learning differences are often just processing a question by the time the answer is given. Teachers may use strategies such as asking a question, letting the student know he or she will be asked for the answer, then coming back to the student.
- Assessment should be scaffolded to measure understanding. Students' disabilities can interfere with their demonstration of knowledge and understanding. These students may have difficulty with vocabulary, expressing their ideas, or using language adequately. Rather than asking a student to write an explanation of a concept, have him list the features of the concept or label a graphic organizer that is provided, ask the student to complete an outline rather than generate a summary or essay, or select examples from a list provided rather than producing examples.

- Differentiate the curriculum to students' needs, such as modifying the number of items the learner completes, increasing the amount of personal assistance, providing different materials to meet a learner's individual needs, or allotting a different amount of time for learning, task completion, or testing.
- Be sensitive to frustration levels. Students with special needs often have a lower frustration threshold than typical learners, which may result in outbursts or giving up easily. A structured learning environment, scaffolded instruction, and opportunities to experience success help alleviate frustration.
- For secondary students with behavior problems, one promising approach is school-wide positive behavior supports (SW-PBS) (Hawkin, 2005). This approach has six key components:
    1. School staff agree upon three to five positively stated expectations (e.g., Be There, Be Ready; Hands and Feet to Self; Be Respectful).
    2. All staff members throughout the school teach expectations, directly and intensively, at the beginnng of the school year and consistently throughout the year.
    3. A continuum of rewards or incentives is established to acknowledge students following expectations.
    4. A range of consequences is established for students who do not follow expectations.
    5. Data (e.g., office discipline referrals, attendance rates, suspensions) are gathered to evaluate SW-PBS efforts.
    6. A team, including a school administrator, is in charge of leading SW-PBS and evaluating its effectiveness.

  All of these suggestions for assisting students with learning and behavior problems have commonalities: They must be used consistently, data are used to monitor student learning, student well-being is the focus, and there is a commitment to enhancing learning for all students.

Summary

One of the most critical issues facing educators is delivering an instructional program appropriate for *all* students in their classes: those with limited English proficiency, those who excel academically, those who are performing at grade level, those with low academic levels, those who find reading difficult, those who have experienced persistent failure, those who work hard but continue to struggle academically, and those with problematic behaviors.

This chapter provided an overview of issues related to reading and special education, including how linguistic differences in home languages and English may cause English learners difficulty with literacy development. When classroom teachers implement the features of the SIOP® Model, many students with reading and learning difficulties find success. Very often, students' academic difficulties have more to do with the curriculum, teaching methods, and classroom setting than with any deficit in the student. That said, some students will still struggle with reading and learning despite best practices in teaching. We recommend the kinds of interventions used in a tiered service delivery model so that appropriate supports are afforded struggling students. Most importantly, we want to avoid labeling students with reading problems or disabilities and instead provide them with the most appropriate and effective instructional context possible.

Discussion Questions

1. Select an English learner in your class who is having difficulty with reading and/or content learning. Reread the questions in this chapter on page 198. Begin with the first question: What evidence do you have that a particular student is having difficulty with reading? Try to provide answers to the other questions as they relate to your identified student. If questions 3.a–e are answered negatively, what are the implications for your instruction of this student, and for the other teachers who work with him or her? Now examine Figure 10.1. From your work with this student, using your best guess as well as any assessment findings you have—including a measure of English language proficiency that you may need to obtain from your school's ESL specialist—see if any of the descriptions of Language Differences and/or Language Learning Disabilities match your student. For older English learners, what are some possible next steps for meeting students' language, literacy, and academic needs?
2. Analyze your school and/or district's assessment program in reading and language arts. Are reading specialists available to help with the assessment and instruction of students with reading problems? If not, who has the expertise for helping teachers and administrators design an effective assessment program for secondary learners? What happens to teachers' district-required literacy assessment results? Are they used for designing appropriate instruction for students, including English learners? Are professional development programs in place to assist secondary teachers and administrators in increasing their knowledge and skills in teaching reading? These are critical questions to consider when planning literacy instruction for English learners (and all students, for that matter), and they should be asked when designing schoolwide and district inservice and professional development.
3. In this chapter we have discussed some of the reasons why minority children, including many English learners, are over- and underrepresented in special education. For your own school or district, determine the number (percent) of English learners who are designated as receiving special education services (this information should be available at your district office). Are there disproportionate numbers of ELs in special education compared to their percent of the population? How can RtI help ensure that English learners are receiving an appropriate education and that proper services are offered as needed?
4. How would you respond to a teacher who says, "Well, if I follow the SIOP® Model and make sure my ELs are able to access content using these activities, techniques, and approaches, my on-level kids and native English speakers will be bored." Do you agree with this statement? Why or why not? How can teachers with only a few English learners in their classrooms organize instruction so that all students' needs are met? Which, if any, of the activities, methods, or SIOP® features in this book are inappropriate for some students, such as accelerated learners? Or are all of these instructional features appropriate for all students? Obviously, we believe that all students benefit from the instruction that is integral to the SIOP® Model. But from our experience, some teachers think otherwise. Prepare a response to these teachers' concerns.

chapter 11

Effective Use of the SIOP® Protocol

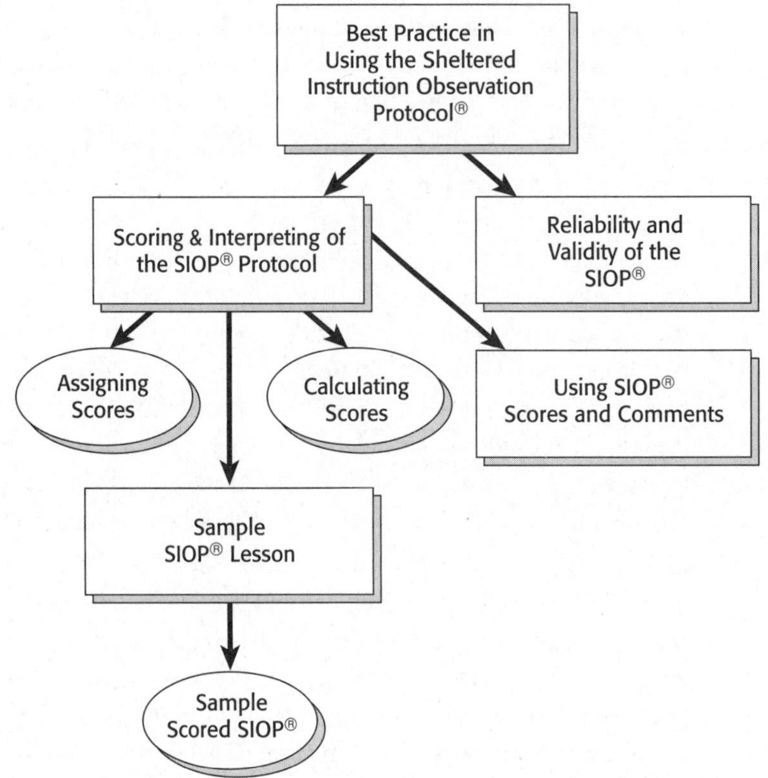

Objectives

After reading, discussing, and engaging in activities related to this chapter, you will be able to meet the following content and language objectives.

Content Objectives

Examine how all the SIOP® features fit into one lesson plan.

Use the Sheltered Instruction Observation Protocol to score and assess a teacher's lesson.

Language Objectives

Discuss SIOP® scores as a postobservation conference with the teacher whose lesson was rated.

Explain the value of observing and rating teachers over time on the SIOP®.

Since its inception, the SIOP® Model has been used as a lesson planning and instructional delivery system for teaching ELs effectively. Sample lesson plan formats can be found in Chapter 2, Appendix B, and at www.siopinstitute.net.

The SIOP® protocol, our observation instrument, has also been useful to educators in a number of ways. The SIOP® Model and protocol have been used in school districts and universities around the country since the 1990s with measurable success. We have interviewed many school personnel who have told us their stories of SIOP® implementation (Echevarria, Short, & Vogt, 2008). From their stories we suggest the following uses of the SIOP® protocol.

Best Practice in Using the SIOP® Protocol

Initially we developed the SIOP® protocol because we found that school personnel and researchers wanted and needed an objective measure of high-quality sheltered instruction for ELs. Over time, uses of the SIOP® protocol have expanded.

The SIOP® protocol provides a tool for gauging the quality of teaching. Qualitative and quantitative information written on the protocol documents lesson effectiveness and shows areas that need improvement. This information may be used by teachers, administrators, university faculty, and researchers.

Teachers find the SIOP® protocol useful for improving their own practice through self-reflection and/or peer coaching. Some schools reported that their teachers regularly used the

protocol to reflect on their lessons, completing the protocol after they taught a specific lesson. More effective is the practice of videotaping lessons and scoring the lessons on their various SIOP® features. The objectivity the camera provides is valuable to teachers in recognizing their areas of strength and areas that need attention.

Some schools used peer coaches to assist teachers in SIOP® implementation. In one school district, a coach modeled a SIOP® lesson for a group of three to five peers. Using the SIOP® protocol with the rating numbers removed, the group debriefed the lesson and discussed the components of the SIOP®. The focus of the debriefing and discussion was around the comments written on the protocol. Participants wrote what they saw the coach do and described it on the protocol under each corresponding feature. At the conclusion of the session, one of the teachers in the group volunteered to model a lesson during the following quarter (two-month period). Because of the nonevaluative nature of the feedback, it wasn't difficult to get teachers to volunteer. The coach assisted the teacher volunteer in planning the lesson that was later modeled for the group. Feedback from the group was always limited to positive comments and a discussion of how the lesson matched SIOP® features. After each teacher in the group had a turn in modeling a SIOP® lesson for the group, the individuals then became coaches for another small group of teachers. In this way, a large number of teachers learned and practiced using the SIOP® Model and had the opportunity to understand the model deeply (Echevarria, Short, & Vogt, 2008).

A number of sources have reported that schoolwide use of the SIOP® Model and protocol provides a common language and conceptual framework from which to work and develop a community of practice. School site administrators commented that the features of the SIOP® bring together in one place many of the ideas and techniques staff have learned through district professional development efforts. For example, a school staff may have received inservice training in cooperative learning, Thinking Maps, or differentiated instruction, but teachers struggle with how to incorporate these varied ideas into their daily teaching practice. The SIOP® Model provides a framework for systematically addressing and incorporating a variety of techniques into one's teaching practice.

The SIOP® protocol is useful for administrators because it provides them with a way of understanding instruction for ELs. Administrators typically do not have the same opportunity to learn about effective instruction for ELs as the teachers on their staff (Short, Vogt, & Echevarria, 2008). Yet the administrator is responsible for observing and providing feedback to teaching personnel. The SIOP® protocol gives administrators a means for providing clear, concrete feedback to the teachers they observe. The format allows for rating of lessons but, more important, has space for writing comments that will be constructive for improving instruction for English learners.

University faculty have also found the SIOP® Model and protocol to be useful in courses that specifically address the needs of English learners. Faculty who supervise field experience find that the SIOP® protocol assists in providing concrete examples of techniques necessary for making instruction comprehensible for English learners. Feedback on the rating and comments sections of the instrument assists student teachers in their professional development.

Finally, the SIOP® protocol is a tool researchers can use to determine the extent to which SIOP® instruction is implemented in a given classroom. It can also be used to measure consistency and fidelity of implementation.

Scoring and Interpreting the SIOP® Protocol

The heading on the first page of the SIOP® protocol is fairly self-explanatory (see Figure 11.1). It is intended to provide a context for the lesson being observed. There is space for the observer's name and the date of the observation. Other information, such as the teacher's name, school, grade of the class being observed, ESL level of the students, and the academic content area, is also included. We recognize that an observation at one point in time does not always accurately represent the teacher's implementation of SIOP® strategies and techniques. Therefore, there is a place for the observer to indicate if the lesson is part of a multiday unit or is a single-day lesson.

In using the SIOP® protocol, we have found that it is most useful to videotape a lesson and analyze it later. Teachers, supervisors, and researchers alike have found this to be an effective way of recording and measuring teachers' growth over time. The tape number may be written on the heading to indicate its corresponding lesson.

Finally, there is a box for the total score the teacher received on the SIOP®. It is most useful to represent a teacher's score as a percentage because NA affects a total score number (see next section for an explanation of scoring).

When scoring a lesson is appropriate, an observer may assign scores in a number of ways: (1) during the observation itself, as individual features are recognized; (2) after the observation, as the observer reflects on the entire lesson, referring to observational field notes; or (3) after the observation while watching a videotape of the lesson. The third option is often useful so that the teacher and observer are able to share the same point of reference when discussing the lesson.

It is important to stress that not all features on the SIOP® will be present in every lesson. However, some features, such as items under Preparation, Comprehensible Input, Interaction, and Review and Assessment, are essential for each lesson. Over the course of time (several lessons, a week), all features should be represented in one's teaching.

Assigning Scores

An observer determines the level of SIOP® implementation, guided by the scenario descriptions in this book. Each chapter's scenarios were designed to show a clear example for each feature with scores ranging from 4 to 0. The SIOP® protocol provides a five-point scale as well as space for qualitative data. It is recommended that the observer use the "Comments" section to record examples of the presence or absence of each feature. That way, both the observer and the teacher have specific information, besides a score,

FIGURE 11.1 *SIOP® Heading*

The Sheltered Instruction Observation Protocol (SIOP®)
(Echevarria, Vogt, & Short, 2000, 2004, 2008)

Observer(s): ______________ Teacher: ______________
Date: ______________ School: ______________
Grade: ______________ Class/Topic: ______________
ESL Level: ______________ Lesson: Multiday Single-day *(circle one)*

Total Points Possible: 120 (Subtract 4 points for each NA given) ________
Total Points Earned: ________ Percentage Score: ________

Directions: Circle the number that best reflects what you observe in a sheltered lesson. You may give a score from 0–4 (or NA on selected items). Cite under "Comments" specific examples of the behaviors observed.

to use in their postlesson discussion. More information may be added to the Comments section during review of the SIOP®, documenting the content of the discussion for future reference, which is particularly useful as subsequent lessons are planned. In any case, sufficient notes with examples of how the feature was addressed should be included to provide concrete feedback with each score.

Naturally, there is an element of subjectivity to interpreting the features and assigning scores. Observers must be consistent in their scoring. For example, one person may think that for Feature #3 (Content concepts appropriate for age and educational background level of students), only grade-level materials are appropriate, while another observer may feel that the same content found in materials for lower grade levels can be used because of the students' low reading levels or because students have interrupted educational backgrounds. In either case, observers must be consistent in their interpretation and scoring across settings.

We suggest that, to assist in more accurate scoring, the observer ask the teacher for a copy of the lesson plan in advance of observing the class. Ideally, the teacher and observer would meet for a preobservation conference to discuss the lesson plan and provide the observer with background about the lesson. In this way, the observer is better able to score the lesson, especially the Preparation section, and NA items.

Not Applicable (NA) Category

The Not Applicable (NA) scoring option is important because it distinguishes a feature that is "not applicable" to the observed lesson from a score of "0," which indicates that the feature should have been present but was not. For example, Mr. Leung taught a five-day unit on the solar system. During the first few lessons of the unit, Mr. Leung concentrated on making the rather dense information accessible to his students. He adapted the text to make it understandable for them and provided ample opportunities for students to use strategies. On the final day of the unit, an observer was present. Mr. Leung wrapped up the unit by having the students complete an enjoyable hands-on activity wherein they applied the concepts they had learned. It was obvious that the students had learned the content and were able to use it in the activity. However, because of the nature of that particular lesson, there was no observed adaptation of content (Feature #5). Mr. Leung was not penalized by receiving a score of "0" because the lesson did not lend itself to that item and Mr. Leung had covered that item on another day. A score of NA would be correct in this case.

In the case of Mrs. Nash, however, it would be appropriate to score this feature as "0." Mrs. Nash also taught a unit on the solar system. On the first day of the unit, she showed a video about the solar system and had a brief oral discussion following the movie. The next day an observer was present as she read from the text and then had students answer chapter questions. There was no evidence that any of the content had been adapted to the variety of student proficiency levels in her class. In fact, many students appeared to be confused as they tried to answer questions based on readings from the grade-level textbook.

The distinction between a "0" and "NA" is an important one because a score of "0" adversely affects the overall score for the lesson, while an "NA" does not because a percentage is to be used.

Calculating Scores

There are 30 features on the SIOP®, each with a range of possible scores from 0 to 4, or NA. After scoring each feature, the observer tallies all numeric scores. The score is written

FIGURE 11.2 *The Step-by-Step Process for Tallying Scores*

1. Add the lesson's scores from all features.
2. Count the number of NAs, multiply by 4, then subtract this number from 120.
3. Divide the number from step 2 into the number from step 1 (the adjusted possible score into the lesson's score).

over the total possible score, usually 120 (30 features × a score of 4). So an example of a total score would be written 115/120. Because of the NA, adding the individual scores for a grand total is meaningless. It is more informative to know the total score based on the total possible score.

Let's take a step-by-step look at how a lesson's total score is calculated.

Mr. Leung's lesson received a score of 4 on 20 features, a score of 3 on 5 features, a score of 2 on 4 features, and 1 NA. The sum of those scores is 103.

$$\begin{aligned} 20 \times 4 &= 80 \\ 5 \times 3 &= 15 \\ 2 \times 4 &= \ \ 8 \\ \textbf{Total score} &= \overline{\textbf{103}}\textbf{/116} \end{aligned}$$

The score of 116 was derived in this way: If the lesson had received a 4 on each feature of the SIOP® (a perfect score), it would have had a total score of 116.

$$29 \times 4 = 116$$

The number of features is 29 instead of 30 because one feature was not applicable (NA); the lesson was rated on only 29 features.

Mr. Leung's lesson received a total score of 103/116. The total score can be converted to a percentage, if that form is more useful. Simply divide the numerator by the denominator: 103 ÷ 116. In this case, the SIOP® was implemented at a level of 88 percent. You can see the importance of distinguishing between a score of 0 and NA. For Mr. Leung's lesson, a 0 score would have changed the total score from 88 percent to 85 percent. Let's see how.

$$\begin{aligned} 20 \times 4 &= 80 \\ 5 \times 3 &= 15 \\ 2 \times 4 &= \ \ 8 \\ 1 \times 0 &= \ \ 0 \\ \textbf{Total score} &= \overline{\textbf{103}}\textbf{/120} \end{aligned}$$ [1]

The step-by-step process for tallying scores is shown in Figure 11.2.

Sample Lesson

In this section of the chapter, we will describe an entire science lesson conducted by a sixth-grade teacher and show how it was scored on the SIOP® protocol. Ms. Clark received training and has been using the SIOP® for lesson planning and delivery for

[1]The highest possible score on the SIOP® for all 30 features is 120 (30 items × a score of 4). If Mr. Leung's lesson were rated on all 30 features, the total score would be 103/120, or 85 percent.

about 16 months. This lesson took place at the end of the first quarter of the school year. The class consisted of beginning ESL students from varying language backgrounds and countries of origin. The class has been studying a unit on minerals and visited a local natural history museum. The students have examined rocks in class as well. Ms. Clark provided us with a lesson plan before we conducted the observation.

In the classroom, the desks were arranged in three circular groups. Some students had to turn around to see the board and overhead screen at the front of the room. The class objectives and agenda were written on a whiteboard at the side. Two bulletin boards in the back of the room displayed the students' work for a language arts project and a science project. A Spanish-speaking bilingual aide assisted the teacher and also helped newly arrived Spanish-speaking students. The class period was 45 minutes long.

The teacher began the class by complimenting the students for their performance on a test they had taken on minerals and singled out one student who received the highest A grade in the class. She then asked the students to read the objectives and activities for the day silently while she read them aloud:

> *Content Objective:* Today we will develop an understanding of what volcanoes are and why they erupt.
>
> - First, I will demonstrate how rocks could move and what happens when they move.
> - Second, you will use a semantic web worksheet to recall what you know about volcanoes.
> - Third, I will use a model to show how a volcano erupts.
> - Fourth, you will make predictions about the story *Pompeii . . . Buried Alive*, and then read pages 4 to 9 silently.
> - Fifth, you will refer to information on page 6 in the book to write on a worksheet the steps that happen before a volcano erupts.
> - Your homework is to draw a volcano and label the parts. The vocabulary words and terms for the day are: melts, blast, mixture, rumbles, straw, pipe, shepherd, giant, peddler, crater, lava, magma, magma chamber.

The teacher then demonstrated for the class what happens when rocks move against each other, using two stacks of books. After placing the stacks side by side on a desk, she pushed against one stack so the other stack slid off the desk and scattered onto the floor. She asked the students what happens when one set of rocks moves another set of rocks. The students responded that the rocks break.

The aide distributed semantic web worksheets to the students and asked them to write "Volcano" in the center circle. Then, in the other spaces, students were to write everything they already knew about volcanoes. While the students worked, the teacher and aide circulated to monitor the students' understanding of the task and to see how they were progressing.

After the students filled in their webs, the teacher led them in a discussion of what they had written and wrote some of their comments on the whiteboard:

- Lava melts and explodes
- When it erupts, all that force comes from the middle of the earth

- Volcanoes are formed deep inside the earth
- When a volcano is under water, the lava comes out and makes an island

The teacher repeated that she was going to make a model volcano and asked the class what a "model" is. One student answered that it is an example, not a real volcano. All of the students were watching as the teacher showed them a bottle and explained it would be like the magma chamber that is inside a volcano. She poured a cup of warm water inside the bottle. While it cooled slightly, she showed the class a diagram of the model for the experiment, with the corresponding volcano parts labeled. They discussed each part of the volcano and in doing so emphasized some of the key vocabulary word and terms: crater, magma pipe, lava, magma, magma chamber, basin.

The teacher returned to the model and placed a few drops of liquid dish detergent in the warm water. Next, she picked up an object and asked the students to identify it. One student said it was a measuring spoon. The teacher measured a teaspoon of baking soda and put it into the water and detergent mixture. She asked the students to identify where she was putting it. The students responded, "magma chamber." She put in a second teaspoon of baking soda, then held up the bottle for the students to observe, and then they reviewed the ingredients. To speed up the process, she added vinegar to the bottle. She asked them, "When was the last time we used vinegar?" The students said they had used it on the previous day. The "volcano" began to erupt, and the teacher displayed the bottle so that the students could see the foam overflowing.

The class reviewed the process and the ingredients for the model volcano. Individual students were called to the front to participate in a second volcano demonstration, each one completing one of the steps to produce another "eruption." The second "lava" flow was a bit larger than the first.

The teacher asked the whole class to think about "What causes a volcano to erupt?" and added, "We used warm water. What will happen to heat in a chamber?" One student answered, "Heat rises." The teacher explained that it was not just the heat that caused the eruption and asked them to think of the other ingredients and what happened when they were mixed. The teacher went on to explain, "The mixture of gases produces carbon monoxide," and wrote "carbon monoxide" and its chemical symbol on the board. She also asked them what they knew about plants and said, "They breathe in carbon monoxide. We breathe out carbon monoxide; we breathe in oxygen." [This part was an error, but the teacher did not realize her mistake in calling carbon dioxide (for plants and humans), carbon monoxide.]

One student wanted to know why rocks come out of volcanoes and another student offered an explanation, "The volcano is inside of a mountain of rocks." The teacher commented that whatever is inside the chamber when it erupts will come out with the lava, and if they had put small bits of material inside their model, those bits also would have come out when it erupted.

The teacher and aide handed out the storybooks *Pompeii . . . Buried Alive*, to the students, and they began prereading activities. The teacher focused their attention on the title and asked them to predict what they thought the book would be about. One student said, "Volcanoes erupting." The teacher asked, "Where do you think it takes place?" Students guessed various places: Nicaragua, Rome, Greece, England. The teacher commented on the togas in the cover's picture. She then directed their attention to the back cover and read the summary aloud, stating the story took place 2,000 years ago in Italy. She asked, "Is it a true story?" Some students guessed yes; others no. "How do you know it's true?" They discussed that the term "took place" and the use of a specific time in history meant that it was true. The teacher then asked for a student volunteer to point out Italy on the wall map, and the class discussed the location of Italy in southern Europe.

The teacher asked how many of the students came from countries with volcanoes. Students from Ethiopia, El Salvador, and Guatemala said they knew about volcanoes in their countries. One student asked if it had to be a hot country to have a volcano. The teacher asked if they knew where the most recent eruption had occurred. She told them it was Montserrat in the Caribbean and that volcanoes often occur in warm countries, but not all are in warm countries. She asked if they knew about a volcano in the United States and told them about Mt. St. Helens in Washington, a state that is cold in winter. She showed them Washington on the map. One student commented on the way precipitation forms and tried to compare it with what happens in the formation of a volcano.

The teacher directed the students to read pages 4 to 9 silently for two minutes. While they were reading, she distributed worksheets with a sequencing exercise to describe what happens before a volcano erupts. The instructions told students to put the sentences in order according to what they read on page 6. They could refer back to the reading.

The teacher began to read the passage aloud slowly about three minutes later, although some students indicated that they had not yet finished reading it silently. As she read, she again displayed the transparency with the model volcano diagram on the overhead and referred to it and to the key vocabulary as she read. She also paused from time to time to ask comprehension questions. Students were able to answer questions orally, using the model and naming the parts of a volcano. They discussed unknown words in the reading, such as peddler, rumbled, and shepherd, as they went along.

As the period drew to a close, the teacher told the students they would complete the sequencing worksheet the next day. She reminded them of the homework—draw a volcano in their journal and label the parts. They were also told to place the webs they had completed in their journals. The teacher then led a brief wrap-up of the lesson, asking questions about a volcano, which students answered.

On the following pages (Figure 11.3) you will see how Ms. Clark was scored on the SIOP® items and the Comments that provide evidence for her score.

Using SIOP® Scores and Comments

Scores can be used "as is" to serve as a starting point for a collaborative discussion between a teacher and a supervisor or among a group of teachers. If lessons are rated, comments supporting the scores are essential. We have found that videotaping a lesson, rating it, and discussing it with the teacher provides an effective forum for professional growth. We also get valuable information from teachers explaining a student's behavior or why something may not have taken place despite the lesson plan that included it, for example. The discussion may take place between the teacher and the observer, or a group of teachers may meet on a regular basis to provide feedback to one another and assist in refining their teaching.

FIGURE 11.3 *The Sheltered Instruction Observation Protocol (SIOP®)*

The Sheltered Instruction Observation Protocol (SIOP®)
(Echevarria, Vogt, & Short, 2000, 2004, 2008)

Observer(s): J. Cruz
Date: 4/3
Grade: 6
ESL Level: 6

Teacher: Ms. Clark
School: Cloverleaf
Class/Topic: Science
Lesson: Multiday (Single-day) *(circle one)*

Total Points Possible: 120 (Subtract 4 points for each NA given) 120
Total Points Earned: 94 Percentage Score: 78%

Directions: Circle the number that best reflects what you observe in a sheltered lesson. You may give a score from 0–4 (or NA on selected items). Cite under "Comments" specific examples of the behaviors observed.

Lesson Preparation

(4)	3	2	1	0
1. **Content objectives** are clearly defined, displayed and reviewed with students		**Content objectives** for students implied		No clearly defined **content objectives** for students

Comments: Content objectives were written and stated at the beginning of the lesson.

4	3	(2)	1	0
2. **Language objectives** are clearly defined, displayed and reviewed with students		**Language objectives** for students implied		No clearly defined **language objectives** for students

Comments: No specific language objective was written or stated. Key vocabulary was listed, but the language skills to be targeted were listed and stated as activities and not written as objectives.

4	3	(2)	1	0
3. **Content concepts** appropriate for age and educational background level of students		**Content concepts** somewhat appropriate for age and educational background level of students		**Content concepts** inappropriate for age and educational background level of students

Comments: Students seemed to understand the concepts. However, several students mentioned that they studied volcanos in elementary school. It is unclear why volcanos were taught when these concepts had been introduced previously.

(*continued*)

FIGURE 11.3 *continued*

(4)	3	2	1	0	NA
4. **Supplementary materials** used to a high degree, making the lesson clear and meaningful (e.g., computer programs, graphs, models, visuals)		Some use of **supplementary materials**		No use of **supplementary materials**	

Comments: Good use of supplementary materials to enhance students' understanding of volcanoes such as copies of semantic maps, pull-down maps, a book, Pompeii . . . Buried Alive, *a transparency indicating the parts of a volcano, stacks of books to demonstrate rocks pushing against each other, household items to illustrate a volcanic eruption.*

(4)	3	2	1	0	NA
5. **Adaptation of content** (e.g., text, assignment) to all levels of student proficiency		Some **adaption of content** to all levels of student proficiency		No significant **adaption of content** to all levels of student proficiency	

Comments: All students were given the same text with which to work. There were no specific adaptations made to the text itself to address the varying levels of language proficiency. However, the teacher had prepared a sequencing activity for students to complete where she identified sentences that explained the process of a volcanic eruption and students were required to put the steps in order. In addition, she began reading the text aloud to the students and paused frequently to ask questions and to check for clarification.

(4)	3	2	1	0
6. **Meaningful activities** that integrate lesson concepts (e.g., surveys, letter writing, simulations, models) with language practice opportunities for reading, writing, listening, and/or speaking		**Meaningful activities** that integrate lesson concepts but provide little opportunity for language practice with opportunities for reading, writing, listening, and/or speaking		No **meaningful activities** that integrate lesson concepts with language practice

Comments: There were a lot of meaningful and interesting activities that provided students with language practice (e.g., participation in building the model volcano, discussing information from their semantic maps about volcanoes, and reading authentic text).

Building Background

(4)	3	2	1	0	NA
7. **Concepts explicitly linked** to students' background experiences		**Concepts loosely linked** to students' background experiences		**Concepts not explicitly linked** to students' background experiences	

Comments: The teacher tapped into students' understanding of volcanoes by asking them to complete a semantic mapping exercise writing everything they knew about volcanoes.

4	3	②	1	0
8. **Links explicity made** between past learning and new concepts		**Few links made** between past learning and new concepts		**No links made** between past learning and new concepts

Comments: There were few links made between past learning and its connection to new concepts. The teacher initiated the class by reminding the students of the visit to the Museum of Natural History and also reminded them of the rocks they had brought in. However, she did not explain how the visit or the collection of rocks related to that day's lesson about volcanoes.

④	3	2	1	0
9. **Key vocabulary** emphasized (e.g., introduced, written, repeated, and highlighted for students to see)		**Key vocabulary** introduced, but not emphasized		**Key vocabulary** not introduced or emphasized

Comments: The key vocabulary words used for this lesson were written on the board, stated to the students at the beginning of the lesson, and reiterated throughout the lesson, particularly when the teacher and students constructed the model volcano.

Comprehensible Input

④	3	2	1	0
10. **Speech** appropriate for students' proficiency level (e.g., slower rate, enunciation, and simple sentence structure for beginners)		**Speech** sometimes inappropriate for students' proficiency level		**Speech** inappropriate for students' proficiency level

Comments: The teacher explained tasks well and modeled the demonstrations first before the students participated.

④	3	2	1	0
11. **Clear explanation of** academic tasks		**Unclear** explanation of academic tasks		**No** explanation of academic tasks

Comments: The teacher explained tasks well and modeled the demonstrations first before the students participated.

(*continued*)

FIGURE 11.3 *continued*

(4)	3	2	1	0
12. A **variety of techniques** used to make content concepts clear (e.g., modeling, visuals, hands-on activities, demonstrations, gestures, body language)		Some **techniques** used to make content concepts clear		No **techniques** used to make content concepts clear

Comments: A variety of techniques were used in this lesson: the use of the overhead transparency with a diagram of a volcano and the labeled parts, brainstorming in the semantic mapping activity, demonstrating a model of a volcanic eruption, and reading about the topic after exploring it orally and visually. Used sequencing steps to check reading comprehension.

Strategies

4	(3)	2	1	0
13. Ample opportunities provided for students to use **learning strategies**		Inadequate opportunities provided for students to use **learning strategies**		No opportunity provided for students to use **learning strategies**

Comments: The teacher used various strategies with students such as accessing prior knowledge and having them make predictions. Students, however, used these strategies with the teacher, not with other students.

(4)	3	2	1	0
14. **Scaffolding techniques** consistently used, assisting and supporting student understanding (e.g., think-alouds)		**Scaffolding techniques** occasionally used		**Scaffolding techniques** not used

Comments: The teacher used various scaffolding techniques throughout the lesson to promote and assess students' comprehension of content concepts by means of questions, visuals, models, graphic organizers, prereading predictions, and demonstrations.

4	(3)	2	1	0
15. A variety of **questions or tasks that promote higher-order thinking skills** (e.g., literal, analytical, and interpretive questions)		Infrequent **questions or tasks that promote higher-order thinking skills**		No **questions or tasks that promote higher-order thinking skills**

Comments: Most of the questions for this beginning level consisted of more factual/identification questions. In some cases, more elaborated responses were required of students; for example, "What happens when one set of rocks moves against another?" "Can you think of other places in the world where eruptions have occurred?" "Tell me about volcanoes in your country." "How do you know this is a true story?"

Interaction

	4	(3)	2	1	0
16.	Frequent opportunities for **interaction** and discussion between teacher/student and among students, which encourage elaborated responses about lesson concepts		**Interaction** mostly teacher-dominated with some opportunities for students to talk about or question lesson concepts		**Interaction** teacher-dominated with no opportunities for students to discuss lesson concepts

Comments: The teacher engaged the students in discussions about volcanoes throughout the class period. The semantic mapping exercise, the demonstration, and the prereading activity were all means that facilitated student interaction. The majority of interactions were teacher-student.

	4	3	(2)	1	0
17.	**Grouping configurations** support language and content objectives of the lesson		**Grouping configurations** unevenly support the language and content objectives		**Grouping configurations** do not support the language and content objectives

Comments: Although students were seated in groups, there was little opportunity for them to interact to practice their language skills. The whole-class setting supported the demonstration about volcanic eruption.

	4	(3)	2	1	0
18.	Sufficient **wait time for student responses** consistently provided		Sufficient **wait time for student responses** occasionally provided		Sufficient **wait time for student responses** not provided

Comments: At times there were students who wanted to respond but were overlooked, perhaps because the period was running out of time. For those students selected to respond, the teacher allowed them time to articulate their thoughts.

	(4)	3	2	1	0	NA
19.	Ample opportunities for students to **clarify key concepts in L1** as needed with aide, peer, or L1 text		Some opportunities for students to **clarify key concepts in L1**		No opportunities for students to **clarify key concepts in L1**	

Comments: Only a few students could be identified as using their L1 during the lesson, and they were seated in the far left corner of the classroom where the bilingual aide assisted them. The other students in the classroom did not seem to need to use their L1 text.

(*continued*)

FIGURE 11.3 *continued*

Practice/Application

4	(3)	2	1	0	NA
20. **Hands-on materials and/or manipulatives** provided for students to practice using new content knowledge		**Few hands-on materials and/or manipulatives** provided for students to practice using new content knowledge		**No hands-on materials and/or manipulatives** provided for students to practice using new content knowledge	

Comments: The lesson involved manipulatives. During the experiment/demonstration for the volcanic eruption, for example, the teacher used materials such as a bottle, liquid detergent, warm water, measuring spoons, baking soda, and vinegar. Only a few students, though, used these materials themselves.

4	(3)	2	1	0	NA
21. Activities provided for students to **apply content and language knowledge** in the classroom		Activities provided for students to **apply** either **content or language knowledge** in the classroom		No activities provided for students to **apply content or language knowledge** in the classroom	

Comments: For the most part, students applied content and language. More student–student interactions would have been beneficial and provided better opportunities for assessment.

4	(3)	2	1	0
22. Activities integrate all **language skills** (i.e., reading, writing, listening, and speaking)		Activities integrate some **language skills**		Activities do not integrate **language skills**

Comments: The lesson allowed students an opportunity to use all language skills (some more than others) such as listening, speaking, and reading. Writing was evident mostly in the semantic mapping activity. Some predicting and scanning for information was part of the reading skills practiced.

Lesson Delivery

4	(3)	2	1	0
23. **Content objectives** clearly supported by lesson delivery		**Content objectives** supported somewhat by lesson delivery		**Content objectives** not supported by lesson delivery

Comments: The demonstration and discussion along with the constant repetition of key vocabulary served to accomplish most of the content objectives for the lesson. While students seemed to indicate an understanding of what volcanoes are, it is not certain that they fully understand what causes them to erupt.

	4	3	2 (circled)	1	0
24.	**Language objectives** clearly supported by lesson delivery		**Language objectives** somewhat supported by lesson delivery		**Language objectives** not supported by lesson delivery

Comments: Most of the language objectives were supported by the delivery. Students did not have a chance to complete the sequencing activity based on the reading in order to assess their reading comprehension.

	4 (circled)	3	2	1	0
25.	**Students engaged** approximately 90% to 100% of the period		**Students engaged** approximately 70% of the period		**Students engaged** less than 50% of the period

Comments: Students were on task throughout the lesson activity.

	4	3	2 (circled)	1	0
26.	**Pacing** of the lesson appropriate to students' ability levels		**Pacing** generally appropriate, but at times too fast or too slow		**Pacing** inappropriate to the students' ability levels

Comments: The pacing seemed fine, but was a little rushed at times, which prevented students from completing some activities such as the individual silent reading and sequencing activity.

Review/Assessment

	4	3	2 (circled)	1	0
27.	Comprehensive **review of key vocabulary**		Uneven **review of key vocabulary**		No **review of key vocabulary**

Comments: Teacher reviewed key vocabulary at the beginning of the lesson and reinforced it throughout. No final review took place at the end of the lesson.

	4	3 (circled)	2	1	0
28.	Comprehensive **review of key content concepts**		Uneven **review of key content concepts**		No **review of key content concepts**

Comments: The key content concepts were reviewed throughout the lesson, but there was no comprehensive review to wrap up the lesson, other than the final question posed to students at the end of the class, "What is a volcano?"

(*continued*)

FIGURE 11.3 *continued*

	4	(3)	2	1	0
29.	Regular **feedback** provided to students on their output (e.g., language, content, work)		Inconsistent **feedback** provided to students on their output		No **feedback** provided to students on their output

Comments: The teacher gave positive feedback to students' responses in most cases. In some instances, when time was short, she did not always respond to students whose hands were raised. She guided the brainstorming and prereading discussions.

	4	3	(2)	1	0
30.	**Assessment of student comprehension and learning** of all lesson objectives (e.g., spot checking, group response) throughout the lesson		**Assessment of student comprehension and learning** of some lesson objectives		No **assessment of student comprehension and learning** of lesson objectives

Comments: Throughout the lesson, the teacher checked students' understanding of some concepts and of the instructional tasks. She monitored the classroom to answer questions and to provide assistance. During the reading activity, however, students were not allotted sufficient time to read individually, and the sequencing activity was moved to the following day. Therefore, it is unclear how she was able to assess individual student comprehension before she began reading the text to students.

Teacher	Observation 1 Score/Date	Observation 2 Score/Date	Observation 3 Score/Date

FIGURE 11.4 *SIOP® Lesson Rating Form*

Scores can also be documented on a SIOP® Lesson Rating Form over time to show growth (see Figure 11.4). Using percentages, teachers can see how their implementation of the SIOP® features improves. This type of documentation is also useful for research purposes to document systematic implementation of the SIOP® and fidelity of implementation.

Further, plotting scores on a graph, as seen in Figure 11.5, is a very effective way to illustrate strong areas as well as areas that require attention, or areas teachers have highlighted as important for their own growth. If a lesson consistently shows low scores on certain features, that provides the teacher with clear feedback for areas on which to focus. Staff developers and teacher educators can use the scores to determine areas for further discussion and practice in workshops and course sessions if several teachers are having difficulty with the same feature or component.

Finally, while the SIOP® protocol is a useful tool for professional development, scores should be used with caution. Many variables affect the success or failure of a given lesson such as time of day, time of year, dynamics between students, and the like. Rather than just doing one observation and scoring of a lesson, several lessons should be rated over time for a more complete picture of the teacher's implementation of sheltered instruction.

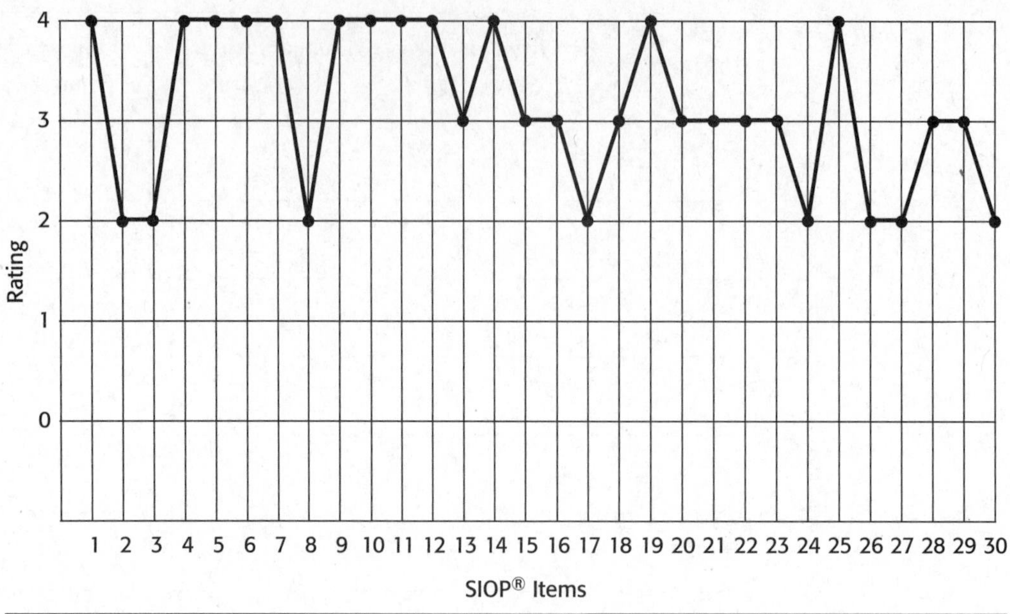

FIGURE 11.5 *Ms. Clark's Scores*

Reliability and Validity of the SIOP®

After several years of field-testing and refining the SIOP®, a study was conducted (Guarino, Echevarria, Short, Schick, Forbes, & Rueda, 2001) to establish the validity and reliability of the instrument. The findings of the study indicated that the SIOP® is a highly reliable and valid measure of sheltered instruction (see Appendix C for a discussion of the study).

Summary

This book has been developed for teachers, supervisors, administrators, teacher education faculty, professional developers, and researchers as a resource for increasing the effectiveness of instruction for adolescent English learners. We have presented a research-based, professional development model of sheltered instruction, the SIOP®, that can be used as an observation instrument, as well as a lesson planning guide.

The SIOP® Model and protocol provide concrete examples of the features of effective instruction for ELs, and the book has been written as a way to illustrate and elucidate those features by describing how real teachers might actually teach SIOP® lessons in grades 6–12. The use of vignettes allows readers to "see" what each feature might look like in a classroom setting. The features of the SIOP® Model represent best practice for teaching English learners.

Discussion Questions

1. The SIOP® has a number of uses by different constituencies (e.g., teachers, supervisors, administrators, and researchers). How can you begin using the SIOP®? What additional uses might it have for you or other constituencies?

2. Reread the sample lesson on pages 213–216. Would you score this lesson differently from the sample SIOP® scores? On what items would you differ? What was the basis of your disagreement?
3. Look at the sample SIOP® protocol and change any two scores to 1. What would be the total score and percentage score on the revised and recalculated SIOP®?
4. Imagine that you and a supervisor have just watched a videotape of your SIOP® lesson. You are discussing the SIOP® rating sheet that each of you scored independently. What would be the most collaborative way to approach the discussion of your teaching? What would yield the most useful information for improving your teaching?

appendix a: The Sheltered Instruction Observation Protocol (SIOP®)

Observer(s): ______________________ Teacher: ______________________
Date: ______________________ School: ______________________
Grade: ______________________ Class/Topic: ______________________
ESL Level: ______________________ Lesson: Multi-day Single-day (*circle one*)

Total Points Possible: 120 (Subtract 4 points for each NA given: ________)
Total Points Earned: ________ Percentage Score: ________

Directions: Circle the number that best reflects what you observe in a sheltered lesson. You may give a score from 0–4 (or NA on selected items). Cite under "Comments" specific examples of the behaviors observed.

LESSON PREPARATION

4	3	2	1	0
1. **Content objectives** clearly defined, displayed and reviewed with students		**Content objectives** for students implied		No clearly defined **content objectives** for students

Comments:

4	3	2	1	0
2. **Language objectives** clearly defined, displayed and reviewed with students		**Language objectives** for students implied		No clearly defined **language objectives** for students

Comments:

4	3	2	1	0
3. **Content concepts** appropriate for age and educational background level of students		**Content concepts** somewhat appropriate for age and educational background level of students		**Content concepts** inappropriate for age and educational background level of students

Comments:

4	3	2	1	0
4. **Supplementary materials** used to a high degree, making the lesson clear and meaningful (e.g., computer programs, graphs, models, visuals)		Some use of **supplementary materials**		No use of **supplementary materials**

Comments:

(Echevarria, Vogt, & Short, 2000, 2004, 2008)

4	3	2	1	0	NA
5. **Adaptation of content** (e.g., text, assignment) to all levels of student proficiency		Some **adaptation of content** to all levels of student proficiency		No significant **adaptation of content** to all levels of student proficiency	

Comments:

4	3	2	1	0
6. **Meaningful activities** that integrate lesson concepts (e.g., interviews, letter writing, simulations, models) with language practice opportunities for reading, writing, listening, and/or speaking		**Meaningful activities** that integrate lesson concepts but provide few language practice opportunities for reading, writing, listening, and/or speaking		No **meaningful activities** that integrate lesson concepts with language practice

Comments:

BUILDING BACKGROUND

4	3	2	1	0	NA
7. **Concepts explicitly linked** to students' background experiences		**Concepts loosely linked** to students' background experiences		**Concepts not explicitly linked** to students' background experiences	

Comments:

4	3	2	1	0
8. **Links explicitly made** between past learning and new concepts		**Few links made** between past learning and new concepts		**No links made** between past learning and new concepts

Comments:

4	3	2	1	0
9. **Key vocabulary** emphasized (e.g., introduced, written, repeated, and highlighted for students to see)		**Key vocabulary** introduced, but not emphasized		**Key vocabulary** not introduced or emphasized

Comments:

COMPREHENSIBLE INPUT

4	3	2	1	0
10. **Speech** appropriate for students' proficiency levels (e.g., slower rate, enunciation, and simple sentence structure for beginners)		**Speech** sometimes inappropriate for students' proficiency levels		**Speech** inappropriate for students' proficiency levels

Comments:

4	3	2	1	0
11. **Clear explanation** of academic tasks		**Unclear** explanation of academic tasks		**No** explanation of academic tasks

Comments:

4	3	2	1	0
12. **A variety of techniques** used to make content concepts clear (e.g., modeling, visuals, hands-on activities, demonstrations, gestures, body language)		Some **techniques** used to make content concepts clear		No **techniques** used to make concepts clear

Comments:

STRATEGIES

4	3	2	1	0
13. Ample opportunities provided for students to use **learning strategies**		Inadequate opportunities provided for students to use **learning strategies**		No opportunity provided for students to use **learning strategies**

Comments:

4	3	2	1	0
14. **Scaffolding techniques** consistently used, assisting and supporting student understanding (e.g., think-alouds)		**Scaffolding techniques** occasionally used		**Scaffolding techniques** not used

Comments:

4	3	2	1	0
15. A variety of **questions or tasks that promote higher-order thinking skills** (e.g., literal, analytical, and interpretive questions)		Infrequent **questions or tasks that promote higher-order thinking skills**		No **questions or tasks that promote higher-order thinking skills**

Comments:

INTERACTION

4	3	2	1	0
16. Frequent opportunities for **interaction** and discussion between teacher/student and among students, which encourage elaborated responses about lesson concepts		**Interaction** mostly teacher-dominated with some opportunities for students to talk about or question lesson concepts		**Interaction** teacher-dominated with no opportunities for students to discuss lesson concepts

Comments:

4	3	2	1	0
17. **Grouping configurations** support language and content objectives of the lesson		**Grouping configurations** unevenly support the language and content objectives		**Grouping configurations** do not support the language and content objectives

Comments:T

4	3	2	1	0
18. Sufficient **wait time for student responses** consistently provided		Sufficient **wait time for student responses** occasionally provided		Sufficient **wait time for student responses** not provided

Comments:

4	3	2	1	0	NA
19. Ample opportunities for students to **clarify key concepts in L1** as needed with aide, peer, or L1 text		Some opportunities for students to **clarify key concepts in L1**		No opportunities for students to **clarify key concepts in L1**	

Comments:

PRACTICE & APPLICATION

4	3	2	1	0	NA
20. **Hands-on materials and/or manipulatives** provided for students to practice using new content knowledge		Few **hands-on materials and/or manipulatives** provided for students to practice using new content knowledge		No **hands-on materials and/or manipulatives** provided for students to practice using new content knowledge	

Comments:

4	3	2	1	0	NA
21. Activities provided for students to **apply content and language knowledge** in the classroom		Activities provided for students to **apply** either **content or language knowledge** in the classroom		No activities provided for students to **apply content and language knowledge** in the classroom	

Comments:

4	3	2	1	0
22. Activities integrate all **language skills** (i.e., reading, writing, listening, and speaking)		Activities integrate some **language skills**		Activities do not integrate **language skills**

Comments:

LESSON DELIVERY

4	3	2	1	0
23. **Content objectives** clearly supported by lesson delivery		**Content objectives** somewhat supported by lesson delivery		**Content objectives** not supported by lesson delivery

Comments:

4	3	2	1	0
24. **Language objectives** clearly supported by lesson delivery		**Language objectives** somewhat supported by lesson delivery		**Language objectives** not supported by lesson delivery

Comments:

4	3	2	1	0
25. **Students engaged** approximately 90% to 100% of the period		**Students engaged** approximately70% of the period		**Students engaged** less than 50% of the period

Comments:

4	3	2	1	0
26. **Pacing** of the lesson appropriate to students' ability levels		**Pacing** generally appropriate, but at times too fast or too slow		**Pacing** inappropriate to students' ability levels

Comments:

REVIEW & ASSESSMENT

4	3	2	1	0
27. Comprehensive **review of key vocabulary**		Uneven **review of key vocabulary**		No **review of key vocabulary**

Comments:

4	3	2	1	0
28. Comprehensive **review of key content concepts**		Uneven **review of key content concepts**		No **review of key content concepts**

Comments:

4	3	2	1	0
29. Regular **feedback** provided to students on their output (e.g., language, content, work)		Inconsistent **feedback** provided to students on their output		No **feedback** provided to students on their output

Comments:

4	3	2	1	0
30. **Assessment of student comprehension and learning** of all lesson objectives (e.g., spot checking, group response) throughout the lesson		**Assessment of student comprehension and learning** of some lesson objectives		No **assessment of student comprehension and learning** of lesson objectives

Comments:

The Sheltered Instruction Observation Protocol (SIOP®)

(Echevarria, Vogt, & Short, 2000, 2004, 2008)

Observer(s): ____________ Teacher: ____________________
Date: ________________ School: ____________________
Grade: ________________ Class/Topic: __________________
ESL Level: ____________ Lesson: Multi-day Single-day *(circle one)*

Total Points Possible: 120 (Subtract 4 points for each NA given) _______
Total Points Earned: _____ Percentage Score: _____

Directions: Circle the number that best reflects what you observe in a sheltered lesson. You may give a score from 0–4 (or NA on selected items). Cite under "Comments" specific examples of the behaviors observed.

	Highly Evident		Somewhat Evident		Not Evident	
Preparation	**4**	**3**	**2**	**1**	**0**	
1. **Content objectives** clearly defined, displayed, and reviewed with students	❑	❑	❑	❑	❑	
2. **Language objectives** clearly defined, displayed, and reviewed with students	❑	❑	❑	❑	❑	
3. **Content concepts** appropriate for age and educational background level of students	❑	❑	❑	❑	❑	
4. **Supplementary materials** used to a high degree, making the lesson clear and meaningful (e.g., computer programs, graphs, models, visuals)	❑	❑	❑	❑	❑	**NA**
5. **Adaptation of content** (e.g., text, assignment) to all levels of student proficiency	❑	❑	❑	❑	❑	❑
6. **Meaningful activities** that integrate lesson concepts (e.g., surveys, letter writing, simulations, constructing models) with language practice opportunities for reading, writing, listening, and/or speaking	❑	❑	❑	❑	❑	
Comments:						
Building Background	**4**	**3**	**2**	**1**	**0**	**NA**
7. **Concepts explicitly linked** to students' background experiences	❑	❑	❑	❑	❑	❑
8. **Links explicitly made** between past learning and new concepts	❑	❑	❑	❑	❑	
9. **Key vocabulary** emphasized (e.g., introduced, written, repeated, and highlighted for students to see)	❑	❑	❑	❑	❑	
Comments:						
Comprehensible Input	**4**	**3**	**2**	**1**	**0**	
10. **Speech** appropriate for students' proficiency level (e.g., slower rate, enunciation, and simple sentence structure for beginners)	❑	❑	❑	❑	❑	
11. **Clear explanation** of academic tasks	❑	❑	❑	❑	❑	
12. **A variety of techniques** used to make content concepts clear (e.g., modeling, visuals, hands-on activities, demonstrations, gestures, body language)	❑	❑	❑	❑	❑	
Comments:						
Strategies	**4**	**3**	**2**	**1**	**0**	
13. Ample opportunities provided for students to use **learning strategies**	❑	❑	❑	❑	❑	

	Highly Evident		Somewhat Evident		Not Evident	
	4	3	2	1	0	
14. **Scaffolding techniques** consistently used assisting and supporting student understanding (e.g., think-alouds)	❑	❑	❑	❑	❑	
15. A variety of **questions or tasks that promote higher-order thinking skills** (e.g., literal, analytical, and interpretive questions)	❑	❑	❑	❑	❑	
Comments:						
Interaction	4	3	2	1	0	
16. Frequent opportunities for **interaction** and discussion between teacher/student and among students, which encourage elaborated responses about lesson concepts	❑	❑	❑	❑	❑	
17. **Grouping configurations** support language and content objectives of the lesson	❑	❑	❑	❑	❑	
18. Sufficient **wait time for student responses** consistently provided	❑	❑	❑	❑	❑	
						NA
19. Ample opportunities for students to **clarify key concepts in L1** as needed with aide, peer, or L1 text	❑	❑	❑	❑	❑	❑
Comments:						
Practice & Application	4	3	2	1	0	NA
20. **Hands-on materials and/or manipulatives** provided for students to practice using new content knowledge	❑	❑	❑	❑	❑	❑
21. Activities provided for students to **apply content and language knowledge** in the classroom	❑	❑	❑	❑	❑	❑
22. Activities integrate all **language skills** (i.e., reading, writing, listening, and speaking)	❑	❑	❑	❑	❑	
Comments:						
Lesson Delivery	4	3	2	1	0	
23. **Content objectives** clearly supported by lesson delivery	❑	❑	❑	❑	❑	
24. **Language objectives** clearly supported by lesson delivery	❑	❑	❑	❑	❑	
25. **Students engaged** approximately 90% to 100% of the period	❑	❑	❑	❑	❑	
26. **Pacing** of the lesson appropriate to students' ability level	❑	❑	❑	❑	❑	
Comments:						
Review & Assessment	4	3	2	1	0	
27. Comprehensive **review of key vocabulary**	❑	❑	❑	❑	❑	
28. Comprehensive **review of key content concepts**	❑	❑	❑	❑	❑	
29. Regular **feedback** provided to students on their output (e.g., language, content, work)	❑	❑	❑	❑	❑	
30. **Assessment of student comprehension and learning** of all lesson objectives (e.g., spot checking, group response) throughout the lesson	❑	❑	❑	❑	❑	
Comments:						

SIOP® Lesson Plan Template 1

Date: ______________________ **Grade/Class/Subject:** ______________________

Unit/Theme: ______________________ **Standards:** ______________________

Content Objective(s): ____

____

Language Objective(s): ____

____

Key Vocabulary	**Supplementary Materials**

SIOP® Features

Preparation	**Scaffolding**	**Grouping Options**
___ Adaptation of Content	___ Modeling	___ Whole class
___ Links to Background	___ Guided practice	___ Small groups
___ Links to Past Learning	___ Independent practice	___ Partners
___ Strategies incorporated	___ Comprehensible input	___ Independent
Integration of Processes	**Application**	**Assessment**
___ Reading	___ Hands-on	___ Individual
___ Writing	___ Meaningful	___ Group
___ Speaking	___ Linked to objectives	___ Written
___ Listening	___ Promotes engagement	___ Oral

Lesson Sequence

Reflections:

SIOP® Lesson Plan Template 2

STANDARDS:

THEME:

LESSON TOPIC:

OBJECTIVES:
Language

Content

LEARNING STRATEGIES:

KEY VOCABULARY:

MATERIALS:

MOTIVATION:
(Building background)

PRESENTATION
(Language and content objectives, comprehensible input, strategies, interaction, feedback)

PRACTICE & APPLICATION:
(Meaningful activities, interaction, strategies, practice/application, feedback)

REVIEW & ASSESSMENT:
(Review objectives and vocabulary, assess learning)

EXTENSION:

SIOP® Lesson Plan Template 3

<table>
<tr><td>Topic:</td><td>Class:</td><td>Date:</td></tr>
<tr><td>Content Objectives:</td><td colspan="2">Language Objectives:</td></tr>
<tr><td>Key Vocabulary:</td><td colspan="2">Materials (including supplementary and adapted):</td></tr>
<tr><td colspan="3">Higher-Order Questions:</td></tr>
<tr><td>Time:</td><td colspan="2">Activities

Building Background

Links to Experience:

Links to Learning:

Key Vocabulary:</td></tr>
</table>

(*Continued on next page*)

<table>
<tr><td>Time:</td><td>Student Activities (Check all that apply for activities throughout lesson):

Scaffolding: ❑ Modeling ❑ Guided ❑ Independent
Grouping: ❑ Whole Class ❑ Small Group ❑ Partners ❑ Independent
Processes: ❑ Reading ❑ Writing ❑ Listening ❑ Independent
Strategies: ❑ Hands-on ❑ Meaningful ❑ Links to Objectives

Review and Assessment (Check all that apply):
Individual ❑ Group ❑ Written ❑ Oral ❑

Review Key Vocabulary:

Review Key Content Concepts:</td></tr>
</table>

(Developed by John Seidlitz. Used with permission.)

SIOP® Lesson Plan Template 4

SIOP® Lesson Content Standards:		Grade:
Key Vocabulary: Nigher-Order Thinking Skills (HOTS):		Visuals/Resources:
Connections: Prior Knowledge/Building Background/Prior Learning:		
Content Objective(s): Language Objective(s):	Meaningful Activities: Lesson Sequence	Review & Assessment:

(Developed by Melissa Castillo & Nicole Teyechea. Used with permission.)

(*Continued on next page*)

	Lesson Sequence (*continued*)	**Review & Assessment (*continued*)**
Wrap-up:		

(Developed by Melissa Castillo & Nicole Teyechea. Used with permission.)

appendix c: Research on the SIOP® Model

The original research study that developed the SIOP® Model, "The Effects of Sheltered Instruction on the Achievement of Limited English Proficient Students," was a seven-year project (1996–2003) conducted for the Center for Research on Education, Diversity & Excellence (CREDE), a national research center funded by the U.S. Department of Education, Office of Educational Research and Improvement (now known as the Institute of Education Sciences). This project worked with middle school teachers in four large metropolitan school districts—two on the East Coast and two on the West Coast—to identify key practices for sheltered instruction and develop a professional development model to enable more teachers to use sheltered instruction effectively in their classrooms. Dr. Jana Echevarria of California State University, Long Beach, and Dr. Deborah Short of the Center for Applied Linguistics in Washington, DC, were co–project investigators.

Although sheltered instruction had been widely advocated as an effective instructional strategy for language minority students, when this study began there had been little agreement among practitioners as to what sheltered instruction should look like in the classroom, and few research investigations measuring what constituted an effective sheltered lesson. This project therefore set the following goals: (1) develop an explicit model of sheltered instruction, (2) use that model to train teachers in effective sheltered strategies, and (3) conduct field experiments and collect data to evaluate teacher change and the effects of sheltered instruction on LEP students' English language development and content knowledge.

The specific research questions posed by this project follow:

1. What are the characteristics of sheltered instruction, and how does it differ from high-quality nonsheltered instruction?
2. What are the characteristics of an effective professional development program for implementing quality sheltered instruction to a high degree?
3. Does sheltered instruction improve the achievement of LEP students in content areas such as social studies?
4. Are there significant differences in achievement data (reading scores, writing samples, attendance) for students of project teachers versus students in sheltered classes whose teachers have not received SIOP® training?

This research project involved the active collaboration of practicing middle school teachers both in refining the model of sheltered instruction and in implementing it in their classrooms. In the first two years of the project we identified, based on literature review and classroom research, effective teaching strategies involved in sheltered instruction. The model began as a research observation instrument, the Sheltered Instruction Observation Protocol (SIOP®), so that researchers could determine how well teachers were including these features of effective sheltered instruction in their lessons. Drawing from the literature on best practices, the SIOP® protocol incorporated topics such as scaffolding, learning strategies, literacy techniques, and use of meaningful curricula and materials. Our goal was to determine which combination of best practices in one instructional framework, the SIOP®, would yield positive achievement results for English learners. With feedback from the teachers, the protocol evolved into a lesson planning and delivery approach, the SIOP® Model (Echevarria, Vogt, & Short, 2000, 2008; Short & Echevarria, 1999). It is composed of 30 items grouped into 8 components essential for making content comprehensible for English learners—Lesson Preparation, Building Background, Comprehensible Input, Strategies, Interaction, Practice & Application, Lesson Delivery, and Review & Assessment. The SIOP® Model shares many features recommended for high-quality instruction for all students, but adds key features for the academic success of students learning through a second language, such as including language objectives in every content lesson, developing background knowledge among the students, and attending to specific academic literacy skills. This model can be applied in ESL classes as well as all content area classes because it offers a framework for instruction that incorporates best practices for teaching both language and content.

After several years of field-testing the SIOP® protocol, a study was conducted to establish the validity and reliability of the observation instrument. It was found to be a highly reliable and valid measure of sheltered instruction (Guarino, Echevarria, Short, Schick, Forbes, & Rueda, 2001). Experienced observers of classroom instruction (e.g., teacher education faculty who supervise student teachers) who were *not* specifically trained in the SIOP® Model were able to use the protocol to distinguish between high and low implementers of the model. A statistical analysis revealed an interrater of correlation 0.99.

As part of the research design, student data in the form of a writing assessment based on the IMAGE (Illinois Measure of Annual Growth in English) Test were gathered and analyzed. The IMAGE was the standardized test of reading and writing used by the state of Illinois to measure annual growth of these skills in their limited English proficient students in grades 3–12. It was correlated to and a predictor of scores on the IGAP (the state standardized test of achievement) that was given to all students in Illinois, except those exempted for linguistic development reasons or learning disabilities. The IMAGE Writing Test provides separate scores for five features of writing: Language Production, Focus, Support/Elaboration, Organization, and Mechanics, as well as an overall score.

During the 1998–99 school year, researchers gave prompts to middle school English language learning students that required expository writing, once in the fall (pretest) and then again in the spring (posttest). Two distinct, but similar, cohorts of English learners in sheltered classes participated: students whose teachers were trained in implementing the SIOP® Model (the treatment group), and students whose teachers had no exposure to the SIOP® Model (the comparison group). The students in both groups were in grades 6–8 and represented mixed proficiency levels.

Results showed English learners in sheltered classes with teachers who had been trained in implementing the SIOP® Model to a high degree improved their writing and outperformed the students in control classes by receiving overall higher scores for the spring assessment (Echevarria, Short, & Powers, 2006). They also made greater gains from the fall to spring administrations of the test. These findings were statistically significant. The results indicated that students whose teachers implemented the SIOP® Model of sheltered instruction improved significantly in all areas of writing over students in sheltered classes whose teachers were not familiar with the SIOP® Model. These results match the findings from the 1997–98 school year when a similar administration of a writing assessment requiring narrative writing was given. Secondary analyses of the data revealed that special education

TABLE C.1 *Mean Scores, Standard Deviations, and Sample Size for Treatment and Comparison Groups*

	SIOP®(Treatment)		Comparison	
	Pretest	Posttest	Pretest	Posttest
Total Score				
M	13.55	16.36	14.61	15.81
SD	3.42	3.33	3.36	3.45
N	238	238	77	77
Language Production				
M	2.65	3.22	2.77	3.09
SD	.78	.79	.78	.73
N	240	240	77	77
Focus				
M	2.81	3.30	3.01	3.17
SD	.87	.98	.88	.94
N	239	239	77	77
Support/Elaboration				
M	2.65	3.26	2.83	3.18
SD	.78	.72	.70	.81
N	241	241	77	77
Organization				
M	2.77	3.31	3.16	3.21
SD	.96	.78	.92	.71
N	241	241	77	77
Mechanics				
M	2.72	3.28	2.84	3.17
SD	.88	.87	.86	.94
N	241	241	77	77

students who constituted a subset of the English learners made significant improvement overall in their writing as well, with both the narrative and expository assessments.

Specifically, with the 1998–99 assessment, analysis of treatment and comparison groups' total scores (i.e., aggregated across the five subscales) found the participants whose teachers were trained in the SIOP® Model made statistically significantly better gains than the control group in writing ($F(1,312) = 10.79$; $p < 0.05$). Follow-up analyses on student performance on the various subtests of the writing assessment found that the treatment group performed at a significantly higher level in language production ($F(1,314) = 5.00$; $p < 0.05$), organization ($F(1,315) = 5.65$; $p < 0.05$) and mechanics ($F(1,315) = 4.10$; $p < 0.05$) than those in the comparison group, whose teachers had not received the study-developed training and support in delivering sheltered instruction (see Tables C.1 and C.2). The treatment group did not make significant gains over the comparison group in their performance on the writing focus and elaboration subtests.

The project also developed and field-tested a professional development program for the SIOP® Model that incorporated key features of effective teacher development as recommended by Darling-Hammond (1998) and Garet, Porter, Desimone, Birman, &

TABLE C.2 *Analysis of Covariance of Posttest Writing Results by Treatment Condition*

Variable	*df*	*M Square*	*F-ratio*	*p*
Total Score	1	78.276	10.785	.001*
Language Production	1	2.133	5.004	.026*
Focus	1	2.904	3.706	.055
Support/Elaboration	1	1.247	2.680	1.03
Organization	1	2.842	5.651	.018*
Mechanics	1	2.065	4.101	.044*

Note: Pretest scores for each measure served as the covariate for posttest dependent measures.
* $p < .05$*

Yoon (2001). In this project, it has been found that through sustained, intensive interaction and coaching among staff developers and teachers—for at least one year—teachers can modify their pedagogy to promote both language and content learning among English learners. Two professional development videos (Hudec & Short, 2002a; 2002b), training manuals (Echevarria & Vogt, 2006; Short, Hudec, & Echevarria, 2002), and other materials have been developed to support this program, and institutes to prepare staff developers and teacher educators to coach others in the SIOP® Model have been held across the United States. (See www.siopinstitute.net for more details.)

Since the SIOP® Model was first published in 2000, the following uses for the observation tool and professional development program have been realized:

- Teacher lesson plan checklist and self-reflection guide
- Classroom observation tool for administrators
- Supervision tool for faculty to observe student teachers
- Research observation tool for fidelity of model implementation
- Program of professional development

Summary: Selected Findings from the SIOP® Research Project

- After five years of collaboration with practicing teachers, CREDE researchers developed a model of high-quality sheltered instruction, known as the SIOP® Model. This model takes into account the special language development needs of English language learners, which distinguishes it from high-quality nonsheltered teaching.
- A study conducted to establish the validity and reliability of the Sheltered Instruction Observation Protocol found that the instrument is a highly reliable and valid measure of sheltered instruction (Guarino, Echevarria, Short, Schick, Forbes, & Rueda, 2001).
- 1997–98: Researchers compared English language learning students in classes whose teachers had been trained in implementing the SIOP® Model to a high degree to a comparison group (taught by teachers not trained in the SIOP® Model) using a prompt that required narrative writing. They scored the prompt using the writing rubric of the Illinois Measure of Annual Growth in English (IMAGE) Test. The English learners in

classes whose teachers had been trained in implementing the SIOP® Model to a high degree demonstrated significantly higher writing scores than the control group.

- 1998–99: Researchers compared English learners in classes whose teachers had been trained in implementing the SIOP® Model to a high degree to a comparison group (taught by teachers not trained in the SIOP® Model) using a prompt that required expository writing. They scored the prompt using the writing rubric of the Illinois Measure of Annual Growth in English (IMAGE) Test. The English learners in classes whose teachers had been trained in implementing the SIOP® Model to a high degree demonstrated significantly higher writing scores than the comparison group and made greater gains from the pretest to the posttest. See the results in Tables C.1 and C.2.

Current and Recent SIOP® Research Studies

Since we conducted the original SIOP® research for CREDE, additional investigations have taken or are taking place. Some school districts have implemented the SIOP® Model and have evaluated their results. In addition, some large-scale quasi-experimental and experimental studies have taken place or are in progress. We describe them briefly here but encourage you to look at www.cal.org and www.siopinstitute.net for updates and final results.

Academic Literacy Through Sheltered Instruction for Secondary English Language Learners was a quasi-experimental research study conducted in the two districts in New Jersey. Funded by the Carnegie Corporation of New York and the Rockefeller Foundation from 2004–07, researchers from the Center for Applied Linguistics collected and analyzed data to investigate the relationship between professional development in the SIOP® Model and the academic achievement of secondary English language learners. One school district received the SIOP® Model as the professional development treatment; the other was a comparison site. Both school districts have two middle schools and one high school with similar multilingual English learner populations. More than 500 ELs were in the treatment district, approximately 225 in the comparison site. Each district follows an ESL program design in grades 6–12 with some designated sheltered courses.

In the treatment site, math, science, social studies, language arts, ESL, and technology teachers participated in ongoing SIOP® Model training: approximately 35 teachers for 2 years (cohort 1) and an additional 25 for 1 (cohort 2). Each cohort had 7 days for workshops spread throughout the year, and cohort 1 had 3 follow-up days in the second year. The teachers in the comparison site did not receive any SIOP® Model training. The treatment teachers also had part-time on-site coaches who primarily facilitated after-school meetings and offered guidance in lesson design and material resources. Some coaches were able to make classroom visits. Ongoing support was also provided via closed Listserv, a project dedicated website, and online chats.

Researchers collected teacher implementation data (two classroom observations each year, one in the fall, the other in the spring) using the SIOP® protocol at both sites. Analyses showed that the number of high implementers of the SIOP® Model increased to a greater extent in the treatment district than the comparison district. After one year of SIOP® professional development in the treatment district, 56% of cohort 1 and 74% of cohort 2 teachers implemented the model to a high degree. After two years, 71% of cohort 1 reached a high level. In contrast, only 5% of the teachers reached a high level of implementation after one year at the comparison site and only 17% after two years (Center for Applied Linguistics, 2007).

In addition, pre- and post-SIOP® lesson plans were collected at the treatment site to measure how well teachers incorporated SIOP® Model components in their preparation. The incorporation of SIOP® features in the teachers' lesson plans improved by more than 50 percent.

The researchers collected and analyzed results on the state's English language proficiency assessment, which at that time was the IDEA Proficiency Test (IPT), for all ELs in grades 6–12 who were in ESL programs. Analyses showed that, on average, students with SIOP-trained teachers (in the treatment district) outperformed students without SIOP-trained teachers (in the comparison district) to a statistically significant level ($p < .05$) when comparing average mean scores on the IPT oral, writing, and total tests in the second year of the intervention (2005–06). There was no significant difference in the first year. However, SIOP students in the treatment district made greater gains in average mean scores on all IPT tests from the baseline year (2003–04) to the final year (2005–06) than the students in the comparison district did.

An examination of student performance within the treatment district revealed that, on average, SIOP students outperformed non-SIOP students to a statistically significant level ($p < .05$) in both the first and second year of the intervention, when comparing mean scores on the IPT oral, reading, writing, and total tests (Center for Applied Linguistics, 2007).

The researchers also collected and analyzed student content area achievement data from New Jersey state tests in reading, math, social studies, and science for grades 6–7; reading, math, and science for grade 8; and reading and math for grade 11 (or grade 12 for some ELs), although this was complicated by the fact that New Jersey changed tests during the study. (In the second year, students in grades 6 and 7 had a new test, and were tested only in reading and math.) The analyses were further limited by the fact that the students in the treatment and comparison districts took these tests only once, and the number of student subjects was very small for each test; therefore, the results are not generalizable. The results showed a significant difference ($p < .05$) in mean scores in favor of SIOP students in the treatment district on six state content tests: grade 6 reading, language arts, and total proficiency score for 2004–05 and grade 6 language arts, grade 7 language arts, and grade 11 mathematics in 2005–06. There was a significant difference ($p < .05$) in mean scores in favor of students in the comparison district on one state content test, grade 7 social studies in 2004–05. There were no significant differences between groups on the other 19 content tests (Center for Applied Linguistics, 2007). The content achievement results indicate some promise for the SIOP Model, but further research and larger sample sizes are needed.

Optimizing Educational Outcomes for English Language Learners is a five-year experimental study conducted by the University of Houston, the University of Texas at Austin, the Center for Applied Linguistics, and the University of Miami (2003–08). It is supported by the U.S. Department of Education. Within this research project, the SIOP® Model is part of a larger intervention design to enhance academic language/literacy development and content knowledge in elementary school students in ESL and bilingual programs.

The project follows a longitudinal, experimental design to evaluate traditional and enhanced models of ESL and bilingual programs in grades K–3. Approximately 12 schools in one district are participating. Some offer a bilingual (Spanish-English) program model; others, an ESL program. Students have been randomly assigned to traditional or intervention classes, and the study follows the same students over four years as they progress from kindergarten to grade 3. The intervention consists of the following elements:

- Tier I (core instruction)
  –Enhanced language enrichment in English and/or Spanish for phonics and reading (grades 1–3)
  –SIOP® Model instruction with a focus on mathematics classes in English or Spanish (grades K–3)
  –Additional language development using authentic text and focusing on vocabulary in English and/or Spanish (grades K–3)
- Tier II
  –Classroom-based supplemental reading instruction (offered in small groups to identified students, grades K–3)
- Tier III
  –Intensive small-group, pull-out intervention for reading (grades 2–3)

Intervention teachers participate in professional development on all interventions. The training is distributed throughout each school year to the targeted grade level. External mentors offer ongoing mentoring with biweekly classroom visits and meetings. Additional pedagogical materials and curriculum units are developed by the research staff and given to the teachers for use in the classrooms.

Data collection consists of classroom observations using the SIOP® protocol and other researcher-developed measures to determine the teachers' level of implementation. In addition, student data is collected: pre- and post-assessments for literacy/language development in grades K–3, which include early reading (letter names, letter sounds, phonological awareness), vocabulary, word reading, and listening comprehension. When students reach grade 3, they are also assessed with the state reading and mathematics tests.

Findings from this study should be available in 2009.

The Impact of the SIOP® Model on Middle School Science and Language Learning is another five-year study funded by the U.S. Department of Education. It is one of several studies in the national Center for Research on the Educational Achievement & Teaching of English Language Learners (CREATE). This SIOP® research is conducted by researchers at California State University Long Beach, the Center for Applied Linguistics, and the University of Houston (2005–10). This study uses a randomized experimental design to investigate the impact of the SIOP® Model on student academic achievement in middle school science. Researchers are developing science curriculum units with SIOP® lesson plans and science language assessments that focus on the acquisition of science concepts and language development among English learners.

The study is being conducted in phases. Phase 1 was a pilot study designed to develop and refine science curriculum lessons that incorporate the SIOP® Model features and to field-test academic science language assessments. Phase 2 involves two one-year studies. In the first year, approximately 10 schools will participate as treatment or control sites. Treatment teachers will receive SIOP® training, the SIOP® science lessons, and coaching. In the second year, approximately 15 schools in another district will participate as Treatment 1, Treatment 2, or control sites. Treatment 1 teachers will receive SIOP® training, SIOP® science lessons, and coaching. Treatment 2 teachers will receive SIOP® training and coaching. The analyses will examine if SIOP® lessons help teachers learn the SIOP® Model faster and/or better. Phase 3 will occur in the final two years of the research center: data gathered from years 1–3 will be combined with the research findings from other CREATE research studies and will be tested as a school reform intervention for English learners in several sites across the United States.

Data collection and analyses for Phases 2 and 3 will be of teacher implementation ratings using the SIOP® protocol and student state test results in reading, science, and English language development. In addition, the researchers are collecting data from local district content tests and the project-developed science language tests.

Findings from this study should be available in 2011.

References

Center for Applied Linguistics. (2007). *Academic literacy through sheltered instruction for secondary English language learners.* Final Report to the Carnegie Corporation of New York. Washington, DC: Center for Applied Linguistics.

Darling-Hammond, L. (1998). Teacher learning that supports student learning. *Educational Leadership, 55,* 6–11.

Echevarria, J., Short, D., & Powers, K. (2006). School reform and standards-based education: An instructional model for English language learners. *Journal of Educational Research, 99*(4), 195–211.

Echevarria, J., & Vogt, M. E. (2008). *The SIOP® Model SIOP I Institute training manual.* Glenview, IL: Pearson.

Echevarria, J., Vogt, M. E., & Short, D. (2000). *Making content comprehensible for English language learners: The SIOP® Model.* Needham Heights, MA: Allyn & Bacon.

Echevarria, J., Vogt, M. E., & Short, D. (2008). *Making content comprehensible for English learners: The SIOP® Model* (3rd ed.). Boston: Pearson/Allyn & Bacon.

Garet, M. S., Porter, A. C., Desimone, L., Birman, B. F., & Yoon, K. S. (2001). What makes professional development effective? Results from a national sample of teachers. *American Educational Research Journal, 38*(4), 915–945.

Guarino, A. J., Echevarria, J., Short, D., Schick, J. E., Forbes, S., & Rueda, R. (2001). The sheltered instruction observation protocol. *Journal of Research in Education, 11*(1), 138–140.

Hudec, J., & Short, D. (Prods). (2002a). *Helping English learners succeed: An overview of the SIOP® Model.* [Video]. Washington, DC: Center for Applied Linguistics.

Hudec, J., & Short, D. (Prods). (2002b). *The SIOP® Model: Sheltered instruction for academic achievement.* [Video]. Washington, DC: Center for Applied Linguistics.

Short, D., & Echevarria, J. (1999). *The sheltered instruction observation protocol: A tool for teacher-researcher collaboration and professional development* (Educational Practice Rep. No. 3). Santa Cruz, CA, and Washington, DC: Center for Research on Education, Diversity & Excellence.

Short, D., Hudec, J, & Echevarria, J. (2002). *Using the SIOP® Model: Professional development manual for sheltered instruction.* Washington, DC: Center for Applied Linguistics.

glossary

Academic language: Language used in formal contexts for academic subjects. The aspect of language connected with literacy and academic achievement. This includes technical and academic terms (*see* Cognitive/Academic Language Proficiency–CALP).

Additive bilingualism: Rather than neglecting or rejecting students' language and culture, additive bilingualism promotes building on what the child brings to the classroom and adding to it.

Alignment: Match among the ESL and content standards, instruction, curriculum, and assessment.

Assessment: The orderly process of gathering, analyzing, interpreting, and reporting student performance, ideally from multiple sources over a period of time.

Basic Interpersonal Communicative Skills (BICS): Face-to-face conversational fluency, including mastery of pronunciation, vocabulary, and grammar. English language learners typically acquire conversational language used in everyday activities before they develop more complex, conceptual language proficiency.

Bilingual instruction: School instruction using two languages, generally a native language of the student and a second language. The amount of time that each language is used depends on the type of bilingual program, its specific objectives, and students' level of language proficiency.

Cognitive Academic Language Learning Approach (CALLA): An instructional model developed by Chamot and O'Malley (1987, 1994) for content and language learning that incorporates student development of learning strategies, specifi cally metacognitive, cognitive, and socioaffective strategies.

Cognitive/Academic Language Proficiency (CALP): Language proficiency associated with schooling, and the abstract language abilities required for academic work. A more complex, conceptual, linguistic ability that includes analysis, synthesis, and evaluation.

Communicative competence: The combination of grammatical, discourse, strategic, and sociolinguistic competence that allows the recognition and production of fluent and appropriate language in all communicative settings.

Content-based ESL: An instructional approach in which content topics are used as the vehicle for second language learning. A system of instruction in which teachers use a variety of instructional techniques as a way of developing second language, content, cognitive, and study skills, and is often delivered through thematic units.

Content objectives: Statements that identify what students should know and be able to do in particular content areas. They support school district and state content standards and learning outcomes, and they guide teaching and learning in the classroom.

Content standards: Definitions of what students are expected to know and be capable of doing for a given content area; the knowledge and skills that need to be taught in order for students to reach competency; what students are expected to learn and what schools are expected to teach. May be national, state, or local-level standards.

Cross-cultural competence: The ability to understand and follow the cultural rules and norms of more than one system. The ability to respond to the demands of a given situation in a culturally acceptable way.

Culture: The customs, lifestyle, traditions, behavior, attitudes, and artifacts of a given people. Culture also encompasses the ways people organize and interpret the world, and the way events are perceived based on established social norms. A system of standards for understanding the world.

Dialect: The form of a language peculiar to a specific region. Features a variation in vocabulary, grammar, and pronunciation.

Differentiated instruction In order to create a learning environment that addresses the diversity represented in a typical classroom, teachers change the pace, amount, level, or kind of instruction to meet the individual needs of each learner.

Engagement: When students are fully taking part in a lesson, they are said to be engaged. This is a holistic term that encompasses listening, reading, writing, responding, and discussing. The level of students' engagement during a lesson may be assessed to a greater or lesser degree. A low SIOP® score for engagement would imply frequent chatting, daydreaming, nonattention, and other off-task behaviors.

English learners (ELs): Children and adults who are learning English as a second or additional language. This term may apply to learners across various levels of proficiency in English. ELs may also be referred to as English language learners (ELLs), non–English speaking (NES), limited English proficient (LEP), and a non-native speaker (NNS).

EO: Used in some regions, English-only or EO refers to students whose native language is English.

ESL: English as a second language. Used to refer to programs and classes to teach students English as a second (additional) language.

ESOL: English speakers of other languages. Students whose first language is not English and who do not write, speak, and understand the language as well as their classmates.

Evaluation: Judgments about students' learning made by interpreting and analyzing assessment data; the process of judging achievement, growth, product, processes, or changes in these; judgments of education programs. The processes of assessment and evaluation can be viewed as progressive: first, assessment; then, evaluation.

Formative evaluation: Ongoing collection, analysis, and reporting of information about student performance for purposes of instruction and learning.

Grouping: The assignment of students into groups or classes for instruction, such as by age, ability, or achievement; or within classes, such as by reading ability, proficiency, language background, or interests.

Home language: The language, or languages, spoken in the student's home by people who live there. Also referred to as first language (L1), primary language, or native language.

Informal assessment: Appraisal of student performance through unstructured observation; characterized as frequent, ongoing, continuous, and involving simple but important techniques such as verbal checks for understanding, teacher-created assessments, and other nonstandardized procedures. This type of assessment provides teachers with immediate feedback.

Instructional conversations (IC): An approach to teaching that is an interactive dialogue with an instructional intent. An IC approach encourages thoughtful discussion around a concept or idea with balanced participation between teacher and students.

Inter-rater reliability: Measures of the degree of agreement between two different raters on separate ratings of one assessment indicator using the same scale and criteria.

L1: First language. A widely used abbreviation for the primary, home, or native language.

Language competence: An individual's total language ability. The underlying language system as indicated by the individual's language performance.

Language minority: In the United States, a student whose primary language is not English. The individual students' ability to speak English will vary.

Language objectives: Statements that identify what students should know and be able to do while using English (or another language). They support students' language development, often focusing on vocabulary, functional language, questioning, articulating predictions or hypotheses, reading, writing, and so forth.

Language proficiency: An individual's competence in using a language for basic communication and for academic purposes. May be categorized as stages of language acquisition (*see* Levels of language proficiency).

Levels of language proficiency: Students learning language progress through stages. The stages or levels are labeled differently across geographic regions. For example, the WIDA Consortium (World-class Instructional Design and Assessment) uses the terms Entering (Level 1), Beginning (Level 2), Developing (Level 3), Expanding (Level 4), and

Bridging (Level 5). Krashen and Terrell, 1983, 1984 describe the stages as the following:

Preproduction: Students at this stage are not ready to produce much language, so they primarily communicate with gestures and actions. They are absorbing the new language and developing receptive vocabulary.

Early production: Students at this level speak using one or two words or short phrases. Their receptive vocabulary is developing; they understand approximately one thousand words. Students can answer "who, what, and where" questions with limited expression.

Speech emergence: Students speak in longer phrases and complete sentences. However, they may experience frustration at not being able to express completely what they know. Although the number of errors they make increases, they can communicate ideas and the quantity of speech they produce increases.

Intermediate fluency: Students may appear to be fluent; they engage in conversation and produce connected narrative. Errors are usually of style or usage. Lessons continue to expand receptive vocabulary, and activities develop higher levels of language use in content areas. Students at this level are able to communicate effectively.

Advanced fluency: Students communicate very effectively, orally and in writing, in social and academic settings.

Limited English Proficient (LEP): A term used to refer to a student with restricted understanding or use of written and spoken English; a learner who is still developing competence in using English. The federal government uses the term *LEP*, while *EL* or *ELL* is more commonly used in schools.

Mnemonics: From the Greek *mnemon,* meaning "mindful." Mnemonics are devices to jog the memory. For example, steps of a learning strategy are often abbreviated to form an acronym or word that enables the learner to remember the steps.

Multilingualism: The ability to speak more than two languages; proficiency in more than two languages.

Native English speaker: An individual whose first language is English.

Native language: An individual's first, primary, or home language (L1).

Non–English speaking (NES): Individuals who are in an English-speaking environment (such as U.S. schools) but who have not acquired any English proficiency.

Nonverbal communication: Paralinguistic messages such as intonation, stress, pauses and rate of speech, and nonlinguistic messages such as gestures, facial expressions, and body language that can accompany speech or be conveyed without the aid of speech.

Performance assessment: A measure of educational achievement in which students produce a response, create a product, or apply knowledge in ways similar to tasks required in the instructional environment. The performance measures are analyzed and interpreted according to preset criteria.

Portfolio assessment: A type of performance assessment that involves gathering multiple indicators of student progress to support course goals in a dynamic, ongoing process. Portfolios are purposeful collections of student performance that evince students' efforts, progress, and achievement over time.

Primary language: An individual's first, home, or native language (L1).

Pull-out instruction: Students are "pulled-out" from their regular classes for special classes of ESL instruction, remediation, or acceleration.

Realia: Real-life objects and artifacts used to supplement teaching; can provide effective visual scaffolds for English learners.

Reliability: Statistical consistency in measurements and tests, such as the extent to which two assessments measure student performance in the same way.

Rubrics: Statements that describe indicators of performance, which include scoring criteria, on a continuum; may be described as "developmental" (e.g., emergent, beginning, developing, proficient) or "evaluative" (e.g., exceptional, thorough, adequate, inadequate).

Scaffolding: Adult (e.g., teacher) support for learning and student performance of the tasks through instruction, modeling, questioning, feedback, graphic organizers, and more, across successive engagements.

These supports are gradually withdrawn, thus transferring more and more autonomy to the child. Scaffolding activities provide support for learning that can be removed as learners are able to demonstrate strategic behaviors in their own learning activities.

SDAIE (Specially Designed Academic Instruction in English): A term for sheltered instruction used mostly in California. It features strategies and techniques for making content understandable for English learners. Although some SDAIE techniques are research based, SDAIE itself has not been scientifically validated. (*See* Sheltered instruction.)

Self-contained ESL class: A class consisting solely of English speakers of other languages for the purpose of learning English; content may also be taught. An effective alternative to pull-out instruction.

Sheltered instruction (SI): A means for making content comprehensible for English learners while they are developing English proficiency. The SIOP® is a validated model of sheltered instruction. Sheltered classrooms, which may, in a mix of native English speakers and English learners or only ELs, integrate language and content while infusing sociocultural awareness. (*See* SDAIE and SIOP®.)

SIOP® (Sheltered Instruction Observation Protocol): A scientifically validated model of sheltered instruction designed to make grade-level academic content understandable for English learners while at the same time developing their English language. The protocol and lesson planning guide ensure that teachers are consistently implementing practices known to be effective for English learners.

Social language: Basic language proficiency associated with fluency in day-to-day situations, including the classroom. (*See* Basic Interpersonal Communicative Skills [BICS].)

Sociocultural competence: The ability to function effectively by following the rules and behavioral expectations held by members of a given social or cultural group.

Sociolinguistic competence: The degree to which a language is used and understood in a given situaion. The use of appropriate comments and responses in conversation. (*See* Communicative competence.)

Standard: *See* Content standards.

Standard American English: "That variety of American English in which most educational texts, government, and media publications are written in the United States; English as it is spoken and written by those groups with social, economic, and political power in the United States. Standard American English is a relative concept, varying widely in pronunciation and in idiomatic use but maintaining a fairly uniform grammatical structure" (Harris and Hodges, 1995, p. 241).

Standards-based assessment: Assessment involving the planning, gathering, analyzing, and reporting of a student's performance according to the ESL and/or district content standards.

Strategies: Mental processes and plans that people use to help them comprehend, learn, and retain new information. There are three types of strategies—cognitive, metacognitive, and social/affective—and these are consciously adapted and monitored during reading, writing, and learning.

Subtractive bilingualism: The learning of a new language at the expense of the primary language. Learners often lose their native language and culture because they don't have opportunities to continue learning or using it, or they perceive that language to be of lower status. Loss of the primary language often leads to cultural ambivalence.

Summative evaluation: The final collection, analysis, and reporting of information about student achievement or program effectiveness at the end of a given time frame.

Task: An activity that calls for a response to a question, issue, or problem.

Validity: A statistical measure of an assessment's match between the information collected and itsstated purpose; evidence that inferences from evaluation are trustworthy.

Vignette: A short sketch that gives a description of aninstructional process drawn from real-life classroom experiences.

references

Abedi, J., & Lord, C. (2001). The language factor in mathematics tests. *Applied Measurement in Education, 14*(3), 219–234.

Afflerbach, P., Pearson, P. D., & Paris, S. G. (2008). Clarifying differences between reading skills and reading strategies. *The Reading Teacher, 61*(5), 364–373.

Allen, J. (2007). *Inside words: Tools for teaching academic vocabulary, grades 4–12*. Portland, ME: Stenhouse Publishers.

Alvarez, M. C. (1990). *Knowledge activation and schema construction*. Paper presented at the Annual Meeting of the American Educational Research Association, Boston, MA, 1990, 25p. [ED 317 988]

Anderson, L. W., & Krathwohl, D. R. (Eds.). (2001). *Taxonomy for learning, teaching, and assessing: A revision of Bloom's Taxonomy of Educational Objectives*. Boston: Longman.

Anderson, R. C. (1984). Role of the reader's schema in comprehension, learning, and memory. In R. C. Anderson, J. Osborn, & R. J. Tierney (Eds.), *Learning to read in American schools: Basal readers and content texts.* Hillsdale, NJ: Erlbaum.

Anderson, R. C. (1994). Role of the reader's schema in comprehension, learning, and memory. In R. Ruddell, M. Ruddell, & H. Singer (Eds.), *Theoretical models and processes of reading* (4th ed.). Newark, DE: International Reading Association.

Artiles, A. (1998). Overrepresentation of minority students: The case for greater specificity or reconsideration of the variables examined. *Journal of Special Education, 32*(1), 32–36.

ASCD. (2008). *Educational leadership: Reshaping high schools, 65*(8). (Themed journal).

August, D. A. (2006). How does first language literacy development relate to second language literacy development? In E. Hamayan & R. Freeman (Eds.), *English language learners in school: Over 50 experts answer YOUR questions* (pp. 71–72). Philadelphia: Caslon Publishing.

August, D., & Hakuta, K. (Eds.). (1997). *Improving schooling for language minority children: A research agenda.* Washington, DC: National Academy Press.

August, D., & Shanahan T. (Eds.). (2006a). *Developing literacy in second-language learners: A report of the National Literacy Panel on Language-Minority Children and Youth.* Mahwah, NJ: Lawrence Erlbaum Associates.

August, D., & Shanahan, T. (2006b). *Executive summary. Developing literacy in second-language learners: Report of the National Literacy Panel on Language-Minority Children and Youth.* Mahwah, NJ: Lawrence Erlbaum Associates. Available at http://www.cal.org/projects/archive/nlpreports/Executive_Summary.pdf

Bailey, A. (Ed.). (2007). *The language demands of school: Putting academic English to the test.* New Haven, CT: Yale University Press.

Bailey, A., & Butler, F. (2007). A conceptual framework of academic English language for broad application to education. In A. Bailey (Ed.), *The language demands of school: Putting academic English to the test* (pp. 68–102). New Haven, CT: Yale University Press.

Baker, L. (2004). Reading comprehension and science inquiry: Metacognitive connections. In E. W. Saul (Ed.), *Crossing borders in literacy and science instruction: Perspectives on theory and practice* (pp. 239–257). Newark, DE: International Reading Association; Arlington, VA: National Science Teachers Association (NSTA) Press.

Baker, L., & Brown, A. L. (1984). Metacognitive skills and reading. In P. D. Pearson (Ed.), *Handbook of reading research*. New York: Longman.

Barnes, C., Mercer, G., & Shakespeare, T. (1999). *Exploring disability: A sociological introduction.* Cambridge: Polity Press.

Barnhardt, S. (1997). Effective memory strategies. *NCLRC Language Resource, 1*(6), http://www.nclrc.org.

Bartolome, L. I. (1994). Beyond the methods fetish: Toward a humanizing pedagogy. *Harvard Educational Review, 64*(2), 173–194.

Barton, M. L., Heidama, C., & Jordan, D. (2002). Teaching reading in mathematics and science. *Educational Leadership, 60*(3), 24–28.

Batalova, J., Fix, M., & Murray, J. (2005). *English language learner adolescents: Demographics and literacy achievements.* Report to the Center for Applied Linguistics. Washington, DC: Migration Policy Institute.

Baumann, J. F. (2005). Vocabulary-comprehension relationships. In B. Maloch, J. V. Hoffman, D. L. Schallert, C. M. Fairbanks, & J. Worthy (Eds.), *54th Yearbook of the National Reading Conference.* Oak Creek, WI: National Reading Conference, Inc.

Baumann, J., Jones, L., & Seifert-Kessell, N. (1993). Using think-alouds to enhance children's comprehension monitoring abilities. *The Reading Teacher, 47*(3), 184–193.

Bean, T. W. (2000). Reading in the content areas: Social constructivist dimensions. In M. L. Kamil, P. B. Mosenthal, P. D. Pearson, & R. Barr (Eds.), *Handbook of reading research.* (Vol. III, pp. 629–644). Mahwah, NJ: Lawrence Erlbaum Associates.

Bear, D. R., Helman, L., Invernizzi, M., Templeton, S., & Johnston, F. (2007). *Words their way with English learners: Word study for spelling, phonics, and vocabulary instruction.* Boston: Merrill Prentice Hall.

Bear, D. R., Invernizzi, M., Templeton, S., & Johnston, F. (2007). *Words their way: Word study for phonics, vocabulary, and spelling instruction* (4th ed.). Upper Saddle River, NJ: Merrill Prentice Hall.

Bear, D. R., Templeton, S., Helman, L. A., & Baren, T. (2003). Orthographic development and learning to read in different languages. In G. Garcia (Ed.), *English learners: Reaching the highest level of English literacy.* Newark, DE: International Reading Association.

Beck, I. L., & McKeown, M. G. (2006). *Improving comprehension with Questioning the Author: A fresh and expanded view of a powerful approach*. New York: Scholastic.

Beck, I. L., & McKeown, M. G. (2002). Questioning the author: Making sense of social studies. *Educational Leadership, 60*(3), 44–47.

Beck, I., McKeown, M., & Kucan, I. (2002). *Bringing words to life: Robust vocabulary.* New York: Guilford Press.

Beck, I. L., Perfetti, C., & McKeown, M. G. (1982). Effects of long-term vocabulary instruction on lexical access and reading comprehension. *Journal of Educational Psychology, 74*, 506–521.

Berliner, D. C. (1984). The half-full glass: A review of research on teaching. In P. L. Hosford (Ed.), *Using what we know about teaching* (pp. 51–77). Alexandria, VA: Association for Supervision and Curriculum Development.

Berman, P., McLaughlin, B., Minicucci, C., Nelson, B., & Woodworth, K. (1995). *School reform and student diversity: Case studies of exemplary practices for LEP students.* Washington, DC: National Clearinghouse for Bilingual Education.

Biancarosa, G., & Snow, C. (2004). *Reading next: A vision for action and research in middle and high school literacy.* Report to the Carnegie Corporation of New York. Washington, DC: Alliance for Excellent Education.

Bickel, W. E., & Bickel, D. D. (1986). Effective schools, classrooms and instruction: Implications for special education. *Exceptional Children, 52*(6), 489–500.

Biemiller, A. (2004). Teaching vocabulary in the primary grades. In J. F. Baumann & J. E. Kame'enui (Eds.), *Vocabulary instruction: Research to practice*. New York: Guilford Press.

Biemiller, A. (2005). Vocabulary development and instruction: A prerequisite for school learning. In D. Dickinson & S. Neuman (Eds.), *Handbook of early literacy research,* Vol. 2. New York: Guilford Press.

Blachowicz, L. Z., & Fisher, P. (2000). Vocabulary instruction. In R. L. Kamil, P. B. Mosenthal, P. D. Pearson, & R. Barr (Eds.) *Handbook of Reading Research,* Vol. 3. (pp. 503–523). Mahwah, NJ: Lawrence Erlbaum Inc.

Bloom, B., Engelhart, M., Furst, E., Hill, W., & Krathworl, D. (Eds.). (1956). *Taxonomy of educational objectives: The classification of educational goals. Handbook I: Cognitive domain*. New York: David McKay Co.

Borko, H. (2004). Professional development and teacher learning: Mapping the terrain. *Educational Researcher, 33*(8), 3–15.

Bottle biology: An idea book for exploring the world through plastic bottles and other recyclable materials. (1993). Dubuque, IA: Kendall/Hunt Publishing Company.

Bransford, J. (1994). Schema activation and schema acquisition: Comments on Richard C. Anderson's remarks. In R. Ruddell, M. Ruddell, & H. Singer (Eds.), *Theoretical models and processes of reading* (4th ed.). Newark, DE: International Reading Association.

Brown, J. E., & Doolittle, J. (2008). *A cultural, linguistic, and ecological framework for response to intervention with English language learners.* The National Center for Culturally Responsive Educational Systems (NCCREST). Retrieved December 10, 2008 from http://www.nccrest.org/

Brown, R. (2008). The road not yet taken: A transactional strategies approach to comprehension instruction. *The Reading Teacher, 6*(7), 538–547.

Buck, B., Carr, S., & Robertson, J. (2008). Positive psychology and student engagement. *Journal of Cross-Disciplinary Perspectives in Education, 1*(1), 28–35.

Buehl, D. (2009). *Classroom strategies for interactive learning* (3rd ed.). Newark, DE: International Reading Association.

Burke, J. (2002). The Internet reader. *Educational Leadership, 60*(3), 38–42.

California Department of Education, Educational Demographics Unit. (2004). Statewide Stanford 9 test results for reading: Number of students tested and percent scoring at or above the 50th percentile ranking (NPR). Retrieved February 23, 2004, from www.cde.ca.gov/dataquest.

Callahan, R. (2005). Tracking and high school English learners: Limiting opportunity to learn. *American Educational Research Journal, 42*(2), 305–328.

Cañado, M. L. P. (2005). English and Spanish spelling: Are they really different? *The Reading Teacher, 58*(6), 522–530.

Cantoni-Harvey, G. (1987). *Content-area language instruction: Approaches and strategies.* Reading, MA: Addison-Wesley.

Carrell, P. (1987). Content and formal schemata in ESL reading. *TESOL Quarterly, 21*(3), 461–481.

Cazden, C. (2001). *Classroom discourse: The language of teaching and learning* (2nd ed.). Portsmouth, NH: Heinemann.

Center for Applied Linguistics. (2007). *Academic literacy through sheltered instruction for secondary English language learners.* Final Report to the Carnegie Corporation of New York. Washington, DC: Author.

Chamot, A. U., & O'Malley, J. M. (1987). The cognitive academic language learning approach: A bridge to the mainstream. *TESOL Quarterly, 21*(2), 227–249.

Chamot, A. U., & O'Malley, J. M. (1994). *The CALLA handbook: Implementing the cognitive academic language learning approach.* Reading, MA: Addison-Wesley.

Chiesi, H., Spilich, G., & Voss, J. (1979). Acquisition of domain-related information in relation to high- and low-domain knowledge. *Journal of Verbal Learning and Verbal Behavior, 18*, 257–274.

Christen, W. L., & Murphy, T. J. (1991). *Increasing comprehension by activating prior knowledge*. ERIC Digest. Bloomington, IN: ERIC Clearinghouse on Reading, English, and Communication. [ED 328 885]

Colburn, A., & Echevarria, J. (1999). Meaningful lessons. *The Science Teacher, 66*(2), 36–39.

Collier, V. P. (1987). Age and rate of acquisition of language for academic purposes. *TESOL Quarterly, 21*(4), 677.

Coltrane, B. (2002). *English language learners and high-stakes tests: An overview of the issues*. ERIC Digest. Washington, DC: ERIC Clearinghouse on Languages and Linguistics, Center for Applied Linguistics.

Comer, J. P. (1984). Home-school relationships as they affect the academic success of children. *Education and Urban Society, 16*(3), 323–337.

Cooper, J. D., Pikulski, J. J., Au, K., Calderon, M., Comas, J., Lipson, M., Mims, S., Page, S., Valencia, S., & Vogt, M.E. (2003). *Invitations to literacy*. Boston: Houghton Mifflin Company.

Coxhead, A. (2000). A new academic word list. *TESOL Quarterly, 34*(2), 213–238.

Crandall, J. A. (1993). Content-centered learning in the United States. *Annual Review of Applied Linguistics, 13*, 111–126.

Crawford, A. N. (2003). Communicative approaches to second language acquisition: The bridge to second-language literacy. In G. G. Garcia (Ed.), *English learners: Reaching the highest level of English literacy.* Newark, DE: International Reading Association.

Crossley, S., McCarthy, P., Louwerse, M., & McNamara, D. (2007). A linguistic analysis of simplified and authentic texts. *The Modern Language Journal, 19*(2), 15–30.

Cummins, J. (1984). *Bilingualism and special education: Issues in assessment and pedagogy.* Clevedon, England: Multilingual Matters.

Cummins, J. (2000). *Language, power and pedagogy*. Clevedon, England: Multilingual Matters.

Cunningham, P. M. (2004). *Phonics they use: Words for reading and writing* (4th ed.). New York: Harper-Collins College Press.

Dale, E. (1965). Vocabulary measurement: Techniques and major findings. *Elementary English, 42,* 82–88.

Dale, E., & O'Rourke, J. (1981). *Living word vocabulary*. Chicago: World Book/Childcraft International.

Darling-Hammond, L. (1998). Teacher learning that supports student learning. *Educational Leadership, 55*(5), 6–11.

Davis, S. J., & Winek, J. (1989). Improving expository writing by increasing background knowledge. *Journal of Reading 33*(3), 178–181.

Day, R. (Ed.). (1986). *Talking to learn: Conversation in second language acquisition.* Cambridge, MA: Newbury House Publishers.

DeLeeuw, H. (2008). *English language learners in Washington State.* Executive Summary. Report to the Washington State Board of Education, Olympia, Washington, January 10, 2008.

Delpit, L. (1995). *Other people's children: Cultural conflict in the classroom.* New York: New Press.

Dermody, M., & Speaker, R. (1995). Effects of reciprocal strategy training in prediction, clarification, question generation, and summarization on fourth graders' reading comprehension. In K. A. Hinchman, D. Leu, & C. K. Kinzer (Eds.), *Perspectives on literacy research and practice*. Chicago: National Reading Conference.

Deschenes, C., Ebeling, D., & Sprague, J. (1994). *Adapting curriculum and instruction in inclusive classrooms: A teacher's desk reference*. Bloomington, Indiana: Institute for the Study of Developmental Disabilities, Indiana University.

Deshler, D., & Schumaker, J. (2006). *Teaching adolescents with disabilities: Accessing the general education curriculum*. Thousand Oaks, CA: Corwin Press.

Diamond, L., & Gutlohn, L. (2006). *Vocabulary handbook.* Berkeley, CA: Core Literacy Library.

Dole, J., Duffy, G., Roehler, L., & Pearson, P. D. (1991). Moving from the old to the new: Research in reading comprehension instruction. *Review of Educational Research, 61*, 239–264.

Duff, P. A. (2005). ESL in secondary schools: Programs, problematics, and possibilities. *Annual Review of Applied Linguistics*, 45–63.

Duffy, G. G. (2002). The case for direct explanation of strategies. In C. C. Block & M. Pressley (Eds.), *Comprehension instruction: Research-based best practices.* New York: Guilford Press.

Dunn, L. (1968). Special education for the mildly retarded: Is much of it justifiable? *Exceptional Children*, *34*, 5–22.

Echevarria, J. (1995a). Sheltered instruction for students with learning disabilities who have limited English proficiency. *Intervention in School and Clinic, 30*(5), 302–305.

Echevarria, J. (1995b). Interactive reading instruction: A comparison of proximal and distal effects of instructional conversations. *Exceptional Children, 61*(6), 536–552.

Echevarria, J. (1995c). Interactive reading instruction: A comparison of proximal and distal effects of instructional conversations. *Exceptional Children, 61*(6), 536–552.

Echevarria, J. (1998). *A model of sheltered instruction for English language learners.* Paper presented at the conference for the Division on Diversity of the Council for Exceptional Children, Washington, DC.

Echevarria, J., & Graves, A. (2007). *Sheltered content instruction: Teaching English language learners with diverse abilities* (3rd ed.). Boston: Allyn & Bacon.

Echevarria, J., Greene, G., & Goldenberg, C. (1996). *A comparison of sheltered instruction and effective non-sheltered instruction on the achievement of LEP students.* Pilot study.

Echevarria, J., Powers, K., & Elliott, J. (2004). Promising practices for curbing disproportionate representation of minority students in special education. *Issues in Teacher Education: Themed Issues on Special Needs Education, 13*(1), 19–34.

Echevarria, J., & Short, D. (in press). Programs and practices for effective sheltered content instruction. In D. Dolson & L. Burnham-Massey (Eds.). *Improving education for English learners: Research-based approaches*. Sacramento, CA: California Department of Education.

Echevarria, J., Short, D., & Powers, K. (2006). School reform and standards-based education: An instructional model for English language learners. *Journal of Educational Research, 99*(4), 195–211.

Echevarria, J., Short, D., & Vogt, M.E. (2008). *Implementing the SIOP® Model through effective professional development and coaching*. Boston: Pearson/Allyn & Bacon.

Echevarria, J., & Vogt, M.E. (2008). *The SIOP® model, SIOP® I institute training manual.* Glenview, IL: Pearson.

Echevarria, J., Vogt, M.E., & Short, D. (in press). *The SIOP® Model for teaching mathematics to English learners.* Boston: Allyn & Bacon.

Echevarria, J., Vogt, M.E., & Short, D. (2008). *Making content comprehensible for English learners: The SIOP® model* (3rd ed.). Boston: Pearson/Allyn & Bacon.

Echevarria, J., Vogt, M.E., & Short, D. (2004). *Making content comprehensible for English learners: The SIOP® Model* (2nd ed.). Boston: Pearson/Allyn & Bacon.

Echevarria, J., Vogt, M.E., & Short, D. (2000). *Making content comprehensible for English language learners: The SIOP® Model*. Needham Heights, MA: Allyn & Bacon.

Edley, C., Jr., & Wald, J. (2002, December 16). The grade retention fallacy. *The Boston Globe.*

Edwards, P. A., Turner, J. D., & Mokhtari, K. (2008). Balancing the assessment *of* learning and *for* learning in support of student literacy achievement. *The Reading Teacher, 61*(8), 682–684.

Erickson, F., & Shultz, J. (1991). Students' experience of the curriculum. In P. W. Jackson (Ed.), *Handbook of research on curriculum*. New York: Macmillan.

Fathman, A., & Crowther, D. (Eds.). (2006). *Science for English language learners: K–12 classroom strategies*. Arlington, VA: NSTA Press.

Fillmore, L. W., & Snow, C. (2002). What teachers need to know about language. In C. T. Adger, C. E. Snow, & D. Christian (Eds.), *What teachers need to know about language* (pp. 7–53). McHenry, IL: Delta Systems and Center for Applied Linguistics.

Fillmore, L. W., & Valadez, C. (1986). Teaching bilingual learners. In M. C. Wittrock (Ed.), *Handbook of research on teaching* (pp. 648–685). New York: Macmillan.

Fisher, D., & Frey, N. (2008a). *Better learning through structured teaching*. Alexandria, VA: Association for Supervision and Curriculum Development.

Fisher, D., & Frey, N. (2008b). *Wordwise & content rich: Five essential steps to teaching academic vocabulary*. Portsmouth, NH: Heinemann.

Fisher, D., Frey, N., & Williams, D. (2002). Seven literacy strategies that work. *Educational Leadership, 60*(3), 70–73.

Flood, J., Lapp, D., Flood, S., & Nagel, G. (1992). Am I allowed to group? Using flexible patterns for effective instruction. *The Reading Teacher, 45*, 608–616.

Ford, D. (1998). The underrepresentation of minority students in gifted education: Problems and promises in recruitment and retention. *Journal of Special Education, 32*(1), 4–14.

Fordham, D. (2006). Crafting questions that address comprehension strategies in content reading. *Journal of Adolescent & Adult Literacy, 49*(5), 391–396.

Francis, D., Rivera, M., Lesaux, N., Kieffer, M., & Rivera, H. (2006). *Research-based recommendation for serving adolescent newcomers*. Portsmouth, NH: RMC Research Corporation, Center on Instruction.

Fuchs, D., Fuchs, L. S., & Bahr, M. W. (1990). Mainstream assistance teams: A scientific basis for the art of consultation. *Exceptional Children, 57*, 128–139.

Futrell, M., & Gomez, J. (2008). How tracking creates a poverty of learning. *Educational Leadership, 65*(8), 74–78.

Gall, M. (November 1984). Synthesis of research on teachers' questioning. *Educational Leadership*, 40–47.

Gandara, P., Maxwell-Jolly, J., & Driscoll, A. (2005). *Listening to teachers of English language learners: A survey of California teachers' challenges, experiences, and professional development needs*. Santa Cruz, CA: The Center for the Future of Teaching and Learning.

Garcia, G. E., & Godina, H. (2004). Addressing the literacy needs of adolescent English language learners. In T. Jetton and J. Dole (Eds.), *Adolescent literacy: Research and practice* (pp. 304–320). New York: The Guilford Press.

Gardner, H. (1993). *Multiple intelligences: The theory in practice*. New York: Basic Books.

Genesee, F. (1994). *Educating second language children: The whole child, the whole curriculum, the whole community*. New York: Cambridge University Press.

Genesee, F. (Ed.). (1999). *Program alternatives for linguistically diverse students*. Educational Practice Report No. 1. Santa Cruz and Washington, DC: Center for Research on Education, Diversity & Excellence.

Genesee, F., Lindholm-Leary, K., Saunders, W., & Christian, D. (2006). *Educating English language learners: A synthesis of research evidence*. New York: Cambridge University Press.

Gersten, R., Baker, S., Shanahan, T., Linan-Thompson, S., Collins, P., & Scarcella, R. (2007). *Effective literacy and English language instruction for English learners in the elementary grades: A practice guide* (NCEE 2007–4011). Washington, DC: National Center for Education Evaluation and Regional Assistance, Institute of Education Sciences, U.S. Department of Education. Retrieved from http://ies.ed.gov/ncee.

Geva, E. (2006). Second-language oral proficiency and second-language literacy. In D. August & T. Shanahan (Eds.). *Developing literacy in second-language learners: Report of the National Literacy Panel on Language Minority Children and Youth*. Mahwah, NJ: Lawrence Erlbaum Associates.

Gibbons, P. (2002). *Scaffolding language, scaffolding learning*. Portsmouth, NH: Heinemann.

Gibbons, P. (2003). Mediating language learning: Teacher interactions with ESL students in a content-based classroom. *TESOL Quarterly, 37*(2), 247–273.

Gibson, V., & Hasbrouck, J. (2008). *Differentiated instruction: Grouping for success*. New York: McGraw-Hill.

Glick, J. E., & White, M. J. (2004). Post-secondary school participation of immigrant and native youth: The role of familial resources and educational expectations. *Social Science Research, 33*, 272–299.

Goldenberg, C. (1992–93). Instructional conversations: Promoting comprehension through discussion. *The Reading Teacher, 46*, 316–326.

Goldenberg, C. (2008). Teaching English language learners: What the research does and does not say. *American Educator, 32*(2), 8–23, 42–44. Retrieved from http://www.aft.org/pubs-reports/american_educator/index.htm

Goldenberg, C. (Summer 2008). Teaching English language learners: What research does—and does not—say. *American Educator, 32*(2), 8–23, 42–44.

González, J. M., & Darling-Hammond, L. (1997). *New concepts for new challenges: Professional development for teachers of immigrant youth*. McHenry, IL: Delta Systems and CAL.

Goodlad, J. (1984). *A place called school: Prospects for the future*. New York: McGraw-Hill.

Graff, G. (2003). *Clueless in academe*. New Haven: Yale University Press.

Graves, A., Gersten, R. & Haager, D. (2004). Literacy instruction in multiple-language first-grade classrooms: Linking student outcomes to observed instructional practice. *Learning Disabilities Research & Practice, 19*(4), 262–272.

Graves, M. F., & Fitzgerald, J. (2006). Effective vocabulary instruction for English-language learners. In C. C. Block, & J. N. Mangieri (Eds.), *The vocabulary-enriched classroom: Practice for improving the reading performance of all students in grades 3 and up.* New York: Scholastic.

Gray, W. S., & Leary, B. E. (1935). *What makes a book readable?* Chicago: The University of Chicago Press.

Guarino, A. J., Echevarria, J., Short, D., Schick, J. E., Forbes, S., & Rueda, R. (2001). The Sheltered Instruction Observation Protocol. *Journal of Research in Education, 11*(1), 138–140.

Gunderson, L. (1991). *ESL literacy instruction: A guidebook to theory and practice.* Englewood Cliffs, NJ: Regents/Prentice Hall.

Gunderson, L., & Siegel, L. S. (2005). The evils of the use of IQ tests to define learning disabilities in first- and second-language learners. In S. B. Barrentine & S. M. Stokes (Eds.), *Reading assessment: Principles and practices for elementary teachers* (2nd ed.). Newark, DE: International Reading Association.

Guthrie, J. T., & Ozgungor, S. (2002). Instructional content for reading engagement. In C. C. Block & M. Pressley (Eds.). *Comprehension instruction: Research-based best practices* (pp. 275–288). New York: Guilford Press.

Gutiérrez, K. D. (2004). Literacy as laminated activity: Rethinking literacy for English learners. In C. M. Fairbanks, J. Worthy, B. Maloch, J. V. Hoffman, & D. L. Schallert (Eds.), *53rd Yearbook of the National Reading Conference*. Oak Creek, WI: National Reading Conference.

Haager, D., Dimino, J. A., & Windmueller, M. P. (2007). *Interventions for reading success.* Baltimore, MD: Brookes Publishing.

Hakuta, K., Butler, Y., & Witt, D. (2000). *How long does it take English learners to attain proficiency?* Policy Report 2000–1. Santa Barbara: University of California, Linguistic Minority Research Institute.

Harris, T. L., & Hodges, R. E. (Eds.). (1995). *The literacy dictionary: The vocabulary of reading and writing.* Newark, DE: International Reading Association.

Harry, B. (1992). Restructuring the participation of African-American parents in special education. *Exceptional Children, 59*(2), 123–131.

Hart, B., & Risley, T. R. (2003). The early catastrophe: The 30 million word gap. *American Educator, 27*, 4–9.

Hawkin, L. (2005). Behavior programs for older students: What's helpful in secondary schools? *The Special Edge, 19*(1), 1–5.

Hayes, D. A., & Tierney, R. J. (1982). Developing readers' knowledge through analogy. *Reading Research Quarterly 17*(2), 256–280.

Helman, M., & Buchanan, K. (1993). *Reforming mathematics instruction for ESL literacy students.* NCBE Program Information Guide Series, Number 15, Fall 1993. (www.ncela.gwu.edu/ncbepubs/pigs/pig15.htm)

Henry, M. K. (1990). *TUTOR 3.* Los Gatos, CA: Lex Press.

Hiebert, E. H. (1983). An examination of ability grouping for reading instruction. *Reading Research Quarterly, 18*, 231–255.

Hinkel, E. (2006). Current perspectives on teaching the four skills. *TESOL Quarterly, 40*(1), 109–131.

Honea, J. M. (1982, December). Wait-time as an instructional variable: An influence on teacher and student. *Clearing house, 56*(4), 167–170.

Hudec, J., & Short, D. (Prods.). (2002a). *Helping English learners succeed: An overview of the SIOP Model.* (Video). Washington, DC: Center for Applied Linguistics.

Hudec, J., & Short, D. (Prods.) (2002b). *The SIOP Model: Sheltered instruction for academic achievement.* (Video). Washington, DC: Center for Applied Linguistics.

Hunter, M. (1982). *Mastery teaching: Increasing instructional effectiveness in secondary schools, college, and universities.* El Segundo, CA: TIP Publications.

Ima, K., & Rumbaut, R. G. (1989). Southeast Asian refugees in American schools: A comparison of fluent-English-proficient and limited-English-proficient students. *Topics in Language Disorders, 9*(3), 54–77.

IRA & NICHD. (2007). *Key issues and questions in English language learners literacy research.* Washington, DC: International Reading Association and National Institute of Child Health and Human Development. Retrieved from http://www.reading.org/downloads/resources/ELL_paper_071022.pdf

Jamieson, A., Curry, A., & Martinez, G. (2001). *School enrollment in the United States—Social and economic characteristics of students.* Current Population Reports, P20–533. Washington, DC: U.S. Government Printing Office.

Jensen, E. (2005). *Teaching with the brain in mind* (2nd ed.). Alexandria, VA: Association for Supervision and Curriculum Development.

Jiménez, R. T. (2004). More equitable literacy assessments for Latino students. *The Reading Teacher, 57*(6), 576–578.

Jiménez, R. T., Garcia, G. E., & Pearson, P. D. (1996). The reading strategies of bilingual Latina/o students who are successful English readers: Opportunities and obstacles. *Reading Research Quarterly, 31*(1), 90–112.

Johnson, E., & Smith, L. (2008). Implementation of response to intervention at middle school: Challenges and potential benefits. *Teaching Exceptional Children, 40*(3), 46–52.

Kamil, M. (2003). *Adolescents and literacy: Reading for the 21st century.* Washington, DC: Alliance for Excellent Education.

Kauffman, D., & Apple, G. (2000). *Oxford picture dictionary for the content areas.* Oxford, England: Oxford University Press.

Kea, C., & Utley, C. (1998). To teach me is to know me. *Journal of Special Education 32*(1), 44–48.

Keene, E. O., & Zimmerman, S. (1997). *Mosaic of thought: Teaching comprehension in a reader's workshop.* Portsmouth, NH: Heinemann.

Kindler, A. (2002). *Survey of the states' limited English proficient students and available educational programs and services. 2000–01 summary report.* Washington, DC: National Clearinghouse for English Language Acquisition.

Klinger, J., & Harry, B. (2006). The special education referral and decision-making process for English language learners: Child study team meetings and staffings. *Teachers College Record, 108*, 2247–2281.

Kober, N., Zabala, D., Chudowsky, N., Chudowsky, V., Gayler, K., & McMurrer, J. (2006). *State high school exit exams: A challenging year*. Washington, DC: Center on Education Policy.

Krashen, S. (1985). *The input hypothesis: Issues and implications.* New York: Longman.

Krashen, S. (2003). Three roles for reading for minority-language children. In G. Garcia (Ed.), *English learners: Reaching the highest level of literacy learning.* Newark, DE: International Reading Association.

Krashen, S., & Terrell, T. (1983). *The natural approach: Language acquisition in the classroom.* Englewood Cliffs, NJ: Alemany/Prentice Hall.

Kukic, S. J. (2002). *The complete school for all.* Keynote presentation at the 2nd Annual Pacific Northwest Behavior Symposium, Seattle, WA.

Leafstedt, J., Richards, C., Gerber, M. (2004). Effectiveness of explicit phonological-awareness instruction for at-risk English learners. *Learning Disabilities Research & Practice, 19*(4), 252–261.

Lee, J. (2006). *Teaching achievement gaps and assessing the impact of NCLB on the gaps: An in-depth look into national and state reading and math outcome trends.* Cambridge, MA: The Civil Rights Project at Harvard University.

Lee, J., Grigg, W., & Dion, P. (2007). *The nation's report card: Mathematics 2007* (NCES 2007–494). U.S. Department of Education, Institute of Education Sciences, National Center for Education Statistics. Washington, DC: U.S. Government Printing Office.

Lee, J., Grigg, W., & Donahue, P. (2007). *The nation's report card: Reading 2007* (NCES 2007–496). U.S. Department of Education, Institute of Education Sciences, National Center for Education Statistics. Washington, DC: U.S. Government Printing Office.

Lesaux, N., & Geva, E. (2006). Synthesis: Development of literacy in language-minority students. In D. August & T. Shanahan (Eds.), *Developing literacy in second-language learners.* Mahwah, NJ: Lawrence Erlbaum.

Leinhardt, G., Bickel, W., & Pallay, A. (1982). Unlabeled but still entitled: Toward more effective remediation. *Teachers College Record, 84*(2), 391–422.

Lemke, J. (1988). Genres, semantics, and classrom education. *Linguistics and Education 1,* 81–99.

Lenski, S. D., Ehlers-Zavala, F., Daniel, M. C., & Sun-Irminger, X. (2006). Assessing English-language learners in mainstream classrooms. *The Reading Teacher, 60*(1), 24–34.

Lenters, K. (2005). No half measures: Reading instruction for young second-language learners. *The Reading Teacher, 58*(4), 328–336.

Leu, D. (2005). *Literacy research for lives with literacy*. Presidential address given at the National Reading Conference 55th Annual Meeting, Miami, FL.

Limbos, M., & Geva, E. (2002). Accuracy of teacher assessments of second-language students at risk for reading disability. *Journal of Learning Disabilities, 34,* 137–151.

Linan-Thompson, S., Cirino, P. T., & Vaughn, S. (2007). Determining English language learners' response to intervention: Questions and some answers. *Learning Disabilities Quarterly, 30,* 185–195.

Lindholm-Leary, K., & Borsato, G. (2006). Academic achievement. In F. Genesee, K. Lindholm-Leary, W. Saunders, & D. Christian (Eds.), *Educating English language learners: A synthesis of research evidence* (pp. 176–221). New York: Cambridge University Press.

Lipson, M., & Wixson, K. (2008). *Assessment and instruction of reading and writing difficulties: An interactive approach* (3rd ed.). New York: Longman.

Losen, D., & Orfield, G. (2002). *Racial inequity in special education.* Cambridge, MA: Harvard Education Publishing Company.

Lucas, S. R. *Tracking inequality: Stratification and mobility in American high schools.* New York: Teachers College Press.

MacMillan, D., & Reschly, D. (1998). Overrepresentation of minority students: The case for greater specificity or reconsideration of the variables examined. *Journal of Special Education, 32*(1), 15–24.

Macon, J., Buell, D., & Vogt, M.E. (1991). *Responses to literature: Grades K–8.* Newark, DE: International Reading Association.

Manzo, A. J., Manzo, U. C., & Thomas, M. T. (2005). *Content area literacy: Strategic thinking for strategic learning* (4th ed.). New York: John Wiley & Sons.

Marshall, J. (2000). Research on response to literature. In R. L. Kamil, P. B. Mosenthal, P. D. Son, & R. Barr (Eds.). *Handbook of Reading Research,* Vol. 3 (pp. 381–402). Mahwah, NJ: Lawrence Erlbaum.

Marzano, R., Pickering, D. & Pollock, J. (2001) *Classroom instruction that works.* Alexandria, VA: Association for Supervision and Curriculum Development.

Mastropieri, M. A., & Scruggs, T. E. (1994). *Effective instruction for special education.* Austin, TX: PROED.

McCormick, C. B., & Pressley, M. (1997). *Educational psychology: Learning, instruction, assessment.* New York: Longman.

McIntyre, E., Kyle, D., & Moore, G. (2006). A primary teacher's guidance toward small group dialogue. *Reading Research Quarterly, 41*(1), 36–66.

McLaughlin, M. (2003). *Guided comprehension in the primary grades.* Newark, DE: International Reading Association.

McLaughlin, M., & Allen, M. B. (2002). *Guided comprehension: A teaching model for grades 3–8.* Newark, DE: International Reading Association.

McLaughlin, M., & Kennedy, A. (1993). *A classroom guide to performance-based assessment.* Princeton, NJ: Houghton Mifflin.

McLaughlin, M., & Vogt, M.E. (1996). *Portfolios in teacher education.* Newark, DE: International Reading Association.

McLaughlin, M., & Vogt, M.E. (2000). *Creativity and innovation in content area teaching: A resource for intermediate, middle, and high school teachers.* Norwood, MA: Christopher-Gordon Publishers.

McNeil, L. M., Coppola, E., Radigan, J., & Vasquez Heilig, J. (2008). Avoidable losses: High-stakes accountability and the dropout crisis. *Education Policy Analysis Archives, 16*(3). Retrieved February 24, 2008 from http://epaa.asu.edu/epaa/v16n3/.

Menken, K. (2008). *English learners left behind: Standardized testing as language policy.* Clevedon, England: Multilingual Matters.

Miholic, V. (1990). Constructing a semantic map for textbooks. *Journal of Reading 33*(6), 464–465.

Mohan, B. A. (1986). *Language and content.* Reading, MA: Addison-Wesley.

Mohan, B., Leung, C., & Davison, C. (Eds.). (2001). *English as a second language in the mainstream.* Harlow, England: Pearson.

Mokhtari, K., Rosemary, C. A., & Edwards, P. A. (2008). Making instructional decisions based on data: What, how, and why. *The Reading Teacher, 61*(4), 354–359.

Muth, K. D., & Alvermann, D. E. (1999). *Teaching and learning in the middle grades* (2nd ed.). Needham Heights, MA: Allyn & Bacon.

Nagel, G. (2001). *Effective grouping for literacy instruction.* Boston: Allyn & Bacon.

National Association of Secondary School Principals. (2005). *Creating a culture of literacy: A guide for middle and high school principals.* Reston, VA: NASSP.

National Center for Education Statistics (NCES). (1997). *A profile of policies and practices for limited English proficient students: Screening methods, program support, and teacher training* (The 1993–94 Schools and Staffing Survey). Washington, DC: U.S. Department of Education, OERI.

National Center for Education Statistics. (2002). *Schools and staffing survey, 1999–2000: Overview of the data for public, private, public charter, and Bureau of Indian Affairs elementary and secondary schools.* (NCES 2002–313). Washington, DC: U.S. Department of Education, National Center for Educational Statistics.

National Center for Educational Statistics (NCES). (2004). *Language minorities and their educational and labor market indicators—Recent trends,* NCES 2004–09.Washington, DC: U.S. Department of Education.

National Clearinghouse for English Language Acquisition (NCELA). (2008). *NCELA frequently asked questions.* Retrieved October 3, 2008 from www.ncela.gwu.edu/expert/ faq/08leps. html

National Commission on Teaching and America's Future (NCTAF). (1997). *Doing what matters most: Investing in quality teaching.* New York: Columbia University, Teachers College.

National Governors Association. (2005). *A governor's guide to adolescent literacy.* Washington, DC: NGA, Center for Best Practices.

National Institute of Child Health and Human Development (NICHD). (2000). *Report of the National Reading Panel. Teaching children to read: An evidence-based assessment of the scientific research literature on reading and its implications for reading instruction.* (NIH Publication No. 11–4769). Washington, DC: U.S. Department of Health and Human Services.

Neal, L., McCray, A., Webb-Johnson, G., & Bridgest, S. (2003). The effects of African American movement styles on teachers' perceptions and reactions. *Journal of Special Education 37*(1), 49–57.

Neufeld, P. (2005). Comprehension instruction in content classes. *The Reading Teacher, 59*(4), 302–312.

New York City Department of Education. (2004). *The class of 2000 final longitudinal report: A three year follow-up study.* New York: New York City Department of Education, Division of Assessment and Accountability.

No Child Left Behind Act of 2001. 107th Congress of the United States of America. Retrieved December 1, 2002, from www.ed.gov/legislation/ESEA02/107-110.pdf.

Oakes, J. (1985). *Keeping track: How schools structure inequality.* New Haven, CT: Yale University Press.

Office of Special Education Programs (2002). *Twenty-sixth annual Report to Congress on the implementation of the Individuals with Disabilities Education Act.* Washington DC: U.S. Department of Education.

Ogle, D. (1986). K-W-L: A teaching model that develops active reading of expository text. *The Reading Teacher, 39,* 564–570.

O'Malley, J. J., & Chamot, A. U. (1990). *Learning strategies in second language acquisition.* Cambridge: Cambridge University Press.

O'Malley, J. M., & Pierce, L. V. (1996). *Authentic assessment for English language learners: Practical approaches for teachers.* Reading, MA: Addison-Wesley.

Orfield, G., Losen, D., & Edley, Jr., C. (2001). *The Civil Rights Project.* Cambridge, MA: Harvard University.

Ortiz, A. (2002). Prevention of school failure and early intervention. In A. Artiles & A. Ortiz (Eds.). *English language learners with special education needs* (pp. 31–50). Washington DC: Center for Applied Linguistics.

Palinscar, A. C., & Brown, A. L. (1984). Reciprocal teaching of comprehension-fostering and comprehension monitoring activities. *Cognition and Instruction, 1,* 117–175.

Paris, S. (2001). Classroom applications of research on self-regulated learning. *Educational Psychologist, 36*(3), 89–102.

Paris, S. G., Lipson., M. Y., & Wixson, K. (1983). Becoming a strategic reader. *Contemporary Educational Psychology, 8,* 293–316.

Parish, T., Merikel, A., Perez, M., Linquanti, R., Socias, M., Spain, M., et al. (2006). *Effects of the implementation of Proposition 227 on the education of English learners, K–12: Findings from a five-year evaluation.* Palo Alto, CA: American Institutes for Research.

Patton, J., & Townsend, B. (1999). Ethics, power and privilege: Neglected considerations in the education of African American learners with special needs. *Teacher Education and Special Education. 22*(4), 276–286.

Peregoy, S. F., & Boyle, O. F. (2005). *Reading, writing, and learning in ESL: A resource book for K–12 teachers* (4th ed.). New York: Longman.

Perie, M., Grigg, W. S., & Donahue, P. L. (2005). *The Nation's Report Card: Reading 2005* (NCES 2006–451). U.S. Department of Education, Institute of Education Sciences, National Center for Education Statistics. Washington DC: U.S. Government Printing Office.

Podell, D. M. & Soodak, L. C. (1993). Teacher efficacy and bias in special education referrals. *Journal of Educational Researcher, 86*(4), 247–253.

Poldrack, R., Clark, J., Pare-Blagoev, E., Shohamy, D., Creso Moyano, J., Myers, C., & Gluck, M. (2001). Interactive memory systems in the human brain. *Nature, 414,* 546–550.

Powers, K., (2001). Problem solving student support teams. *The California School Psychologist, 6,* 19–30.

Pressley, M. (2000). What should comprehension instruction be instruction of? In M. L. Kamil, P. B. Mosenthal, P. D. Pearson, & R. Barr (Eds.), *Handbook of reading research* (Vol. III, pp. 545–562). Mahwah, NJ: Lawrence Erlbaum Associates.

Pressley, M. (2002). Comprehension strategies instruction: A turn-of-the-century status report. In C. C. Block & M. Pressley (Eds.), *Comprehension instruction: Research-based best practices* (pp. 11–27). New York: Guilford.

Pressley, M. (2005). *Literacy-instructional effective classrooms and schools . . . And why I am so worried about comprehension instruction even in places like these!* Keynote address presented to the Research Institute of the 51st International Reading Association Annual Convention, Chicago, IL.

Pressley, M., Johnson, C., Symons, S., McGoldrick, J. A., & Kurita, J. A. (1989). Strategies that improve children's memory and comprehension of text. *The Elementary School Journal, 90,* 3–32.

Pressley, M., & Woloshyn, V. (Eds.) (1995). *Cognitive strategy instruction that really improves children's academic performance.* Cambridge, MA: Brookline Books.

Ramirez, J., Yuen, S., Ramey, D., & Pasta, D. (1991). *Executive summary: Final report: Longitudinal study of structure English immersion strategy, early-exit and late-exit transitional bilingual education programs for language-minority children.* (Contract No. 300087–0156). Submitted to the U.S. Department of Education. San Mateo: Aguirre International.

Raphael, T. E. (1984). Teaching learners about sources of information for answering comprehension questions. *Journal of Reading 27,* 303–311.

Raphael, T. E., Highfield, K., & Au, K. H. (2006). *QAR now: A powerful and practical framework that develops comprehension and higher-level thinking skills.* New York: Scholastic.

Rasinski, T., & Padak, N. (2004). *Effective reading strategies: Teaching children who find reading difficult.* Upper Saddle River, NJ: Pearson Merrill Prentice Hall.

Readence, J. E., Bean, T. W., & Baldwin, R. S. (2001). *Content area literacy: An integrated approach* (8th ed.). Dubuque, IA: Kendall/Hunt.

Readance, J., Bean, T., & Baldwin, R. S. (2001). *Teaching reading in the content areas* (8th ed.). Dubuque, IA: Kendall Hunt.

Reiss, J. (2008). *102 Content strategies for English learners: Teaching for academic success in grades 3–12.* Upper Saddle River, NJ: Pearson/Merrill Prentice Hall.

Reutzel, D. R., & Morgan, B. C. (1990). Effects of prior knowledge, explicitness, and clause order on children's comprehension of causal relationships. *Reading Psychology 11*(2), 93–109.

Rinaldi, C., & Samson, J. (2008). English language learners and response to intervention: Referral considerations. *Teaching Exceptional Children, 40*(5), 6–14.

Rosenblatt, L. M. (1991). Literacy theory. In J. Flood, J. Jensen, D. Flood, & J. Squire (Eds.), *Handbook of research on teaching the English-language arts.* New York: Macmillan.

Ruddell, M. R. (2007). *Teaching content reading and writing* (5th ed.). Hoboken, NJ: John Wiley & Sons, Inc.

Ruddell, M. R., & Shearer, B. A. (2002). "Extraordinary," "tremendous," "exhilarating," "magnificent": Middle school at-risk students become avid word learners with the Vocabulary Self-Collection Strategy (VSS). *Journal of Adolescent and Adult Literacy, 45*(4), 352–363.

Ruiz-de-Velasco, J., & Fix, M. (2000). *Overlooked and underserved: Immigrant students in U.S. secondary schools.* Washington, DC: Urban Institute.

Rumelhart, D. E. (1980). Schemata: The building blocks of cognition. In Rand J. Spiro et al. (Eds.), *Theoretical Issues in Reading Comprehension* (pp. 33–58). Hillsdale, NJ: Erlbaum.

Rumelhart, D. E. (1994). Toward an interactive model of reading. In R. B. Ruddell, M. R. Ruddell, & H. Singer (Eds.), *Theoretical models and processes of reading* (4th ed.). Newark, DE: International Reading Association.

Saunders, W., & Goldenberg, C. (2007). The effects of an instructional conversation on English Language Learners' concepts of friendship and story comprehension. In R. Horowitz (Ed.), *Talking texts: How speech and writing interact in school learning* (pp. 221–252). Mahwah, NJ: Erlbaum.

Saunders, W., Goldenberg, C., & Hamann, J. (1992). Instructional conversations beget instructional conversations. *Teaching and Teacher Education, 8*(2), 199–218.

Saunders, W., & O'Brien, G. (2006). Oral language. In F. Genesee, K. Lindholm-Leary, W. Saunders, & D. Christian, (Eds.), *Educating English language learners: A synthesis of research evidence* (pp. 14–63). New York: Cambridge University Press.

Saville-Troike, M. (1984). What really matters in second language learning for academic achievement? *TESOL Quarterly, 18,* 117–131.

Schleppegrell, M. (2004). *The language of schooling: A functional linguistic perspective.* Mahwah, NJ: Lawrence Erlbaum Associates.

Schleppegrell, M., Achugar, M., & Orteíza, T. (2004). The grammar of history: Enhancing content-based instruction through a functional focus on language. *TESOL Quarterly, 38*(1), 67–93.

Schmoker, M. (2001) *The results fieldbook: Practical strategies from dramatically improved schools.* Alexandria, VA: Association for Supervision and Curriculum Development.

Schmoker, M. (2006). *Results now.* Alexandria, VA: Association for Supervision and Curriculum Development.

Shearer, B. A., & Ruddell, M. R. (2006). Engaging students' interests and participation in learning. In D. Lapp, J. Flood, & N. Farnan (Eds.), *Content area reading and learning* (3rd ed.). Mahwah, NJ.: Erlbaum.

Shearer, B. A., Ruddell, M. R., & Vogt, M.E. (2001). Successful middle school intervention: Negotiated strategies and individual choice. In T. Shanahan & F. V. Rodriguez (Eds.), *National Reading Conference Yearbook, 50*. National Reading Conference.

Sheppard, K. (1995). *Content-ESL across the USA (Volume I, Technical Report)*. Washington, DC: National Clearinghouse for Bilingual Education.

Short, D. (1994). Expanding middle-school horizons: Integrating language, culture and social studies. *TESOL Quarterly, 28*(3), 581–608.

Short, D. (1999). Integrating language and content for effective sheltered instruction programs. In C. Faltis & P. Wolfe (Eds.), *So much to say: Adolescents, bilingualism, and ESL in the secondary school* (pp. 105–137). New York: Teachers College Press.

Short, D. J. (2002). Language learning in sheltered social studies classes. *TESOL Journal 11*(1), 18–24.

Short, D. (2006). Content teaching and learning and language. In K. Brown (Editor-in-Chief), *Encyclopedia of Language and Linguistics*, 2nd ed. (Vol. 3, pp. 101–105). Oxford: Elsevier.

Short, D., & Boyson, B. (2004). *Creating access: Language and academic programs for secondary school newcomers*. McHenry, IL: Delta Systems, Inc.

Short, D., & Echevarria, J. (2004). Teacher skills to support English language learners. *Educational Leadership, 62*(4), 9–13.

Short, D. J., & Echevarria, J. (1999). *The sheltered instruction observation protocol: Teacher-researcher collaboration and professional development*. Educational Practice Report No. 3. Santa Cruz, CA, and Washington, DC: Center for Research on Education, Diversity & Excellence.

Short, D., & Fitzsimmons, S. (2007). *Double the work: Challenges and solutions to acquiring language and academic literacy for adolescent English language learners*. Report to Carnegie Corporation of New York. Washington, DC: Alliance for Excellent Education.

Short, D., Hudec, J., & Echevarria, J. (2002). *Using the SIOP® Model: Professional development manual for sheltered instruction*. Washington, DC: Center for Applied Linguistics.

Short, D., Vogt, M.E., & Echevarria, J. (in press). *The SIOP® Model for teaching history/social studies to English learners*. Boston: Allyn & Bacon.

Short, D., Vogt, M.E., & Echevarria, J. (in press). *The SIOP® Model for teaching science to English learners*. Boston: Allyn & Bacon.

Short, D., Vogt, M.E., & Echevarria, J. (2008). *The SIOP® Model for administrators*. Boston: Pearson/Allyn & Bacon.

Siegel, H. (2002). Multiculturalism, universalism, and science education: In search of common ground. *Science Education, 86*, 803–820.

Sirotnik, K. (1983). What you see is what you get: Consistency, persistency, and mediocrity in classrooms. *Harvard Educational Review, 53*, 16–31.

Slater, W. H., & Horstman, F. R. (2002). Teaching reading and writing to struggling middle school and high school students: The case for reciprocal teaching. *Preventing School Failure (46)*4, 163–167.

Slavin, R. E., & Cheung, A. (2004). How do English language learners learn to read? *Educational Leadership, 61*(6), 52–57.

Smith, D. (2001). *Introduction to special education: Teaching in an age of opportunity* (4th ed.). Boston: Allyn & Bacon.

Snow, C. E., Cancino, H., De Temple, J., & Schley, S. (1991). Giving formal definitions: A linguistic or metalinguistic skill? In E. Bialystok (Ed.), *Language processing and language awareness by bilingual children* (pp. 90–112). New York: Cambridge University Press.

Snow, C. E., Burns, S., Griffin, P. (Eds.) (1998). *Preventing reading difficulties in young children*. Washington, DC: National Academy Press.

Snow, C. E., Griffin, P., & Burns, M. S. (Eds.). (2005). *Knowledge to support the teaching of reading: Preparing teachers for a changing world*. San Francisco: Jossey-Bass.

Solano-Flores, G., & Trumbull, E. (2003). Examining language in context: The need for new research and practice paradigms in the testing of English language learners. *Educational Researcher, 32*(2), 3–13.

Stahl, S., & Nagy, W. (2006). *Teaching word meanings*. Mahwah, NJ: Erlbaum.

Stanovich, K. E. (1986). Matthew effects in reading: Some consequences of individual differences in the acquisition of literacy. *Reading Research Quarterly, 21*, 360–406.

State of New Jersey Department of Education. (2006). *Preliminary analysis of former limited English proficient students' scores on the New Jersey language arts and literacy exam, 2005–2006*. Trenton, NJ: State of New Jersey Department of Education, New Jersey State Assessment Office of Title I.

Stauffer, R. (1969). *Teaching reading as a thinking process*. New York: Harper & Row.

Stauffer, R. (1980). *The language-experience approach to the teaching of reading* (2nd ed.). New York: Harper & Row.

Steinberg, A., & Almeida, C. (2004). *The dropout crisis: Promising approaches in prevention and recovery*. Boston: Jobs for the Future.

Stenner, A. J., & Burdick, X. (1997). *The objective measurement of reading comprehension*. Durham, NC: Metametrics.

Stoller, F. (2004). Content-based instruction: Perspectives on curriculum planning. *Annual Review of Applied Linguistics 24*, 261–283.

Sullivan, P., Yeager, M., O'Brien, E., Kober, N., Gayler, K., Chudowsky, N., Chudowsky, V., Wooden, J., Jennings, J., & Stark Rentner, D. (2005). *States try harder, but gaps persist: High school exit exams 2005*. Washington, DC: Center on Education Policy.

Swain, M. (1985). Communicative competence: Some roles of comprehensible input and output in its development. In S. Gass & C. Madden (Eds.), *Input in second language acquisition* (pp. 235–256). Rowley, MA: Newbury House.

Swift, J. N. & Gooding, C. T. (1983). Interaction of wait time feedback and questioning instruction on middle school science teaching. *Journal of Research in Science Teaching, 20*, 721–730.

Taboada, A., & Guthrie, J. T. (2006). Contributions of student questioning and prior knowledge to construction of knowledge from reading information text. *Journal of Literacy Research, 38*(1), 1–35.

Tabors, P. O., & Snow, C. E. (2005). Young bilingual children and early literacy development. In R. B. Ruddell & N. J. Unrau (Eds.), *Theoretical models and processes of reading*

(5th ed.), pp. 240–267. Newark, DE: International Reading Association.

Tatum, A. (2008). Toward a more anatomically complete model of literacy instruction: A focus on African American males and texts. *Harvard Educational Review, 78*(1), 155–180.

Teachers of English to Speakers of Other Languages, Inc. (TESOL) (2001). *Scenarios for ESL standards-based assessment.* Alexandria, VA: Author.

Teachers of English to Speakers of Other Languages, Inc. (2006). *PreK–12 English language proficiency standards.* Alexandria, VA: Author.

Tharp, R., & Gallimore, R. (1988). *Rousing minds to life: Teaching, learning and schooling in social context.* Cambridge: Cambridge University Press.

Thomas, W. P., & Collier, V. P. (2002). *A national study of school effectiveness for language minority students' long-term academic achievement.* Santa Cruz, CA, and Washington, DC: Center for Research on Education Diversity & Excellence.

Tierney, R., & Pearson, P. D. (1994). Learning to learn from text: A framework for improving classroom practice. In R. Ruddell, M. Ruddell, & H. Singer (Eds.), *Theoretical models and processes of reading* (4th ed.). Newark, DE: International Reading Association.

Tilly, D. (2006). Response to Intervention: An overview. *The Special Edge, 19*(2), 1–5.

Tobin, K. (1987). The role of wait time in higher cognitive level learning. *Review of Educational Research, 57,* 69–95.

Tolchinsky, L., & Teberosky, A. (1998). The development of word segmentation and writing in two scripts. *Cognitive Development 13,* 1–24.

Tomlinson, C. (2005). *How to differentiate instruction in mixed-ability classrooms.* (2nd ed.). Upper Saddle River, NJ: Pearson.

Tompkins, G. E. (2006). *Literacy for the 21st century: A balanced approach* (4th ed.). Upper Saddle River, NJ: Merrill Prentice Hall.

Torgesen, J., Houston, D., Rissman, L., Decker, S., Roberts, G., Vaughn, S., Wexler, J., Francis, D., Rivera, M., & Lesaux, N. (2007). *Academic literacy instruction for adolescents.* Portsmouth, NH: RMC Research Corporation, Center on Instruction.

Trent, S., Kea, C., & Oh, K. (2008). Preparing preservice educators for cultural diversity: How far have we come? *Exceptional Children, 74*(3), 328–350.

Uribe, M., & Nathenson-Mejia, S. (2008). *Literacy essentials for English language learners: Successful transitions.* New York: Teachers College Press.

Vacca, R. T. (2002). From efficient decoders to strategic readers. *Educational Leadership 60*(3), 6–11.

Vacca, R., & Vacca, J. A. (2004). *Content area reading: Literacy and learning across the curriculum* (7th ed.). New York: Longman.

Vaughn, S., Linan-Thompson, S., Kouzekanani, K., Pedrotty-Bryan, D., Dickson, S., & Blozis, S. (2003). Reading instruction grouping for students with reading difficulties. *Remedial and Special Education, 24*(5), 301–315.

Vogt, M.E. (1989). *A study of the congruence between preservice teachers' and cooperating teachers' attitudes and practices toward high and low achievers.* Unpublished doctoral dissertation submitted to the University of California, Berkeley.

Vogt, M.E. (1992). Strategies for leading readers into text: The pre-reading phase of a content lesson. In C. Hedley & D. Feldman (Eds.), *Literacy across the curriculum.* New York: Ablex.

Vogt, M.E. (1995). *Jumpstarting: Providing support in advance rather than remediation.* Paper presented at the Annual Conference of the International Reading Association, Anaheim, CA.

Vogt, M.E. (1997). *Intervention strategies for intermediate and middle school students: Three models that appear to work.* Paper presented at the Research Institute of the Annual Conference of the California Reading Association, Anaheim, CA.

Vogt, M.E. (2000). Content learning for students needing modifications: An issue of access. In M. McLaughlin and M.E. Vogt (Eds.), *Creativity and innovation in content area teaching: A resource for intermediate, middle, and high school teachers.* Norwood, MA: Christopher Gordon Publishers.

Vogt, M.E. (2002). *SQP2RS: Increasing students' understandings of expository text through cognitive and metacognitive strategy application.* Paper presented at the 52nd Annual Meeting of the National Reading Conference.

Vogt, M.E. (2005). Improving achievement for ELLs through sheltered instruction. *Language Learner, 1*(1), 22, 25.

Vogt, M.E., & Echevarria, J. (2008). *99 ideas and activities for teaching English learners with the SIOP® Model.* Boston: Allyn & Bacon.

Vogt, M.E., Echevarria, J., & Short, D. (in press). *The SIOP® Model for teaching English-language arts to English learners.* Boston: Allyn & Bacon.

Vogt, M.E., & McLaughlin, M. (2005). *Teaching and learning in a global society: Examining changing definitions of literacy.* In M. Pandis (Ed.), Proceedings from the European Reading Conference (Tallinn, Estonia). Newark, DE: International Reading Association.

Vogt, M.E., & Nagano, P. (2003). *Turn it on with Light Bulb Reading! Sound-switching strategies for struggling readers, 57*(3), 214–221.

Vogt, M.E., & Shearer, B. A. (2007). *Reading specialists and literacy coaches in the real world* (2nd ed.). Boston: Allyn & Bacon.

Vygotsky, L. (1978). *Mind and society: The development of higher psychological processes* (M. Cole, V. John-Steiner, S. Scribner, & E. Souberman, Eds. and trans.). Cambridge, MA: Harvard University Press.

Walqui, A. (2006). Scaffolding instruction for English language learners: A conceptual framework. *The International Journal of Bilingual Education and Bilingualism, 9*(2), 159–180.

Watson, K., & Young, B. (1986). Discourse for learning in the classroom. *Language Arts, 63*(2), 126–133.

Weiss, I. R., & Pasley, J. D. (2006). *Scaling up instructional improvement through teacher professional development: Insights from the local systemic change initiative.*

Philadelphia, PA: Consortium for Policy Research in Education (CPRE) Policy Briefs. http://www.cpre.org/Publications/rb44.pdf

WIDA (World-class Instructional Design and Assessment) Consortium. (2007). *Assessing Comprehension and Communication in English State-to-State for English Language Learners* (*ACCESS for ELLs*®). Madison, WI: The Board of Regents the University of Wisconsin System on behalf of the WIDA Consortium.

WIDA Consortium. (2007). *English language proficiency standards and resource guide, 2007 ed. prekindergarten through grade 12.* Madison, Wisconsin: The Board of Regents of the University of Wisconsin System.

Wiggins, G., & McTighe, J. (2008). *Understanding by design.* Upper Saddle River, NJ: Prentice Hall.

Wilen, W. (1990). Forms and phases of discussion. In W. Wilen (Ed.), *Teaching and learning through discussion* (pp. 3–24). Springfield, IL: Charles C Thomas.

Wong-Fillmore, L., & Valadez, C. (1986). Teaching bilingual learners. In M. C. Wittrock (Ed.), *Handbook of research on teaching* (pp. 648–685). New York: Macmillan.

Yoon, B. (2008). Uninvited guests: The influence of teachers' roles and pedagogies on the positioning of English language learners in the regular classroom. *American Educational Research Journal, 45*(2), 495–522.

Ysseldyke, J., & Marston, D. (1999). Origins of categorical special education services in schools and a rationale for changing them. In D. J. Reshchly, W. D. Tilly, & J. P. Grimes (Eds.), *Special education in transition: Functional assessment and noncategorical programming.* Longmont, CO: Sopris West.

Zabala, D., Minnici, A., McMurrer, J., & Briggs, L. (2008). *State high school exit exams: Moving toward end-of-course exams.* Washington, DC: Center on Education Policy.

Zike, D. (2000a). *The big book of science for middle and high school.* San Antonio, TX: Dinah-Might Adventures.

Zike, D. (2000b). *The big book of world history for middle and high school.* San Antonio, TX: Dinah-Might Adventures.

Zike, D. (2003). *The big book of math for middle and high school.* San Antonio, TX: Dinah-Might Adventures.

Zike, D. (2004). *The big book of United States history for middle and high school.* San Antonio, TX: Dinah-Might Adventures.

name index

subject index